# CLASSROOM ASSESSMENT IN ACTION

CLASSROOM ASSESSMENT IN ACTION

MARK D. SHERMIS AND
FRANCIS J. DI VESTA

ROWMAN & LITTLEFIELD PUBLISHERS, INC.
Lanham • Boulder • New York • Toronto • Plymouth, UK

Published by Rowman & Littlefield Publishers, Inc.
A wholly owned subsidiary of The Rowman & Littlefield Publishing Group, Inc.
4501 Forbes Boulevard, Suite 200, Lanham, Maryland 20706
http://www.rowmanlittlefield.com

Estover Road, Plymouth PL6 7PY, United Kingdom

British Library Cataloguing in Publication Information Available

Library of Congress Cataloging-in-Publication Data
Shermis, Mark D., 1953–
   Classroom assessment in action / Mark D. Shermis and Francis J. Di Vesta.
      p. cm.
   Includes bibliographical references and index.
   ISBN 978-1-4422-0836-0 (cloth : alk. paper)—ISBN 978-1-4422-0837-7 (pbk. : alk. paper)—
ISBN 978-1-4422-0838-4 (electronic)
   1. Educational tests and measurements. I. Di Vesta, Francis J. II. Title.
   LB3051.S47 2011
   371.27—dc22   2010051258

Printed in the United States of America

Contents

Preface

THIS BOOK EVOLVED because it had to. We had both been teaching assessment courses to young, enthusiastic teacher candidates, but had been subjecting them to one of two kinds of texts. The first kind of textbook arose out of the traditional psychometric approach. It was chock full of formulas and distinctions that seemed unimportant (or seemingly irrelevant) to the construction of a fifth-grade social studies exam. Sure, classroom teachers need to know something about the consistency of scores their students receive on the assessments they construct, but mastery of this concept probably doesn't require the memorization of KR-20 or coefficient alpha formulas. Yes, classroom teachers should understand how student scores relate to a test they just administered, but whether these teacher candidates need to comprehend the definition of *consequential* validity is a slightly different matter. These texts tended to emphasize the *content* domain of testing.

At the other end of the spectrum were those textbooks that focused primarily or solely on the *processes* associated with assessment. For example, one challenge for aspiring teachers is to develop expectations as to what constitutes *excellent, good, fair,* and *poor* performance levels for the grades they might be teaching. Would they know a good seventh-grade essay if they saw it? Should a fifth grader be expected to incorporate perspective in a pencil drawing? These texts tended to emphasize the relationships between the curricula being taught and how assessments in those areas might be conceived or calibrated, but sometimes at the expense of ignoring the actual mechanics of testing.

What we were looking to create was a text that provided a strong rationale for integrating assessment and instruction into a functional process, one that offered concrete guidelines on how to construct various common assessments, a set of procedures to evaluate and improve assessments once they were constructed, and a discussion of the factors that might impact test score interpretation. To the degree possible, we also wanted to expose teacher candidates to upcoming technologies that they might encounter in building their repertoire of assessments. Whether it be incorporating automated essay scoring or using electronic portfolios, prospective teachers should feel comfortable working with these new technologies. Finally we felt it was important that teachers be able to work with students and parents in explaining assessment results, whether they are from a high-stakes statewide assessment or the grading philosophy to which they ascribe. Almost all of these attributes are embodied in statewide guidelines that govern how teachers should be prepared.

For teacher candidates our hope is that this textbook and the experiences that you have in your assessment class will foster the transition you have embarked on from that of a *consumer* of assessments to a fully-informed *producer* of such instruments armed with the ability to employ assessment fully in curriculum and instruction within the framework of understanding its many impacts on education. Our wish is that your students, in turn, will come to look forward to opportunities to demonstrate what they know rather than fear or dread such events. We further hope that you find the text informative, useful, easy to digest, and current. For those who are instructors of assessment courses, we trust there is a close match in the way we approach assessment and the way that you do. The text and supplemental materials available from the publisher, Rowman & Littlefield, are designed to engage students, generate ideas on in-class activities and exercises, and provide resources for conducting the class. Our vision is that the instructor can seamlessly integrate his or her experiences in assessment to provide a unique stamp on a comprehensive set of instructional resources. Please let us know how we can make both the text and supplements of greater use to you.

Supplementary teaching and learning tools have been developed to accompany this text. Please contact Rowman & Littlefield at textbooks@rowman.com for more information on the following:

- *PowerPoint Presentations.* Instructional approaches for each chapter, answers to activities and text questions, and downloadable slides of text figures and tables.
- *Test Bank.* Available only through the book's password-protected website.
- *Student Web Resources.* Student exercises and activities, supplemental readings, and a guide to websites on hot issues.

Acknowledgments

PUTTING TOGETHER this book has been a long-term labor of love, and in many ways operationally defines the term *delayed gratification*. There are a number of individuals who we wish to thank in making this book possible. First, none of this would have materialized without the trust and confidence of our editor Patti Belcher. We are grateful to her and the staff of Rowman & Littlefield for giving us the opportunity to bring this project to fruition. Those working with Patti include Jin Yu and our production editor, Julia Loy. Their professionalism and guidance has made this a much better book than it would have been if left to our own devices. During the preproduction and production phases of the book Sharon Apel was instrumental in moving this project along, and we are convinced that she has a shining academic career ahead of her. Many thanks go to Susan Hughes, who helped coordinate our activities and pitched in for final proofs. Finally, the senior author wishes to express his gratitude to his family—Becky and Ryan—for their support and sacrifices in allowing him to bring this project to conclusion. Further we, the authors, are each grateful for the collegial cooperation we have had over many years.

A Note to the Reader: Theory to Practice

THIS BOOK FEATURES special sidebars throughout, identified by an apple icon. We call them "Theory to Practice."

Understanding the theories of education is one thing, but knowing how to apply them in real-life situations is invaluable. We help you make that initial connection through the "Theory to Practice" examples, and we have made them easy to find with the apple icon. Use these examples as the first step to applying this knowledge in your own way and in your particular circumstances. Refer to them when observing teachers and discuss them in your courses. By doing so, your knowledge of education and teaching will grow, and your success as a teacher will follow as well.

Pay special attention! The apple will alert you to methods that can be implemented in a classroom situation based on theories being discussed in the text.

CHAPTER 1

Orientation to Assessment

MORE THAN you may realize, your everyday experience has provided you with a foundation for understanding assessment as you will be using it in your classroom. Even before your kindergarten years you used and experienced the outcomes of many types of assessments including, but certainly not limited to, the taking of tests. Retrospectively, you may recognize that assessment has been beneficial by providing you with feedback, even though you may not have recognized it as assessment—for instance, when you asked a parent what they thought about an essay, or when your parent asked you for some information about a current topic such as conservation or sustainability to test your understanding of the concept. Feedback associated with specific skills in math or social studies may have affected your career choice. The information provided in course grades, that is, as an assessment of your progress, may have affected your study habits or strategies, or the level of the grade might have affected your self-efficacy (feeling of competence to perform specific tasks) in a subject-matter area.

On the flip side, you not only have been assessed in home, school, and other settings, but have probably been an assessor yourself, even without being aware of assessing another person. You may have conducted assessment informally by watching another person perform a task and then offering an appraisal of their performance, or you may have used deliberate questioning aimed at finding out what a person knew or understood. You have undoubtedly assessed people in a number of social interactions, whether deliberately or informally, and gained an impression of their social skills or, perhaps, even made judgments of their personality from a number of observations leading to the conclusion that "he or she is an introvert" or "he or she is an extrovert." You may also have administered measures more formally in teaching situations and ranked students from excellent to average. And, whether we are concerned with preschool, elementary, or high school teaching, we all agree on the need for a seamless integration of assessment with teaching and learning.

■ A Definition of Assessment

In this chapter we hope to orient you to assessment from a number of vantage points to provide you with a broad perspective of its many facets. The orientation will provide a basis for understanding a formal definition of assessment. Considering the many uses of assessment, we obviously need a fairly broad definition. Here is a definition of assessment (see for example, Atkin, Black, & Coffey, 2001; Popham, 2008; Stiggins & Chappuis, 2006), extended to a definition of classroom assessment, that provides a useful framework for teaching:

> **Assessment** is (a) a set of procedures (b) designed to provide information about students' development, growth, and achievement (c) as compared with a standard.

> **Classroom Assessment** is the planned collection of information about the outcomes of teaching on student learning. The assignment of grades serves to inform stakeholders about the educational progress of students and achievement of curricular goals within the context of student readiness characteristics. Feedback from assessment helps in making decisions regarding:

> - Effectiveness of instruction
> - Identification of the need for changes in instructional methods
> - Adaptation to or accommodation of individual differences
> - Monitoring teaching in terms of student progress
> - Setting of appropriate curricular goals in terms of content standards
> - Remedial strategies needed to fix ineffective instructional methods

These are general definitions and suggest a multitude of procedures that will be developed in more detail throughout this book. But, for the moment, you can see that assessment involves the use of data from informal observations, student products, formal and systematic tests, and other measurements and evaluations that are typically used in educational settings. Our concern is not merely with the collection of data but with the kinds of measures available, how they are used, how they are constructed, and how they are interpreted to yield educationally worthwhile decisions. Of special importance in the assessment process is the interpretation of data obtained from the various procedures—interpretations that are essential for understanding variables related to educational achievement. Decisions made on the basis of these interpretations require an integration of pedagogical knowledge and understandings—knowledge about cognitive processes, teaching, and teaching special content as well as about content areas (science, social studies, music, and so on). As a result of knowing more about assessment you will gain conceptual understanding of the procedures, the design of assessments, and the standards.

■ The Components of Assessment

The many components of assessment with which we will be concerned can be outlined as shown in Figure 1.1. They are as

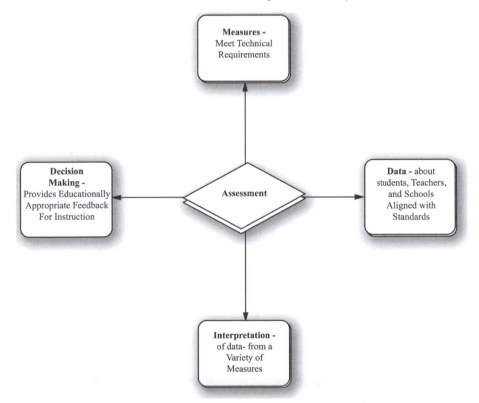

Figure 1.1. An outline view of the components of assessment.

follows: obtaining *data* about students, teachers, or schools by well-constructed *measures*; *interpreting* the meaning of scores (data) for such outcomes as student progress or instructional effectiveness; and using the interpreted scores for making decisions regarding the best ways to facilitate student learning.

For assessment to be characterized in the ways shown in Figure 1.1, the design and overall plan must be technically accurate. This requires an understanding of how the assessment is used by different users and for different purposes. Jo Ann, a teacher at Elmwood Elementary School, asks such questions as: "How do I ensure that my testing practices will be well-planned and of high quality? Are the tests used in these assessments the ones that will work for these particular students? Are there some students with special needs that I need to consider? Who will be using the results of this assessment? What questions will be asked about them (e.g., how will my tests and the way they are scored appear from their unique perspectives)?"

The answer to such questions as these will be developed in the chapters that follow. The details of steps in which teachers eventually engage during assessment are shown in Figure 1.2. The figure provides illustrations of ways the components of assessments may be employed.

■ Who Uses Classroom Assessment and Why?

You can appreciate the importance of assessment when you recognize that teachers and students, of course, are concerned with assessment, but so are the students' families, the community, school administrators, and educational policy makers at the state and national levels. These are known as the stakeholders as the assessments are made and implemented. Each attends to different forms of assessment and does so in substantially different ways, as well as with different bases for interpretation. For example, as a teacher you will use measures to assess student progress and your instructional effectiveness. Parents will use the measures in similar ways but probably focusing on what you are doing to help students meet their potential. Administrators such as the school principal might focus on the adequacy of instruction and the curriculum in using assessments. Although there is some overlap in the interests of different groups, they are distinctively different in the emphases given and the level of understanding in interpretations and decision making.

The fact that so many different parties are involved in educational assessment generates the need to understand the process of assessment as an integral part of teaching within the

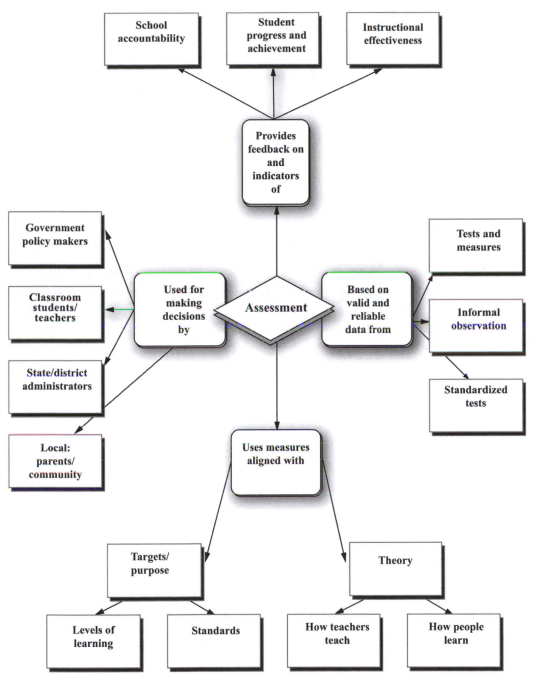

Figure 1.2. A more detailed illustration of the ways in which assessment components are employed in education.

contexts of a multitude of influences or pressures from beyond the classroom. It is also important to see from the outset that you can't speak about education at any level without speaking about how it is used not only for one group but for a variety of groups differentiated by language use, ethnicity, culture, or special needs. An understanding of all considerations of this sort will enhance your overall understanding of assessment. Whatever distinctions or commonalities are observed, all are linked to instruction and the improvement of the student's educational experience.

How Teachers Use Assessment

A currently popular perspective on assessment suggests that assessment differs with the stage of teaching a particular unit or lesson. The stages may be usefully considered as (a) *before* learning, (b) *during* learning, and (c) *after* learning. Each stage provides its own objectives and information that is useful in determining student knowledge status and the subsequent steps to be taken in instruction, as well as the quality of student performance at the end of a unit or lesson. The following are some illustrations:

- *Before learning.* Assessment before learning provides information that helps teachers determine the *readiness* of students for learning in any given class. Knowing what the class already knows (or doesn't know) is an important prerequisite for planning what to teach and at what level the material is to be taught in order to achieve course objectives.
- *During learning.* Assessment during learning provides information that helps you monitor student progress against the effectiveness of the instructional methods you are using. It is important to examine the reasons why instruction succeeds or fails—whether you are teaching the right content, skills, or attitudes at the right level and at the right time during the course of the learning. At this stage, you seek answers to questions regarding the monitoring of instruction—what should be taught next, whether some material needs to be reviewed or developed further, and, perhaps, what you do not need to teach despite your initial intentions. In addition, planned assessments during learning enable teachers to judge whether students need more involvement in instruction, which students need more or different instruction, and which are proceeding well enough to be assigned enrichment instruction.

- *After learning.* This is the time assessment is used for decisions regarding determination and assignment of grades—weighing the importance and use of assessments collected earlier in the teaching of a unit, reporting on ways students are assessed, and reporting and interpreting assessment results. After learning is also the time to reconsider ongoing discussion regarding instruction and curricular revisions—such issues as the adequacy of measures being used, whether the curriculum is satisfactory for meeting school and community objectives, and the adequacy of the curriculum in meeting subject matter standards.

The tasks associated with the teacher's use of assessment as they might appear in practice are summarized in Theory to Practice Box 1.1. These tasks will be discussed in greater detail as you proceed with your study of assessment.

How Others Use Assessment

Aside from teachers, other users of assessment include administrators (school officials, principals, superintendents of schools); the public (parents, community members, school boards, the media); and government officials in their role as policy makers. Let's see who some of these people are and how they use assessment (Dietel, Herman, & Knuth, 1991).

School Administrators

School administrators use assessment measures to *monitor program effectiveness*. That is, on the basis of assessment results, administrators (e.g., principals and school superintendents):

- Examine school programs in terms of their strength and weaknesses in meeting community needs
- Judge the priorities of the school within the district
- Assess whether there is a need for alternative programs
- Plan and improve existing programs
- Formulate standards in all subject-matter areas as well as standards for achievement levels in content
- Evaluate progress of teachers and schools

Principals use assessment to determine the effectiveness of procedures used by teachers in their schools. Such assessments can provide a useful basis for decision making in helping teachers function more effectively within the school context.

Theory to Practice Box 1.1
AN INTERMEDIATE SCHOOL TEACHER'S VIEW OF ASSESSMENT

Bill Burton, a teacher in the middle grades, felt that he learned one important perspective about assessment that he did not really appreciate before his training. He came to the realization that teachers spend much of their time in assessment, not simply at the end of a unit or lesson but at many different stages of learning and for quite different purposes. Here is the way he considered the measures that he would use at the different stages of teaching a lesson.

- *Assessment Before Learning*. In planning a lesson on "insect-eating plants." Bill wanted to learn what his students already knew. From everyday experience they may have some acquaintance with the plants and the names for the plants such as Venus Flytraps or Pitcher Plant. They may know something about the plants' physiology. Bill gathers information for helping him diagnose the needs of individual students. He recalls from his college courses that he must consider the influences on learning of student diversity, background, and motivation. These data will help to identify students with special needs and who need accommodations for those needs, e.g., using larger print for students with visual difficulties or giving more time to complete the tests for students who have difficulty in focusing their attention on a task. The time is well spent on this early data-gathering; it provides information that will help in establishing a starting point for efficient teaching.
- *Assessment During Learning*. Based on what he knows about plants and what his students already know, Bill has decided to begin teaching at a little higher level than he originally thought would be necessary. He begins by using analogies for reviewing the way the insect-eating plants trap their prey: flypaper, pitfall, and snaptraps. He will be able to introduce some new terms which students may not have associated with plants before and, in the course of doing so, teach a little physiology. He compares carnivory and respiration in plants and animals. He introduces terms such as photosynthesis.

  As you might expect, he collects data during instruction, perhaps by questioning, about how the students are progressing and how well his lesson plan is working. He has decided to ask students to keep a portfolio of products they have produced—e.g., collections and labeling of pictures of insect-eating plants, articles read about these plants, pictures of dissected plants to show the different trappings, essays that explain the physiology of plants including insectivores, and so on. He monitors student progress to track whether students are emphasizing the goals or objectives of his lesson: e.g., can they identify different forms of insect-eating plants from pictures? Have any of the students purchased insect-eating plants for home? Do they know the characteristics of these plants that differentiate them from non-carnivorous plants? Do they understand how these plants fit into the scheme of the botanical world? (Note that these assessments require him to know much about botany as well as much about instruction and learning.)

• *Assessment After Learning.* Of course, Bill is concerned about the final achievement of his students. He asks, "To what extent have they achieved the objectives both he and they set out to do?" What might these end-of-unit data look like? In particular he wants to see how much they remembered from the lesson; how well they understand the "science" or physiology behind the nurture of insect-eating plants; whether they can correctly identify plants that use the different methods of feeding; all standards he expects. This information will be useful in assigning a "final grade" but, as importantly, he also uses it for feedback to the students to show what they have accomplished and to correct any misconceptions they might still have. He also uses the measures to provide information that will help him determine whether his teaching method was effective or whether it will need to be changed the next time he teaches the unit.

Parents and Students

Teachers work with parents and students outside of the classroom either in individual conferences or in meetings of groups such as the PTA. They may communicate through letters to parents, face-to-face contact, or parent–teacher meetings. For some parents e-mail may be the way to go. Teachers address such matters as the individual needs of students, student objectives (including grades to be earned and how they are to be graded), learning outcomes to be achieved, and homework requirements as well as student and parental roles in the child's education. In particular, teachers need to be prepared to answer questions raised by parents regarding grading procedures, the reasons why their children are not progressing as well as expected, how to help the student at home, reasons for statewide tests in addition to school tests, and what grades mean and how to interpret scores.

Parents (and students) rely on assessments to:

• *Judge children's progress in learning.* Parents make judgments regarding their child's success as well as judgments about the student's strengths and weaknesses (e.g., high grades in science and lower grades in English).
• *Judge the school's role in children's progress.* Parents make decisions about schools in which the student is placed (public schools, private schools, charter schools, and so on) and cooperatively work with schools and teachers in both the children's education and the educational process presented in the school and the district in which it is located.

- *Judge the school's effectiveness.* Parents seek to understand and determine the school's effectiveness (or accountability, i.e., whether the school is doing as well as expected) and to understand how the school helps the student make informed educational and career choices.
- *Judge the educational plans for children with special needs.* Parents expect assessment to provide information that will help in planning educational experiences of their children, for example, in the development of educational plans for children with special needs. They seek an understanding of the placement of students (for instance, grasping why a student is assigned to a special class or program).

If parents and students are to use assessments for these purposes, it is obvious that they must be accurately informed about the nature of assessments and how they are used, the conditions under which they are used, and their limitations. Clearly, you will have an important role in providing this information as the need arises.

Community Members and the Media

You will see that many of the uses of assessment by the community and the media are very similar to, or extensions of, the ways assessment is used by other users. For the most part, the media attempt to report objective data regarding assessment. They do make influential interpretations through editorial policy. Reading the daily newspapers in your community over a period of time will certainly reveal articles paralleling one or more of the facets of assessment described above:

- Reporting to parents and administrators on the ways schools use assessment for making policy changes that affect educational practice
- Evaluating and recommending ways of improving forms of assessment
- Reporting of assessment results and related issues
- Helping to understand functions of assessment, forms of assessment, related issues, and outcomes
- Reorienting individuals socialized in traditional evaluation roles and expectations to the newer approaches as they appear
- Interpreting assessment data within the context of diversity, poverty, school budgets, school plans, and so on

- Showing where schools have opportunities to intervene in improving the welfare of the community

■ Policy Makers' Use of Assessment: The No Child Left Behind (NCLB) Act

In taking this initial approach to assessment, we caution you to notice that in today's educational setting, other parties (especially legislators), seemingly far removed from the school, are also interested in assessments of school performance. You will be employing tests imposed by policy makers under such legislation as the No Child Left Behind (NCLB) Act.

A common misunderstanding is that this legislation is unrelated to the school. However, such legislation is intended to hold educators and students responsible for what the students are learning. In this context, assessment measures, together with statewide standardized tests, help policy makers:

- Set standards and goals for statewide educational policy
- Monitor educational quality and assign quality grades to schools or districts
- Reward successful practices and allocate financial resources to deserving schools that meet the statewide standards
- Formulate general policy

The Legislation

As an illustration of how legislation affects schooling, NCLB mandates that all children have a fundamental right to a high-quality education and that they should be proficient in basic learning areas by the academic year 2013–2014. The central focus of NCLB requires states to (a) ensure that highly qualified teachers are in every classroom, (b) use research-based practices as the foundation of instruction, (c) develop tests to assess students so that data-driven decisions become a key component of the educational system, and (d) hold schools accountable for the performance of all students (Yell & Dragsow, 2005).

This legislation strongly determines the way states get graded for the performance of their schools. Because assessments affect school performance at the local level as well as at the state level, considerable debate persists about the overall effectiveness of such legislation. The policies indirectly and directly affect how you view your future role as a teacher within the system, how you will assess your students, and how you will budget time for assessment.

Pros and Cons of the Legislation

From both idealistic and political viewpoints, it is difficult indeed to argue against the basic premises of NCLB. All people want children to learn in schools with high-quality teachers and excellent resources. It would be reassuring to know that the curriculum, instructional methods, and assessments employed in the school were formulated from information discovered using scientific methodology. And certainly we all want to believe that our tax dollars are well spent in achieving these goals. Whether immediately attainable or not, the goals of NCLB seem worthy of pursuit.

What NCLB Means to You

The demand to adapt to cognitive and noncognitive needs is highly complex, but NCLB clearly implies that teachers must work around any limitations that might challenge the performance of students (Yell & Drasgow, 2005). One part of the debate centers on the position of some lawmakers that the legislation is too punitive toward students who fail to meet program goals. Accordingly, it will probably undergo some revision by the incumbent president's administration. Such revisions will require studies of failures and successes resulting from the legislation, both for the improvement of instruction and for making certain school grades are fairly assigned. Because this legislation is so important to assessment in today's schools and affects teaching in so many ways, we will extend this brief introduction in more detail in a later chapter.

■ How You Will Incorporate Assessment in Instruction

An understanding of how stakeholders use information about students will enable a better understanding of what assessment will do for you and suggest ways that you can approach testing, measurement, and assessment in your classroom. These suggestions will prove useful as a starting point in the use of measurement and are briefly described in the paragraphs that follow. More details on each step will be detailed in subsequent chapters. You may also want to review Theory to Practice Box 1.1 to understand how these tasks are related to the overall assessment plan.

- *Know and understand the reasons for your assessments.* Are you concerned merely with acquisition of factual information? Or are you as concerned about student concepts, understanding, and organization regarding that information? To what extent are you focused on how students *use* information in some applied situation that calls on higher-order abilities such as decision making and problem solving?

- *Plan the assessment procedure.* For each purpose teachers adapt assessments accordingly. They identify their objectives in teaching specific units. They consider the kind of test most useful for the content being taught—for instance, whether oral question and answers, paper and pencil, or performance measures should be used. Also, they think about the students to be tested—their special attributes that need to be considered when planning assessments.

- *Identify and choose methods that will meet your objectives and yield the information you need.* Keep in mind that our definition didn't focus on a single assessment method such as tests. Rather, it emphasized "a set of procedures." Good assessment might involve anything from an observation checklist to scores on a standardized achievement test to developing a portfolio or organizing an in-basket (the pile of memos, letters, and instructions that accumulate on a teacher's or principal's desk). Sometimes you may be concerned with the administration of a statewide test and will not be constructing a test but administering one already developed for use in all school districts within the state. In such cases you will want to understand the purposes for which the test was developed and how it is to be used.

- *Identify how and to what extent a targeted objective is to be measured.* This is a complex step: It involves thinking about your instruction, about the students' background and understanding, and about the objectives. For example, you may want to teach students about the use of conjugations in Spanish. At the beginning level, you may want to teach specific conjugations of verbs. With that background, you may want to proceed to how those conjugations apply to all verbs, how they apply to regular verbs and then to irregular verbs, and then how they appear in preterites and other grammatical forms. Sometimes you will need only a single test that is highly reliable and valid. Other times you may need to get information from *many sources*, or you may want to sample behavior in a *number of situations* or at *several points in time* to assess students' growth or progress. You will need to consider the level of the assessment, such as the facts you want students to know or the way they organize the facts into concepts or categories and how that information will be used. You should consider whether the assessment will be by means of a teacher-made test, by a portfolio (a collection of student products), or by performance (e.g., of a skill such as a backhand in tennis or a cognitive activity such as taking a position in a debate).

- *Carefully interpret the data you receive.* All data are important but stakeholders will be most concerned with those data (performance scores) that have some meaning to them. Accordingly, a first important step in using data is to return to your original reasons for conducting the assessment. Then select the appropriate assessment data and interpret it to determine whether your intention was supported. Does the score imply that the individual was good (or poor) at a task? That some part of a task was performed well (or poorly)? Or that some criterion has (or has not) been met?
- *Communicate the results.* Part of a teacher's job is to communicate assessment results in a form suitable for the receiver of that information. You communicate assessment results to the student, to parents, and to the school. A student's portfolio (or other quality indicator) may be an objective indicator of his or her performance, but you should realize that it is not understood (interpreted) in the same way by all people. Your perception of the score may be that it represents the success or failure of your instructional method. You might communicate to the student that the score was an indication that his or her study strategy worked well, or that a learning process or strategy needs more work if he or she is to succeed in future assignments. A score might be communicated to an administrator as a need for more resources to support instruction. You might emphasize to a parent the student's level of accomplishment as a reflection of the student's potential for further development or a need or opportunity for enrichment or remediation. The variations in interpretation of scores are many.

■ Your Knowledge about Assessment

Even if you never knowingly administered a test in school, you have assessed and evaluated your environment thousands of times before you even thought of entering a teacher preparation program. Quite simply, in high school you may have decided on a college preparatory rather than a general high school curriculum; you rejected participating in social events; you selected one kind of fruit over others in your diet; you bought used instead of new texts for your college courses; you chose a career in teaching rather than a career in law—all choices or decisions were probably never considered as assessment but certainly were based on a tacit understanding of assessment, that is, based on criteria typically associated with assessment, criteria that you probably understood but were unable to express in verbal form or recognize as assessment by the usual standard of "grades on a report card."

Exploring Classroom Assessment

Think of these previous experiences as entry experiences, experiences that provided you with the basis for an exploration of classroom assessment. Outcomes such as making good choices or decisions or gaining the ability to use information in new situations are infrequently associated with assessment by newcomers to the field, who typically think of classroom assessment in terms of percentage points on report-card grades.

Whether you collect data by informal observations of students on the playground or in the chemistry laboratory or by paper-and-pencil multiple-choice tests, the elements of assessment are ever present. If the aim, for example, is to examine the outcome of a teaching approach in middle school, such elements include *collecting* data by *observing* student performance, *interpreting* that information in view of the purposes for which the information is being collected, *evaluating* the usefulness of the interpretations for *available choices* and decisions, and *implementing* the best alternatives for such activities as improving classroom instruction or guiding students to improve their study strategies.

As we move through this process, your time spent working with children and adolescents now and in the past will provide you with numerous examples of how to apply your newly found understandings of assessment. On the other hand, if you haven't yet spent much time working with real children and teachers in real schools, you may have to do a little deliberate vicarious (imaginary) experiencing based on recall of children you know as well as your own childhood, but the relevant experiences for helping you understand assessment are still there.

You probably have already guessed that a professional understanding of assessment goes far beyond grades, the assignment of numerical scores, or a simple evaluative comment or two. It is a critically important and positive activity that benefits the key participants (stakeholders) in education—participants that include students, teachers, administrators, family members, and the community.

Assessment in Everyday Teaching

You may eventually move your thinking from a position where assessment is recognized only as one part of a cycle of teaching phases, such as the end-of-the-month report card, to a position in which assessment is an integral part of everyday instruction as it is used for continuous improvement of teaching and learning. Classroom assessment, at its best, is a positive collaborative activity between teacher and students. Whatever your experience, you will come to use assessment because of its importance for finding out something about the status of your teaching and its effect on your students.

Assessment Grounded in Instruction

The current view of assessment in the classroom is that it is closely grounded in instruction. The sequence is reasonably structured: Your objectives are *aligned to standards* of the content field (science, math, literacy, and so on) for any given grade level; even the student in first grade has some notions, however intuitive they may be, about the taxonomy of insects, for example. Your instruction will be geared to helping students *achieve those objectives* through the learning processes they use and the content they master. You will, through assessment, *find clues to student mistakes* (misconceptualizations) in their responses and performances on the tasks you give them as tests of their achievement. By using tests in a timely fashion, the results are available in sufficient time to make adjustments to your instruction—whether in the middle of a class period or near the end of a unit.

The short cycle will permit making adjustments in how you teach and/or help students to alter how they are learning. Properly used, such assessments will not only achieve the end results of better learning but will also enhance scores on external accountability measures. Note that assessments given at the end of a course or as an accountability measure (such as a state comprehensive examination) typically come too late to provide feedback for instructional improvement immediately, although, of course, they may help in planning instruction in the future.

Diagnostic Assessment

Your assessments will also help you find out what you can do to help the students learn or how you should interact with the students. Whatever the reason for assessment, the data you obtain has the potential for assisting you in making a decision about the student based on his or her preference for a way of learning (e.g., visual, auditory, or "doing"), about the content being taught (e.g., social organizations of ants), about the tasks to be used in teaching (making diagrams), about the delivery (e.g., lectures, Socratic dialogue, computers), or about the management of the classroom (e.g., pairing, groups).

Diagnosing student progress and instructional effectiveness are the main reasons why assessment is critical to educators at all levels. This information helps when you have to make decisions—decisions about educational policy, about what to teach, about how to teach effectively, and about facilitating student learning. In the course of conducting these activities you will be continually aware of both your role in the process and the dependence on others on effective assessment. In current educational assessment, students play a vital role: Their perceptions, their use of assessment, and the ways they are involved—or can be involved—in doing the assessment are important considerations.

At times, assessment may seem an inconvenience to you and your students—an interruption of the major job of teaching. We sometimes would rather teach than test, or we may think that making assessments somehow hinders or blocks attainment of some goal by misdirecting study to "passing the test." As teachers, we sometimes think that testing takes away from valuable time needed for instruction. However, these perceptions are distortions of the true functions of assessment—they are based on the assumption that somehow teaching, learning, and testing are separate and unrelated classroom activities and that assessment is testing, a necessary evil in the classroom, with its sole purpose being to give a grade. Rather, as shown in Figures 1.1 and 1.2, assessment is closely linked to instruction and involves all stakeholders in the educational process.

Assessment and Improvement of Learning

It is well documented that even testing alone, without other considerations, improves learning (memory) beyond any improvement the student would get by repeated studying (Roediger & Karpicke, 2006). The direct effect on learning of assessment alone probably comes from a number of conditions: Students make choices regarding what to study, acquire learning strategies, and learn techniques that not only have positive effects on taking classroom tests but that transfer to improved performance on statewide comprehensive tests (Roediger & Karpicke,

Text Box 1.1. A Preliminary Checklist of Teachers' Use of Assessment: What Is Needed to Obtain Assessment Data Useful for Educational Decisions.

- *Reasons for Making Assessments.* You obtain data essential to understanding your students' learning processes, outcomes, and performance. Your data should help you determine whether your:
  - Instructional objectives have been reached
  - Instructional methods are effective
  - The instructional method you selected is the best one to facilitate learning
  - Data are viable for recording grades on report cards

- *Engaging Students in Assessment.* Do your students play a role in determining:
  - Educationally relevant instructional objectives?
  - The best measures of their achievement?
  - Qualitative criteria in achieving learning outcomes?
  - The effectiveness of their own studying and learning strategies?
  - Instructional strategies that work for them?

- *What You Achieve by Studying Assessment.* By studying assessment have you learned that:
  - Different assessment methods serve different educational purposes?
  - Objective criteria will facilitate the reliability of authentic assessment?
  - Assessment data is needed by others outside the classroom for making educationally relevant decisions?
  - Student assessment data can be useful to administrators for supporting the in-service development of teachers?

2006). In addition, the expectation of a test or other assessment augments motivation and attention by modifying students' engagement in a task. The tests direct student expectations, encouraging them to spend more time on task. They promote attentive engagement in the learning tasks. They help students to select information that meets learning objectives and to learn strategies for adapting to stress (test anxiety) sometimes associated with taking tests or being assessed.

Teacher Use of Assessment

These advantages, spoken and unspoken, do not go unrecognized in the everyday experience of teachers. They report spending about a third of their time in the classroom dealing with some aspect of assessment. Their educational decisions are made on the basis of data—data that comes from an understanding of the assessment process. A well-developed program in your school will have an assessment plan that evaluates student achievement of learning outcomes or objectives on which the teachers and administrators agree. As teachers, we want to express goals for ourselves and students, how we intend to reach those goals, and the ways we know that those goals have been achieved. Along the way, we use assessment to determine our progress in achieving those goals. If students aren't doing as well as expected, we use repair (remedial) strategies to align instruction to the intended objectives.

Diversity of Assessment Practices

Our purpose in this book is to show the diversity of assessment practices beyond testing and how that diversity can lead to good decisions about instruction at any educational level. You will learn that the form of assessment methods changes over grades. Teachers in lower grades use more frequent and diverse assessments (testing, observation, evaluation, case studies) of individual students than do teachers in the upper grades. You will also learn that diversity in assessment practices is reflected in the forms of testing; paper-and-pencil formats seem more useful for recall of facts, whereas the management of portfolios containing a record of accomplishments may reflect organization ability as well as performance ability. Assessments that involve problem solving may demonstrate ability to use information as well as understanding. The diversity in assessment that occurs at different educational levels or that occurs in formats and inferences made reflects changes in (a) expectations of students, (b) outcomes or standards associated with student levels of experience, (c) the kind of feedback teachers want to provide students (e.g., on acquisition, learning strategies, or management of learning settings), and (d) the kind of feedback teachers want to improve their instruction.

Our focus will be on the purposes for which assessment is conducted by you, the various ways data can be collected, and the ways the data are used for making informed decisions. Knowing about assessment at a professional level is essential for ensuring that it is used effectively and appropriately as one part of teaching woven into the fabric of instruction and learning.

■ The Consequences of Poor Assessment Practices

As you learn about assessment, you will become sensitive to some precautions that will help in avoiding mistakes often made in using assessment results. The illustrations in this section will help make you aware that assessment practices are not all good or bad, their value depending in part on how they are used. Further, as these illustrations are used mainly to build awareness, they will be discussed in more detail in later chapters to show what can be done in avoiding mistakes in the use of assessment practices.

Teachers can learn to recognize the several sources of poor assessment practices. Sometimes poor practice is built into the test. Other times it is what is communicated through the test administration. Still other times, poor practice may be found in the way the results are interpreted and used.

It is worthwhile to keep in mind that communications are not only presented differently to different users of assessment reports but are also perceived (received) differently by them. Timothy Slater (2005), a teacher of physics, has written, "While I was a graduate teaching assistant . . . I sympathized with students who told me that there were two ways of taking courses: One was to learn and understand the material and the other was to get an 'A.' " This all-too-familiar refrain suggests that if, indeed, there is little or no relationship between learning and getting a high grade, then, somewhere in the course of events, the assessment process has broken down.

A basic requirement of good assessment is that standards, course objectives, lesson objectives, and content are *aligned*. That is, your assessment must match your instruction. Moreover, this alignment must be apparent to your students. It is certainly unfair to penalize students for not learning what they have not expected to learn or had the opportunity to learn.

Assessment has deep effects on students' learning not only from the standpoint of feedback on how well they reached some objective, but also from the standpoint of their attributions for success or failure. To illustrate: an assigned grade, however viable it may be, is taken seriously by the student and clearly affects his or her approach to learning, leading him or her to set higher or lower goals based on a feeling of encouragement or frustration. Continual or frequent discouragement may have the effect of convincing the students that they can't learn. Such students often give up rather than feel challenged. Conversely, high grades may engender an unwarranted feeling of superlative ability and reduce students' effort in future tasks.

Teachers want assessments to inform them whether students have learned what the objectives are as well as whether the objectives have been achieved. If students don't play a role in framing course or unit objectives, they may try to infer them from the tests that they take. It is not unusual to find students saying, "To earn a good grade in this course, you have to memorize facts." Or, "Ms. Kim likes long answers on her essay tests." On the other hand, teacher objectives, generally, are content or process oriented rather than oriented toward the mechanical features of responding.

We have all known teachers who use exams for other purposes than those oriented toward meaningful objectives. Some teachers, for example, have personal reasons for making tests that are easy or difficult; they may construct exams so difficult that few students earn an "A" rather than exams concerned with whether students have achieved some learning objective. This orientation sometimes reflects an emphasis on acquiring a reputation of being a "tough grader" or "showing the students how little they know." Such orientations may seem on the surface to be trivial as attempts to challenge students or attempts to "making students motivated to do better next time." But if a test is constructed so that most students do poorly, what useful information is the teacher gaining? What will the teacher learn from this information in order to make the instruction more effective?

These illustrations are of events that contribute to what psychometricians (professional test makers) call error score. Although all measures have some degree of error, error can be minimized by understanding the principles of good assessment. For example, testing based on incorrect premises and done for the wrong reasons may hinder teacher effectiveness (Nichols & Berliner, 2007). In the case of using standardized tests (such as statewide tests or commercially produced tests), an undue focus on the goal of attaining high standardized test scores may be addressed by spending time on "practicing the test" (teaching to the test items) without regard for the standards or objectives on which the test is based.

The pressure on schools to achieve high test scores is sometimes so demanding that some teachers and administrators have been found to falsify student standardized test scores (Levitt & Dunbar, 2005). And, often, when cheating is detected in a middle school classroom, students will see the teacher as creating conditions where cheating can be rationalized as acceptable (Murdock & Anderman, 2006). For example, cheating is rated as more acceptable by students in classrooms where the structure or climate is focused on extrinsic recognition or rewards (performance), such as those reflected in test results, rather than on intrinsic rewards and personal integrity. We believe that a careful study of this text will help you avoid such problems by understanding assessment and its role in instruction.

We have introduced some poor assessment practices here with the intention of helping you to recognize the shortcomings of being uninformed or misinformed about assessment. Other illustrations will be described in more detail in other chapters where poor assessment practices appear.

■ Contemporary Classroom Assessment

At one time you might have thought of assessment as testing students, either objectively (such as by true-false or multiple-choice tests) or subjectively (such as by essay exams) at the end of a period of instruction, conducting tests to obtain a score that tells the teacher and parent "how well the student did." This is known as summative assessment, which means that the assessment represents an estimate of the sum total of what the student has achieved, or otherwise described as the "assessment *of* learning" (Stiggins & Chappuis, 2006). This prevalent perception of assessment is little more than a "snapshot" of what the student knows. Little if any emphasis is placed on different kinds of learning (e.g., learning facts, learning skills, comprehension, understanding, or critical thinking). It was rarely used as a measure of progress (although it was interpreted as a measure of progress), and it was rarely if ever the case that the assessments were used to inform the quality of instruction—to inform the teacher whether the teaching method was obtaining the expected results, whether it was the most appropriate teaching method for the purpose, or whether instruction was adapted to differences in the way students learn. In most use, the interpretation was that the student didn't learn.

The Changing Role of Assessment

Contemporary approaches to classroom assessment are more constructive as represented in the rephrasing of "assessment *of* learning" to the phrase "assessment *for* learning" (Stiggins & Chappuis, 2006). Thus, the approach puts the emphasis on the fact that assessment is used to provide information that will lead to the facilitation of learning.

The theme throughout this chapter, and indeed throughout this book, is the characterization of assessment as a part of a system composed of the loop Assessment → Instruction → Learning. The feedback provided in assessment *of* learning changes the orientation to assessment *for* learning, thereby incorporating assessment as an integral part of instruction. In the process of achieving this outcome, the concern is that a variety of assessment measures are necessary for educational decision making; no single form of measurement or single test, regardless of its length or technical excellence, is sufficient to provide a well-rounded appraisal of student progress and instructional excellence. Nor is the measure of a single outcome sufficient, for there are many possible outcomes, even for a single lesson. They include acquisition of subject-matter content and facts, cognitive and psychomotor skills, attitudes or dispositions, conceptual understanding, critical thinking, and decision making.

For this array of outcomes there are many possible assessments; teachers are no longer restricted to a few traditional measures. Several important kinds of assessments are illustrated in the following chapters. Some of these, such as performance and portfolio assessment, have often been called *alternative assessments*—alternatives to traditional testing. However, they have become a standard part of contemporary teaching and assessment. Since you will be using most if not all of them in your classroom at one time or another they will be discussed in more detail in later chapters.

■ Summary

Instruction and assessment are seamlessly integrated in the classroom, just as assessment and decision making are seamless activities in other facets of everyday life. In our daily lives, if there was not some ongoing, even subconscious, assessment, how would we determine with whom to associate, whether to take a particular job, what clothes to wear, which groceries to buy, and so on? In the classroom, similarly, assessment is always occurring, whether formally or informally, deliberately or inadvertently. We are always in the process of making measurements whether we are aware of them or not. Without some assessment, how would you know that learning has occurred? How would you know how to handle individual differences among students? How would you know whether your instruction was effective or not as effective as it might be?

In addition to its use by teachers, assessment is used by school administrators who monitor program effectiveness, state and federal officials who make educational policy, students who make educational decisions and career choices, and parents who hold their local schools accountable for results. The media and community are interactive, one providing a voice to the other, and in many ways they represent one another. The media report assessment outcomes and communicate activities and ways the community can serve to enhance the value of school-driven educational opportunities. They provide a mechanism for communication to the broader community at the local or higher (state or national) levels. The community makes its needs known through its town meetings, school board meetings, and other "voices," on which the media reports and editorializes.

Poor assessment practices can create problems for all who are seriously concerned with the process, whether teachers, parents, or students. To avoid such difficulties, you should always know the reasons for your assessments before you begin. It would be irresponsible, for example, simply to spring a test on students in your class without a good reason for doing so. You should plan assessment procedures thoroughly by selecting the most appropriate methods to produce the information you need, by determining the extent of the measurement including the objective(s) and level(s), by carefully interpreting the data you receive (from the standpoint of all stakeholders), and by communicating the results in an appropriate way.

In your teaching career you will use many varieties of assessment including both conventional and alternative forms. In addition to tests that you or your colleagues create, your assessment repertoire will include observation (formal and informal), performance assessment, portfolio assessment, and standardized tests. Some tests will use special forms of assessment outside the realm of this textbook, but will include measures of capacity, special abilities, and personality. Moreover, whatever forms of assessment you will use, for whatever objectives, you will need to be sensitive to issues of equity and diversity, making certain that students from all ethnic groups and cultures are being assessed fairly. You should also pay attention to the ways assessment results affect public policy—and, in turn, how public policy affects your classroom.

Exercise 1.1
How many ways have *you* been assessed as a student? Think about teacher-made tests, standardized tests, tests for placement, tests for selection, and informal observations by peers or by teachers. Try to make a complete list.

Exercise 1.2
Look for articles in the daily newspaper that relate to classroom assessment, school assessment, and assessment in the military or in industry. Keep a scrapbook of such items for evaluation during the course. Share the articles with your class for discussion.

Exercise 1.3
Interview a teacher, perhaps your supervising teacher or a friend who is a teacher, regarding his or her perspective on assessment

in teaching. You might ask such questions as these: Do you plan for measures to be used? Do you use a number of measures? Which ones? How frequently are students assessed? What is your view of statewide tests? How do you handle parents' questions about student achievement? Write a brief constructive critique regarding the teacher's perspective from the viewpoint of concerns in this chapter.

■ References

Atkin, J. M., Black, P., & Coffey, J. (Eds.). (2001). *Classroom assessment and the National Science Education Standards*. Washington, D.C.: National Academy Press.

Dietel, R. J., Herman, R. L., & Knuth, R. A. (1991). What does research say about assessment? Available from www.ncrel.org/sdrs/areas/stw_esys/4assess.htm.

Levitt, S. D., & Dunbar, S. J. (2005). *Freakanomics: A rogue economist explores the hidden side of everything*. New York: Morrow.

Murdock, T., & Anderman, E. M. (2006). Motivational perspectives on student cheating: Toward an integrated model of academic dishonesty. *Educational Psychologist, 41*(3), 129–145.

Nichols, S. L., & Berliner, D. C. (2007). *Collateral damage: How high-stakes testing corrupts America's schools*. Cambridge, MA: Harvard Education Press.

Popham, W. J. (2008). *Classroom assessment: What teachers need to know* (5th ed.). Boston, MA: Allyn and Bacon.

Roediger, H. L., III, & Karpicke, J. D. (2006). The power of testing memory: Basic research and implications for educational practice. *Perspectives on Psychological Science, 1*(3), 181–210.

Slater, T. F. (2005). Field-tested learning assessment guide. Retrieved May 6, 2005, from www.flaguide.org/cat/perfass/perfass1.php.

Stiggins, R., & Chappuis, J. (2006). What a difference a word makes: Assessment FOR learning rather than assessment OF learning helps students succeed. *JSD, 27*(1). Retrieved January 15, 2010, from www.nsdc.org/library/publications/jsd/stiggins271.cfm.

Yell, M. L., & Drasgow, E. (2005). *No Child Left Behind: A guide for professionals*. Upper Saddle River, NJ: Pearson Merrill Prentice Hall.

CHAPTER 2

Planning Assessments

EFFECTIVE CLASSROOM assessments do not simply happen. To make your assessments successful, you need to plan them well in advance. Obviously you will consider the content of the unit of instruction and the level of the performance you expect from your students. In addition, good planning involves considering factors like the following:

- The purposes to be served by the assessment—for example, the kinds of inferences you want to make about students' learning
- The kinds of assessments that will best serve your purposes
- How the assessment outcomes will affect your instruction
- When and with what frequency you want to get measures of your students' achievement

Focusing on these key elements, this chapter offers a step-by-step guide for planning assessments in your classroom.

■ Scores and Their Interpretation

We begin thinking about plans for a test or other assessment by looking at the end product, the kinds of interpretations the scores support. The interpretation is important for communicating instructional outcomes to parents and students as well as for your own use in improving instruction.

The way a score is interpreted leads to different implications for teaching and learning. A raw score is simply a unit of measure. Alone, it has no independent meaning. For instance, if you are told "you had 20 correct answers" on that test or "you had 75 percent correct on that test," you know essentially nothing unless you have a way of interpreting those results.

With but a few qualifications, scores become the basis of several kinds of interpretations and inferences. At this point, we will describe two kinds of interpretation that are essential to know about in making assessments: criterion-referenced and norm-referenced. Criterion-referenced scores can be used to identify levels of achievement in specific areas. Norm-referenced scores can be used to compare an individual score with a norm—a typical performance of a defined group on the same measure. The following sections describe these two types of measures in more detail.

■ Criterion-Referenced Assessments

In *criterion-referenced assessment*, a score is interpreted by comparing it to a performance standard. The interpretation—the set of inferences you make about the student—is based on clearly specified, concrete instructional objectives and standards. In planning a criterion-referenced assessment, you define levels of competence, criteria for having passed or failed, and cut-off points for mastery levels of the skills you are trying to measure (Popham, 1978a).

To illustrate one application, a criterion-referenced report card (see Figure 2.1) might have the following elements:

- A list of subject-matter areas
- Specific competencies under each area, using verbs such as *understands* (concepts and principles), *uses* (good writing skills), *explains* (cause and effect), *contributes* (to class discussions), *completes* (homework assignments), *interacts* (skillfully in social situations), and *creates* (novel artistic designs)
- A rating scale, such as 1 = mastery, 2 = nearing independent performance, 3 = making progress, 4 = needs improvement or remedial help

Criterion levels are set by the teacher (for classroom assessment) or by the school (for reporting performance levels). A report card can use various terms to indicate levels of excellence achieved by the student; for example:

- For test work: "Essay exams are well organized."
- For projects: "The student makes theme-oriented exhibits."

JACKSON MIDDLE SCHOOL
GRADE 6

Student ——————— Teacher —————— Principal —————— Quarter 2   3   4

E = Excellent   S = Satisfactory   P = Making Progress   N = Needs Improvement

READING & WRITING

—— Reads with understanding
—— Is able to write about what has been read
—— Completes reading work
—— Shows interest in reading
Reading Skills
—— Decodes new words
—— Understands new words
Independent Reading Level:
Below   At Grade Level   Above

SPELLING & GRAMMAR

——Uses oral language effectively
——Listens carefully
——Masters weekly spelling
Writing skills
——Understands writing process
——Creates a rough draft
——Makes meaningful revisions
——Creates edited, final draft
Editing skills
——Capitalizes
——Punctuates
——Uses complete sentences
——Uses paragraphs correctly
——Uses dictionary correctly

Writing skills level:
Below   At Grade Level   Above

MATHEMATICS
Problem Solving
—— Solves program problems
—— Solves homework problems
—— Solves story problems
Interpreting Problems
—— Uses correct strategies
—— Can use multiple strategies
—— Explains strategies in written form
—— Explains strategies orally
Math Concepts
   Understands Fractions
Beginner Developing Sophisticated
   Multiplication, Basic facts
Beginner Developing Sophisticated
   2 Digit Multiplication
Beginner Developing Sophisticated
   Division
Beginner Developing Sophisticated
   Geometry
Beginner Developing Sophisticated
Overall Math Skill Level:
Beginner Developing Sophisticated
Attitude/Work Skills
—— Welcomes a challenge
—— Persistence
—— Learns from others
—— Listens to others
—— Participates in discussions
It Figures
Is working on: ——————
Goal: ——————————
Is working on achieving goal:
————————————

HISTORY
—— Understands subject matter
—— Shows curiosity & enthusiasm
—— Contributes to class discussions
—— Uses map skills
—— Understands readings by interpreting text
Topics covered: Individual cultures, Columbus - First English colonies

SCIENCE
—— Shows interest in scientific subject matter
—— Asks scientific questions
—— Shows knowledge of scientific method of investigation
—— Uses knowledge to set up and run experiments
—— Makes good scientific observations
—— Has researched scientific topic
Topic(s)
I Wonder
Is currently working on:

LEARNING SKILLS
—— Listens carefully
—— Follows directions
—— Works neatly and carefully
—— Checks work
—— Completes work on time
—— Uses time wisely
—— Works well independently
—— Works well in a group
—— Takes risks in learning
—— Welcomes a challenge

HOMEWORK
—— Self-selects homework
—— Completes work accurately
—— Completes work on time

PROJECTS
_____
_____

CITIZENSHIP
—— Shows courtesy
—— Respects rights of others
—— Shows self-control
—— Interacts well with peers
—— Shows a cooperative and positive attitude in class
—— Shows a cooperative attitude when asked to work with other students
—— Is willing to help other students
—— Works well with other adults (subs, student teacher, parents, etc.)

Attendance

	1st	2nd	3rd	4th
Present				
Absent				
Tardy				

Placement for next year:
_____

Figure 2.1. A report card illustrating some components of criterion-referenced assessment. *Source:* **Lake & Kafka, 1996.**

- For homework assignments: "The student completes assignments neatly and accurately."
- For laboratory work: "The student sets up laboratory experiments from manual, but is unable to design his or her own experiment."

Align Assessments with Objectives

When used properly, criterion-referenced assessments represent clearly stated objectives. They can be particularly useful for programs in which such objectives predominate—for example, reading skill programs, mastery learning programs, and developmental programs in science and math. Because they are based on what the student is able to do, criterion-referenced assessments help teachers make instructional decisions. These tests are also useful for diagnosing students' need for remedial help.

Align Tests and Test Items with Criteria

Well-developed criterion-referenced interpretation depends on the clarity with which objectives are stated. If your objectives are fuzzy, your assessment will not be useful. Similarly, you need to make sure that your objectives or performance criteria are well represented in the test items. In other words, there must be good correspondence between the targeted objectives and the actual items on the test.

Plan Defensible Communication of Grades

Your planning should also include the way grades will be communicated and explained. The levels of achievement you choose as cut-offs for rating levels (such as excellent, average, mediocre, or low performance) must be defensible when questioned by administrators, parents, or students.

■ Norm-Referenced Assessments

A *norm-referenced assessment* is one based on an average of a specified group of other people, called a peer group, a cohort, or a norm group. Such groups may range from the other students in the classroom to an age group or a given ethnic group. For instance, in addition to saying that a student achieved a specific performance criterion, a teacher could compare the student's score with the typical performance of classmates. Thus, the difference between criterion-referenced and norm-referenced tests lies not in the bases of test construction but in the kinds of inferences made from the scores (Nitko & Brookhart, 2006).

The *norm* is the typical achievement, the typical performance, of a group judged to be similar in some defined way to the individual whose score is being interpreted. A norm-referenced score is interpreted according to a student's standing in the norm group and is communicated by such statements as "The score is in the bottom 8 percent of a group of college freshmen who have taken the test."

Norm-referenced inferences about a test score derive from its position within the group with which it is being compared. Interpreted in this way, *the score is not a measure of the amount or quality of a performance or competency*. In our example of a score in "the bottom 8 percent of a group of college freshmen," the "8 percent" does not refer to the number or percentage of correct answers. Rather, the "8 percent" refers to the ranking within the norm group.

Grading "on the Curve"

One way of using norm-referenced scores is the assignment of grades, usually letter grades, based on the normal distribution curve. Called *grading on the curve*, this was a popular approach during the last century for assigning grades in large college and university classes. Its use is illustrated in Theory to Practice Box 2.1 and Figure 2.2.

The Determination of Grades Based on Grading on the Curve

Because grading on the curve is based on the distribution of scores and not on the magnitude of scores, the range of raw scores is immaterial; the distribution is the basis for assigning grades. This characteristic may lead to an ambiguous interpretation of the score. For example, assume a hypothetical class composed of above-average students who studied well for an exam. The examination results might show that the scores ranged from 75 percent to 95 percent correct. Accordingly, despite the relatively high scores, the grades assigned would be distributed according to their place on the curve: A few students would earn As or Fs, a larger number would earn Bs and Ds, and most would earn Cs.

Now assume another class has been administered the same test. Assume further that this second class is composed of less-prepared students of average ability. Their scores, which range from 50 percent to 75 percent correct, are also assigned letter grades of A through F based on grading on the curve. There will be the same numbers of As and Fs in this class as in the previously described class, even though the number of correct answers is definitely lower.

Limitations of Grading on the Curve

Obviously, this procedure raises questions about how to compare grades from one class to another. It also implies that, in principle at least, there will always be Fs as well as As regardless of how well the group as a whole did. Fortunately, there are other ways of assigning norm-referenced scores, and we will discuss several of these in the following sections.

Theory to Practice Box 2.1
GRADING ON THE CURVE

The *normal curve* has the characteristics shown in Figure 2.2. It has central tendency and regular dispersion (frequency) of cases around the average. Percentages of cases are shown for each part of the curve.

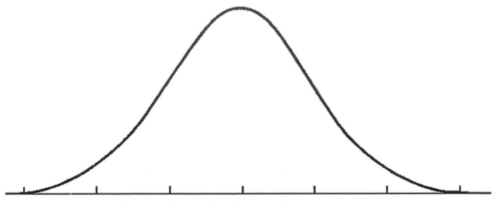

Figure 2.2. The "bell-shaped" normal curve.

The normal curve is bell shaped. The base is divided into equal segments according to the range of scores. The center portion is the average score. The twin segments on either side of the average contain equal frequencies.

In grading on the curve the greatest proportion of students receives grades of C– which, incidentally, before the era of grade inflation, had the reputation of being a respectable grade.

Using the normal curve as a basis for the assignment of grades to a class of students, you might follow this procedure: Regardless of the range or magnitude of the scores, assume they will be normally distributed as shown in the figure. For any test or end-of-semester scores, a small percentage (assume about 2–3 percent) will be at each of the extremes (very high and very low). Assign these scores As and Fs, respectively. Next, there will be a larger percentage intermediate between those groups and the cluster of center or middle scores. These will consist of about 13–14 percent at each end of the curve. They will be assigned Bs and Ds, respectively. The greatest number of cases exists at the center of the curve around the middle or average. There will be about 34 percent on either side of the "peak" or average of the bell. Assign those scores the average grade of C or, if you wish, give the lower half C– and the upper half C+.

Percentiles and Similar Methods

Percentiles place a raw score within a distribution of 100 percent, according to the percentage of people who earned the same score or a lower score. For example, if Mary's raw score of 55 percent correct is reported to be in the 72nd percentile, it would mean that 72 percent of the people within her peer group (norm) received a score at or lower than her score. You should remember that a percentile refers to a *position in the distribution* of scores. It does *not* represent the percentage or the number of correct answers.

Other ways of reporting scores are closely related to percentiles. You may see references to quartiles, quintiles, deciles, stanines, and the like. In each case, the distribution of scores is divided into sections: quarters for quartiles, fifths for quintiles, tenths for deciles, and ninths for stanines (a term derived from "standard nines"). Thus, a score reported in the top *quartile* refers to a score in the top 25 percent of all the scores reported; a score in the second *decile* refers to a score in the second tenth of all scores reported; and, a score in the second *stanine* is in the second ninth of all scores reported.

Any of these methods might be used in grading on the curve. For example, the stanine is a way of dividing the normal curve into nine sections. The lowest or highest 4 percent of the scores would be assigned very poor or very excellent grades, respectively. The next 7 percent of the lowest and highest scores would be assigned poor or good grades; and so on for sections containing 12 percent and 17 percent. The middle or "average" section would contain 20 percent of the scores.

Grade-Equivalent Scores

In using standardized tests in most areas, including statewide tests, you will often see results reported as *grade equivalent scores.* These are like percentiles and other similar scores in that they are based on norms. However, in this case the norm is the average for a grade level. So if the average of seventh graders in all schools in the state for the Reading subtest of the XCAT is 92, and the average for teacher John Brown's class is 92 on the same test, his class is reported as reading at the seventh-grade level. In other words, the grade-level score is the average of the norm group at that grade level. Sometimes these scores are reported with decimals for refining interpretations: A score of 7.5 would mean "better than the performance of the average seventh grader" or "halfway to reading at the level of eighth graders." Scores of individuals who are substantially out of grade level are difficult, if not impossible, to interpret. A sixth grader who scores 9.0 on a sixth-grade reading test may not actually be reading at the ninth-grade level.

Using Norm-Referenced Scores

You can see by now that interpreting any norm-referenced score requires understanding the characteristics of the norm group and the scoring system. Most developers of standardized tests provide norms based on *disaggregated* distributions of scores. This means that the total distribution is separated into subgroups or "cohorts" so that norms can be based on distinctive statistical or demographic factors, such as ethnicity, race, age, and gender groups and geographical location—factors that may expose students to distinctive instructional experiences.

Knowing the characteristics of the norm group will prevent unfair comparisons based on an inappropriate norm group. In using any distribution, note also that the ranges of scores do not have the same intervals within each section of the curve. The range of scores in the average or center portion is smaller that the range of scores at the extremes. For instance, a difference of four points at the center of the distribution represents more percentile points than does a difference of four points at the high end or low end.

Be especially wary in using and interpreting single test scores. The use of single scores for grading purposes is common. For example, it is quite common to report a single grade for language and another single grade for science. Obviously, these areas are composed of many components (see the example in Theory to Practice Box 2.2). Any one student might be good in one component and average in another component, thereby suggesting different forms of remediation.

Another point to keep in mind is that students motivated by norm-referenced scores will tend to be competitive, striving for higher scores than their peers or becoming anxious when their grades are lower than their peers' grades. Too often, with this kind of grading system, status within a group becomes more important than attainment of learning objectives.

■ Making Plans for Assessments

Knowing the kinds of scores used to report test results and how you might interpret them is one way of thinking about the end result of assessment. Now let's look at a framework you can use for planning assessments.

An Assessment Model

Our assessment model consists of these components:

- *Targeted objectives.* What do you want students to learn in the lesson(s)? What are the targets of instruction, the outcomes to be achieved? What are the behavioral, attitudinal, or cognitive manifestations of these objectives?

- *Instructional methods and content.* What will you do to achieve your targets? What instructional methods, learning tasks, and learning contexts will you use?
- *Assessment tasks and measures.* How will you know whether your targets have been achieved? Have you considered the full range of assessment tools? Have you thought about both formal and informal measures of student ability or achievement?

The three components should be in balance, as shown by the assessment triangle in Figure 2.3. They should interact in such a way that instruction guides progress toward achieving the objectives on the one hand, but is guided by objectives on the other. Assessments are based on observation of behaviors or skills targeted in the objectives. The findings from assessments provide feedback about the adequacy of instruction so that either the instruction or the objectives may be revised if necessary. Given reasonable targets and instruction to reach these targets, the assessments will make the success or failure of the instruction apparent.

Theory to Practice Box 2.2
THE INFORMATION HIDDEN BY SINGLE SCORES

The following questions from a quiz in introductory chemistry require different kinds of skills and represent different levels of understanding. The objective is shown in parentheses following the question. A single score such as percent right would likely conceal information about a student's specific strengths and weaknesses.

- What are the valences of these elements: carbon, oxygen, chlorine, hydrogen, sodium, and sulfur? *(memory of content knowledge)*
- What are the characteristics of the elements in isolation? *(memory of content knowledge)*
- What compounds could you make from these elements by simply combining them? *(analysis)*
- What compounds could you make from these elements by applying heat? *(analyzing relations)*
- What are the characteristics of the compounds you formed (1) without heat and (2) with heat? *(analyzing relations)*
- Can you develop a compound that would act on metal from these elements? *(induction and deduction)*
- Can you develop a compound that would neutralize the compound that would dissolve the metal? *(problem solving)*

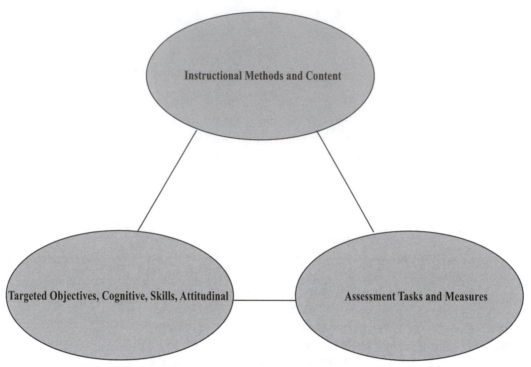

Figure 2.3. The assessment triangle.

■ Steps in Assessment and Reporting

Figure 2.4 offers a graphic overview of the way assessment integrates with instruction and student learning. In this section we develop a detailed outline of steps for achieving that integration. These steps reflect the components of the assessment triangle and the work of a number of researchers (for instance, Johnson & Johnson, 1996; Stiggins, 2007). These steps also provide a preview of assessment topics to be discussed in more detail later in this text.

Specify the End Product
- Begin by focusing on assessment of instruction and learning, not on scoring or on selecting students for special classes.
- Specify objectives. Decide what students are to achieve. In addition to the content of learning, you may also want to consider the processes of learning and attitudes toward the subject matter.

Align Instruction with Indicators of Learning Progress
- Specify guidelines for the instructional unit. Align the objectives and instructional methods with assessments of student progress toward objectives. Begin with knowing where your students are—that is, what they know before instruction—and

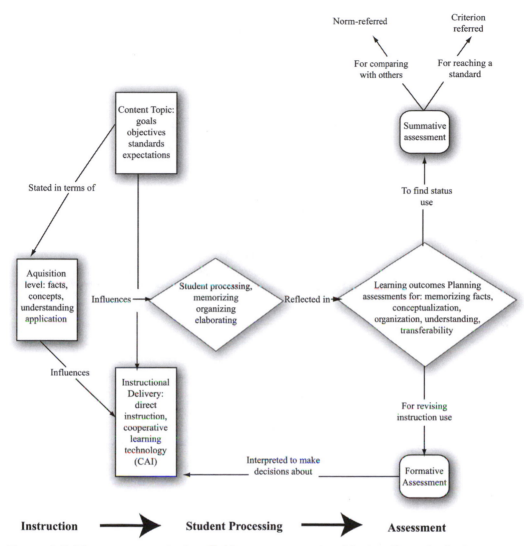

Figure 2.3. The assessment plan, linking components of instruction, student processing, and assessment.

gear your instruction to that level. Don't repeat material that they already know. But do provide remedial instruction or initiate instruction at a lower level if students aren't ready for the level you anticipated as a start.

• Identify the performances—the indicators or pointers—that show what level of progress has been made in reaching the expectations.

Plan to Communicate Assessment Targets and Procedures

• Share objectives with students (parents, administrators, and others). Don't keep expectations about student learning a secret. Don't make the mistake of holding this knowledge from students so you can surprise them on a test. Even the youngest students will take an interest in what you want them to achieve. Ask their opinion about how they can demonstrate what they know. Justify procedures you use based on good assessment practices. In the process you provide initial experiences for developing students' self-regulation of learning and realistic evaluations of self-efficacy.

Develop and Schedule Assessment Measures
- To assess how much students have learned, measure both the quality and quantity of achievement. In addition to traditional paper-and-pencil tests, consider performance-based assessment that requires demonstration of what students can do with their knowledge. They can submit compositions, exhibitions, projects, reports, demonstrations, surveys, or even actual job performances.
- Create clearly articulated sets of criteria or rubrics to serve as the basis for scoring or grading. That is, rather than grading a project as a whole (with grades of A through F, for example), grade the quality of individual components. For example, if problem-solving ability is to be evaluated, the performance measure might be based on several dimensions: use of prior knowledge, analysis of the problem, use of systematic strategies in arriving at a solution, and adequacy of the solution statement.
- Make a schedule of times when assessments are to be administered. It is appropriate to give an assessment at the conclusion of an instructional unit, but often teachers give more tests than necessary. Administer tests at points when students have had an opportunity to demonstrate improvement of learning.

Decide on the Format of the Assessment Measures
- In each instance, decide on the best format for the assessment measure, for instance, whether it will be a performance measure, such as demonstrating a skill, or a test; and if the latter, whether it will be objective or essay based.
- State the setting or context in which assessment will take place. Most tests do not require a particular setting and can be performed in the abstract; for instance, an arithmetic test with problems in simple addition can be performed as an abstract problem ($2 + 3 = 5$). As word problems, a situation is provided to supplement the requirements for solving the abstract problem. For example, the contextual (word) counterpart of the simple abstract problem might be: "If John has two marbles and Mary has three, how many marbles are there?" Or,

"You have written two checks at one bank and three at the other; how many checks have you written?"

Authentic assessments require students to demonstrate skill levels or procedures in everyday settings, or similar detailed contexts involving simulated real-life tasks or real-life problems. To assess a science unit, you could evaluate students' conduct of an experiment to see the effect of light on plant growth. To measure skills in journalistic writing, you could have students write a report on a current event.

- Even when assessments are based on dimensions of performance, it is unrealistic to measure every dimension, if for no other reason than that it would be overly time consuming. Accordingly, you should make decisions about *sampling* dimensions and establishing criteria for evaluating the quality of performance.

Use the Feedback from Assessment Results
- Finally, close the assessment loop, as shown at the bottom of Figure 2.4. Once the assessment has been made, use the feedback it provides for instructional improvement. When assessments are given before the instruction, they provide information about the students' instructional readiness—whether they have the required skills or knowledge to learn from your lessons. When assessments are given during the learning, they provide information about adjustments you need to make to facilitate learning. When given at the end of a period of learning (a lesson, unit, or time period), assessments provide a basis for evaluating how well your expectations about student achievement have been met.

■ Creating Blueprints for Specific Assessments

In this section we will provide additional guidance in applying the steps we have just described. We'll talk in detail about objectives and test construction. Before writing objectives, though, you need to visualize what a successful student performance would be.

Visualizing Performance

In planning a specific assessment, it helps to be able to visualize performance of your objectives in different ways or different settings. If you are an elementary school teacher, do you know what good writing is at the fourth-grade level? If you are going to teach piano, would you know what constitutes outstanding performance for a second-year learner? Would it make a difference if the second-year learner were an adult? Can you develop a questionnaire that would show a student's self-efficacy in geometry? Simple listing of steps in defining the characteristics of good performance is often helpful in this stage of planning.

Appropriate performance can be defined by written goals and objectives, but can only be recognized with practice and experience. If you don't have a good sense of appropriate target behavior, it is virtually impossible to develop a good assessment. Theory to Practice Box 2.3 provides a brief exercise to help you evaluate your ability to visualize.

Specifying Objectives

Visualizing an outcome will help you generate an appropriate target to begin the assessment process. The target then needs to be translated into a task.

Behavioral objectives provide good illustrations of how to implement this requirement. Such objectives provide a set of expectations of what students should be able to do, under prescribed circumstances, to achieve a stated criterion. These objectives supply both students and teachers with a common vocabulary to negotiate the process. An illustration of a behavioral objective is:

The student will be able to set up a laboratory experiment using appropriate chemicals and apparatus to produce and prove the production of oxygen.

Did you see that this objective has a setting, a task to perform, a stated outcome of the task, and criteria for acceptable performance? Notice that an objective of this sort clearly suggests both the instructional method to be used and the context in which the learning is to be demonstrated.

Mager (1975) discusses the three components of well-written objectives:

1. *Conditions* under which the performance must occur ("Given the equipment and materials of a chemistry lab . . .")
2. *Performance indicators* (". . . the student will choose appropriate apparatus and chemicals to produce oxygen . . .")
3. *Level of proficiency* reached (". . . and will successfully conduct the experiment and demonstrate that oxygen has been produced.")

Theory to Practice Box 2.3
A VISUALIZATION EXERCISE

The following are some test questions taken from textbooks that cover grades K–12. In each example, try to guess what grade level the material is taken from.

1. When calculating global population growth, the death rate is

    a. Added to the birthrate.
    b. Subtracted from life expectancy.
    c. Multiplied by 100.
    d. Subtracted from the birthrate.

2. Think of the missing letter or letters in each Elephant Word. Write each word.

    a. __ ny
    b. s __ __ d

3. Why was the binomial nomenclature system developed by Linnaeus an improvement over earlier systems for naming organisms?
4. Write a paragraph or two in answer to one of the following questions.

    a. What were the most important reforms of Florida's governors between 1905 and 1917?
    b. What were the complaints of passengers and farmers against the railroads?

5. Write balanced chemical equations for each of these reactions. Classify each as to type.

    a. Aluminum reacts with sulfuric acid to produce hydrogen and aluminum sulfate.
    b. Heating sulfuric acid produces water, oxygen, and sulfur dioxide.
    c. Pentane, C_5H_{12}, reacts with oxygen.
    d. Sodium iodide reacts with phosphoric acid to form hydrogen iodide and sodium phosphate.
    e. Potassium oxide reacts with water to form potassium hydroxide.

Answers: (1) grades 6–11, (2) grades 1–2, (3) grades 6–9, (4) grade 4, (5) grades 9–12.

For assessments of most academic tasks, these three components require some serious consideration. For example, if you require students to make calculations for a math test, will the use of a calculator be permitted or will you require students to perform those functions from memory? For assessing students' proficiency, will a paper-and-pencil alternative response test serve as well as a performance measure? In everyday situations, would it make a difference?

Without careful attention to specificity, objectives may be too broad. Instruction is best guided by objectives that focus precisely on targeted changes expected in student behavior and achievement. But is it possible for objectives to be *too* specific? Theory to Practice Box 2.4 offers some insight into this question.

Bloom's Taxonomy

Bloom's Taxonomy of Educational Objectives (Bloom & Krath-wohl, 1956) provides a classic description of various levels of learning. The importance of Bloom's taxonomy (and others like it) is that taxonomies call attention to potentially different instructional outcome levels. They point out the difference between acquisition of factual knowledge at a basic level and the ability to analyze and synthesize information at a more advanced level. That is, rather than placing a premium on rote learning of discrete facts, taxonomies help us see the importance of higher-order learning and the sequential emergence of understanding. They also call attention to the patterns of thinking underlying the responses to assessment items.

Teachers who understand the different levels of learning can use that information in selecting the type of assessment to use and in making decisions about additional instruction to help students who perform poorly. The following list shows five levels of objectives that can be applied to any content domain. These levels are based on Bloom's taxonomy, reorganized by imposing a thinking-level category based on Newmann and associates (1996):

- *Knowledge.* Knowledge is composed of facts that the student knows. Assessment at this level involves finding out whether the student knows specific information, such as the definition of a term or the characteristics of a triangle. At this lowest level of understanding, an objective might use verbs such as *names, knows, selects,* and *labels.*
- *Comprehension/Understanding.* At a more advanced level, specific information is related to other information. For example, are small creeping things classified as bugs or insects? Eventually, these connections lead to deeper knowledge so that the student can understand and work with the basic ideas of a subject-matter area. Assessment of comprehension involves determining whether or how the student links information into patterns, such as networks of information

Theory to Practice Box 2.4
THE SPECIFICITY OF OBJECTIVES

The degree of specificity of objectives has important implications for both instruction and assessment. Let's start with a broadly stated goal:

> Students should be able to perform basic operations in mathematics.

This statement might appear in a statewide set of curricular guidelines, but it fails to inform an instructor about what to teach. Perhaps it can be revised to be a bit more specific:

> Students should be able to multiply real numbers.

This statement has more focus (multiplication) but, again, little instructional utility. Let's make it even more specific:

> Students should be able to multiply two 2-digit real numbers together.

Now we are reaching a level of specificity at which we would be able to plan meaningful instruction.

Using this last objective, we might write a test item like this:

$$11 \times 22 = ?$$

How do you feel about this item as a measure of the domain covered by the objective? Most people would evaluate the item as not being fair. Why? When pressed, they would say that it does not involve the process of carrying over or regrouping. In that sense, it would be qualitatively different from this item:

$$45 \times 67 = ?$$

This multiplication task derives from the same objective, but different processes are involved in calculating the solution. So should we go back to the objective and write it even more specifically? We might revise it as follows:

> Students should be able to multiply two 2-digit real numbers
> together in a way that involves the process of carrying over.

At this level of specificity, however, we may have gone too far. The objective is getting so detailed that items on a test will be *defined* by it. When objectives become this cumbersome, they are also hard to manage, difficult to teach, and restrictive in their assessment. Popham (1978b) might suggest that the behavior objective needs to be reigned in or "lassoed." Popham recommends that objectives should be specific, but not overly specific.

or classifications of concepts. Objectives for this deeper level of understanding use verbs such as *comprehends*, *estimates*, *understands*, and *predicts*.

- *Synthesis.* At this level of thinking and understanding, we move into what is often called higher-order thinking. Here, the student can take a number of specific ideas and put them together into theories and generalizations. An example may be seen in students who conduct doctoral dissertations. They often consider a set of variables that are described as demographic variables. These are often strung out as a list, for instance as intelligence, aptitude, socioeconomic class, ethnicity, race, religion, high school grades, and so on. Very often they fail to consider that these variables can be grouped (synthesized) into classes; for example, a nuclear family can consist of one or two parents or any number of children; ethnicity can consist of race, religion, and country of origin as well as status (immigrant or first generation); and social demographics can consist of socioeconomic status, career, friendships, and so on. Assessment tasks to measure synthesis may require students to organize, elaborate, explain, categorize, reconstruct, or summarize.

- *Analysis.* At this level of understanding the student is expected to break down an idea into its structure or component parts and explain the way the structure is organized. For example, the class of objects we call animals is composed of birds, reptiles, fish, and mammals. All share such attributes of living, mobility, reproduction, and so on. Yet they are vastly different, and students at this level of understanding would be able to explain both similarities and differences. Assessment of ability to analyze can be made by testing understanding of underlying causes and effects, or it might focus on comparisons, differentiation, or outlining of specific elements, relations, or principles.

- *Application: making new connections.* At this level, the student can apply information to other contexts inside and outside the classroom. Assessments of this ability often require performance-based or criterion-based assessments. They might involve any of the assessments used for other levels of objectives, adding to them different contexts than those used in instruction. Assessment of thinking beyond the classroom is often considered an important component of authentic measures.

Each level in the taxonomy implies a different method of assessment, instruction, and achievement. If you wanted to assess students' ability to analyze, for example, you would not construct a test that focused solely on facts. Keeping the taxonomy in mind will help you create assessments appropriate to the full range of your teaching.

Examples of Behavioral Objectives

As mentioned before, a good behavioral objective has three parts: (1) conditions under which the behavior occurs, (2) a specification of the *observable* behavior, and (3) some criterion that must be met. This latter part may be explicit or implicit. So for example in performance assessment, we would expect that the pilot would "land the plane safely 100 percent of the time." Other examples include:

- "Given two 2-digit numbers, the student will be able to correctly multiply them 80 percent of the time."
- "Given lab apparatus, hydrochloric acid, and zinc, the student will be able to produce hydrogen gas in three out of four attempts."
- "Given the results of four experimental conditions, the student will correctly analyze them to the second decimal place."

Notice that all of the verbs in the examples above (*multiply*, *produce*, *analyze*) are in some way directly observable. Other verbs, however, do not lend themselves to direct observation and are therefore weak choices for well-stated behavior objectives. For example:

- The student will *understand* the three elements of combustion.

How do you know when a student "understands" or "knows" something? You really do not. So, alternatively, you would state, more precisely, the objectives you want to achieve, as in the following examples:

- The student will correctly *state* the three elements of combustion.
- Given the elements of heat, fuel, and oxygen, the student will correctly *predict* under what conditions combustion will occur.
- Given a stalled car, the student will correctly *diagnose* the likely cause of the problem.

The three alternative versions of the behavioral objective do contain observable verbs (sometimes known as action verbs) and are therefore preferable.

Table 2.1 is a listing of verbs that approximately correspond to a given level of Bloom's taxonomy. While the verb itself does not indicate how the behavior will be measured, it does indicate the level of cognitive complexity with which a task is performed.

■ Test Blueprints

Let's say that you have determined that a paper-and-pencil exam is the best way to test student progress on a particular unit you've been teaching. Your next step will be to plan the test. But where should you begin?

We suggest you begin with a test blueprint that maps out a technically proficient set of components to describe what a student will see on the test. Most instructors take one of two approaches to this task:

1. Create a matrix that lists the number of items linked to their instructional objectives and taxonomic level (according to Bloom's taxonomy). Table 2.2 illustrates this approach for a unit on statistics and sampling.
2. List the topics (and number of items for each topic) linked to the objectives in an outline form, as shown in Table 2.3.

You can also combine these two approaches, as Table 2.4 illustrates.

The test blueprint might be considered a cognitive road map of the test. It is often employed as part of a grade-level team approach to constructing tests. A team leader constructs the test blueprint and passes it to the team members for review and validation. Once consensus has been achieved on the test's content and format, individual team members take sections of the test to construct test tasks appropriate to the objectives. The final assembly and review of the test are then coordinated by the team leader. Using this coordinated approach, no one teacher is saddled with constructing an entire test, but rather each can make contributions in his or her areas of expertise or interest.

Based on the test blueprint in Table 2.4, the following multiple-choice item might be generated to match the objective "mean versus median":

1. What would be the relationship of the mean and median for income on a sample taken from a college town?
   a. The mean and median would be the same.
   b. The mean would be smaller than the median.
   c. The mean would be larger than the median.
   d. The answer depends on the size of the sample.

Table 2.1. Instrumentation of the Taxonomy of Educational Objectives: Cognitive Domain

Taxonomy Classification	Key Words	
	Examples of Infinitives	*Examples of Direct Objects*
1.00 Knowledge		
1.10 Knowledge of Specifics		
1.11 Knowledge of Terminology	To define, to distinguish, to acquire, to identify, to recall, to recognize	Vocabulary, terms, terminology, meaning(s), definitions, referents, elements
1.12 Knowledge of Specific Facts	To recall, to recognize, to acquire, to identify	Facts, factual information, sources, names, dates, events, persons, places, time periods, properties, examples, phenomena
1.20 Knowledge of Ways and Means of Dealing with Specifics		
1.21 Knowledge of Conventions	To recall, to identify, to recognize, to acquire	Form(s), conventions, uses, usage, rules, ways, devices, symbols, representations, style(s), format(s)
1.22 Knowledge of Trends Sequences	To recall, to recognize, to acquire, to identify	Action(s), processes, movement(s), continuity, development(s), trend(s), sequence(s), causes, relationship(s), forces, influences
1.23 Knowledge of Classifications and Categories	To recall, to recognize, to acquire, to identify	Area(s), type(s), feature(s), class(es), set(s), division(s), arrangements(s), classification(s), category/categories
1.24 Knowledge of Criteria	To recall, to recognize, to acquire, to identify	Criteria, basics, elements
1.25 Knowledge of Methodology	To recall, to recognize, to acquire, to identify	Methods, techniques, approaches, uses, procedures, treatments
1.30 Knowledge of the Universals and Abstractions in a Field		

(continued)

Table 2.1. (continued)

Taxonomy Classification	Key Words	
	Examples of Infinitives	Examples of Direct Objects
1.32 Knowledge of Theories and Structures	To recall, to recognize, to acquire, to identify	Theories, bases, interrelations, structure(s), organization(s), formulation(s)
2.00 Comprehension		
2.10 Translation	To translate, to transform, to give in own words, to illustrate, to prepare, to read, to represent, to change, to rephrase, to restate	Meaning(s), sample(s), definitions, abstractions, representations, words, phrases
2.20 Interpretation	To interpret, to reorder, to rearrange, to differ, to differentiate, to distinguish, to make, to draw, to explain, to demonstrate	Relevancies, relationships, essentials, aspects, new view(s), qualifications, conclusions, methods, theories, abstractions
2.30 Extrapolation	To estimate, to infer, to conclude, to predict, to differentiate, to determine, to extend, to interpolate, to extrapolate, to fill in, to draw	Consequences, implications, conclusions, factors, ramifications, meanings, corollaries, effects, probabilities
3.00 Application	To apply, to generalize, to relate, to choose, to develop, to organize, to use, to employ to transfer, to restructure, to classify	Principles, laws, conclusions, effects, methods, theories, abstractions, situations, generalizations, processes, phenomena, procedures
4.00 Analysis		
4.10 Analysis of elements	To distinguish, to detect, to identify, to classify, to discriminate, to recognize, to categorize, to deduce	Elements, hypotheses/hypotheses, conclusions, assumptions, statements (of fact), statements (of intent), arguments, particulars

Taxonomy Classification	Key Words	
	Examples of Infinitives	*Examples of Direct Objects*
4.30 Analysis of Organizational Principles	To analyze, to distinguish, to detect, to deduce	Form(s), pattern(s), purpose(s) point(s) of view, techniques, bias(es), structure(s), theme(s), arrangement(s), organization(s)
5.00 Synthesis		
5.10 Production of a Unique Communication	To write, to tell, to relate, to produce, to constitute, to transmit, to originate, to modify, to document	Structure(s), pattern(s), product(s), performance(s), design(s), work(s), communications, effort(s), specifics, composition(s)
5.20 Productions of a Plan or Proposed Set of Operations	To propose, to plan, to produce, to design, to modify, to specify	Plan(s), objectives, specification(s), schematic(s), operations, way(s), solution(s), means
5.30 Derivation of a Set of Abstraction Relations	To produce, to derive, to develop, to combine, to organize, to synthesize, to classify, to deduce, to develop, to formulate, to modify	Phenomena, taxonomies, concept(s), scheme(s), theories, relationships, abstractions, generalizations, hypothesis/hypotheses, perceptions, ways, discoveries
6.00 Evaluation		
6.10 Judgments in Terms of Internal Evidence	To judge, to argue, to validate, to assess, to decide	Accuracy/accuracies, consistency/ consistencies, fallacies, reliability, flaws, error, precision, exactness
6.20 Judgments in Terms of External Criteria	To judge, to argue, to consider, to compare, to contrast, to standardize, to appraise	Ends, means, efficiency, economy/economies, utility, alternatives, courses of action, standards, theories, generalizations

Source: Metfessel, N. S., Michael, W. B., and Kirsner, D. A. (1969). Instrumentation of Bloom's and Krathwol's taxonomies for writing of educational objectives. *Psychology in the Schools, 6,* 227–231.

Table 2.2. A Matrix Listing of Objectives to Form a Test Blueprint for High School Statistics

	Number of Items		
Level of Objectives	Statistical Techniques	Selecting a Sample	Total Number of Items
Knowledge	3	3	6
Comprehension	1	2	3
Application	2	2	4
Analysis	2	1	3
Synthesis			0
Evaluation		1	1
Number of Items	8	9	17

Table 2.3. An Outline Listing of Objectives to Form a Test Blueprint

III. Statistical Techniques (8 items)	IV. Selecting a Sample (9 items)
a. Quantitative versus qualitative data	a. The results of a study
b. Types of derived scores	b. Sampling strategies
c. Mean versus median	c. Target generalizing population
d. Characteristics of score distributions in a normal curve	d. Population validity Stratified sample
e. Alpha levels	e. When small samples can be used
f. Increasing statistical power	f. Qualitative sampling designs (2 items)
g. Sample statistics and population parameters	g. Qualitative sampling designs (2 items)
h. How to handle missing data	h. Characteristics of volunteers

■ Assessment Modalities and the Role of Observation

The multiple-choice test format we have just illustrated is only one possibility. You will want to use different assessment formats—often known as *modalities*—depending on the kind of assessment you are planning.

For example, essay tests and other writing tasks open up a variety of ways for students to demonstrate what they know, how they reason, or how they feel about something. Performance assessment is likely to be the preferred way to convince a science teacher that a student could set up a laboratory experiment or a social studies teacher that a student has the social skills for effective leadership. Formal or informal conversations with students can also serve as assessments, with the advantage that the teacher can accomplish them "on the fly." Later chapters will illustrate these modalities, among others.

The assessment modalities are all based on the concept of observation and the skills that are required to become a good

Table 2.4. A Combination of the Test Blueprint Formats from Tables 2.2 and 2.3

| Level of Objectives | Topics | | Number of Items |
	Statistical Techniques	Selecting a Sample	
Knowledge	• Mean versus median • Types of derived scores • Alpha levels	• Sampling strategies • Target population • Population validity	6
Comprehension	• Increasing statistical power	• When small samples can be used • Characteristics of volunteers	3
Application	• Quantitative versus qualitative data • Sample statistics and population parameters	• Qualitative sampling designs (2 items)	4
Analysis	• Characteristics of score distributions in a normal curve • How to handle missing data	• Sampling strategies	3
Synthesis			0
Evaluation		• Generalizing the results of a study	1
Number of Items	8	9	17

observer. In the next chapter we lay the foundation for formal assessment procedures by discussing this most basic of assessment techniques—observation.

■ Summary

A student's raw score on any assessment is simply a unit of measure with no independent meaning. To give scores meaning, assessments are usually either criterion-referenced or norm-referenced. In criterion-referenced assessment, a score is interpreted by comparing it to a performance standard. In norm-referenced assessment, the interpretation is based on the average scores of a specified group of other people.

One type of norm-referenced scoring is the practice known as grading on the curve, in which grades are based on the bell-shaped normal curve. Norm-referenced scores can also be reported in terms of percentiles, quartiles, quintiles, stanines, and grade equivalent scores. Interpreting any norm-referenced score requires understanding the characteristics of the norm group and the scoring system. By itself, understanding grading on the curve usefully contributes to understanding the statistical characteristics of scoring procedures, but it is severely limited by the difficulty encountered in its interpretations, which in turn has restricted its practicality for widespread use.

One useful way to conceptualize assessment is with the assessment triangle, which shows three components linked interactively: (a) the teacher's targeted objectives, (b) the instructional methods and content, and (c) the assessment tasks and measures.

The steps in creating assessments include specifying the end product, aligning instruction with indicators of learning progress, planning ways to communicate assessment targets and procedures, developing and scheduling the assessment measures, deciding the format of the assessment measures, and using the feedback from assessment results.

To construct an individual test, begin by visualizing the performance you expect from your students. Next, create specific objectives, using Bloom's taxonomy or a similar model to make sure you address different levels of knowledge and understanding. From these objectives, construct a test blueprint, and then write individual items to address each of your objectives and topics.

Exercise 2.1

You have been asked to create a unit on photosynthesis. Using the proper format, write three to five behavioral objectives on the topic. Make sure that at least one of the objectives is at the evaluation level and one at the application level.

Exercise 2.2

Using the behavioral objectives that you generated for Exercise 2.1, create a test blueprint for an upcoming test of at least 20 items. Distribute the objectives across the different levels of Bloom's Taxonomy by employing one of the templates from Tables 2.2 through 2.4.

Exercise 2.3

In thinking about the test blueprint that you generated for Exercise 2.3, what are the best ways to assess the skills, knowledge, or dispositions you specified in your behavioral objectives? How many of them require a performance of some kind? What resources would you need to ensure that students could demonstrate their mastery through a performance of some kind?

■ References

Bloom, B. S., & Krathwohl, D. (1956). *Taxonomy of educational objectives: Handbook 1. Cognitive domain.* New York: Longman, Green.

Johnson, D. W., & Johnson, R. T. (1996). The role of cooperative learning in assessing and communicating student learning. In T. R. Guskey (Ed.), *1996 ASCD Yearbook: Communicating student learning* (pp. 25–46). Alexandria, VA: Association for Supervision and Curriculum Development.

Lake, K., & Kafka, K. (1996). Reporting methods in grades K–8. *ASCD Yearbook*, 90–118.

Mager, R. F. (1975). *Preparing instructional objectives* (2nd ed.). Belmont, CA: Fearon.

Newman, F. M., et al. (1996). *Authentic achievement: Restructuring schools for intellectual quality.* San Francisco, CA: Jossey-Bass Publishers, Inc.

Nitko, A. J., & Brookhart, S. M. (2006). *Educational assessment of students* (5th ed.). Columbus, OH: Allyn & Bacon/Merrill Education.

Popham, W. J. (1978a). *Criterion-referenced measurement.* Englewood Cliffs, NJ: Prentice-Hall.

Popham, W. J. (1978b, October). *A lasso for runaway test items.* Paper presented at the First Annual Johns Hopkins University National Symposium on Educational Research, Washington, DC.

Stiggins, R. J. (2007). *An introduction to student-involved assessment for learning* (5th ed.). Columbus, OH: Allyn & Bacon/Merrill Education.

CHAPTER 3

Observation: Bases of Assessment

OBSERVATION IS A basic tool in assessment. It begins with knowing how to make straightforward observations of pupil behavior in a variety of settings and of the products of that behavior, some of which we have come to know as *artifacts*. You have already used the process by observing how children, adolescents, or your peers do assignments; how they interact with other students; how they interpret, understand, and use instructions to carry out assignments; and how they solve problems. In the course of these activities, you have observed their achievement, their affective reactions to frustration or dilemmas, their feelings of adequacy (or inadequacy) in task performance, and their motivations. In many ways, the assessment process we use as teachers parallels the use of everyday purposeful observation. (See Theory to Practice Box 3.1.)

■ Making Observations

The classroom is a dynamic flow of information emerging from the interaction of students and teachers. The data needed to describe these interactions and to monitor their effectiveness come initially from direct observation, anecdotal evidence, and work samples. As time progresses data collection becomes focused on indirect observation by employing classroom tests and formal tests developed for specific purposes (e.g., math achievement, use of the scientific method, and so on).

Understanding the Purposes of Observation

The purposes of using any measures, whether based on direct observations or formal tests, vary according to the stage of

Theory to Practice Box 3.1
EVERYDAY OBSERVATION

Observation is more than the simple act of seeing. You want to learn as much about the student as needed with the aim of understanding his or her progress in learning and what steps might be taken to improve that progress, if necessary. Direct observation requires the skills important to all assessment:

- *Planning. What purposes are served in making planned observations? What can you observe?* The range of potential targets includes such features as the strategies students use while learning, the details of their expertise (proficiency), their reaction to feedback, and what they know and how they use what they know. Determine which of these require direct observation or observation through such tools as tests, rating scales, or other devices.
- *Developing skills. Skill in observation involves understanding what to look for in specific contexts.* You will find out information related to different aspects of student learning and behavior in different situations. Not all behaviors in which you are interested are manifested in all situations. Both obvious and subtle details of behavior are important.
- *Learn the psychological meaning(s) underlying student behaviors.* Know and understand the signs of good and poor learning and the behavioral signs related to motivation, use of feedback, engagement in tasks, motivations, and so on.
- *Integrate observations with knowledge about the pros and cons of observation as well as what you already know about the student.* It is inevitable that you will seek the meaning behind behaviors (the "why" of a student's behavior). The full use of informed observation will depend on information from a variety of sources (including tests and reports of others—parents, teachers, peers) and settings in which you observe the student (e.g., classroom, playground, social settings). Sophisticated interpretations rely on a rich knowledge base.
- *Understand the implications of your judgment.* Of course, this is why you collected information in the first place. You will use all information collected. Based on this information you will cautiously consider the behavior-in-context for its potential in drawing implications or conclusions—such as for remediation or for enrichment. Relate the products of direct observations to your knowledge about the purposes of collecting information by direct observation as well as the purposes served by observation. Make certain that you have considered the potential limitations of the data you have collected.
- *Interpret the behaviors with reference to the specific context.* For instance, a student quietly studying, disengaged from talking to other students in a library, would be an expected, normal behavior. On the other hand, a quiet pupil totally disengaged in a social group or isolated during recess periods is potentially uncharacteristic of typical adolescent behavior.
- *Evaluate the information you have within the context of implications and judgments you have made.* Of particular importance, make certain you have

sufficient data from the right contexts to enable useful feedback. Have your observations suggested the need for other information? Do you need more information? Should you observe the student in other contexts (situations)? What additional sources will provide the best information? Do you need counterchecks? Do you need to make repeat observations to determine if you have missed important details? Any conclusions about which you are uncertain or about which you feel you have insufficient data should be designated as tentative or needing more information.

- *Record your final use of the observations into a record that can be used in talking to parents, school psychologists, committees, and others who have a legitimate interest in the record.* Such records may take the form of a case study in which all information and implications are organized and integrated into a meaningful whole—a focused and unified explanatory description. More simply it might take the form of a story or an anecdote.

  Descriptions of this sort are frequently developed with the help of professionals (other teachers, school psychologists, administrators, parents) working as a group. Alternatively, you could make a running report beginning with a statement of the reasons why you decided to make observations for a specific purpose. Then follow up this initial statement by sequentially incorporating into your report the kind of observations made, the data from these observations, interpretations of the data (categorizations, comparisons, implications), and the need for further data collection if required (people with whom you might have consulted, reports to be made, and tentative conclusions).

Source: Based on Pelligrino, Chudowsky, and Glaser (2001).

learning (e.g., Gronlund & James, 2005). Before learning they provide information about what pupils know when they begin learning and what pupils need to know and learn as they pursue curricular objectives. During learning they provide information about how pupils learn or are learning, their learning styles or strategies, and their struggles to learn. After learning the measures provide information about how much pupils have learned and the quality of pupils' learning, for example, the judgments one typically finds on report cards. Although these after-learning measures may be viewed as status or summary measures, they may also be used to suggest appropriate feedback for instruction and remediation for areas that need improvement.

Collecting Information

The basic procedures used for knowing about student progress begin with (1) *direct observation* through looking at and listening to children's, adolescents', or adults' everyday behavior; (2) the *products* produced in classwork such as essays, letters, and news articles; (3) *archived information* (information stored from one class to the next such as that which might be kept in school files); and (4) *anecdotal reports by others (teachers or peers)* of student progress.

Skill in using these data sources is critical to reliable (consistent) and valid (accurate) interpretations and inferences based on observation. More formal assessment instruments, whether tests, interviews, surveys, portfolios, or standardized tests, are sophisticated, technically accurate extensions of direct observation and most often are used when informal observation is inadequate. These formal measures are used when the variables affecting behaviors are known but direct observation is beyond the available skills of the observer; when the behaviors occur so infrequently that specific measurements must be taken; and when the behaviors are so complex that they may require multiple measures. Measures that go beyond direct observation, such as tests, place students in specific situations (test situations) characterized by specific task demands not easily seen in informal settings or which require particular forms of responses or performances.

The Observer's Knowledge Base

The requirements for making observations imply that teachers' deliberate use of observations is guided by a scholarly knowledge base (Driscoll, 2005). Which behavioral characteristics are observed, selected, and recorded from direct observation in informal settings (e.g., behaviors that arise in normal classroom or play situtions) are influenced by the expertise of the observer. In other words, the knowledge base informs the teacher, as observer, what to look for, the purposes of seeking specific information, and the methods of making plausibly useful interpretations of what is observed.

Products in Observation

Within a sociological or anthropological framework, artifacts are products that remain as representative of a culture (Webb, Campbell, Schwartz, & Sechrest, 2000). They are human-made objects, give information about the person who made them, and may be all manner of objects including weapons, tools, cooking utensils, ornaments, or writings. You are probably most familiar with these from reports of objects that anthropologists find in "digs." These products provide information about the person or persons who made them, how they were made, how they were used, and who used them.

Behavioral Artifacts

Students produce products from seatwork, homework, or other assignments, even notes or doodles, that can be used in assessments. They are important because they form a representation of the student's typical performance. You could learn about the student's motivations and special interests by the things they write about, things they know how to use (like computers or iPods), things they have posted on the bulletin board, and the time they spend on the variety of behaviors that comprise the uniqueness of the learner.

Adjunct Question

What other artifacts of student work can you identify? How can you set up deliberate assignments as collections of artifacts (*Hint:* portfolios, trunks, collections)? When you pool these with all ideas from other students, what does the list contain? Can you classify them as artifacts related to student culture, artifacts that are products of an individual student's behaviors, and artifacts that are the result of the student's social activity?

Classroom Assignments

Artifacts are also products produced in the ordinary course of classroom work. Many are useful indicators of the students' ability. In the course of ordinary assignments students produce specific products such as a paper on "insecticides for biting and sucking insects" or on "chemical reactions in waste disposal," or "the social consequences of the cell phone." Although such papers may have been assigned, initially, for improving literacy, they may also be used for other purposes including making inferences about neatness, prior knowledge, procedural knowledge, or organizational ability.

Whatever their nature, everyday products of this sort can be collected into portfolios, adding to the sources available for assessment. When deliberately produced in response to an assignment for inclusion in a portfolio, they may be useful for appraisals, but should be recognized as possessing different qualitative attributes (e.g., time spent, care in producing products such as essays, embellishments, and so on) than those associated with normally or spontaneously produced products in everyday settings or in response to normal classroom assignments.

Everyday Situations

You can capitalize on informal opportunities for assessment by observing students behavior outside of the classroom. Situations such as study halls, library, dining room, recess periods, playground, and so on provide rich opportunities for unobtrusive observation of social skills, leisure-time activities, intellectual orientations, or leadership capacities (Webb et al., 2000).

Products produced in the course of everyday behaviors or for usual assignments may have a degree of authenticity not present in a requirement to use a given behavior, as exists in formal observations such as those provided by tests. Their production is influenced by a variety of variables such as the setting, the context, and the situation that modifies the behavior from the way it might have been used in the classroom (Wiggins, 1993). Examples include such behaviors as those used in a laboratory experiment for a technical report compared to those used in a demonstration experiment for a science fair; writing a letter for a summer job would employ a different set of skills than one written in response to an English class assignment or a personal letter to a friend; and procedures for planning a budget with debit and credit sheets in a business class would be different from those used for personal budgeting or in maintaining a checkbook or credit card account.

■ Direct Observation

Over time, experienced teachers become sharp observers of students. They look for typical behaviors that characterize students and for atypical behaviors that separate students from one another. Teachers keep in memory or writing a running record identifying specific students who might require special attention. As these separate records are merged they may eventually become consolidated as characteristic impressions, such as "he is a very *good* student," "she does much *better than her brother* in mathematics," "he seems to be *introverted*," "she is clearly a *leader*," or "he is a *struggling reader* but can be helped by teaching him some reading strategies."

Direct Observation in Informal Settings

With professional training, we become more skilled as observers. We can initiate deliberate observation (direct observation) of some specific behavior. If we want to find out more about a student's interests we might make note of what he or she chooses to do in leisure time (collecting stamps, reading sports magazines, or learning new computer programs). (*Informal* is used here simply to indicate settings that are outside of classroom settings.) Systematic observations might include records (or reports) made by the observer (teacher) of the following factors:

- Number of visits made to the library
- Bases used to make book selections (color of cover, pictures, reading chapter titles)
- Grade level of books selected and read
- Topics
- Genre of books read
- Favorite author
- Number of books read within a time period
- Attentiveness during reading
- Amount of time the student spends in reading

You have probably noted that each of these data sources (number of visits, time spent in reading) informs you of something different about the pupil's reading habits, including his or her prior knowledge, reading strategies, attitude toward reading, interests, and motivation for reading.

When Direct Observation Is Used

The opportunities for direct observation are present in every contact with the student, or you can make your own opportunities to observe behaviors when they don't occur frequently. Some observation activities that you can use for initiating useful observation include (Gall, Gall, & Borg, 2006):

- Observe at periodic intervals.
- Choose settings for observation.
- Sample settings in which the behavior is likely to occur, such as interaction with other students, on a playground, in the classroom, and in social settings; observe when the student is working on assignments in class as well as in a study hall.
- Record typical behavior(s) as well as behaviors that may warrant attention.
- Use checklists (see Theory to Practice Box 3.2) of behaviors important to understanding the student.
- Ask questions or require performance of tasks to permit observing infrequently occurring behaviors.

Some considerations in what to look for in observing student behaviors related to good or effective reading are displayed in Theory to Practice Box 3.2. You will note that some of the behaviors are related to the strategies or styles used by good readers. Others of the behaviors are related to *attitudes toward self as a reader* as well as *attitudes toward the reading material*, thereby providing the opportunity for making analytical interpretations. The behaviors noted in the items are capable of being observed by an observer who understands the purpose of making these observations, who is well informed in the subject

---

Theory to Practice Box 3.2
EXAMPLE OF AN OBSERVATION CHECKLIST

Instructions to observer: Before using this checklist, become familiar with all of the items for easily locating any one of them as the need arises. Note that the items on the left represent behaviors associated with learning strategies and those on the right represent behaviors associated with self-perceptions. Check (with a checkmark) on the line before any item that describes a behavior that you observed during the period of observation. Please be sure to restrict your observations to those listed. If you infer a behavior but do not observe it directly, and wish to make a record of that inference, do so on another piece of paper.

Two Facets of a Student Reader's Behavior

Procedures Used in Reading	*Affective Behaviors during Reading*
____ Makes hypotheses (guesses) about the story scheme	____ Views self solely as follower of teacher assignments
____ Establishes goals in reading as they are related to the assignment	____ Evaluates interest in the selection
	____ Provides personal editorials about agreement with ideas or characters
____ Monitors progress in terms of such goals as understanding and comprehension	____ Discusses personal evaluation of selection with peers
____ Uses repair strategies when comprehension is hampered (e.g., review)	____ Engages in critique of selection in class
____ Looks for main ideas related to the reading goal	____ Relates the details of the selection to his or her own experiences
____ If reading a story, summarizes the behaviors of characters— what they stand for	
____ Effectively summarizes or abstracts the content of the passage read	

Source: This abbreviated checklist and modifications are based on Tucson Unified School District (n.d.).

matter, and who understands student behaviors related to the subject-matter goals.

■ Teachers as Observers

As in all learning, initial attempts at learning to make observations for understanding student behaviors are certain to be awkward and less informative than later attempts. Such initial attempts are typically based on a collection of salient, easily observed cues, sometimes lacking sophisticated or meaningful organizational patterns of behavior. Initial observations, even those made by experts, may include "noise," that is, irrelevant, redundant information that is extraneous to the focus of the observation. As one progresses toward expertise in observation it can be seen as a complex process. Expert observers depend upon a wealth of background information and finely tuned skills. They are led to focus on relevant information. They disregard irrelevant details. Unlike the novice, the expert observer's information processing is smooth and rapid from the time the information is selected to the time the conclusions or predictions are made.

Use Context Information

Distraction may occur as a result of the context or settings that modify the meaning of an observed behavior. Biased interpretations are formed because the contextual contributions to meaning are ignored and, in doing so, may diminish the importance of a given behavior. For example, a simple gesture, such as a wave of the hand (a nonverbal behavior), frequently cannot be taken at face value; its meaning depends in large part on the setting, the vigor of the movement, the location of the hand, the recipient, and the characteristics (e.g., ethnicity) of the person waving his or her hand—all of which contribute to the purpose of that gesture. The inferences made from that observation within context may be that it is a scoffing gesture, a good-bye, or a greeting. Consider the multitude of meanings that might be attached to pointing a finger at another person in view of who does the pointing (boy, girl, parent), the social context (counseling, brawl, gossip, play, debate), and the characteristics of the person, such as emotionality (worry, interest, evaluative feedback) and ethnicity. A student who speaks softly may, on the surface, appear to be of little importance and not warrant remembering or interpreting. On the other hand, with further knowledge of the student and the context in which the behavior occurs, speaking softly may have other meanings; it may emerge because of a self-perception of being isolated or of little self-worth, of not knowing an answer when called upon, or simply of an intent to be polite.

With differences in context, observed behaviors may take on a variety of meanings. The meanings of some behaviors are influenced by the immediate situations (e.g., an interaction between student and teacher). Some behaviors are influenced by broader cultural values (e.g., some cultures favor higher levels of interaction during learning than do American schools). Contexts serve to influence affective behaviors such as confidence, uncertainty in oneself, and respect for others as well as cognitive behaviors. Thus, attending only to surface cues may interfere with making useful interpretations. Behaviors that on the surface seem similar take on different meanings when contexts are considered.

Observe Organization and Patterns of Behavior

Experience and knowledge in a content area or in a behavioral science can facilitate making worthwhile observations. They add to observational skill by providing reasons underlying behavior differences. Consider the not-infrequent conflict of a spectator's interpretation of an umpire's judgment. Often your judgment and his or hers do not coincide. Experience adds to the details of the observation and allows the anticipation of the outcome of a behavior before it actually occurs (e.g., the expert referee can make reasonable predictions about the outcome of a high dive—entry into the water—at the time of the approach by observing the quality of the hold, the height of the diver at the apex of the dive, and postural elements such as body position).

Similarly, when observing pupils in the classroom, knowing the reasons for different or changed behaviors allows you to make predictions of future behavior, performance, and learning. Improvement in observational skill adds to the facility with which available information can be used and influences how the information is used (patterns and configurations). Often the details or patterns go unnoticed by the beginning observer—for instance, a student who continually twists a lock of hair around his or her finger only while speaking to an adult may suggest a degree of uncertainty, lack of confidence, or anxiety.

Observing consistent subtle behavioral details and patterns that enable making valid predictions is a mark of observational expertise. Skilled observers use relevant cues, even minimal ones, for determining expectations of what is to be observed as well as in making inferences from the observational data. As suggested in the preceding paragraphs, expert observers, such as referees and umpires, anticipate good performance on the basis of form moments before the activity itself is performed.

In brief, the experienced observer understands the pattern of behavior by knowing what to observe and the consequences of different forms that the behavior might take. In the early development of observation skills, interpretations depend on explicit surface or salient characteristics. With added experience, well-developed observational skills lead to interpretations based on meaningful patterns and subtle (tacit) configurations of behavior observed (Bransford, Brown, & Cocking, 2000; Wagner, 1987). Some frequently overlooked naturalistic settings and the potential observations that can be made in those settings are described in Theory to Practice Box 3.3.

Interpreting Observations

People look for certain kinds of behaviors and their consistency in observable situations or contexts. They relate one kind of behavior to another behavior—looking for a smile that signals approval, a frown that signals rejection, or a grimace that conveys hostility. Observing and interpreting behavior is a common part of human activity, for instance, "that person seems elated," or "he is compulsive," or "I think he is angry."

Context frames the interpretations of observations made within some perspective such as the culture of the classroom. We have provided illustrations of how events as simple as a frown may fail to convey the same meaning in every circumstance. Although a frown may imply disapproval in the context of a student behaving unconventionally, it may mean "I don't understand what you are saying" in the context of giving an explanation. As another example, when students delay in giving an answer to a question in the classroom, teachers or parents sometimes interpret the delay as the student not knowing the information. Conversely, when students respond quickly, as they might in responses to flashcards, the rapidity in answering is simply interpreted as knowing the answer. However, within a more technical framework, the rapidity with which a response is made is considered as a "window to the mind" and is a measure of a degree of processing, that is, thinking going on—the person is not simply answering a question but is thinking about the alternatives at arriving at the answer and has an idea about how he or she arrives at the answer (a metacognition; Flavell, 1979). A long delay may indicate that the student has insufficient

Theory to Practice Box 3.3
SOME ILLUSTRATIONS OF DIRECT OBSERVATION TECHNIQUES

I. Unstructured or Less-Structured Observation Settings

Naturalistic settings provide informal opportunity for collecting information about student readiness for learning or progress in learning. You can observe ongoing behavior wherever it may occur, whether in the classroom, on the playground, or in the dining hall; for individual students working alone or with other students; and in peer-to-peer interactions or in interactions with an authoritative figure. Observations of this nature can be made from:

- *Writing samples*. When students write anything on specific topics, in newspapers or newsletters, collages, doodling, notes in workbooks, or stories, the writing can be analyzed for writing ability as well as for interest.
- *Homework*. Although done in response to class assignments, the content and organization of answers may provide useful information about (a) response to teacher guidance, (b) self-remediation of errors identified in diagnoses, and (c) interest, ability, or motivational effort over time.
- *Logs or journals*. When keeping a periodic (daily, weekly, or monthly) record of events, the entries are certain to be colored by self-appraisals, interests, background knowledge, and so on. These can be reviewed (with permission of the student, of course) for students' perceptions regarding their accomplishments, the way they shape their ideas, or difficulties with which they may be struggling.
- *Games*. Observations of participation in computer or other games are often useful sources of data for understanding student readiness and progress as well as attitudes toward learning. Look for ways in which students prepare for participation, how they approach the game, how methodical they are in the use of strategies, and the like.
- *Debates*. Debating and discussion formats provide observational settings for evaluating oral presentation skills, ability to understand concepts, and ability to communicate ideas in an orderly fashion.
- *Brainstorming sessions*. This technique simply requires open-ended responses to such questions as, "How can we promote conservation in our community?" It can be used successfully by children of all ages in virtually all courses to determine what may already be known about a particular topic. Students may feel free to participate because there is no criticism or judgment; the responses are made with impunity.
- *Retelling of stories, newspaper or other articles, passages, and so on*. Retelling may be either oral or written. Careful observation of student performance can provide information on a wide range of cognitive abilities such as recall of facts, conceptualization, organization of ideas, comparison, and so on. Teachers can use the opportunity to determine whether children understood the point of an article or story and what problems children have in organizing the elements of the story into a coherent whole. This also can be used to

share cultural heritage when children are asked to retell a story in class that is part of their family heritage, and teachers can observe such characteristics as self-attitudes, feeling of confidence, pride, loyalty, and motivations.

II. Structured Observational Settings for Informal Assessments

Some aids are helpful in providing guides for what to observe as well as providing a basis for keeping records over time. They help in focusing on performance attributes that might otherwise be neglected or go unnoticed. They are helpful in compensating for the possibility that natural settings won't provide opportunities for behaviors to be observed.

- *Checklists.* The checklist is a list of student behaviors, the presence (or absence) of which are observed or checked. An example is shown in Theory to Practice Box 3.2. Checking the presence or absence of a behavior typically provides reliable data (different people will make the same rating)and is relatively easy. Used over time, checklists can be used to document students' rate and degree of accomplishment within the curriculum. They can be used by teachers in observing their students, or students can use them to check the presence or absence of their own behaviors.
- *Rating scales.* These are sometimes used as an extension of the checklist. Rather than recording the presence or absence of a behavior or skill, the observer subjectively rates each item according to some dimension of interest. For example, students might be rated on proficiency in elements related to making oral presentations. Each element may be rated on a bipolar scale (scales bounded by opposites) of 1 to 5 (e.g., proficiency level: 1 = low and 5 = high).
- *Questionnaires.* Questionnaires can be constructed to be used by observers or by the one being observed for self-reporting of behaviors. Items can be written in a variety of formats. They may provide alternatives, as in the following example:

Which is of most interest to you? (a) collecting stamps, (b) hiking, (c) studying a new topic, (d) being with other people.

Or they might be open-ended, allowing the student to answer questions in their own words, as in the following example:

What activities are of most interest to you? List them in order of interest. Put the ones in which you are most interested first.

Alternative assessments of achievement or language proficiency may ask students for such reports as how well they believe they are performing in a particular subject or areas in which they would like more help from the teacher. An interesting variation is a questionnaire (which assumes that the student can read in the native language) that students with English as a second language

(continued)

Theory to Practice Box 3.3
(Continued)

check off in the first language the kinds of things they can do in English. This format, of course, could be extended to a variety of behaviors and settings. For a questionnaire to provide accurate information, students must be able to read the items, have the information to respond to the items, and have the writing skills to respond.

- *Structured interviews.* Structured interviews are essentially oral interview questionnaires. Used as an alternative assessment of achievement or language proficiency, the interview could be conducted with a student or a group of students to obtain information of interest to a teacher. As with written questionnaires, interview questions could provide alternatives or be open-ended. Because the information exchange is entirely oral, it is important to keep interview questions (including response alternatives for forced-choice items) as simple and to-the-point as possible.

Source: Adapted from Navarete, Wilde, Nelson, Martínez, & Hargett (1990). This list was reproducible provided its source is documented. It has been reproduced with modification from the original.

information, has difficulty in accessing information, is using an ineffective process, or is searching for a potentially fruitful complex reasoning skill he or she thinks may be required.

Observing permits you to learn much about the students' learning. But you don't merely observe. You also have to assess the information you got from the observation. Then you decide whether something more needs to be done in your teaching. You can observe students in everyday activities such as playing in the school gymnasium or shopping (see Theory to Practice Box 3.3 for other settings). But, obviously, these have disadvantages because you may not be there at the right time or the situations don't permit some important behaviors to be manifested. One way of handling these disadvantages is to establish situations and carefully observe the students' behavior, assess the behaviors, and make decisions based on those assessments.

The Influence of Cultural Expectations: The Observer and the Observed

Cultures emphasize different characteristics, and these differences affect the behavior of the one being observed—*what is observed by the observer*—as well as the interpretation or meaning of the behavior observed (Sternberg & Grigorenko, 2002). Cultural background contributes to the knowledge base of both the participant and the observer.

From the standpoint of the observer, cultural expectations have the potential of affecting what is observed (direct behaviors or anecdotes from others), how it is observed (visual or auditory), what is seen (identified), what is selected as important, how it is interpreted (its meaning), and how it is evaluated (its implications). There may be cultural differences in expectations regarding importance or preferences in what to look for and how the behaviors are to be identified (e.g., by hearing and listening or by seeing and looking).

It is critical that the observer consider cultural differences among students and how those differences affect the behavior of students as they engage in both learning and social situations. As we have already noted, among these differences are distinctions in patterns of verbal and nonverbal behaviors. They differ, for example, in frequency (some groups use expressive behaviors more frequently as accompaniments of speaking than another), intensity (some groups speak more loudly than others), and in variety (groups vary in the "color" or formality of the language they use). There are enormous cultural differences in speech, whether in inflections, intonation, loudness, or rapidity; all play a part. Nonverbal accompaniments of speaking such as hand waving, pointing, posturing, and the like add emphasis to the spoken word and are clearly identified with group membership. Also, context plays a part for many children who arrive to our classrooms from different parts of the world. You may observe that Chinese children in an American classroom prefer choral rather than independent answers. Knowing that these are preferred learning styles in the Chinese culture (Wang & Murphy, 2004) is essential to correctly interpreting the behavior. It may be observed that Chinese children may be reluctant to answer individually, giving the impression that they do not know the answer to questions raised by the teacher. However, when given opportunities to provide choral answers they do so willingly and correctly.

In summary, cultural differences may not only contribute to differences in the meanings of student behavior, but also contribute to observer bias. A candid oral report of an eyewitness (observer), in the absence of an understanding of the role of ethnicity and culture, must be viewed with caution and, to some extent, with skepticism.

■ Components and Purposes of Observation

Observation requires that you know what to look for and what to expect. But that doesn't mean that observation is a single procedure with a single purpose, such as simply "looking to see what happens." It involves observing, evaluating, assessing, and decision making.

Observing Student Behavior in Teaching

An example of this process may be seen in Theory to Practice Box 3.4, in which instruction using a common experimental demonstration of air pressure was used. In that process, student reactions to the demonstration are observed by the teacher. The teacher assesses the information the observations provide about students' behaviors. This information, in turn, is the basis for decision making about next steps in instruction. (The observations illustrated in Theory to Practice Box 3.4 are coordinated with broader levels of educational objectives to be discussed in later chapters.) As in earlier chapters, we continue to caution that, in actual teaching situations, decisions should not be made on the basis of a single observation or tests but on observations of students in a variety of situations over time.

Describing Student Behavior

Initially specific events or behaviors are observed for their details, something like snapshots or sequences—as in photographs or movie scenes. Patterns are formed by taking note of the setting of the behavior, of the student or performer, and of the task being performed.

Data are obtained to describe behaviors as they occur. Observers seek important details on which later inferences depend. Observers "see what they know"; if the significance of the details are not known, are ignored, or are neglected the significance or meaning of a behavior may be overlooked, particularly if it is subtle (lacks saliency).

Making Inferences from Observational Data

Once data are obtained, the observation process moves from the ordinary seeing of an event to understanding it. Inference, important to every phase of assessment, is an attempt to understand and explain, to find reasons underlying the event. Doing so often results in a conceptualization, a pattern of the student's

Theory to Practice Box 3.4
OBSERVE, ASSESS, INTERPRET

Jane L., a teacher, uses a common demonstration of air pressure in a general science class. She boils a small amount of water in a gallon can until steam escapes through the spout and then caps the spout. She observes that the students are watching intently as the sides collapse when she plunges the can in cold water. She asks students for their general reactions, which she will observe and assess for making possible decisions. Some responses related to different educational objectives are illustrated here:

- *Problem-solving skills.* John is the first to ask a question. Rather than explanations, he openly questions the effects, asking, "Why did the sides collapse? How did you make that happen? Did plunging into the water somehow push the sides in?" Jane L. uses this information to assess John's problem-solving skills. One of the first requisites for good problem solving is to ask, "What is the principle involved?" But John also shows that his questions may be misdirected, as he thinks the water (into which the can was immersed to cool it off) may be pushing the sides in.
- *Analysis and synthesis.* Ann is quite thoughtful and takes into consideration the what, how, and why of the problem. She says, "Usually air pressure is the same inside and outside the can, but when the water was boiled, it turned to steam. The molecules in steam are very far apart and, in addition, they pushed the air out of the can (steam displaced the air). When the can was capped and the air cooled down, the steam vapor condensed, creating a partial vacuum in the can, leaving the pressure inside the can lower than the pressure outside. This difference (discrepancy) in pressure caused the sides to push in."
- *Prior knowledge: Misconceptions and preconceptions.* Pete reacts to the original question, but ignores Ann's comment completely. He overconfidently states that he knows why the sides collapsed. He says, "I am sure the steam is sucking the sides in. Air doesn't have anything to do with it. Air is all around us and doesn't have any way of pushing the sides in, especially when the metal is so strong." Jane L., the teacher, assesses Pete's behavior as unwarranted feeling of overconfidence that keeps him from correctly using what he has learned. He comes to snap judgments without thinking. He is satisfied with partial answers and explanations whether they are correct or incorrect. Jane L. will have to work on his approach to skills in solving problems.
- *Application of previously learned information.* At various points in the discussion, several students chimed in with attempts at making applications. Gene says that he has seen high school kids take an empty aluminum cola can and crush it by squeezing it. Paco thinks the principle in the demonstration has a counterpart in tornados and hurricanes. Alice thinks that air has weight. "After all," she says, "pressure in tires is recorded in weight."

(continued)

Theory to Practice Box 3.4
(Continued)

- *Evaluation.* Evaluation is the questioning of the validity of explanations, of the principles. Jorge says, "I think this is like a suction cup. It is the suction that holds it to the surface." Jane L. thinks that the class will require a more thorough explanation of how suction cups work. (The role of suction is a common misconception. It is not suction that holds the cup to a surface; it is the difference in pressure. First, all the air is pushed out from underneath the cup, causing a discrepancy in pressure, with the 14.7 psi on the outside holding it to the surface.) Donna thinks there is an analogy with a hot air balloon. The fire that heats the air at the bottom causes the molecules to become more diffuse, pushing much of the air out of the balloon and thereby reducing the weight inside. The pressure from the air outside pushes it up. Still another student thinks there is an analogy with drinking from a straw. She says that the crushing of the sides of the can was similar to her observation of how people's cheeks went in when they drank through a straw.
- *Jane L.'s decision.* All told, Jane L. thinks the students have reached the lesson objectives. However, she will follow up on Pete with the possibility of providing him direct instruction on problem-solving skills. She will provide further illustrations in the class on applications such as explanations of tornados and suction cups.

Note: The components of the observation processes illustrated are described in more detail below (see e.g., Gall, Gall, and Borg, 2004).

behavior. Be warned not to make hasty conclusions in labeling the behavior. Early establishment of a label for the behavior tends to result in finality of the judgment, stopping further evaluative efforts prematurely. It is better to postpone a judgment than to summarize a hasty judgment.

Inferences are based on:

- *Sophisticated technical knowledge* about the meaning of the behavior. Inferences are represented in assumed, not directly observed, variables or patterns, called psychological concepts.
- An *integration of information* from several frameworks (personal, social, contextual) and sources (observation, tests, reports, documents) of information.

Evaluating, Explaining, and Interpreting Behavior: Comparison with a Standard

Once observational data have been collected and inferences made, the outcome is evaluated; the inferred behavior (learning, confidence, self-efficacy) might be rated as adequate (inadequate) or excellent (poor), or assigned a letter grade or other mark. Evaluations are difficult to make reliably without carefully stated bases for acceptable definitions.

Evaluating the behaviors you observed in a student may require a comparison of the behavior with some standard. The standard might be an implicit criterion, an explicitly stated standard of performance, or a carefully considered comparison with another student or group of students.

What Summaries of Observations Don't Show

No measure, whether made by informal observation or by formal tests, answers all questions about ability or performance. A single or even a few observations will usually be insufficient for providing enough information on which to make valid judgments (Linn & Burton, 1994; Mehrens, 1992). At best, a few observations are limited samples of all behavior, with the consequence that interpretations are also limited. Adequate interpretations require more perspectives than is possible when the data are derived from a single source (Gall et al., 2004).

■ Making Observations

Although observation is a general skill, expertise in educational setting varies with experience. As an acquired skill it is facilitated and enhanced by training and experience aimed at knowing those characteristics and processes of observations that lead to useful data collection and interpretation about yourself and your students (Gall et al., 2004; Gall et al., 2006; Winsor, 2003).

The ingredients for making skilled observations can be summarized as follows (in parallel with Figure 3.1):

- *Know behavioral patterns.* Experts attend to salient, easily observed behaviors, as does the beginner, but they also attend to other, tacit (less observable, more comprehensive and encompassing) behaviors that correspond to the depth of their understanding (Polanyi, 1966/1983; Wagner, 1987).
- *Plan your observations.* Why you are doing the observation makes a difference in what you will be looking for. Identify the data you want and the purposes for which the data will be used.
- *Take note of the situations or settings in which the behavior occurs.* The behavior in context will certainly affect your inferences. The same behavior in different contexts may be interpreted differently.

	Often	Occasionally	Rarely
1. Talks to others about books	😄	😐	🙁
2. Goes to library on his/ her own	😄	😐	🙁
3. Makes selections based on knowledge of author genre	😄	😐	🙁
4. Selects books for different purposes like learning how to do something, entertainment, or finding information	😄	😐	🙁
5. Knows different venues for getting books	😄	😐	🙁
6. Knows different ways of finding out what the book is about	😄	😐	🙁

Figure 3.1. An observation assessment checklist.

- *Be sensitive to any ethnic or cultural differences.* Culture and ethnicity are so important in your interpretations that you must give special attention to them (Goddard, Hoy, & Hoy, 2004).
- *Identify bases of observation.* Know what to observe. You can't observe everything that goes on in the behavior of all students. In information processing there is always a selection process going on. Taxonomic bases help in this regard. Checklists can help remind you what to look for. An example of one such checklist is shown in Figure 3.1.

Practice Exercise

The items in Figure 3.1 have been developed as a guide for teacher observations. However, if you wish to do so, the items can easily be rephrased to be used as a self-rating scale by a student. As a practice exercise you may wish to change the scale to one which can be used for guiding such self-ratings. (Hint: As an example of how this change might be made, Item 1 might be changed from "Talks to others about books" to "I like to talk to others about books I am reading.") You might also consider changing the scale to observing the student's work on computers, in the laboratory, or in some classroom activity.

- *Use a variety of data sources about students to supplement direct observation.* In addition to direct observation, teachers may search school records, speak with previous teachers who have had the student in their classes, and talk with parents or peers. With care, you can engage the student in conversations about his or her perceptions and feelings regarding a topic. You can also assign the student a situation where performance on academic tasks can be observed and evaluated. Problem-solving situations, shopping, accessing the Internet, and so on provide opportunities for observing behaviors related to decision-making situations. Play situations provide opportunity to observe behavior related to social-interactive skills.
- *Understand how you process observations.* Some of the processes that may occur as you process observations (planning, looking, making inferences, and using the outcomes for improving teaching and learning) are described in Text Box 3.1.

Avoiding Negative Consequences of Direct Observation

Informed, sophisticated observation depends on understanding the variables that influence both the antecedents (preceding events) and the consequences (end results) of behavior. It is more than simply seeing. It is composed of sets of observations (including testing) for collecting information about student behaviors that can be used advantageously for description, inferences, and evaluations of students. That's an important orientation on which to focus. Yet, despite these advantages, there are potential shortcomings that should be addressed. They are as follows:

Potential for Error Due to Lack of Expertise

The techniques of assessment enable obtaining reliable and valid information. Nevertheless, if the basic observations, whether informal or formal, are uninformed because of lack of knowledge, procedures, or understanding (Mayer, 2003), they will be functionally useless. If the observations are carelessly made,

---

Text Box 3.1 Behavior Changes Due to Awareness of Being Observed

Students who are aware of being observed may change their behavior according to that awareness. If they believe a particular behavior is being observed they may try harder at being a good performer to gain your praise. Even young children (or, perhaps, especially young children) perceive subtle signs that they are being observed and change their behavior to gain approval from the observer (Rosenthal & Jacobson, 1968/1992). Make observations as objective as possible so that they are free from bias.

Bias and Expectations of the Observer Affects Observation Results

The experience, attitudes, and motivations of the observer can bias the selection of information. As we have seen in the previous discussion, sometimes biased selection of behavioral data occurs inadvertently, as for example when classes or groups of students are believed to have some characteristic such as "successful," "learning disabled," "goal-directed," or "attractive." Guard against the negative effects of labels on obtaining dependable information for further action such as remediation or enrichment.

A Single Source of Information or Occurrence Is Undependable

The potential danger of using single test scores obtained on a single occasion has already been underlined. This practice may provide atypical data (data that wouldn't be observed again on another occasion). Using observations based on multiple measures in multiple settings provides a better source of data.

---

then inferences, carelessly drawn, will be biased, unreliable, or, at the least, naïve. Useful assessment is dependent on sophisticated observations, attention to critical attributes leading to deeper understanding of given behaviors, and interpretations of clusters of organized information about content, learning, teaching, and testing. To be avoided is the sole dependence on surface observations of the more salient details. Interpretations should be held in abeyance until the obvious details can be integrated with the more important features of behavior into meaningful patterns (e.g., Chi, Feltovich, & Glaser, 1981). Observations can easily become biased by the lack of sensitivity to relevant behaviors, inappropriate discriminations among things observed, inconsistency of the measures taken under different contexts and conditions, and premature jumping to conclusions as shown in the next paragraphs.

Potential for Errors in Interpretation

The observer brings to any situation his or her world of experiences, which enters into the interpretation of even the most closely guarded observation, the most carefully designed test, or the most precisely calibrated test score. All of one's experiences affect the inferences made. For example, the score of a statewide high-stakes test is clearly reported simply as a number or a letter grade. But the meaning of that score and its use is debated widely and differently by several categories of end users. (End users are those responsible for constructing and revising the test, those using the test for policy decisions, and those to whom the test is being given and who will be most affected by the assigned grade.)

As we process information we, of course, see things that are there, but due to biases or leading questions, we sometimes infer that we saw things that aren't there. Like all professionals in assessment, you will want to avoid difficulties intrinsic to uninformed observations by checking the validity and reliability of any observation you make, whether by direct observation or by formal standardized tests.

Potential for Contextual Errors

Humans look for certain kinds of behaviors and the consistency of those behaviors in observable situations or contexts. They jump to conclusions on that basis. They relate one kind of behavior to another behavior—in a setting that offers feedback, they may look for a smile that signals approval, a frown that signals rejection, or a grimace that conveys hostility. Nevertheless, even something as simple as a frown, as we all recognize, conveys a different meaning in different contexts: in an unconventional context, the frown may imply disapproval; in the context of an explanation the frown may mean a lack of understanding; or, in the case of an inappropriate behavior, it may mean a quizzical, "Why did you do that?"

Exercise 3.1 Direct Observations

What decisions have you made that were based on direct observations, perhaps about going to a party with friends, about a lack of confidence in some one of your abilities, or about making a career choice? Having been in a classroom as a student and, perhaps, as a teacher, have you used any artifacts that were related to your formation of opinions or attitudes about other students or about your teachers? What were they? Were you aware of them at the time? How did your role (teacher or student) affect what you observed? Did you make observations in one or many different situations?

Sampling Bias

Data from unobtrusive measures are not free from questions of validity or reliability. In some cases observation may be biased because of inadequate sampling—the behaviors were not observed in a sufficient number of situations. Students' behavior may differ in classrooms that cater to social interests compared to academic interests, in classes taught using different teaching styles, or in different subject-matter areas.

If we collect information in one classroom format (e.g., lecture) it may have different opportunities for remediation, exploration, or enrichment than a classroom taught in another format (e.g., group discussion), thereby having the potential of yielding different behaviors from the same student. Reward systems, too, may vary among teachers. Classroom climates associated with different curricula (e.g. business, vocational, or college) differ in their appeal to different students who make choices in selecting one over another. Also, the clientele who chose them, having different tastes, may express their satisfactions, dislikes, or abilities in different forms of behavior. A curriculum in one district serves a different population than its counterpart in a different district. In addition, it is quite probable that students who have predispositions toward a course, who willingly take a course versus those who are required to take the course, will also exhibit different behaviors.

Biases in sampling can occur in any observation, whether of groups or individuals. Observations might be made in single settings without recognizing the consequences in biased interpretations. Similarly, one could easily overgeneralize to all situations without regard for the uniqueness characterizing a limited context in which a few observations had been made.

Use Several Data Sources

No single method of enhancing or facilitating observation is sufficient to avoid bias, unreliability, or lack of validity. There always exists the need for considering the sampling, the observational method, the analysis of data, and so on.

Using multiple sources of data that cut across and minimize the errors when data come from a single measure is essential with the use of any measure, including unobtrusive measures (Webb et al., 2000). Although the use of archival records, for example, would seem to be free of contamination, it is not; the conditions under which the records are collected must be examined closely for their validity. If the records had been made by poorly trained or poorly disciplined clerks, the posting of data may have been made carelessly, often from delayed recall, resulting in a less-than-accurate account. Such records may also have been intentionally (or unintentionally) altered for biased reasons.

Tests, surveys, interviews, and questionnaires are ancillary to direct observation; their use in education and other social sciences are attempts to elicit otherwise infrequently elicited behaviors or processes underlying observable behaviors. They are intended to obtain systematic observations of how learners perform under clearly specified conditions. Such observations, made by psychometricians, are continually subjected to examination for reliability, validity, psychometric characteristics, and the like to assure that the construction and use is well informed, unbiased, and psychometrically sound.

■ Summary

Observation is a basic source of information. It can be accomplished by observing children in natural settings such as playgrounds, social events, and study periods. These settings provide a rich context in which behavior is displayed without the student's awareness that he or she is being observed.

Direct observation is basic to the construction of instruments, such as tests, for gathering data about the status of student progress in education. Tests are intended to make focused observations of specific attributes (e.g., a test of specific knowledge about gravitational forces) typically in given settings (e.g., as a theoretical principle versus application in understanding space travel). Although direct observations in natural settings can provide much useful information, they do not always provide opportunities for the manifestation of behaviors that are of interest to teachers. Even so frequent an event as comparing the nutritional value of several food products may not be observed in normal settings, and may require formal establishment of test-like opportunities (e.g., comparison of the labels of cereal products in a field trip to a grocery store) for evoking those behaviors. Additionally, when judgments of behavior in such events are defined more technically, such as the extent to which the student has misconceptions about some physical principle, then tests might be constructed for the specific purpose of measuring the effect of misconceptions on the outcomes of making a comparison. In the use of observational data, the roles of the measurement specialist, the test constructor, and the test user are intertwined at least to the extent that each is informed of the other's responsibilities.

Teachers need to be informed about what observations contribute to data obtained by tests in making assessments (e.g., Gronlund & James, 2005). They are expected to:

- Understand the ways direct observation and its products are processed
- Employ direct and indirect observations using whatever instrumentation is needed to reach observational objectives

- Employ the information collected by observation for making useful implications, inferences, and interpretations; these can then become the bases for legitimate applications to the conduct of classroom work aimed at reaching purposeful educational objectives
- Appropriately relate pieces of observational data to relevant features of instruction for improving instruction and student learning

Coincidental with these expectations is the understanding that the observer's knowledge about content and assessment influences observation. Awareness of the features of the observational methods is critical to the effectiveness of observational data for decision making. Properly used, all forms and sources of data contribute to these aims of assessment. Data from well-conducted observations serve purposes of understanding student progress, communicating with parents, and contributing to interpretation and use of policy decisions. Data from direct observation, in conjunction with other assessment practices, is helpful in the appraisal of student progress and reporting grades. Such data is helpful for modifying instruction by demonstrating the effects of instruction on student mastery of course objectives (cognition, skills, and attitudes). Direct observation can become an important source of data for facilitating the alignment of teacher goals with student needs. Observations from parents, coupled with teacher and peer observations, can provide additioinal sources of information for understanding student progress, planning the use of tests in adapting the curricular programs to differences in student needs, and repairing inefficient instructional methods. As supplements to direct and formal measures, expert observations can be useful in amplifying and extending formation of policy and the documentation of the school's performance.

■ References

Bransford, J. D., Brown, A. L., & Cocking, R. R. (2000). *How people learn: Brain, mind, experience, and school.* Washington, DC: National Academy Press.

Chi, M. T. H., Feltovich, P. J., & Glaser, R. (1981). Categorization and representation of physics problems by experts and novices. *Cognitive Science, 5,* 121–152.

Driscoll, M. (2005). *Psychology of learning for Instruction* (3rd ed.). New York: Allyn & Bacon.

Flavell, J. H. (1979). Metacognition and cognitive mentoring: A new area of cognitive-developmental inquiry. *American Psychologist, 34,* 906–911.

Gall, J. P., Gall, M. D., & Borg, W. R. (2004). *Applying educational research: A practical guide* (5th ed.). Boston: Allyn & Bacon.

Gall, M. D., Gall, J. P., & Borg, W. R. (2006). *Educational research: An introduction* (8th ed.). Boston: Allyn & Bacon.

Goddard, R. D., Hoy, W. K., & Hoy, A. W. (2004). Collective efficacy beliefs: Theoretical developments, empirical evidence, and future directions. *Educational Researcher, 33*(3), 3–13.

Gronlund, G., & James, M. (2005). *Focused observations: How to observe children for assessment and curriculum planning.* St. Paul, MN: Redleaf Press.

Linn, R. L., & Burton, E. (1994). Performance-based assessment: Implications of task specificity. *Educational Measurement: Issues and Practice, 13*(1), 5–8, 15.

Mayer, R. E. (2003). *Learning and instruction.* Upper Saddle River, NJ: Merrill Prentice Hall Pearson Education.

Mehrens, W. A. (1992). Using performance assessment for accountability purposes. *Educational Measurement: Issues and Practice, 1*(1), 3–9.

Navarete, C., Wilde, J., Nelson, C., Martínez, R., & Hargett, G. (1990). Informal assessment in educational evaluation: Implications for bilingual education programs. *NCBE Program Information Guide Series,* (3). Retrieved March 4, 2010 from www.ncela.gwu.edu/pubs/pigs/pig3.htm.

Pelligrino, J. W., Chudowsky, N., & Glaser, R. (2001). *Knowing what students know: The science and design of educational assessment.* Washington, DC: National Academy Press.

Polanyi, M. (1966/1983). *The tacit dimension.* Gloucester, MA: Peter Smith (Reprinted from Doubleday & Co., 1966).

Rosenthal, R., & Jacobson, L. (1968/1992). *Pygmalion in the classroom: Teacher expectation and pupils' intellectual development.* New York: Irvington Publishers.

Sternberg, R. J., & Grigorenko, E. L. (2002). *Dynamic testing: The nature and measurement of learning potential.* Cambridge, MA: Cambridge University Press.

Tucson Unified School District. (n.d.). *Components of a balanced literacy program.* Retrieved April 21, 2008, from http://instech.tusd.k12.az.us/balancedlit/handbook/blasmt.htm.

Wagner, R. K. (1987). Tacit knowledge in everyday intelligent behavior. *Journal of Personality and Social Psychology, 52,* 1236–1124.

Wang, T., & Murphy, J. (2004). An examination of coherence in a Chinese mathematics classroom. In L. Fan, N. Y. Wong, J. Cai, & S. Li (Eds.), *How Chinese learn mathematics: Perspectives from insiders* (pp. 107–123). London: World Scientific Publishing.

Webb, E. J., Campbell, D. T., Schwartz, R. D., & Sechrest, L. (2000). *Unobtrusive measures* (Revised ed.). Thousand Oaks, CA: Sage.

Wiggins, G. (1993). Assessment: Authenticity, context, and validity. *Phi Delta Kappan, 75*(3), 200–208, 210–214.

Winsor, A. P. (2003). Direct behavioral observation for classrooms. In C. R. Reynolds & R. W. Kamphaus (Eds.), *Handbook of psychological & educational assessment of children: Personality, behavior, and context* (pp. 248–258). New York: Guilford.

CHAPTER 4

Formative Assessment: Using Assessment for Improving Instruction

I N BEING CLOSELY LINKED with instruction and learning, assessment reaches beyond the use with which you are most familiar, that is, beyond report-card grades (Wiliam, Lee, Harrison, & Black, 2004). This chapter focuses on *formative* assessment to show the ways that teachers use important information about student achievement. The idea here is that assessment can be used to inform teachers of the effectiveness of their teaching and of the effectiveness of student learning as a result of their instructional practices. In other words, your assessments are framed to gather information about student progress that can be used to make inferences about how well your instructional practices are working. The assessments provide feedback based on student performance that can help make valid inferences about facets of instruction such as how much the students already know, how well they can use the new learning, whether they are learning with understanding, and so on. Additionally, students can be helped to understand how to use assessment information for improving their own learning both in and out of school settings. A major component of formative assessment, in these terms, is the orientation that has been described as "assessment *for* learning," a phrase that will be used interchangeably with *formative assessment*.

The following key ideas, among others, will be targeted (see Figure 4.1):

- Assessment is an integral part, not a separate appendage, of instruction.
- Assessment of student progress occurs on a day-to-day, even moment-to-moment basis; it is not simply a grade assigned at

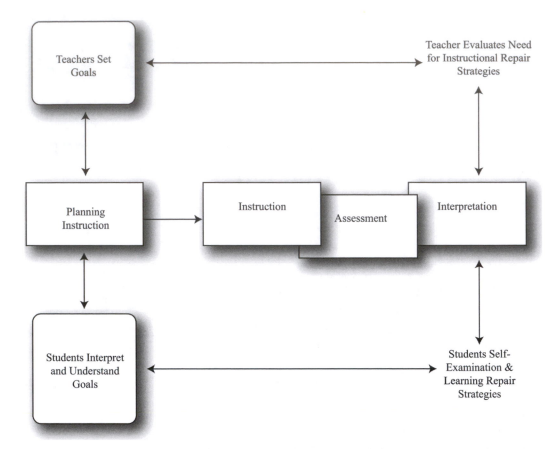

Figure 4.1. Assessment for learning: basic components, processes, and interactions.

the end of month or marking period; all methods of assessment provide key information about student progress.

- The information provided by formal assessments such as statewide or other standardized tests are used by the makers for policy decisions. However, for the classroom, they should be considered as more than status measures; teachers can use information from these measures for (a) improving their own teaching methods, (b) developing curricula, and (c) achieving broader goals of education such as enrichment, transfer, and lifelong learning.

- Feedback about student performance, as an indicator of instructional effectiveness, is a critical part of formative assessment. To be optimally useful, teachers and students interact to communicate their interpretation of grades, scores, or other measures. Such conversations provide a basis for understanding what has been accomplished and how much progress has been made toward the achievement of instructional goals.

- Feedback should also focus on student perceptions of the nature of learning objectives and how the objectives are to be achieved. Misperceptions should be corrected without delay so that both students and teachers are on track regarding what is to be accomplished. The student perceptions about objectives affect learning processes; they may learn, for example, unintended ways to study in order to get good grades. Feedback to the student about learning processes (how to learn) results in learning with understanding to a greater extent than feedback that emphasizes only performance (getting a higher score on an examination).

- Knowing which methods are available for you to use in collecting data about different levels of assessment (e.g., fact, understanding, analysis, synthesis, application) will enable you to collect a range of data that will provide useful informative feedback for both you and your students. Nonproductive feedback can be avoided by emphasizing, to both you and your students, that assessments are geared to learning outcomes. As a result, the consequent benefits for students when they use constructive approaches in reaching those outcomes (e.g., what strategies can be used and how to use them for acquiring different learning goals) can then be identified.

■ Distinctions between Summative and Formative Assessment

Most readers are familiar with assessment as report-card grades received at the end of a marking period. This definition emphasizes what is known as *summative assessment*, a conclusion based on an average or an "average impression" of performance at a stated period of time, which can be referred to as student status. Data about student performance, however, can be used to understand the effectiveness of instruction during the course of a unit of instruction as well as simply at the end of instruction. Useful comments to students, based on assessment data, help direct student learning. For the teacher, assessment data provides a basis for making decisions about teaching methods, such as whether or not to make changes in content, level of content, or delivery. For the students, whether by themselves or in conjunction with teachers, assessment data can help in understanding learning goals, weaknesses and strengths, and useful study methods for achieving goals as well as compensating for difficulties in studying. If some change appears necessary, the teacher may decide to make changes in the instructional method, in the content to be taught, or in the level of course content, or the student can decide how to make changes in what and how to study. All are components of formative assessment.

The use of separate descriptors, *formative* and *summative*, may appear to imply that there are two different kinds of assessment or two different ways of collecting information about students. It would be incorrect to make this interpretation (Harlen, 2005). Rather, the descriptors refer to the use made of data, the interpretations of the data obtained from observations, tests, or other measures. Thus, *formative* refers to the interpretations of data that are useful for improving instruction and learning (thus the phrase, "assessment *for* learning"). The term *summative* refers to interpretations of assessment data in terms that represent a summary of student achievement, that is, what students have learned or achieved at a given point in their education (thus the phrase, "assessment *of* learning").

In either case, the score or grade is a marker of performance; each can be interpreted differently to serve either of the two purposes—formative or summative. The difference between the two labels does not imply two methods for assessing student learning, but, rather, their interpretation. These interpretations underlie the decisions about what evidence is to be collected, the reasons for the information to be acquired, and the way the evidence collected is used.

Summative Assessment

As stated earlier, it is probably true that the kind of assessment that immediately comes to mind when we speak of assessment is summative assessment, and the function of summative assessment with which we are most familiar is the end-of-unit (instructional unit, month, year, or marking period) assessment used to provide summary information about student performance. School administrators might (often) interpret such assessments in terms of a teacher's or a school's success. Parents might interpret the grade in terms of "how well the child is doing in school." When administered for local purposes such as end-of-unit or end-of-marking-period summative grade reports, summative assessments are sometimes used for placement of students in enrichment classes, for promotion, for graduation, or simply for the status (how well the student performed in a given subject or behavioral area) at the end of a marking period. When these are the sole decisions made from assessments, it is apparent that we are speaking about summative assessments, often being grounded in the belief that they automatically improve learning as a result of rewards or punishments that motivate students. Although summative assessment has been an enduring part of education and does serve policy needs, the concept of formative assessment provides a perspective of direct importance to classroom functioning (Harlen, 2006).

High-stakes (accountability) assessments, such as statewide comprehensive examinations, are used for identifying the achievement *status* of students; for example, test scores are used to determine whether the school passes or fails stated achievement standards. The assessment then is used to determine eligibility for additional funding or resources. A salient characteristic of such scores is the finality of the judgments, interpretations, implications, or decisions about schools or students. In an earlier era of the educational enterprise, the summative assessment was based solely on tests; today it might be based on essays, teacher ratings, and other indexes of performance.

From this discussion the reader may get the impression that summative assessments are mainly of negative value. However, for the present, we must recognize that regardless of how it is done, teachers and schools must do some summative assessment. Student performance, work, and achievement status need to be summarized for school records. Reports are needed by school counselors for help in identifying special learning needs of individual students. Future teachers will refer to students' past work to judge readiness for learning new topics. Parents will want to be given reports of their children's educational progress. All stakeholders, including students, have an interest in the information provided in a summary record of a student's achievement. But these goals achieved by summative assessment require measures of educational achievement that goes beyond a simple score as a summary of student achievement.

Formative Assessment

In contrast to summative assessment, formative assessment is composed of assessments integrated with instruction for making instructional decisions (Linn, 1989) during the course of instruction. To do so requires a degree of information regarding instruction and learning that you will acquire in other courses in teacher preparation. These include an understanding of:

- The ways developmental processes impact learning
- The process of curriculum development and goals at different developmental levels

- The nature of instructional goals and methods for achieving them
- The ways different methods of instruction impact learning
- The ways students learn
- The processes students use in different learning environments (Linn, 1989)

Formative assessment is based on the inference that assessment is not an end in itself but can be used constructively by teachers and educators at any point during instruction for identifying whether and where instruction and learning might be improved. The idea is that any or all assessments provide a basis for considering retention or change in your approach. With assessments conducted with students and teachers working cooperatively, teachers retain an approach that is producing satisfactory results, revise instruction to improve its effectiveness, or, when the occasion demands it, abandon an instructional component that is ineffective. Monitoring instruction and learning in these ways is intended to have continual effects on the improvement of instruction.

■ Formal and Informal Formative Assessment

The distinction between informal and formal formative assessment can be made on the basis of the way the information is gathered, how it is perceived, and the purposes for which it is to be used. Ruiz-Primo and Furtak (2004) distinguish the two forms by the processes employed in each (also see Bell & Cowie, 2001; Duschl, 2003b).

Formal Formative Assessment

Formal formative assessment is conducted with deliberate planning and may be used for feedback on curricular matters. At this level, it typically involves standardized tests or tests deliberately made for feedback about such matters as student readiness, diagnosis, remediation, and placement. After assessing how well the students have performed relative to standards and objectives, educators make recommendations for improving learning and instruction.

Thus, formal formative assessment involves (a) deliberate and planned *gathering* of information, (b) *interpreting* that information in terms of goals to be achieved, and (c) *acting* upon the information by restructuring instruction, curriculum, or other characteristics of the system. Assessment shapes the characteristics of student learning and powers the instruction that enables learning progress.

Informal Formative Assessment

The opportunities for *informal formative assessment* are many. They occur in every teacher-student interaction and in all learning contexts where evidence of student learning is displayed. They comprise the instructional settings where teachers make hundreds of decisions daily. Illustrations of contexts in which assessments can be made include:

- A short, simple conversation between student and teacher (verbal context)
- The teacher's observation of the student interacting with another student (social context)
- The teacher's quick check of the student's progress by ratings or tests on an ongoing project (performance context)

Informal formative assessment, being unplanned or loosely planned, is based on a decision to identify "How well are we progressing in this class?" It may involve:

- Observing ongoing behavior
- Eliciting information about the level of student achievement related to goal performance at various points in instruction
- Recognizing that the observed performance provides relevant information about student progress
- Interpreting the information in terms of understanding gaps between the goal and current status
- Making reasonable guesses as to how the gap can be closed
- Using that information for repair of instruction; that is, remediation or reinforcement of some feature of instruction and learning occurring at the time of observation

Distinctions between Formal and Informal Formative Assessment

The characteristics of formal and informal formative assessment overlap in practice. For example, formal formative assessment does include planning observations, and setting up situations that enable eliciting information about the attainment of specifically defined educational goals. On the other hand, informal formative assessment may occur opportunistically with limited planning of the situations in which students are to be observed or tested.

The strength of formal formative assessment is that teachers devise questions, tasks, or challenges ahead of time to have them ready for evoking learning outcomes consistent with their objectives, such as the acquisition of factual understanding, the transfer of learned subject matter to practical situations, or the elaboration of conceptual information. These methods of collecting information are then used at a point during instruction when it seems advantageous to require demonstrations of related cognitive abilities in appropriate performance settings. The information so acquired is interpreted to provide feedback to determine instructional effectiveness, with implications for instructional improvement if necessary.

Some Strategies for Using Formative Assessment

Table 4.1 illustrates the strategies suggested by Ruiz-Primo and Furtak (2004). They describe these as strategies for "recognizing and guiding assessment conversation." Note that these strategies, while designed for informal assessment, can provide the basis for more formal measures, such as tests, observational schedules, and surveys.

■ Interpretation of Feedback in Formative Assessment

Formal assessment typically results in a performance report, often in the form of grades or scores. Sometimes it might be in the form of a case study or similar written report summarizing aspects of student performance. Informal assessment might result in an impression, a speculation, or a suggestion and, if included in a more formally assigned grade or score, the results of informal assessment will appear as a tentative interpretation. But as simple as a grade or score based on a formal assessment may seem, an informed teacher may perceive it from many perspectives capable of uncovering a wealth of information about student needs, motivations, or learning processes. The information can then be used for improving instruction or for helping students understand their learning by making inferences from assessment data.

A major advantage of informal formative assessments is that they can be acquired frequently, unlike summative grades or marks, which may not be obtained with sufficient frequency to enable interpretations for modifying instructions (Harlen, 2006). Additionally, averages represented in summative marks

Table 4.1. Strategies for Recognizing and Guiding Assessment Conversations

Framework	Retrieving	Processing	Applications
Enhancing meaning: Ask questions that require thinking responses.	Ask students what information they would need to make predictions: "what would happen if . . ."	Assess meaning by paraphrased products.	Provide such opportunities for evaluating outcomes as those in debate, controversy, or arguments; help students achieve consensus.
Classifications, categories, concepts: Ask questions that help identify what students know or understand through forming groups or categories of specific instances.	Ask students to provide their own potential or actual definitions. Ask students to compare and contrast.	Construct categories; group objects along known dimensions; make new categories appropriate to a content area.	Evaluate understanding the range of conceptualizations (inclusions and exclusions). For example, what are the consequences for a community when the nesting habits of birds exposed to extinction are destroyed?
Social skills and processes: Ask questions that elicit skills in social processes.	Share everyday experience; explain, review others' ideas.	Make judgments based on social implications, e.g., ethics or values of a community.	Consider the ethics involved in day-to-day school activities such as cheating and plagiarism as well as corporate ethics such as are involved in a current event (corporate, military, legal, and so on).

Source: Adapted from Ruiz-Primo and Furtak (2004).

may be so comprehensive that they fail to enable diagnostic information targeted at the reasons why grades are high or low, including specific considerations such as how students learn, whether what they are learning is on target, and whether their learning expectations coincide with their teacher's expectation (Maxwell, 2004 as cited in Harlen, 2006, p. 107). Conversely, summative evaluations may be erroneously thought to have formative use simply because they appear in black and white on a report card (one outcome of this assumption is the risky practice of teaching to the test).

Inferences about Instruction

Grades or other indicators of student performance can be viewed as having potential for inferring the causes of high or low performance in terms of the instructional method or the students' learning. For example, you can look for:

- *Precursors or predispositions that influence receptivity to instruction.* Are there cultural and socioeconomic factors that modify receptivity to instruction (and content)? Do instruction and assessments require alignment to developmental status?
- *Events that might be related to a grade.* Are there identifiable events that contribute to an outcome? Were there events that were particularly motivating or distracting during learning or at the time of assessment? How did the student go about studying an assignment?
- *The importance of a grade or other outcome.* Was the measure perceived as a useful index of learning by the student or teacher? Was the evaluation taken seriously? For what purposes was the evaluation considered important? Were all users informed about the alignment of the measure to intended objectives or goals?
- *The way grades are used by teachers and students.* How is the evaluation outcome perceived? Does that perception have an effect on the way it is used? Does the outcome of an assessment result in or promote immediate or future remedial action? How does the student's interpretation affect his or her use of the evaluation? What effect will his or her interpretation have on later learning or motivation?

Teacher Perspectives

From the teacher's perspective, constructive interpretations can be used to chart the overall effectiveness of teaching methods, ranging from student placement in special programs to style of teaching and the establishment of classroom climate. These interpretations are essential aids in sequencing curricular content, selecting remedial interventions, and evaluating the effectiveness of special procedures such as the use of group discussions, seatwork, or specific enrichment exercises.

Student Perspectives

From the student's perspective, interpretations of whatever assessments are made of performance provide a source of feedback that guides learning. It affects both what and why students learn and how they learn it. Without teacher guidance, students make their own interpretations. Not uncommon are such judgments (sometimes known as attributions) as the following: "I did well because I studied hard for this test; I'm going to study hard from now on" (attributing success to effort); "This test was on facts, I didn't do well because I spent my time on the general ideas. Next time, I am going to memorize the details" (attributing poor performance to external causes like test difficulty; change is on what he or she will memorize rather than on study procedures); or, "I didn't study for this test at all. I was lucky to barely pass the test. I'll probably do well the next time" (attributing success to luck with no change in study procedure).

Although students will normally draw conclusions about their performance, the teacher's interpretations of performance measures are likely to be more accurate because teachers are more informed about such matters. As much as the grade itself, the interpretation you make to the student may shape his or her reaction to the test, but the final determinant of its effect will be the student's perception, however naïve that might seem to be. Constructive interpretations improve future learning; interpretation of grades and scores that are more formative and less summative will have positive effects on cognitive processes important to educational performance.

Effects on Self-Concept

Interpretations of grades impact students' self-concepts. From their grades, students make inferences about their ability and their potential for performing academic work. Grades can also be important sources of general motivation.

Effects on Learning Strategies

Along with their test results teachers should provide students, whenever possible, with additional information about *why* their performance results were or were not successful. Students can use this information to enhance their success in reaching goals and objectives. By knowing why performance was successful students can verify the usefulness of study strategies; by knowing why performance was less than successful students can be helped to understand what needs to be done, what new or additional strategies can be used or learned to get better results. For example, the young student who has difficulty in finding the main idea of a chapter (thereby getting a low score) may be reading serially from the first word to the end of the chapter (thereby using an inefficient reading process). To improve his or her performance, the teacher might suggest a remedial strategy (repairing the inefficient one) in which the student begins an assignment of a new chapter by surveying the entire chapter and finding the main idea reflected in the organization of headings.

Such information can be constructively focused on the degree to which students have reached their objectives (standards achieved, outcomes, or grades). Feedback may focus on the adequacy of cognitive (learning and studying) skills already acquired or in need of development. Most importantly, your feedback can provide specifics about the kind of modifications students need to make to improve their learning strategies or increase their skills.

With experience in using information from tests, students learn to adapt to distinctions among academic situations. For example, one of the most common acquisitions without teacher or other formal guidance is that students learn, correctly or incorrectly, that the way to study for a multiple-choice test is to memorize details and the way to study for an essay test is to learn generalizations or general ideas, or to memorize lists of ideas under a concept such as the three branches of the government, the functions of each branch of the government or even examples of checks and balances in the democratic system. It can be seen that these examples all provide repair strategies that amount to little more than mindless repetition or memorization of facts. However, with constructive feedback from the teacher each can be understood and learned meaningfully.

■ Using Assessments as Evidence of Progress

The importance of comparing the results of pre- and post-measures is often neglected in grading, but it is as much as part of understanding learning as is the straightforward end-of-unit measure. Thus the contents of a portfolio (for the present consider a portfolio to be something like a container) of accomplishments at the beginning of instruction might be compared with a portfolio after a unit of instruction. Clearly there would be differences not only in the content of the portfolio but the organization of the contents.

Measures used prior to instruction are sometimes employed for diagnostic purposes, to identify students who need to be selected for special instruction (either remediation or enrichment). (We'll elaborate on this point in other sections of the textbook, one of which is called *"Response to Intervention."*)

However, by comparing scores from two identical measures, one before and one after instruction, you can identify differences and trends in student progress. Not only can you find where the student's performance stands at a given point in learning, you can identify the *progress* that has been made in learning a given topic—progress not only in how much he or she has learned, but in how well the student understands, comprehends, or uses the learning. Simply having done well on a test or other measure may provide students an indicator of status, but adding your (and their) informed interpretation and analysis is significant to a better understanding of progress being made. Both together account for the finding that frequent testing enhances learning of the tested material (Dempster, 1997; Roediger & Karpicke, 2006).

■ The Dynamics of Formative Assessment

Now that you are gaining an understanding of the importance of formative assessment, let's look more directly at the process of using it in your classroom. From the vantage point of assessment for learning, instruction often looks very similar to assessment and vice versa (see overlapping components in Figure 4.1). So instruction is more than the mere presentation of information; it involves (a) enhancing motivational interests and involvement and (b) providing opportunities for making assessments by both students and teacher. Theory to Practice Box 4.1 illustrates several activities that provide such opportunities for the teacher, the students engaged in the work, and other observers of the displays of the products.

■ Feedback

As we have seen, a critical component of formative assessment is feedback, information (a) to the *student* about his or her performance, perhaps to help him or her understand successful *learning* techniques, and (b) to the *teacher* for promoting an understanding of successful *teaching* techniques. The aim is to help either understand the "why" of errors that might have been made as well as the reasons for successes. Even students who may feel they have done poorly on a performance measure respond well to feedback regarding their learning potential when they get meaningful feedback (Sternberg, 2006). Feedback should be understood sufficiently well that it becomes functional for both teacher and student in knowing the nature of a difficulty (or success), acquiring the available remedial

Theory to Practice Box 4.1
ILLUSTRATION OF INSTRUCTIONAL ACTIVITIES PROVIDING THE OPPORTUNITY FOR FORMATIVE ASSESSMENT IN SEVERAL SCHOOL CONTENT AREAS

Assessments are used to learn how to solve problems. Students ask questions, find alternative solutions, and make such decisions as illustrated below for different subject-matter areas. Their products can then be assessed for accuracy, meaningfulness, completeness, and usefulness. The activities provide opportunities for the teacher to observe the processes students use to achieve the goals of a unit of instruction.

In a social studies class:
The students in this class will use and share their experience to enhance the extent of a conceptual category. Some things they will do in a unit on safe driving include:

- Students will identify important community values particularly associated with safety.
- Groups of students will share and list all the values they identified.
- Teams will choose a value to research; they will simultaneously identify symbols associated with the value.
- The collection of values becomes a part of a representation for a given team.

In another unit students in this class might demonstrate their thinking by depicting their knowledge of moral values and well-adjusted behavior through the use of graphic representations to show why understanding such different values as honesty, loyalty, civic duty, orderliness, justice, freedom, and so on are important to a society.

In a geography class:
Every day the students see their work as they come into the team area. At the end of the term they will have an expo to show their projects on some region of the world coming into prominence. Different courses will emphasize their unique characteristics. Social studies classes will emphasize people, communities, and values. Science classes will share their research about ecology within these regions. Some things they might do include:

- Identify the wildlife populations of the regions.
- On maps show migratory routes, if any, of species inhabiting the regions. Learn about the reasons for migration.
- Show the relation between animal and plant populations as well as their dependence on climatic change.

In a science class:
Students use learning logs in their classes to demonstrate what they know and what needs further clarification about topics covered. They tell in their learning log how they knew to use a particular form of visual display (web) and how the connections in the web were to be performed.

- Students learn about the scientific method, perform experiments following the scientific method, and develop lab reports to summarize their findings. Keeping a log helps trace their learning from what they knew before taking the course to performing experiments to support claims associated with principles and concepts. They describe what they know and how they go about performing the best experiment for a certain purpose—such as providing evidence for Boyle's or Charles' law or, at a simpler level, the attributes associated with buoyancy of an object.
- Students apply what they learn from class discussions, textbook assignments, and seatwork by using graphic representations such as a web to demonstrate the connections between essential information for describing the scientific method.

In a history class:
Students studying any war (either historic or recent) can demonstrate their knowledge in a number of ways:

- Student design bulletin boards to demonstrate their knowledge of the differences between Northerners and Southerners during the Civil War, the differences between civil wars and revolutionary or other wars, the evolution of technology in wartimes, and so on.
- Other students develop a tour during peace time for a travel agency through the place where the war had been fought. In preparation for making a brochure they might study, select, and justify battle sites to include in their tour. They also determine travel and hotel costs.

In a writing class:
Through written products such as essays, assess the students' level of understanding, skills, interests, needs, and goals. These writing exercises are framed around meaningful topics within content areas:

- Students enhance and extend their knowledge of history while learning to write resumes. They do so by such assignments as researching the work of a famous person, in some historical period, in some area such as invention, science, or mathematics and developing a resume for him or her. The work takes on additional meaning if the student identifies the person and shows the reason for his or her notoriety and how it is related to that period in history.
- Essays can be directed toward meaningful evaluation of one's own plans. Students can write essays about their personal goals as reflected in an understanding of the curriculum in which they are enrolled; the essays might include the instruction that was used, the different measures that were used over the year and why those measures were used, and other relevant information. Or the essay can be written to reflect how the curriculum and its parts were related to their initial goals, the progress toward those goals, and, perhaps, a change in goals.

Source: Based on Jacoby (2002).

strategies, and increasing self-efficacy in using the material. For example, for a lesson in government, you can:

- *Examine the evidence on performance that you have collected.* For example, "The evidence shows that students are able to list branches of government but are unable to see the relationship among their functions."
- *Interpret the evidence in terms of what you know about student learning.* For example, "Because the teacher had presented them as a list of the definitions of the three independent branches, students had depended on rote memory in preparation for the evaluation."
- *Evaluate choices for remedial action from the alternatives you have learned about.* For example, "Graphic displays are particularly useful for showing hierarchical representation with links showing the functional relations between the three branches."
- *Attend to other outcomes such as the effects on motivation, persistence, and confidence.* For example, "Enhance self-efficacy and confidence by increasing understanding and competence in the use of the hierarchical representation."

The Importance of Early Feedback

The most efficiently useable feedback for any learner comes close to the time the performance is assessed. Summative evaluation, for example, informs teachers and students of what happened in the past. If the past is at the end of a unit of time or at the end of a semester, the evaluation is too late for effective remedial measures to be taken. Also, summative assessment is often "of" the recipient; as such, it typically provides few opportunities for self-assessment of studying or learning strategies. Students rarely receive information about what contributed to their scores beyond the mere comparison of their performance with that of others. Instead, they rely on their own interpretations. Only infrequently are they able, with the teacher's help, to examine where and how they could improve. Rarely do they judge their final performance scores in terms of understanding objectives, planning study schedules, setting learning goals, or recognizing when they have achieved learning goals—even lacking in the metacognition of knowing when they have studied enough to pass a test on the material learned.

Frequency and Content of Feedback

Attempts to provide feedback with final grades through such generalized statements as "You can do better if you try" may provide a modicum of motivation but fail to offer guidance to improve learning. Don't wait until the final grade is posted to offer your students feedback that not only motivates but also improves performance. Provide feedback as soon as it is evident that the student might use a better learning strategy or as soon as it is evident that the student has a faulty conceptualization.

To illustrate, instructor Pete Jones knows that student Ellie T. has difficulty with understanding the law of gravity after he sees her responses to these situations:

Question: Explain which would hit the ground first and why in each of these situations:
A. Two objects, identical in all respects except weight, dropped from the same height: one is a 2# weight, the other is a 4# weight.
   a. 2# weight
   b. 4# weight
   c. Neither
   d. Both
   Explain why _____

B. Identical bullets, one shot horizontally from a gun and another dropped at exactly the same moment from the same height as the gun.
   a. Bullet shot from a gun
   b. Bullet dropped from the same height as the gun
   c. Neither
   d. Both
   Explain why _____

(Ellie's answers were "b" in both situations. That is, she answered that the 4-pound weight in the first situation and the bullet dropped from the same height in the second situation were correct. However, the correct answers were that both weights and both bullets will hit the ground at the same time. Discussions of the bullet problem may be found in textbooks or online.)

Good feedback means knowing how understanding is manifested, the standards for good performance, and what feedback is relevant to achieving those standards. For example, knowing only that monarch butterflies migrate seasonally would be insufficient for predicting when, why, or to where they migrate. The student would profit most from knowing the "why's" and "how's" of migration and the routes of butterflies. But to trace the migration route of the monarch butterfly also requires knowledge of the effects of the seasons on migration. Assessing the student's simple knowledge of these characteristics of migration would need to be supplemented by the ability to relate in-depth knowledge and understanding of the developmental stages of butterflies, seasonal effects on butterfly behaviors, and characteristics of migration routes.

Overall, good feedback focuses on elements of achievement that the student will find useful for future learning. Feedback should suggest some information about new learning or teaching strategies coupled with opportunities to use them. It should also help the student to rid him- or herself of older, ineffective strategies. By providing opportunities for self-assessment and practice you will contribute to the development of self-regulated learning. Without these opportunities students may depend on superficial feedback based on their own naïve perceptions (as explained in the next section), or teachers may inadvertently teach students to depend on others (such as parents or peers) for corrective guidance, thereby defeating the development of self-regulated learning.

Dysfunctional Feedback

Any seatwork or computer software exercises, including drill and practice, that may be used to enhance learning provides opportunities for simple and continuous feedback. At a minimum, the student is told whether the answer is correct or incorrect. But, optimally, it should be informative feedback. Using feedback in practice exercises for perceptual motor and cognitive skills facilitates the development of automaticity and fluency in using the skill.

But unless understood, feedback can sometimes lead to wrong inferences. For example, in the early learning stages as a skill is being acquired (as in the initial learning of arithmetic facts), simple feedback without useful information about the "how" and "why" may result in student self-interpretations that are not aligned to school learning. Imagine that your students are just learning to use the addition operator (the plus sign). If your early feedback stresses only the right or wrong nature of the answers, students may arrive at notions like these:

- The main purpose of learning the information is to satisfy the teacher (learning does not have intrinsic value for the student). (I'll learn it for the test, but I'll forget it just as quickly.)
- That's not the way it was in the textbook (students know the information as it appears in the text and believe that the text

is the *only* context in which this knowledge applies). (The information doesn't have any utility beyond the classroom; it's just "book knowledge.")

- I memorized the principle by heart and knew it backward and forward. I don't see how that question on the test was related to the principle. (This is known as inert knowledge; information is learned by rote without an understanding of the underlying principles. There won't be any useful application of the learning.)

- I never could do arithmetic; this is just one more example of how poor my ability is. (This result enhances the belief that learning is an innate ability rather than one that can be improved under the control of the learner. There is no acquisition of self-regulated learning here.)

Negative self-interpretations can also be applied to successes. In that case, they have effects much like those above. For example, students can maintain:

- A less efficient learning strategy like brute force memorization (repetition aimed at rote memory)
- Beliefs that learning is an innate ability that one has or doesn't have and about which one has little control
- Study habits that satisfy external authority (parents or teachers) who provide rewards rather than studying for its intrinsic value
- Study habits that are limited to text presentations, thereby limiting ability to transfer knowledge to other situations (e.g., the student who scores well on classroom arithmetic tests may fail to understand how simple arithmetic operations are used to balance a checkbook)

Feedback for Self-Regulation of Learning

As noted in the foregoing paragraphs, it is desirable to facilitate self-regulation of learning. Given appropriate feedback on different aspects of learning (such as thinking processes, conceptualizations learned, and interactions with others), students can learn to take responsibility for their own learning.

With sufficient informative feedback, learners begin to set their goals realistically, monitor their performance against those goals, and assess their degree of improvement as a consequence of alternative strategies. They also learn how to provide their own remediation of strategies that don't work efficiently. Initially, remediation strategies will be suggested by an outside source, such as the teacher. But, by gradually relinquishing this assistance, the need for using monitoring strategies can be successfully transferred to the student, an essential requirement for the development of self-assessment. Over time, given the responsibility of interpreting assessment outcomes and knowing their relationship to the strategies used, students can learn to identify processes with criteria characteristic of successful learning. With guidance, they can eventually learn to match appropriate learning strategies to learning outcomes, the benefits of which are critical to lifelong learning.

■ Asking the Right Questions in Assessment

Feedback in instruction follows some indicator about performance: number of right or wrong answers; latency of responding (how quickly the students responds); understanding demonstrated in graphic organizers; organization demonstrated in the composition of records constituting a portfolio; and so on. In order to provide useful occasions for feedback, your formative assessments need to be well designed; to put it simply, you need to ask the right questions.

When to Use Questions

Your assessment questions can involve *formal measures* (such as teacher-made tests), *informal on-the-spot dialogues, systematic discussions* (as in Socratic questioning in which the questions target or probe assumptions, rationales, implications, conceptual clarity, perspectives, and so on about a concept or phenomenon), or *performance tasks* in which students perform or act out a task requirement. In either instance, your focus should be on the critical concepts that you want students to address. Good questions also typically present a challenge, moving the student toward another level of understanding or goal. Different forms of questions are asked at different stages of learning. Before learning you might ask questions such as "What do you know about (a scientific principle, a form of government, etc.)?" During learning you might ask, "How does this (form of government, etc.) compare with that (form of government)?" After learning, you might ask, "Can you tell how this (form of government) will handle the (current exchange rate)?"

When a measure is used (whether it is a test score, rating of a written essay, or rating of a lab experiment) for formative assessment, it should reflect the specific challenges posed in the learning task (the difficulties involved, the places where attention is most needed, and the situations where applications are possible). Be sure to focus on understanding rather than on sheer memorization.

Look carefully at what has to be assessed in order to provide useful feedback. For example, in learning how to use scalar units in making scale drawings or in reading maps drawn to scale, it's one thing to know what a blueprint is. It is quite another matter to create a blueprint with size, locations, or distances correctly displayed and drawn to scale. And it is a completely different matter to evaluate the accuracy and utility of the blueprint. Each of these focuses on different (a) *perspectives* (e.g., knowing, understanding, doing, or applying); (b) *characteristics of learning* (e.g., repetition, strategy, finding cause-effect relations); (c) *means of assessment* (e.g., tests, performance, producing a product); and (d) *forms of feedback* (e.g., grading, grading against a standard, grading comparing another's performance).

Stating Questions

Formative assessments begin with student and teacher working out answers to questions like these from the beginning of an instructional unit:

- *What is the activity and why is it being learned?* Possible questions: Why are we studying (adding and subtracting; the dinosaur; the war in _____)? Show students what you are aiming for if they can't come up with a list similar to yours. Conversely, avoid starting a new unit by simply saying, "Today we are going to study (poets; budgets; the multiplication and division operators; the Archimedes principle) and then initiate a lecture presentation.
- *What are the expected learning outcomes?* Establish a goal(s) with students. Questions: What do we want to know when this lesson is over? What are we going to learn? Possible answers: We are learning to use arithmetic operators so we can use them in (shopping; making family budgets; balancing debit and credit sheets).
- *What are the learning contexts?* Questions: What kind of learning experience will be appropriate for this class to achieve the learning outcomes? What are student expectations about what they have to do (e.g., draw a reasonably accurate diagram of an insect)? Possible answers: We will (write sentences using adverbs and adjectives; analyze political reasons for the war; set up laboratory apparatus to produce oxygen;

work out a plan for conservation in the _____ part of the Everglades).

- *What are the criteria for knowing that learning has been achieved by both you and students?* Questions: How will *we* (teachers and students) know that you have learned this? How will *you* (self) know that you have learned this? Possible answers: We will know we have achieved this (because we can retell a story without losing its meaning; because when we use an adjective or adverb the sentence makes sense; because whether we draw a picture of a lobster or a grasshopper all the parts of the body will be clear).

A Summary of the Unique Features of Questions for Formative Assessment

Some unique features of assessments used for formative feedback relate to these kinds of questions:

- Can students go beyond merely repeating back what they know to organizing and transforming what they know?
- Can the students examine their own learning processes? For instance, do they know strategies for accessing information? Do they know it helps to skim the headings before starting to read a chapter?
- Can students relate what they are learning to their own prior knowledge? Are they aware that they already know a lot (or very little) about the subject being studied? Are they aware that their experiences and knowledge schemata contain inadequacies or misconceptions and that these can be corrected by studying?

Once assessments are made, the feedback from them can be used to facilitate the:

- Adequacy of learning outcome statements and expectations
- Effectiveness of instructional strategies, procedures or tasks
- Criteria for knowing what levels or criteria of success have been achieved

Merely telling the students about effective learning processes in a text or lecture format is typically of little value and has little durability. Without a basis in assessment for critiquing and feedback, mere telling may lead to little more than dependence on others for the content and methods of learning. The result is that achievement is inert; the material is learned sufficiently well

Theory to Practice Box 4.2
SAMPLE ITEMS SHOWING DIFFERENT WAYS OF ASSESSING
STUDENT'S LEARNING OF GEOMETRY

Memory
A square has four sides that are the same length. Circle the answer that shows how you would calculate the distance around the outside of a square.

a. $y - y + y - y$
b. $y + y + y + y$
c. $y \times y$
d. $y + y - y$

Analytical
You have two pipe cleaners of the same length. Make a circle with one and an oval with the other. Which shape has the larger area? Why?

Practical
You can have the square piece of your favorite chocolate bar or you can have the rectangular piece. Circle the piece that will give you the most amount of chocolate.

Creative
Young children learn new words best when there is a picture or a symbol for them to remember. You want to help children remember the new word area. Come up with a symbol or simple picture that helps young children remember what area is.

Source: Adapted from Sternberg (2006, p. 32, Figure 1).

to pass a test, but the knowledge is not enduring ("I got an 'A' but can't remember a thing!") or applicable to new situations ("I learned a lot but can't seem to use it").

It is insufficient to say that a question is effective or ineffective, rather it is more meaningful to ask whether a question reveals something about how the student is learning. As illustrated in Theory to Practice Box 4.2, items in content tests can be constructed to measure such different objectives as memory, analytical, practical, and creative skills. Accordingly, it is a matter of defining the ways an item is effective or ineffective rather than simply saying a test is effective or ineffective.

■ Implementing Formative Assessment

By now you should understand the inseparability of teaching and assessment. Perhaps you thought the connection was obvious. Yet, in a formal survey of more than 200 teachers, Stiggins and Collins (1992), insightfully, made a list of a number of things teachers should know about using assessment. However, their study showed that the majority of the teachers didn't know the "why" of assessment, how assessed behaviors actually appear in instruction, ways to prevent difficulties in assessment, methods of providing feedback to the end users, or ways to use assessment for influencing policy.

The Role of Teacher Beliefs

Teachers' beliefs have strong effects on communication of expectations about their students' performance (Black & Wiliam, 1998). These beliefs influence the interpretation of assessment feedback, which in turn affects instructional practices. For example, a teacher who believes that ability to learn is an inherent trait is more likely to interpret good or bad performance in terms of a student's native capacity and is likely not to place much emphasis on what can be done in instruction. On the other hand, teachers who use formative assessment believe that learning is a cumulative ongoing process and that all pupils can learn and profit from feedback about the qualities of their work. These teachers were also found to want to improve their teaching.

Overall, teachers adhering to the belief that student learning ability or intelligence is a fixed, inherent entity, as opposed to the belief that learning is an incremental process, are less likely to employ formative assessment. When teachers (or any other agent such as parents) comment that achievement is dependent on the student's ability and that understanding reasons for learning success or failure seems unnecessary (after all, the student "has or does not have the ability"), they circumvent the need for knowing what to do about learning problems or unsuccessful instruction.

Using Formative Assessment

To use formative assessment, both teacher and students interactively (a) recognize the goals targeted for instruction; (b) monitor or track, through assessment, their progress toward the goal so that they know their present position in achieving the goal; and (c) know how to close the gap between the end product or goal and their present position (Kulik, Kulik, & Bangert-Drowns, 1990; Swing, Stoiber, & Peterson, 1988).

Students found to have lower ability are not ignored or neglected in this process. They can be helped to good advantage by taking part in identifying learning outcomes and by learning study skills such as how to evaluate their work, how to understand why the strategies they were using were or were not effective, how to select appropriate strategies related to objectives or goals, how to understand the criteria by which to judge their work, and how to judge the effectiveness of their study strategies. In other words, these and all students can take part in identifying what is wrong (or right) in their lack of progress and in learning how to make it right. But teachers who believe that some children can never learn are unlikely to engage in formative assessment that reveals the needs of students, and thus are unlikely to modify their teaching.

Overuse of Standardized Tests

Students profit most from feedback when opportunities arise to revise their thinking as they work on assignments. Not only do they learn about content or process, but they learn about values and contexts such as learning to value opportunities to revise or learning the nature of effective learning (such as knowing when a learning is understood, when a reading is comprehended, or when a procedure is appropriately used).

Unfortunately, the overuse of and overdependence on standardized tests sometimes leads to an overemphasis on sheer memorization or strategies for "beating the test" (even to the point of cheating on a test) (Nichols & Berliner, 2006). A case in point is a description by Schonfeld (1988) as cited in Bransford and colleagues (1999) of teachers whose students scored consistently high in examinations (or teachers who received consistently high teacher effectiveness ratings). Upon closer examination it was found that this performance was facilitated by drilling students on math proofs found frequently on examinations. The prompting or coaching seemed to have favorable effects—the coached students earned higher test scores. However, the test emphasized the simple recall of facts. When tested on understanding the processes involved, the coached students did not show improvement. Thus, evaluation of and feedback on knowing the factual content was an insufficient condition for effective problem solving.

School policies are also responsible for promulgating feedback emphasizing rote memory. It is not difficult to find schools that have sidetracked efforts to adapt instruction to individual differences and the needs of diverse students in order to schedule a substantial period (weeks) of preparation for the statewide tests. The time set aside is devoted to teaching to the test, a practice in which students are drilled in the kinds of items and the content that they will encounter on the standardized exam (Nichols & Berliner, 2007). Such teaching offers little promise for learning with understanding and defeats the purposes of formative assessment.

Few educators will admit they believe in teaching to the test. But many assert that, to demonstrate that students are well taught, tests or other measures should correspond to the specifics of instruction, without considering their utility for feedback. As a result, left with ambiguous and vague standards, they may believe their best approach to improving learning is to improve test scores. Under those circumstances the easiest route is to know and teach to approximations of the test items. Not surprisingly, students taught in this manner learn little more than the answers to a single kind of test or test item.

■ Designing Appropriate Formative Tests

Formative assessment conveys the idea of evaluating students against the standards or objectives of a learning unit, and it also provides for a degree of challenge to the students. As students become aware of the objectives being tested and what is required of them, they are motivated to go beyond the basic objectives, perhaps by knowing how to elaborate on the learning (going beyond the textbook) or by using the information in an everyday situation. For example, they might be motivated to use math principles in planning an underground tunnel or finding the height of a building. Challenging tasks are those within the ability of the students; students can be successful in learning them. However, at the same time, such tasks are sufficiently difficult that they leave room for improvement. In solving more difficult tasks or problems, both their ability and motivation for learning increases. Properly developed challenges reduce off-task (distracting) behaviors and thereby contribute to favorable classroom climate.

Nevertheless, an overly challenging (too difficult or extending too far beyond the material that has been taught) task has the potential for creating frustration and anxiety, producing negative motivation that is beneficial to neither the student nor the school. Tests that are too difficult can have the potential of inhibiting learning.

The functional implementation of formative assessment, based on these characteristics and others discussed in this chapter are illustrated in the Theory to Practice Box 4.3, based in part on the careful and thoughtful work of Shavelson (2007).

Theory to Practice Box 4.3
WAYS OF IMPLEMENTING FORMATIVE ASSESSMENT IN
CLASSROOM INSTRUCTION

This case illustrates many of the principles described in this chapter associated with formative assessment. As you read this illustration you will see that the incorporation of assessment into instruction makes the two—instruction and feedback—virtually seamless, that is, indistinguishable parts of instructional events. The focus is on (a) *setting tasks* that will be instructional but also will provide the kind of information you want to know about achieving instructional objectives; (b) *obtaining data* about student performance on these tasks; (c) *interpreting the data* for their implications about the progress students are making; and (d) *making instructional and learning decision*s based on the interpretations of that data.

The instructional target in this illustration is the student's understanding of a concept. It could be any concept in any content area or at any educational level; the underlying principles and structure of the instructional events would be essentially the same. In this example, we emphasize the understanding of the concept of buoyancy, as Shavelson does in the original description. As you know buoyancy is a factor in Archimedes' principle that an object immersed in a fluid is buoyed up by a force equal to the weight of the water it displaces. This principle contains many complexities in understanding such as the fact that a fluid might be a liquid or a gas. It contains the notions of density and specific gravity. The principle applies to submarines (under the water) and to balloons (in the air). As with most complex principles, it can be understood at the fourth-grade level, as it is used here, or at the expert physicist's level of understanding.

The idea behind embedding assessments for formative feedback employs teaching tools to evoke *teachable moments*—opportune times for teaching, times when students want to learn about something and are receptive to finding out all that they can about a topic or skill.

A generally useful technique with both instructional and assessment implications is to ask questions around carefully planned tasks using motivational attractors at the very beginning of the lesson. We use the term *attractors* simply to imply the use of motivation to get the student into the learning situation. In this case, we assume that a focus on answers to such questions as, "Why do things sink and float" will motivate the student to want to learn more. The added benefits in teaching are that such questions require recalling, reflecting, and integrating information they know as well as what they need to know in order to answer questions.

Adjunct Questions: Think Outside the Box

We have selected buoyancy to illustrate how reflective lessons and formative assessments are used. A related question is "Why do things sink and float?" In order to learn applications beyond this example, you may want to begin thinking in terms of your field of specialization or the educational level of your students.

(continued)

Theory to Practice Box 4.3
(Continued)

Substitute concepts from your own field of specialization or from the courses you teach in elementary or high school. For example, a concept in biology might be "living thing." (What does it mean to be alive? Is a plant alive? Is a rolling stone alive? Give examples of things that are not alive. How do you know something is a living thing?) Or select a concept in social studies or history such as "government" (Why did the constitution provide for three branches? Why are the powers separated? What are checks and balances? Do all forms of government, including those in other countries, have the three branches? What happens when the power of one branch or the other is abused? When does a monarchy show abuse of power?)

Teaching to Integrate Formative Assessments

Teachers step back at key points during instruction to check expectations regarding student progress. Convenient points for these checks are (a) the completion of a unit for achieving a designated level of understanding, (b) a transition period from one level to the next such as acquisition of facts, to understanding concepts, to applying principles, or (c) making applications to check the applicability of what they know to other areas or problems. In the process of doing so, both students and teachers reflect on what they have accomplished, what understandings have been achieved, and what more they need to know; they identify the next steps that must be taken to move forward (Shavelson et al., 2007).

Adjunct Question

Assume that students are given the task of predicting whether a bottle will float or sink and that they predict the bottle will sink. Is there sufficient information in this statement alone (e.g., is the bottle capped?). Would it be advisable for the teacher to use another demonstration to make certain the students understand the concept? Is a correct answer to this one problem sufficient proof that the students know the answer? What are some ways of rating an answer besides its correctness? What would be the value of adding another demonstration, if there is a value in doing so? Can you suggest another demonstration?

The assessments used in these lessons are planned (based on Shavelson et al., 2007; cf. Duschl, 2003a, 2003b) to:

- *Make deliberate attempts to find out what students know.* Students' knowledge about the principle surfaces when the teacher asks the focus question, "Why do you think some things sink and other things float?" Sometimes a demonstration of a common or novel situation will permit interesting evaluations of student thinking about deceptively simple problems. Students studying buoyancy, for example, might be presented with this question: "Cooks commonly know that when raw ravioli-like foods are placed in boiling water the ravioli initially sink. The cooks know the ravioli are cooked when they rise to the surface. (In the instructional situation, it will probably be necessary to precede the question with a description of how ravioli is made.) Why does the same object (the ravioli square) sink when raw and then float when it is cooked?"

- *Plan activities that engage students in active learning.* Activities can be planned to help students verbalize what buoyancy (or any concept) means to them. The activities will also provide evidence about the extent to which students know the relation of such features of an object as density to that object's buoyancy. For example, you might have students compare the buoyancy of two objects of the same size and demonstrate that one floats and the other sinks. Or take an object made of the same material but in different form (clay ball vs. clay wafer). Compare their behavior when placed in water—do they float or sink? Why?

- *Know and use alternative teaching strategies.* Instructional strategies differ in both the way they are employed and their outcomes. Group work is useful for learning to share responsibility for completing tasks. Stating problems to be solved helps students become aware of the processes involved in thinking. Questioning with prompts helps reveal students' conceptions and interpretations. Each strategy provides teachers with opportunities for assessing unique features of student performance.

Adjunct Question

The word prompt *refers to the way an answer is to be given, the situation within which it is framed, or how it is to be assessed. Any concept can be cued at some level. Buoyancy can be understood, for example, at the level of "things that float (or sink)," at the conceptual level of density, or at the principle level of Archimedes's principle. It can be applied to engineering in a number of areas such as boat design. Some cues used in assessment of writing are:*

- Descriptive. *Evaluate the accuracy of student descriptions of things that would float and sink in a freshwater lake compared to a salt lake. What do they consider important—is it size? Is it weight? A rhinoceros sinks and immense boats float. Why?*

- Expository. *Evaluate explanations students give for things that are buoyant and those that are not. Are their explanations technical and technically accurate or are they guesses based on incorrect assumptions?*

- Narration. *Evaluate student stories about experiences that affected the way they learned about things that were buoyant, about things that sink of float.*

- Persuasion. *This is a little more difficult, but if you think they are prepared to do so, students can be assigned a task to convince the class that under some conditions things that ordinarily sink will float on a liquid medium (e.g., change the fluidity of the medium such as water or oil).*

(continued)

Theory to Practice Box 4.3
(Continued)

Write a series of questions for a creative problem on buoyancy, each of which incorporates one of the cues. You might ask, for example, "What common objects can float?" "Under what circumstances can things that don't float be made to float?" "How would you design an animal to be able to walk on water?" or, "What is it in the design of a submarine that permits it to float or sink at will?" You might incorporate into your question, for instance, criteria for performing a task—the evidence that the student needs for a good answer to a problem.

- Facilitate interaction of students to facilitate meaningful communication of ideas. *There is always opportunity for students to exchange ideas by telling one another about their findings, by discussing controversial issues, or by debating, to name but a few. The availability of new technological channels such as developing websites facilitates the process further. Such activities engage the processes of retrieving, selecting, and using relevant information associated with cognition. Whether as communicators or recipients of the communication, students provide useful assessment feedback for teachers to evaluate and assess in what they (the students) recall, the importance of information recalled, the selection of information explained, the organization of the material recalled, the applications used in elaborations, and the adequacy of their summary.*
- Critiquing, comparing, and controversy. *Whatever the teaching method employed, student responses reflect whether their conceptions and theories are based on sound evidence and the applicability of conclusions to everyday situations. Look for that evidence in making assessments. Nevertheless, also be aware that such prompts as the following might be needed to obtain a complete reading of what the student knows: "Can this model (e.g., about the relation of weight and volume to the object's displacement of water) be applied to all other cases?" How did your intial model of buoyancy differ from the model proposed in Archimedes' principle?" When evaluating responses, look for the quality of evidence by such questions as, "How do you know that?" and "What evidence do you need to support your explanation?"*

Source: Based on Shavelson et al. (2007).

■ Summary

Formative assessment transforms your classroom into a dynamic laboratory. It becomes replete with opportunities for using assessments to improve student learning and instruction. Throughout this chapter you have seen why formative assessment is sometimes referred to as assessment *for* learning. In most cases, formative assessment means giving students information about their performance at reasonably frequent intervals. It means providing information about remedial measures that might be taken to compensate for weaknesses. It means pointing out the reasons for good or excellent performance. It means pointing out information that will be helpful in self-assessment and in repair strategies. All of these apply to your instruction as well. The more frequently you get information, judiciously determined on the basis of student performance about your teaching the more effective it will be for modifying your instruction if needed.

An important characteristic of formative assessment is the use of functional feedback from assessments. Feedback will be provided when it:

- Will be most beneficial—generally immediately after learning
- Is based on frequent assessments with short intervals rather than when it is based on infrequent assessments at longer intervals
- Provides information about how to take on the specific challenges posed by the instruction or learning
- Is framed in terms of standards or criteria
- Informs teacher (and students) about what needs to be changed, whether learning outcomes, instructional procedures, learning tasks, or criteria for judging or demonstrating that learning has taken place

Effective feedback serves as a basis for self-evaluation of performance and self-correction of poor study strategies. In the long run, it should help students learn to self-regulate their learning.

A salient characteristic of formative assessment is its diagnostic quality. Unlike summative assessment it is planned at the time of teaching and is implemented through self-monitoring by teachers and students to advance learning, to involve them in learning, and to achieve such learning goals as understanding, comprehension, and application. These characteristics are unlike those interpretations made in sheer summative assessments, which examine past achievements to sum up learning, involving mainly marking, that is, assigning single grades (or marks) at periodic intervals for summary evaluations or as status markers of achievement.

All told, assessment involves observation of student performance in classroom activities that range from active discussion to seatwork. Analysis is made of student performance, whether on constructing projects, assembling portfolios, doing homework assignments, or taking tests. When these assessments are used to modify teaching by simply reteaching or by using alternative instructional methods, the assessments are said to be used formatively to facilitate instruction and learning.

Used by teachers who are informed in principles of assessment, formative assessment produces significant learning gains, helping children with learning disabilities as much as it helps children without learning disabilities. Feedback helps both students and teachers to be aware of goals, gaps in achievement of those goals, and constructive ways for closing the gaps. Formative assessment diverts focus from getting the right answer or passing the test to a focus on understanding, comprehending, and application. It emphasizes the importance of learning as a legitimate outcome in its own right and its improvement through *effort* rather than an emphasis on inherent ability or lack of ability.

Although formative assessment is often diagnostic, its functions may differ according to instructional phases. Before instruction, for example, formative assessment emphasizes student readiness for learning a new topic. You may want to know what students know about the topic, how well they know it, and at what level they understand it. Knowing your students' readiness will help you know where to initiate your assignments; you might need to provide for more elaboration and explanation than you had intended or, because your students know more about the topic than you anticipated, you might want to teach at a more advanced level, or you might need to provide remediation by teaching them the basics of processes involved in such tasks as proving theorems or reading strategies.

Assessment before learning also provides the opportunity for learning whether students are ready to put effort into achieving such desirable learning outcomes as understanding, comprehending, and making applications. In comparison, you might learn whether students are overburdened by the motivation of simply achieving a grade by whatever means are available, including the acquisition of inert knowledge (knowledge that is not useable beyond passing a test) by brute force (memorizing facts by repetition). In either case, the assessment will provide information that will help in determining whether you should resort to ways of improving motivation before you deal with instructional content.

During instruction, formative assessment takes on its full meaning. In this phase, assessments are moment-to-moment as well as periodic. They are made through monitoring of goal achievement by teachers and students, which informs them how well the lessons are progressing; how well students are responding to instruction; how well instructional goals are being achieved; whether students are using effective learning strategies; whether alternative instructional methods ought to be used; how effectively learning is monitored by teachers and students; whether effective repair strategies are being used to close gaps between progress and goals; and what still needs to be learned and where remediation is needed on the part of teachers or students.

Although we typically think of assessment after instruction as summative, it can also be used to make inferences that are formative. Assessments after instruction can be used to provide feedback for changing instruction in the future. They can be used to infer how instruction can be adapted to meet the needs of students for their future development, for example, when they are taught a new unit of instruction or when they enter a new grade with a new teacher. Summative assessment can also be turned around on itself to check on its adequacy for the achievement and performance goals, thereby suggesting the need for alternative assessments and observations in the future, measures that might indicate different teaching levels or educational goals based on student needs and readiness.

In summary, formative assessment involves both students and teachers in the process of assessment. It emphasizes quality of instruction as well as quality of learning. Outcomes of understanding, comprehension, and application are emphasized beyond the mere acquisition of a grade at the end of a marking period. Feedback is analyzed constructively. The aim is to improve instruction, in the service of improving learning. The feedback is aimed at the modification of existing practices, or at suggesting the need for alternatives to existing practices. Simple value judgments of instructional methods as "good" or "bad" are avoided and replaced by judgments of how well the students are being served. The progress of individual students is judged relative to their ability and readiness, rather than at a comparison with a group of individuals.

Exercise 4.1

Review Figure 4.1 again. How would you change it to represent summative evaluation? As a start consider whether the instruction and assessment boxes would overlap. Also consider whether feedback loops are needed and whether there might be extensions beyond interpretation and if so, to what.

Exercise 4.2

Take an existing lesson plan and incorporate into it an emphasis on formative assessment and assessment for learning. Begin this exercise with a lesson plan you may have created for a course in general teaching methods or a similar course. Or it might be from some other source such as a textbook, an online course, or one developed by your supervising teacher (in which case you should ask permission to use it). The plan should be a clear and functionally useful statement of the instruction for a given unit. If a plan is not available, then create one for a lesson in your area incorporating the assessment-for-learning components.

■ References

Bell, B., & Cowie, B. (2001). *Formative assessment and science education.* Dordrecht, The Netherlands: Kluwer Academic Publishers.

Black, P., & Wiliam, D. (1998). *Inside the black box.* London: NFER Nelson.

Bransford, J. C., Brown, A. L., & Cocking, R. R. (1999). *How people learn: Brain, mind, experience, and school.* Washington, DC: National Academy Press.

Dempster, F. N. (1997). Using tests to promote classroom learning. In R. Dillon (Ed.), *Handbook on testing* (pp. 332–346). London: Greenwood Press.

Duschl, R. A. (2003a). The assessment of argumentation & explanation: Creating and supporting teachers' feedback strategies. In D. Zeidler (Ed.), *The role of moral reasoning on socio-scientific issues and discourse in science education.* Dordrecht, The Netherlands: Kluwer Academic Press.

Duschl, R. A. (2003b). Assessment of inquiry. In J. M. Atkin & J. Coffey (Eds.), *Everyday assessment in the science classroom* (pp. 41–59). Washington, DC: National Science Teachers Association Press.

Harlen, W. (2005). Teachers' summative practices and assessment for learning: Tensions and synergies. *Curriculum Journal, 16,* 207–223.

Harlen, W. (2006). On the relationship between assessment for formative and summative purposes. In J. Gardner (Ed.), *Assessment and learning* (pp. 103–118). Thousand Oaks, CA: Sage.

Jacoby, S. (2002). Assessing what students know and do at KDES and MSSD. *The Clerc Center Connection, 4*(3). Retrieved December 12, 2006, from http://clerccenter.gallaudet.edu/tpd/news/2002-11/mssd.html.

Kulik, C. L. C., Kulik, J. A., & Bangert-Drowns, R. L. (1990). Effectiveness of mastery learning programs: A meta-analysis. *Review of Educational Research, 60,* 265–299.

Linn, R. L. (1989). Current perspectives and future directions. In R. L. Linn (Ed.), *Educational measurement* (3rd ed.) (pp. 1–10). London: Collier Macmillan.

Maxwell, G. S. (2004). *Progressive assessment for learning and certification: Some lessons from school-based assessment in Queensland.*

Paper presented at the Third Conference of the Association of Commonwealth Examination and Assessment Boards.

Nichols, S. L., & Berliner, D. C. (2006). The pressure to cheat in a high-stakes testing environment. In E. M. Anderman & T. Murdock (Eds.), *Psychological perspectives on academic cheating* (pp. 289–312). New York: Elsevier.

Nichols, S. L., & Berliner, D. C. (2007). *Collateral damage: How high-stakes testing corrupts America's schools.* Cambridge, MA: Harvard University Press.

Roediger, H. L., III, & Karpicke, J. D. (2006). The power of testing memory: Basic research and implications for educational practice. *Perspectives on Psychological Science, 1*(3), 181–210.

Ruiz-Primo, M. A., & Furtak, E. M. (2004). *Informal formative assessment of students' understanding of scientific inquiry* (No. 639). Los Angeles, CA: Center for the Study of Evaluation.

Schonfeld, A. H. (1988). When good teaching leads to bad results: The disasters of well taught mathematics classes. *Educational Psychologist, 23*(2), 145–166.

Shavelson, R. J., Young, D. B., Ayala, C. C., Brandon, P., Furtak, E. M., Ruiz-Primo, M. A., et al. (2007). On the impact of curriculum-embedded formative assessment on learning: A collaboration between curriculum and assessment developers. Retrieved April 23, 2008, from www.stanford.edu/dept/SUSE/SEAL/special/1-On%20the%20Impact%20of%20FA_Submit.doc.

Sternberg, R. J. (2006). Recognizing neglected strengths. *Educational Leadership, 64*(1), 30–35.

Stiggins, R. J., & Collins, N. F. (1992). *In teachers' hands: Investigating the practices of classroom assessment.* Albany: State University of New York Press.

Swing, S. R., Stoiber, K. C., & Peterson, P. L. (1988). Thinking skills versus learning time: Effects of alternative classroom based interventions on students' mathematics problem solving. *Cognition and Instruction, 5*, 123–191.

Wiliam, D., Lee, C., Harrison, C., & Black, P. (2004). Teachers developing assessment for learning: Impact on student achievement. *Assessment in Education: Principles, Policy and Practice, 11*, 49–65.

CHAPTER 5

Performance Assessment

I N THE SECOND EDITION of his book *Preparing Instructional Objectives*, Bob Mager (1976) tells the story of a mythical kingdom in which men wore beards and the practice of barbering had long been forgotten. One day the king decided to get his beard cut, and the search was on for an individual who could provide the ruler with the best possible shave. A commission was assembled to ensure that the king would be exposed to only the best professional. To help identify the royal barber, the commission created a battery of tests to see who would perform with the greatest skill and knowledge. One test asked the candidates to provide the history of barbering, another to describe the techniques of barbering, and a third inventoried the instruments used for the profession. On the basis of test scores in these areas a royal barber was chosen who was subsequently led to the king. After lathering up the king's beard, the royal barber took out his razor and promptly cut off the king's ear. As a penalty for poor performance and judgment, the royal barber and the test commission lost their heads.

The moral of the story is, of course, that if you want to know how someone is going to perform, ask for a performance. In the case of the unfortunate king, a direct test (on somebody else) would have been a better indicator of the royal barber's future work than a paper-and-pencil assessment. In this chapter, we look at how to communicate performance expectations and then discuss the types of assessment situations in which direct assessment might be better than indirect indicators of work. We also look at ways to evaluate performance to ensure that one is measuring the important aspects of it in a consistent way. Finally we address the topic of evaluating group versus individual work performance.

■ Definitions

The terms *performance assessment*, *alternative assessment*, and *portfolio assessment* are often used interchangeably, but have slightly different meanings (Carl & Rosen, 1992; Pierce & O'Malley, 1992; Stiggins, 1987; Tierney, Carter, & Desai, 1991).

Alternative Assessment
- Is any method of finding out what a student knows or can do that is intended to show growth and inform instruction and is not a standardized or traditional test
- Is by definition criterion referenced
- Is authentic because it is based on activities that represent actual progress toward instructional goals and reflect tasks typical of classrooms and real-life settings
- Requires integration of language skills
- May include teacher observation, performance assessment, and student self-assessment

Performance Assessment
- Is a type of alternative assessment
- Is an exercise in which a student demonstrates specific skills and competencies in relation to a continuum of agreed upon standards of proficiency or excellence
- Reflects student performance on instructional tasks and relies on professional rater judgment in its design and interpretation

Portfolio Assessment
- Is the use of records of a student's work over time and in a variety of modes to show the depth, breadth, and development of the student's abilities
- Is the purposeful and systematic collection of student work that reflects accomplishment relative to specific instructional goals or objectives
- Can be used as an approach for combining the information from both alternative and standardized assessments
- Has as key elements student reflection and self-monitoring

The term *alternative assessment* implies the application of something second best. However, that is not the case; alternative assessments are more authentic than traditional (paper-and-pencil) assessments, and their results have a greater likelihood of being valid if the assessments are implemented in a reliable fashion. However, the potential validity comes at a cost as these tests usually take more time, resources, and labor than traditional tests. They may, sometimes, be more vulnerable to sources of invalidity beyond the control of the maker and administrator of the test (teacher). For example, a selection of products for a portfolio may be more carefully prepared than would normally be the case, the selection of ordinary products might be influenced by peers, or a performance of a skill might be influenced by contextual characteristics such as prompting by onlookers. It is often a challenge to develop alternative assessments that match the reliability usually obtained with multiple-choice tests. So the conundrum is often this: Is it better to employ highly reliable multiple-choice tests that are merely correlated with authentic behavior or to employ a more authentic assessment vulnerable to sources of unreliability? Ideally, of course, the goal is to employ a reliable authentic assessment, where feasible. We discuss how to assess reliability later on in this chapter.

■ Performance Assessments

Performance assessment, a subcategory of alternative assessments, is typically accomplished with human raters who use observational schedules (such as checklists of skill components to be observed) to evaluate student performance as it is being done. This permits student performance to be evaluated on the basis of a clearly specified set of objectives from one observer to another or from one performer (student) to another. Thus, whatever tasks or exercises are being evaluated have a direct link to the desired outcome and are clearly known by both the performer and the evaluator.

Portfolios, on the other hand, are collections of student work and performance already done. They serve as a repository where student work can be held and reviewed for summative (final) or formative (continuing) evaluation. They might consist of term papers, photographs, essays on personal feelings, newspaper articles, and so on. They may be held in a looseleaf notebook, in a folder, or a file. Usually they are selected as representative of outcome quality or characteristics of student ability. So, for instance, a video of student teaching might be archived in a portfolio as a stand alone or in conjunction with earlier student teaching videos to permit comparison of progress. The single video would give a potential employer a glimpse of present performance from which to infer future teaching performance. On the other hand, a series of videos might show how the student's teaching has changed over time.

Relationship between Performance Assessment and Other Assessments

You probably have already inferred that any test involves a type of performance. The difference is that some assessments are more direct indicators of some kinds of objective than others. To illustrate, you could generate a written question on how to maintain zero buoyancy underwater or you could require the student to maintain zero buoyancy underwater in a pool or on a scuba dive. Inevitably, you would find the latter to be a better indicator of a student's skill level (or even physics knowledge). Such assessments of actual performances, those that approximate what is expected in real life, are more *authentic* assessments.

The need for authentic assessments is always an important consideration, but which of the alternative assessments is best for your purposes depends on what can be accomplished by each. A lab demonstration that zinc and hydrochloric acid combine to produce hydrogen (which can explode when exposed to a spark) as a byproduct can be an engaging way for students to show what they understand about chemical reactions, but the curriculum may not allow enough time to justify an entire laboratory session on the one topic (although in an earlier era the curriculum did so). It may seem that a computer simulation or mock-up of laboratory tasks may approximate a real task, but upon close analysis you might find that key (and perhaps unarticulated) components may still be missing. For example, the means of collecting the hydrogen may not be noticed, the order of adding the metal with the acid may not be understood, or the means of testing whether one has hydrogen or some other product may not be clear. Simulating a frog dissection on the computer may demonstrate that the student has mastered the organ anatomy of the amphibian, but would likely reveal little, if anything, about the skills associated with dissecting. However, dissecting a frog in a laboratory setting would be virtually a perfect indicator of the ability to dissect a frog in a corporate biological setting. As you can see, there is a real difference between knowing and doing—an important consideration in determining how you will evaluate student performance.

Positive Appeal of Authentic Assessment

The growing interest among some educators in performance assessment is due in part, at least, to the belief that objective (choice) tests fail to assess higher-order and psychomotor skills essential for functioning in school or work settings (Haney

& Madaus, 1989; Neill & Medina, 1989; O'Neil, 1992; Wiggins, 1989). Multiple-choice tests, for example, are said not to be authentic because they do not represent activities students typically perform in classrooms. In addition, multiple-choice tests do not reflect current theories of learning and cognition and are not based on abilities students actually need for future success (Herman, 1992). When tests are too narrowly defined, then classroom activity often takes the form of much practice on questions taken from the previous versions of the test—as in practice for taking the state comprehensive test. The difficulty is that students are taken from the purposes of the curriculum, without learning from assignments and without the problem-solving activities of asking relevant questions, or questioning texts, or writing in-depth thoughtful papers that explain and conceptualize ideas—that is, without activities that are aimed at useable knowledge, that go beyond the rote memory and inert knowledge required to learn a subject. In the worst-case scenario, which is not at all uncommon, the classroom activity in "practicing the test" is totally oriented to the test, the test items, test-taking skills, and so on rather than to the underlying cognitive abilities of thinking and understanding the content and how it is used.

It is important that the perception of the test is not reduced to simply a high or low score. As you know from your own experience, you may know a topic well enough to get a high score on a test, but may be unable to do the thinking and application so essential to understanding. Thus, the conclusion or inference that a student knows history or science because he or she got a high score on a multiple-choice test may not be defensible. Another concern is that standardized tests cannot be used to closely monitor student progress in the school curriculum throughout the year because they are only administered once or twice annually. These concerns are no less valid for educators of language minority students.

Requirements for Good Performance Assessment

Performance assessments are not absent from the requirements of good assessment procedures, including reliability and validity. Like other assessments they require observation of the student's behavior according to acceptable criteria; evaluation of the product that results from that behavior as being due to new learning; and assurance that any inferences about the products are based on clearly articulated criteria. By doing so, a sound professional judgment or inference can be made regarding the student's level of achievement and the proficiency with which the achievement can be employed. Intuitions, impressions, and feelings about student performance are not a part of sound performance assessments.

What may elude the beginning teacher is an appreciation of the degree to which familiar test items will deviate from targeted behavioral objectives. Written objective or essay items (which we cover in subsequent chapters) permit an evaluation of accumulated information about a topic but probably won't allow a robust judgment as to whether a student can or ultimately will perform a task acceptably. In drivers' education, for example, performance on a multiple-choice rules-of-the-road test may say little about one's ability to make lane changes, brake a car, or parallel park. In a government class, a written essay arguing the pros and cons of a democracy has little predictive value as to whether students will vote as soon as they are legally of age.

The authentic assessment movement is consistent with the philosophy of John Dewey (1923) and his exhortation of "learning by doing." He felt that students would be better served by schools that provided instruction on tasks practiced in later life. Note that for many topics, writing may be the authentic task of choice. An aspiring journalist will later spend a majority of his or her professional life conveying descriptions and ideas through the medium of writing. Most professionals communicate through some form of written expression. It is a critical skill, but one of many that students need to master.

In spite of the press for more authentic assessment, it is difficult to generate authentic tasks and still cover a lot of curricular material within the constraints of a typical school day and academic year. If one is required to address the legislative, executive, and judicial branches of government in 180 days, as is typical in 11th-grade social studies, it may be a challenging constraint to spend more than a few days on proposing a bill and taking it through the legislative process even though it could take over a year to accomplish this in a real legislative undertaking. Writing about the process or answering questions on it may be an efficient alternative, but it may lack critical dimensions of the process (the ability to influence others or to forge compromise wording) that would make the task successful in an authentic setting.

What is most likely to occur in classroom assessment is the compromise of authentic assessment for the sake of testing efficiency. However, there are a number of classroom subjects in which performance assessment may come quite naturally. We provide a few examples in the paragraphs below as a way to illustrate the diversity of assessment approaches in this area.

Examples of Authentic Assessment Tasks

Science

Mrs. Olsen teaches seventh-grade science and has asked her class to conduct a scientific experiment to determine which laundry detergent gets clothes the cleanest. In this experiment, conducted at home, students take four washcloths and stain them with equal amounts of cranberry juice. Using their own washing machines and dryers (or a neighbor's if they don't have one), they are asked to wash each washcloth separately with equal amounts of three different detergents (controlling for the concentration level) and the one remaining washcloth with just plain water. Students are then asked to rank the cleaned washcloths with respect to cleanliness and report on their control of water amount, water temperature, cleaning cycles, drying cycles, the care with which they stained the washcloths, and the chemical composition of the detergent, if it can be determined. They present on their experimental results, describe why the procedure they used was better than other sources of information (e.g., commercials), and determine the degree to which the detergent may have a negative environmental impact.

Speech

Mr. Tzeng has created a debate on the topic, "All students should perform some sort of compulsory community service." Students in his speech class are to take a position, pro or con, and create a 10-minute opening statement. The position statement must include appropriate research to support the points made. When matched with a student taking the opposite position, the students are then asked to make a five-minute rebuttal. Students will be evaluated in two ways: first, they are rated on the effectiveness of their opening argument, and then an overall decision will be made as to who of the pair of students won the debate.

Dance

Ms. Diaz teaches high school dance class, which serves as an option to fulfill a statewide physical education requirement. For the upcoming assignment, students are asked to interpret a fairy tale of their choice and choreograph it to modern dance.

Students will be evaluated on their interpretation, the number and difficulty of the dance moves, and the degree to which they execute the planned steps. The dance routine must last a minimum of five minutes.

Art

Ms. Johnson has asked her eighth graders to use charcoal pencil to draw a street scene that portrays a building (or multiple buildings) and human characters. In this assignment, students are asked to pay particular attention to their interpretation of perspective for the street and the building(s) and the emotions displayed by the human characters.

Characteristics of Performance Assessments

The main characteristics of performance measures are categorized by Wiggins (1989):

- Tasks should have a parallel to real-life tasks or some component, including tasks that are representative of those met in dealing with life problems, as self-sufficient members of society. What can the student do?
- The required performance should bear a similarity to some requirement in real life.
- The selection of a task requires attention to how the teaching and learning criteria are to be used in the assessment.
- The performance measures should depend more on *construction of responses* rather than the mere making of binary or multiple choices. One can well imagine, in mathematics, the use of tables, calculators, and the like being permitted in solving problems; computers could be used for accessing information for problem solving on social issues, and laboratory simulations for balancing equations or molecular composition in chemistry, whether inorganic or organic.
- Self-assessment must be understood and incorporated into the task. As in all assessment, student participation is crucial in the process of what is to be evaluated and the criteria for evaluating performance.
- The assessment depends on real-life contextual parallels, including expectations for public presentations of work, writing samples for assessing writing ability, orally and/or verbally displaying findings or conclusions for testing public speaking, and defending points of view for debate. These are sometimes referred to as direct methods.

Text Box 5.1 Example of an Authentic Assessment Task

This final lesson should help you:

- Compare and contrast performance assessments with more common forms of objective assessment.
- Develop "performance tests" and "performance tasks" to measure learning.

What Is Authentic Assessment?

To begin this lesson, carefully review the three samples which follow.

1. Look for things that all three have in common.
2. Notice ways that they are different from more traditional "objective" paper-and-pencil tests. Pay particular attention to the skills and abilities that they are testing.
   - Water Quality (performance test)
   - Designing a Classification System (performance test)
   - Not In My Backyard (performance task)

Sample authentic assessment:

High School Science Course

Objective: Reasonably infer the water sample's source by testing its properties.

1. Collect and record the data using the procedures listed to decrease chance of error.
2. Analyze the data and infer.
3. Create supplementary materials (e.g., tables, graphs) as needed to describe and summarize the data.

Water Quality

There are three samples of water. Using the materials, test for the properties of water: pH, hardness, and suspended solids; record the results. Inferring from the results of the tests, write down the possible source of each sample.

Suggested Materials Needed:

Litmus paper, diluted detergent, three clear vials with lids, graduated cylinder, filter paper, transparent grid beaker, water from various sources

Scoring Scale (out of 100%):

Record of results	20%
Correct pH readings	20%
Correct comparison of hardness	20%
Correct reading of solids	20%
Sources	20%

Source: Adapted from www.usoe.k12.ut.us/curr/Science/Perform/Past5.htm.

- Typical vehicles for carrying out these performances are poster sessions, exhibits, recitals, debate, role playing, consulting with managerial people, and so on.

There are numerous positions with regard to the use of authentic measures, and questions are continually raised with regard to the authenticity of standardized tests. As with any other form of assessment, authenticity is not all good or bad for any purpose. It is not simply a replacement for another form of assessment that may be perceived as being more or less valuable. The distinctive characteristics of authenticity that make it an advantageous form of assessment are relative to educational requirements, having benefits and disadvantages for some objectives more than for others. As in other assessments there are often unforeseen failures in achieving the supposed advantages as well. Thus, as with any test, students can just as easily view a performance as simply a requirement culminating in a grade; its purpose can be misperceived, and it may or may not result in the degree of transfer desired, particularly if students are not involved in the assessment. In addition, the outcomes cannot always be anticipated or taken for granted. For example, an authentic assessment in general science might be framed around performance criteria for maintaining a terrarium, a proxy for a real-life project on maintaining balance in ecosystems. If successful, it is clear that the learner will acquire some knowledge about the components of the terrarium, the way they are organized, the way they interact, the day-to-day care required, and the balancing of components to maintain life in the terrarium. Nevertheless, the outcomes are certain to be different among students who participate in the project, raising the question of "What is learned?" For example, it is possible to maintain the system without learning anything about symbiosis, photosynthesis, physiology of the animals in the terrarium, or the climates involved for life outside of the terrarium. If students learned about the need for light of the green plants, will they learn about the way plants get food? Will students learn about how mushrooms get food? As they learn to maintain a terrarium, will they also learn to maintain an aquarium?

These questions relate to the many facets of making good assessments: making it clear to students what is to be learned from a learning activity and how it is to benefit from assessment; the need for sampling many performances to assure opportunity for the outcome to be performed; knowing and understanding the criteria by which success is judged; assessing the reliability of the observations; understanding the potential biases in making judgments; and, in particular, determining the degree to which we, as assessors of student performance, can generalize from the performance on one task to performance on other tasks. As with other forms of assessments, these are among the considerations that must accompany any new way of testing or scoring.

Validity Criteria for Performance Assessments

In using performance measures one must be aware of the difficulties posed in evaluating their effectiveness. Validity evidence may restrict their adoption for broader policy requirements such as those needed in accountability. Several criteria have been reported by experts in measurement for comparing different means of assessment, including performance assessments.

Consequences

How do different means of testing affect outcomes? Learning? Both intended and unintended consequences are important considerations.

Transfer

Inferences regarding transfer are always a consideration in assessment. We want to make predictions from small samples to larger domains or broader skills. It is as much a requirement for performance measures as it is for traditional measures.

Cognitive Complexity

Performance on a task is not always a guarantee that the individual is capable of using the skill or knowledge with understanding. It is entirely possible that even seemingly complex processes such as solving the binomial theorems can be memorized by rote, as can long procedures such as those in geometry or balancing equations in chemistry. Just what is being assessed is just as critical here as in any measure. The student can run through the routines of a performance, such as dissecting a frog, without ever understanding why or what is being done.

Content Quality

Performance measures are based on single tasks and so content may be limited. The knowledges or content students use is critical to assessing their understanding. For example, in developing proposals for research they may use the terms *important* or *critical* without reference to the specific knowledge underlying the purpose of their research. Or, in balancing equations in chemistry they may have memorized solutions without ever referring to valences of the elements involved. In writing, they may never consider the elements of paragraph or sentence construction, merely stringing out ideas. If the tasks are not meaningful, the learning only contributes to inert (rote, meaningless) learning and reduces the value of any inferences made from judging the performance.

Content Coverage

It should be clear that there is simply insufficient time in the overall curriculum to consider all of the possible tasks encompassed in the curricular objectives. Some degree of generalization (transfer) must be expected. So sampling must be done, and it must be done carefully to adequately represent the major objectives or criteria. If the same tasks are always used from year to year, there will be a tendency to restrict teaching to those tasks and the objectives they represent, thereby narrowing the content to be covered. A caveat is in order here: *Content coverage* as used here refers to facilitating understanding and application of a given set of learning objectives. Content coverage is not the exclusive aim of teaching, particularly when it is done at the expense of understanding.

Cost Effectiveness

Performance, authentic measures, and the like require more effort on the part of the person making the tasks, as well as the student performing the task. Briefly, it takes time to make good tests, and it takes considerable know-how and training in test development. Tasks have to be made worthwhile: carefully constructed, carefully administered, and the behaviors (consequences) carefully scored. All processes require considerably more effort than traditional assessment instruments and are just as prone to negative outcomes.

■ Behavioral Objectives Redux

The key to setting behavioral expectations is the formulation of behavioral objectives. In Chapter 2 we focused on stating behavioral objectives using Bloom's cognitive taxonomy. Most of the illustrations used paper-and-pencil assessments to evaluate proficiencies at the six levels of the cognitive hierarchy.

There are two additional domains of assessment, developed by Bloom and his colleagues (Bloom, Krathwohl, & Masia, 1973). These include behavioral objectives for the affective domain and for the psychomotor domain. Of particular importance, at least for the purposes of performance assessment, are objectives in the psychomotor domain. Table 5.1 illustrates the categories and some examples of behavioral objectives in this latter area.

Other Psychomotor Domains

The Bloom and colleagues committee did not produce a compilation for the psychomotor domain model, but others have. Below are listed two other popular versions.

Dave (1967)
- *Imitation.* Observing and patterning behavior after someone else. Performance may be of low quality. Example: Copying a work of art.
- *Manipulation.* Being able to perform certain actions by following instructions and practicing. Example: Creating work on one's own after taking lessons or reading about it.
- *Precision.* Refining, becoming more exact. Few errors are apparent. Example: Working and reworking something so it will be just right.
- *Articulation.* Coordinating a series of actions, achieving harmony and internal consistency. Example: Producing a video that involves music, drama, color, sound, and so forth.
- *Naturalization.* Having high-level performance become natural, without needing to think much about it. Examples: LeBron James playing basketball, Michelle Wie hitting a golf ball, and so forth.

Harrow (1972)
- *Reflex movements.* Reactions that are not learned
- *Fundamental movements.* Basic movements such as walking, or grasping
- *Perception.* Response to stimuli such as visual, auditory, kinesthetic, or tactile discrimination
- *Physical abilities.* Stamina that must be developed for further development such as strength and agility
- *Skilled movements.* Advanced learned movements as one finds in sports or acting
- *No discursive communication.* Effective body language, such as gestures and facial expressions

Table 5.1. Categories and Examples of Behavioral Objectives in the Psychomotor Domain

Category	Example and Key Words
Perception: The ability to use sensory cues to guide motor activity. This ranges from sensory stimulation, through cue selection, to translation.	**Examples**: Detects nonverbal communication cues. Estimates where a ball will land after it is thrown and then moves to the correct location to catch the ball. Adjusts heat of stove to correct temperature by smell and taste of food. Adjusts the height of the forks on a forklift by comparing where the forks are in relation to the pallet. **Key Words**: chooses, describes, detects, differentiates, distinguishes, identifies, isolates, relates, selects
Set: Readiness to act. Includes mental, physical, and emotional sets. These three sets are dispositions that predetermine a person's response to different situations (sometimes called mindsets).	**Examples**: Knows and acts upon a sequence of steps in a manufacturing process. Recognizes one's abilities and limitations. Shows desire to learn a new process (motivation). NOTE: This subdivision of the Psychomotor domain is closely related with the "Responding to Phenomena" subdivision of the affective domain. **Key Words**: begins, displays, explains, moves, proceeds, reacts, shows, states, volunteers.
Guided Response: The early stages in learning a complex skill that include imitation and trial and error. Adequacy of performance is achieved by practicing.	**Examples**: Performs a mathematical equation as demonstrated. Follows instructions to build a model. Responds to hand signals of instructor while learning to operate a forklift. **Key Words**: copies, traces, follows, reacts, reproduces, responds.
Mechanism: The intermediate stage in learning a complex skill. Learned responses have become habitual and the movements can be performed with some confidence and proficiency.	**Examples**: Uses a personal computer. Repairs a leaking faucet. Drives a car. **Key Words**: assembles, calibrates, constructs, dismantles, displays, fastens, fixes, grinds, heats, manipulates, measures, mends, mixes, organizes, sketches.
Complex Overt Response: The skillful performance of motor acts that involve complex movement patterns. Proficiency is indicated by a quick, accurate, and highly coordinated performance, requiring a minimum of energy. This category includes performing without hesitation and automatic performance. For example, players often utter sounds of satisfaction or expletives as soon as they hit a tennis ball or throw a	**Examples**: Maneuvers a car into a tight parallel parking spot. Operates a computer quickly and accurately. Displays competence while playing the piano. **Key Words**: assembles, builds, calibrates, constructs, dismantles, displays, fastens, fixes, grinds, heats, manipulates, measures, mends, mixes, organizes, sketches. NOTE: The Key Words are the same as for Mechanism, but will have adverbs or

Category	Example and Key Words
football, because they can tell by the feel of the act what the result will produce.	adjectives that indicate that the performance is quicker, better, more accurate, etc.
Adaptation: Skills are well developed and the individual can modify movement patterns to fit special requirements.	**Examples:** Responds effectively to unexpected experiences. Modifies instruction to meet the needs of the learners. Perform a task with a machine that it was not originally intended to do (machine is not damaged and there is no danger in performing the new task). **Key Words:** adapts, alters, changes, rearranges, reorganizes, revises, varies.
Origination: Creating new movement patterns to fit a particular situation or specific problem. Learning outcomes emphasize creativity based upon highly developed skills.	**Examples:** Constructs a new theory. Develops a new and comprehensive training programming. Creates a new gymnastic routine. **Key Words:** arranges, builds, combines, composes, constructs, creates, designs, initiate, makes, originates.

Source: Clark (2004).

All of these might be configured for a particular skill domain (e.g., tennis, golf) incorporating rubrics associated with a range of skill development. So for example,

The student will be able to hit an overhead smash with 90% accuracy.

■ Creating Rubrics

Rubrics are rules by which performances or their artifacts are evaluated. They set criteria for degrees of effective performance. An effective means by which evaluators address quality is to analyze the performance into its key subdomains and assign ratings to each performance dimension.

The example in Theory to Practice Box 5.1 illustrates a rubric for a modern dance topic (recalling and reproducing movement and creating a variation) that has four dimensions (replication, reproduction, and recall; creating a variation of a taught phrase; expressiveness; physical control and coordination). Each point on the rating scale is articulated with a performance definition, and in general, the higher the rating, the more or more completely a subdomain is carried out. A dance judge would sum the scores from the four scales and evaluate the dancer's performance in terms of the overall score total. In the example shown in Theory to Practice Box 5.1, 12 would be the highest possible

Theory to Practice Box 5.1
EXAMPLE OF A RUBRIC

Subject: Fine Arts—Dramatics (four scales as shown below)
Grade(s): 8, 12
Topic: **Recalling and Reproducing Movement and Creating a Variation**

Assignment: The assignment was to repeat a 24-count phrase that was taught (phrase A), improvise a second, 16-count phrase (phrase B), then repeat the initial phrase.

Scale I: Replication, Reproduction, and Recall

Rating of 3: Student repeats the phrase and performs accurately with ease. He or she also performs with confidence and demonstrates clear articulation with all parts of the body. He or she communicates the given phrase to be reproduced.

Rating of 2: Student reproduces the phrase with accurate rhythm, movement, direction, and sequence so that it is clearly recognizable, but with differences from the phrase as demonstrated.

Rating of 1: Student cannot perform the phrase accurately with clarity of movement and body alignment. His or her movements, rhythm, direction, and order of actions are not demonstrated correctly. Student response is more or less random.

Rating of 0: No response. Student doesn't perform.

Scale II: Creation of a Variation of a Taught Phrase

Rating of 3: Student creates the variation B with ease. The phrases that he or she created and performed contrast clearly with the original A phrase. The student demonstrates clearly well-defined movements in both phrases.

Rating of 2: Student-created phrase demonstrates effective use of time, space, force, and body shapes, incorporating choreographic principles. The pattern the student creates is not in contrast to the taught A phrase. He or she struggles some to complete the A and B phrases.

Rating of 1: Student cannot create a 16-count phrase. Student response is more or less random, with starting and stopping before the end of the phrase, or has only a single solution.

Rating of 0: No response. Student doesn't create and perform a variation phrase.

Scale III: Evaluation Criteria for Expressiveness

Rating of 3: Student goes beyond the movement as demonstrated and enhances both the A phrase and his or her own B phrase of the movement with personal feelings. The student communicates clarity and excitement within both movement phrases.

Rating of 2: Student accurately reproduces the movement quality as demonstrated. He or she performs his or her variation with clarity and assurance.

Rating of 1: Student lacks focus and is uncommitted to the movement, both his or her own and that of the given phrase. The movements are small and close to the body and seem tentative and self-conscious. Lacks expressiveness in time, force, and space.

Rating of 0: No response.

Scale IV: Physical Control and Coordination

Rating of 3: Student brings excitement, commitment, and intensity to the performance. The student uses principles of alignment to maintain balance and control. He or she articulates clearly contrasting movement dynamics and fills out the time during the phrases. The student demonstrates careful attention to detail when performing the A and B sequences.

Rating of 2: Student has smooth transitions between levels, directions, and rhythms. He or she fills out the time during sustained movements and maintains correct balance and ending position. The student can use body parts in isolation as appropriate in the phrases.

Rating of 1: Student cannot coordinate the locomotor and other movement demands of the phrase. He or she is off balance and is unable to sustain movements to complete the phrase.

Rating of 0: No response.

Source: Adapted from Council of Chief State School Officers' National Assessment of Educational Progress Fine Arts Consensus Project.

score (4 domains × 3 points max per domain). Note that in this example, each subdomain is weighted equally, but that need not be the case. By weighting dimensions differently, one can communicate the relative importance of one dimension compared to another. If students are aware of the relative subdomain weightings, then they can direct their practice or rehearsal time appropriately. This illustrates another instance where it is essential for students to participate in the assessment process.

How Rubrics Function

In conjunction with behavioral objectives, rubrics define expected or targeted behaviors. They can also help the beginning teacher develop a picture of how students at a particular grade level are likely to perform. Rubrics focus on the critical elements of the task while deemphasizing the more trivial components. Moreover, limiting the number of things a judge has to attend to can help increase the reliability of ratings. However, restricting the focus of rating attention comes at a potential cost of assessment validity. How many times have you heard a recital in which the performer had a complete technical mastery of the notes, but somehow lacked passion or enthusiasm (affectivity or emotionality that contributes to expression). If the assessment rubric simply focuses on the technical aspects of performance (e.g., piece memorized completely, good technique, rhythm, no missed notes), then a student can obtain a good score, yet the performance may be somehow lacking. Sometimes what transforms a good performance to a great performance is difficult to articulate via a rubric, and there may be a difference of opinion by expert judges as to what that additional element might be. Although we mention this possibility here as an interesting sidelight, it is typically not a concern of teachers who are working with beginning learners. Qualities that comprise refinements in performance (such as dynamics in playing the piano, skill in putting together the components of cookery, or the handling of the club in golf to produce a spin on the ball) are typically associated with expertise of coaches, referees, and umpires.

At the other extreme, the teacher might mistakenly include elements unrelated to the performance being evaluated. For example, we often see rubrics that include dimensions like "improvement from past assignments," "work habits," and "effort." To be sure, it could be rationally argued that the development of good work habits will lead to increased or better performance, but the focus of the evaluation should be on the performance itself. There are plenty of art masterpieces that have been produced by individuals with suspect work habits who may not have had to exert much effort in the production of their painting. In fact, one telling trait of being *gifted* is embodied in the notion that the individual doesn't have to work very hard at all to create the performance or product. We revisit the same set of concerns when we present information on grading.

How to Formulate a Good Rubric

Formulating a good rubric, like any other assessment, presents three basic challenges. The first is to *identify a critical dimension of behavior* at a particular developmental level. Drawing from our previous example in art, the relevant questions might be, "What would a picture incorporating perspective look like? What critical elements must be present? Are eighth graders capable of rendering such a picture? How would the range of attempts present itself? What would be the types of errors one might expect at this grade level? Are these errors a function of prior learning experience or do they stem from a lack of innate talent? Are some errors more serious than others?" The key for a beginning teacher is to have a well-developed vision of what to expect in terms of the range of performance. Obviously as one obtains more experience teaching in a particular grade level, these expectations become better defined.

The second challenge is to articulate the rubric to the point where different evaluators can use the descriptions to *obtain consistency in their ratings*. For example, the use of the rating dimension "creativity" borders on meaningless because it takes on an array of definitions ranging from "deviation from the norm" to "a disciplined synthesis of accumulated skills or knowledge." However, "generates plausible variations on a blues theme" might embody what is required for creativity in the field of jazz or music.

While the second challenge is more of a concern for raters, the third (related) challenge is directed towards student learners. That is, the vocabulary used in the rubric must serve as a way to *communicate with learners* what is expected of them. It is not enough to say, "Be creative"; rather the teacher has to provide a bit more guidance: "These are the notes that are consonant with 12-bar blues. If you play a made-up melody using these notes, you will have created a stand-alone riff for this music. You will be evaluated on how well you generate variations of the original riff for a four-minute sequence using the guitar." Using this terminology, the instructor can operationalize what is meant by *creative*.

Rubrics in Content Areas

An Example from Math

To extend the discussion of rubrics, this section provides a number of illustrations of different qualities of rubrics. These are based in large part on discussions by Arter and McTighe (2001) and on how the rubrics are used in actual classroom settings. Table 5.2 for example shows the teaching objective, some expected qualities of student performance after their lessons, and how quality of performance is to be rated in a mathematics unit for high and low levels of performance quality (the intermediate levels have been omitted in this illustration). Importantly, this rubric not only deals with math but with problem solving as well.

An Example from Writing

Table 5.3 displays summaries of what teachers look for in writing. Because writing is so important across all subject-matter areas and at every grade level (from the first grade to college levels) these will have interest to you, beyond your teaching, to evaluating your own products such as term papers and the like. Additionally, keep in mind that in a well-stated rubric elements or qualities are grouped together under a general category. The category is carefully defined by statements that illustrate the quality being observed.

To illustrate how the criteria shown in the table appear when extended into rubrics, an example illustrating what performances characterized high and low scores are shown in Table 5.4 for the characteristic of voice.

As you can see, rubrics are more than mere listings of criteria in checklist format. As we warned earlier, the specific performances are conceptualized into distinct categories with defining characteristics for each. Obviously, such conceptual categories as voice, organization, and so on will be generally acceptable to most teachers, but the specific defining characteristics may not be precisely the same for all schools and all situations. They change according to grade level, age, and experience of the student, as well as with the expertise and training of the teacher. In addition, rubrics vary according to time needed to spend on any one category—for instance, it may take one or two grade levels to internalize some categories (such as voice) at the earliest grade levels, but only hours at the adult level.

Table 5.2. Mathematics Problem-Solving Scoring Rubric: A Guide to Extended Response Items—an Illustration of the Relation of Teaching Objectives, Criteria for Performance Assessment, and the Basis for Different Levels of Ratings

Objective: MATH KNOWLEDGE: Display of math principles and concepts resulting in a correct solution to a problem.	Objective: STRATEGIC KNOWLEDGE: Identification of important elements of the problem and the use of models, diagrams, symbols, and/or algorithms are used to systematically represent and integrate concepts.	Objective: EXPLANATION: Written explanation and rationales translate into words the steps of the solution process and provide justification for each step. Though important, length, grammar, and syntax are not the critical components.
Rating 4: Student • Shows understanding of the math concepts and principles. • Uses correct math terminology and notions including labels. • Executes algorithms completely and correctly.	Rating 4: Student • Identifies important elements of the problem and shows understanding of the relationships among elements. • Reflects appropriate and systematic strategy for solving the problem. • Solution process is nearly complete.	Rating 4: Student • Gives a complete written explanation of the solution process employed: how and why it was solved. • If a diagram is appropriate there is a complete explanation of all the elements in the diagram.
Rating 1: • Has limited to no understanding of the problem's mathematical concepts and theories. • Uses incorrect mathematical terms. • May contain major computational errors.	Rating 1: • Fails to identify important concepts or places; too much emphasis on unimportant elements. • May reflect an inappropriate or inconsistent strategy for solving the problem. • Gives minimal evidence of a solution process; process may be difficult to identify.	Rating 1: • Gives minimal written explanation of solution process; may not explain how and why it was solved. • Explanation does not match presented solution process. • May include minimal discussion of labels in diagram; explanation of significant label is unclear.

Source: Adapted from Illinois Standards Achievement Test: Sample Mathematics Materials 2000 (p. 59). © 2000, Illinois Department of Public Instruction. Retrieved from www.isbe.state.il.us/assessment/pdfs/ERMathRubric.pdf.

Note: The above illustration omits rubrics for categories receiving intermediate ratings of 2 and 3 shown in the original. Readers may wish to try their hands at filling in the appropriate rubrics for those levels.

Table 5.3. Students Know What Teachers Look For in Writing

IDEAS . . .
- Makes sense.
- Gets and holds attention.
- Has a main idea, themes, center, sense of purpose.
- Writer draws on experience.
- Says something new or says it in a fresh ways.
- Is full of details that add important information.
- Is interesting.

WORD CHOICE . . .
- Makes me say, "Yes, that's just the right word or phrase."
- Long after reading, some words still tug at my memory.
- Words are used correctly.
- The writer chooses wisely but isn't afraid to stretch.
- This writer knows the language of the topic—but doesn't try to impress me with phony, bloated phrases.
- Simple language is used when it gets the job done.

ORGANIZATION . . .
- The opening makes we want to keep reading. Has a logical order or pattern.
- I can follow the story or main points.
- Ends well. Ties up loose ends. Doesn't stop abruptly.
- Doesn't repeat what I just read: "now know the three reasons we should fight pollution."
- Pacing is good.

SENTENCE FLUENCY . . .
- It's smooth going—easy on the ear.
- I could easily read this aloud.
- Sentences begin differently.
- Repetition is stylistic, not annoying.
- Some sentences long. Some aren't.
- Sentences aren't choppy. Sentences don't meander.

VOICE . . .
- Sounds like a person wrote it.
- Sounds like this particular writer.
- Writing has style, flavor.
- Reaches out to me the reader. Brings me "inside."
- Makes me respond. Makes me feel.

CONVENTIONS . . .
- The writing is cleanly polished. It looks proofread.
- Most things are done correctly.
- Careful controlled use of conventions makes meaning clear and reading easy.
- "No BIG erers sHOouttat me frm the pg: Hey! Fergt IDEAS and VIOCE! Think? abowt, the mistakes!, A lot!!"
- Spelling, punctuation, grammar, capital letters, and paragraph indenting—this writer has thoughtfully attended to all conventional details.

Source: Arter and McTighe (2001).

■ Advantages of Using Rubrics

Rubrics provide a number of critical advantages for formative evaluation. They provide an opportunity for you and your students to work together in determining the outcomes of instruction and how they are to be assessed. The ratings of a performance provide feedback regarding where more instruction and what kind of instruction is needed for further improvement of

Table 5.4. An Example of Rubrics for Voice in a Written Product

Rating 5. The writer speaks directly to the reader in a way that is individual, compelling, and engaging. The writer crafts the writing with an awareness and respect for the audience and purpose for writing.
- A. The tone of the writing *adds interest* to the message and is *appropriate for the purpose and audience.*
- B. The readers feel a *strong interaction* with the writer, sensing the person behind the words.
- C. The writer *takes a risk* by revealing to you who he or she is consistently through the piece.
- D. Expository or persuasive writing reflects a *strong commitment* to the topic by *showing why the reader needs to know this* and why he or she should care.
- E. Narrative writing is *honest, personal, engaging,* and makes *you think about and react* to the author's ideas and point of view.

Rating 3. The writer seems sincere but not fully engaged or involved. The result is pleasant or even personable, but not compelling.
- A. The writer seems aware of an audience but discards personal insights in favor of *obvious generalities.*
- B. The writing communicates in an *earnest, pleasing, yet safe* manner.
- C. *Only one or two moments here or there intrigue* delight or move the reader. These places may emerge strongly for a line or two but quickly fade away.
- D. *Expository or persuasive* writing *lacks consistent engagement* with the topic to build credibility.
- E. *Narrative* writing is *reasonably sincere* but doesn't reflect unique or individual perspective on the topic.

Rating 1. The writer seems indifferent, uninvolved, or distanced from the topic and/or the audience. As a result, the paper reflects more than one of the following problems.
- A. The writer is *not concerned with the audience.* The writer's style is a *complete mismatch* for the intended reader, or the writing is so short that little is accomplished beyond introducing the topic.
- B. The writer speaks in a kind of *monotone* that flattens all potential highs or lows of the message.
- C. The writing is *humdrum* and *risk free.*
- D. The writing is *lifeless or mechanical*; depending on the topic, it may be overly technical or jargonistic.
- E. The development of the topic is so *limited* that *no point of view is present*—zip, zero, zilch, nada.

Source: Arter and McTighe (2001).

learning. Rubrics do provide specific criteria for judging performance but also provide features to be examined for determining quality of performance (see Tables 5.2, 5.3, and 5.4 for examples). You don't have to consider that you are beginning afresh in identifying rubrics, although the more you know about them the easier it will be for you to determine the specific criteria composing the rubric to be used in judging whether you and the students have reached your objectives (Arter & McTighe, 2001). If you are not an expert, there are examples in the professional literature or from your courses in your subject-matter area that will provide good sources of rubrics. In any case, you will constantly be on the lookout for adaptations, whether it is for the technically unique characteristics of performance related to grade level, previous experience, or cultural diversity. Remember that however you go about writing rubrics it is helpful to have examples of student performance before you, so that you can determine just what characteristics of performance (writing, laboratory work, problem solving, and so on) are missing and what needs to be highlighted or identified at each level of the quality levels. To the extent that you can, pay particular attention to whether the criteria you have listed can be grouped (see Tables 5.2, 5.3, and 5.4).

Developing and Using Rubrics Effectively

As Arter and McTighe (2001) point out, performance criteria are not automatically known by the students. Furthermore, merely writing the rubrics on the board or passing them out on a handout sheet to be placed in their notebooks will be of little help. Students must be brought into the process gradually and consistently. They should have a part in developing the rubrics, and eventually there should be no mystery or ambiguity regarding how the performance is to be judged. Use creative ways to demonstrate to the student what the criteria are about. The advantage, of course, is that the criteria for assessment are now public, clarifying for both teacher and student (and parents as well) what is to be learned and the reasons or explanations for a grade earned by a student.

As we have touched the surface in describing the development of rubrics, you probably brought some other advantages to mind already, such as that students need to know that you will teach them how to look for and use the same criteria as you do. Remove the mystery, the ambiguity, and uncertainty about evaluation. By playing a part in defining performance characteristics, they will soon get to know what the specific criteria (e.g., voice or fluency) mean and how they appear in their writings and writings of others. They will have ideas of what good and poor performance is like, so expect and use feedback from them. Bring definitions of rubrics down to the level of the student. Look for ambiguities and rephrase the rubric to remove the ambiguity. Provide good and poor examples of each rubric category and have students make ratings of the examples, using the rubrics and explaining why the rating was made. Ask students to rewrite or suggest revisions of poor examples. Keep in mind that these will not be grasped in a single hour but will take considerable revisiting over long periods of time. You will need to provide considerable modeling in the writing process (or whatever subject matter is involved) yourself. Ask students to reorganize papers of others or their own. Show different ways to provide for voice, word choice, content, organization, or conventions. Use writing of well-known authors that appeal to the students in the classroom. The idea is to make the objectives of learning and the way it is assessed clear to both you and the students. The aim is to bring the students into the learning process and for them to use that knowledge in improving their own writing in the future.

■ Improving Consistency of Ratings

The reliability of an instrument generally refers to the consistency of its measurement over time. You may have a concern that the way you evaluate a student's performance today will approximate the way you might evaluate it later, assuming it remains unchanged. This shift, sometimes called *drift*, is a natural phenomenon of both learning and boredom. As you learn more about the phenomena you observe, your observations typically will get better. If you tire of the observations, then you will be less attentive and presumably make poorer judgments. Your task as an observer is to remain fresh and motivated to do your best rating job.

In the context of many performance assessment tasks, the issue of consistency also involves agreement of different observers evaluating the same performance. As an instructor, you will want others with your level of expertise to evaluate a performance the same way you do. Otherwise a student will receive inconsistent feedback. As importantly, consider also that the different observers will consist of stakeholders, including parents, other teachers, administrators, and community members, who will want to know the basis of your grading systems.

Here are some steps that can be taken to help improve the consistency of ratings for performance assessment rubrics:

1. Define the behavior accurately, completely, and comprehensively. In assessing a speech, have all the persuasive arguments been put forth or simply a subset? If a student came up with a new type of argument, would your rubric have missed it?
2. Make sure that the behaviors in the rubric are nonoverlapping. For example, in a rubric on writing, it is easy to imagine

that word choice might somehow influence one's perception of sentence fluency. The trick here is to ensure that these two aspects of writing are clear and distinct in the rater's (and students') mind.

3. Create a codebook or rubric scoring sheet. This is something that can help you gauge or anchor your observations. It can also be used to communicate your expectations to students.

4. Develop models or examples of different performance levels. This can help you calibrate what performance might be at different levels. It is also another way to communicate to students what you will be looking for as you evaluate their work.

5. If working with other raters, conduct a review session to obtain consensus on what the observations should be. This typically involves having an experienced rater explain key elements that influenced his or her decision to give the performance a specific rating.

■ Portfolio Assessment

The portfolio is a relatively recent addition to authentic assessment. As a start in understanding the nature of a portfolio, it may help you to think of the way an artist or composer represents him- or herself to the public. He or she develops a portfolio of representative pieces selected to show him- or herself off as competent in certain selected ways. Perhaps one wants to represent him- or herself as an artist who has exceptional capabilities in advertising, or another as a composer of jazz compositions. Either portfolio might contain:

- *Artifacts.* The portfolio generally contains artifacts, or samples of previous work. The artist might include advertising or compositions which best represent his or her accomplishments.
- *Reproductions.* The portfolio might contain some reproductions of earlier work, such as pictures of personal contacts related to the work; for example, photographs of an exhibit or audience, copies of the work as used by others, or guides to the exhibits.
- *Attestations.* Some people keep a file of congratulatory messages. These comprise a collection of documents supporting praiseworthy accomplishments such as news articles praising an artist's work, letters of commendation, critic reviews, or articles in a professional journal regarding an exhibition of his or her work.

How Students Construct Portfolios

Students or professionals who build portfolios build them around the three categories of artifacts, reproductions, and attestations.

Stating Purpose of the Portfolio

Central to the portfolio is the purpose it is to serve. A student's portfolio may consist of evidence regarding his or her achievement, understanding, or ability to use information beyond the classroom. There may be records of books read, essays written, part-time work held while in school, letters of recommendation, letters or records (news articles) of community service projects completed, photographs, worksheets, lab reports, critiques by teachers or peers—almost anything of relevance. It might also be comprised of early products or of bad products to permit comparisons that will demonstrate progress.

Don't think of the portfolio as simply a collection of objects; it is a collection to serve a well-defined purpose. There is no one set of products that specifically apply to the contents of all portfolios for all purposes. A portfolio is a programmatic selection aimed at a given purpose. It is not a random collection of items. Rather it is an organized collection of products assumed to be representative of some objective of the educational experience in a given course or courses. The content of the portfolio reflects what the student has learned and how well it can be used. Basically, it is a set of products that will allow some inferences to be made from the collection.

It is important to recognize that a standard set of portfolio contents can't be specified here. What goes into the portfolio has to be guided by what is appropriate for a given objective, at a given age or grade level, and within a specified course. What a student will include is determined by those objectives and how the portfolio best reflects the student's development over time of his or her understandings, skills, or attitudes—whatever the specifications are. Although we can't list specific items further than in our examples here, it is important that you recognize that the portfolio is not simply a basket full of stuff, a basket full of miscellaneous items that the student collects. We have heard one of our colleagues attempt to enlarge on the idea of portfolio and call it a "trunk." A portfolio implies a systematic collection confined to a particular objective—for instance, an artist's portfolio of paintings or a businessperson's portfolio of advertisements. On the other hand, a "trunk" implies a collection of a variety of artifacts, often simply accumulated with little order, rhyme, or reason.

Structuring Contents of Portfolios

Not only does the portfolio have a systematic relation to course or career objectives, but it might also be in some given order to reflect developmental changes resulting in expertise or changes; it might be in chronological order to reflect improvement or progress; or it might demonstrate transitions in ability to make decisions or solve problems. A portfolio need not be restricted to cognitive abilities, but might be related to skill development (e.g., in the fine arts), social skills (participation in groups, interviewing, or leadership), or attitude change (e.g., preferences).

As with all assessment, the assemblage of products should be made with a clear objective (Collins, 1992). One set of products might be appropriate to a science portfolio and include specific products such as writing; photos of some assemblage such as a laboratory experiment; words of praise by other students, by teachers, or by community leaders; and specific or unique products related to the project such as statements regarding the purpose as stated by teacher objectives; introspective reflections by the student; and perhaps a table of contents or elaborations of the purposes for each segment of the portfolio. It might contain evidence regarding thinking skills, any products such as blackboard displays that had been graded, or a written review of the history of personal experiences in that area. It could contain books read, notes taken, homework completed, applications to problems, part-time work, and any other experiences or products.

Selecting Contents for the Portfolio

As one might suspect, a portfolio may become overloaded. If the student maintains extended files and collections over a long period of time, for example, a year of schooling, it is likely that there will be many items. The teacher might then request the student to make a selection, perhaps of the two or three (or any number) items that best represent the objectives, accomplishments, perspectives, attestations, experiences, or acquired knowledge.

The contents of the portfolio—the products (artifacts)—may include such things as problem-solving projects to demonstrate the levels of problem solving in which the student has engaged; application letters, letters of intent, or essays related to jobs to reflect the kinds of career goals the student may have; presentations to community members or leaders; poster sessions to demonstrate what kinds of activities the student has engaged in; records of work completed such as publications; or records of work in progress to show growth in ability to plan and ability to work with specific activities. It might even include some self-review of the contents of the portfolio over various points in time to demonstrate self-awareness of learning progress, learning capabilities, need for remediation, strengths, and degree of affect associated with learning.

A potential portfolio in elementary grades would contain four kinds of objects (Collins, 1992): artifacts that are specific productions, such as written reports of experiences; reproductions, including pictures or photographs of work done; attestations, which include written letters or other documentation by a person other than a peer or teacher of the reporting on the quality or the nature of the work, perhaps done cooperatively or for some external agency, and perhaps providing constructive feedback in the form of praise, usefulness of the service and the like; and productions. The latter would have been prepared as requirements for inclusion in the portfolio, including self-appraisals of productions, relation of the objects to the purpose of the portfolio, and means for displaying products and outcomes. All would be means of documenting achievement, thinking skills acquired, and ability to transfer learning.

Possible Outcomes of Portfolio Assessment

When one views report cards at their briefest, only a sketchy picture of the student is obtained. It's a letter or other grade designation for some aspect of schooling. Often, it contains a secret—a secret of where or how the grade was assigned. It tells little more than that the student did pretty well if he or she received an A or B, has average achievement if he or she earned a C, or failed, perhaps miserably, with a D or F. On the other hand, the portfolio contains tangible artifacts, things that can be seen and images of actual performance underlying a grade. They are point-at-ables, concrete pieces of evidence that resemble the educational outcomes desired and that could be reproduced by the student. Because they are concrete and reflect the actual performance of the individual, they have the potential of enhancing the student's self-esteem. We have seen a great deal of effort going into imaginative and creative portfolios to which the student points with pride, sometimes to the portfolio itself—"doesn't it look elegant?"—and sometimes to the content—"see my accomplishments?" In fact, as this was being written, we met a student in the elevator who was holding a large and bulging notebook. Taking a chance, we asked, "Is that a portfolio?" The student answered with considerable pride, "Yes, would you like to see it?" Agreeing to do so, the student proceeded to explain each and every article of the contents—PowerPoint slides of a workshop she attended, pictures of students in a class she taught, and letters of recommendation from her supervisors.

Using Portfolios for Grading

Anyone using the portfolio for grading must determine whether such collections, as systematic as they might be, are indeed as valid and reliable as other means that might be used for evaluating student progress, such as those involved in making systematic evaluations against rubrics of student products—of writing, oral presentations, laboratory work, engaging in off-course pursuit of a topic such as reading scientific reports that are not assigned, debates, leadership on the playground or in small groups, and other performances. Obviously, these provide rich bases for assessments of progress that are not captured in assessment portfolios and they do so in much more comprehensive ways.

One may ask, "How effective are portfolios as assessment devices?" Are they as comprehensive as other forms of assessment that we have covered and will cover in this textbook? Inasmuch as the portfolio is constructed by the student, we might ask whether the components are as sophisticated as they might be. There is probably some question as to how independently the student made the selections. Errors can be made in the judgments of the students as to what goes into the portfolios. We have heard students say, for example, "Should we put this or that into our portfolios?" or "How much will this count toward the total?" A portfolio consisting only of reports, letters, summaries, and critiques may show only a small sample of the student's work and even less of the overall quality. All are considerations when developing the rubrics as well as in using the rubrics for scoring purposes.

Using Portfolios for Instructional Feedback

Portfolios can serve the very important purpose of providing feedback on one's teaching. They provide products that the teacher can inspect and can implement to change what goes on in the classroom. They are indicators of what the student has used the most and has made the most progress in, which activities are entertaining but of little use, and which have the worst outcome. Students can also gain some practice in self-assessment and, by examining portfolios of others, can gain some idea of the nature of assessment in general.

Some teachers would claim that portfolio assessments can facilitate the development of metacognitions about the nature of assessment, the practice of assessment, the setting of subject matter standards, and the ways in which standards can be met. Also, by writing critiques of the final contents of the portfolio, the student has the opportunity for self-reflection. The question of "what counts" or "how much it counts toward the total" becomes of secondary importance. Thus, in explaining a particular picture of a laboratory experiment, the student might relate "This photograph is of my laboratory experiment. It was carefully designed and neatly put together. It worked well because I attended to the care a scientist would have put into it. I knew why I used each piece—the flask, rubber stopper, tubing and water jar, funnel, and other parts—together rather than a hasty combination of a jumble of parts that somehow got thrown together as a kind of assemblage of a lot of things."

Most teachers, especially at the younger grades, will not need to worry about artifact authenticity. They are likely to be familiar with the creative and performance levels of their own students and would readily notice anything that would represent an extreme exception to typical student work. However, this is a topic that occasionally emerges with students in the higher grades, who may be tempted to turn in artifacts not of their own creation. We have found that the best way to determine whether a student has included a plagiarized artifact is to simply ask them about it. Those who plagiarize tend to be unable to answer even the simplest questions about how it was created, how long it took, and what it represents.

■ Summary

Assessment is aided and abetted by a variety of measures, not the least of which are performance measures, which make useful supplements to the familiar standardized tests, the objective tests, and the essay (or subjective) tests. The category of performance assessments includes authentic assessments, portfolios, simulations, and demonstrations, all of which have similarities, in varying degrees, to real-life activities (balancing a checkbook in class requires the same operations as in real life) or problems (such as judging which of two cereals is more nutritious). Some, such as dress rehearsals for plays, are so similar to the onstage performances that they become proxies for judging what the first public performance would look like. Others, such as setting up laboratory equipment or simulated jury duty, are mini-replicas of the actual settings used in real-life performances. Writing a business letter in the ninth grade will likely have most of the characteristics of a business letter in real life. The advantage of performance assessments is that they require not only use the abstract knowledge about a subject-matter area (e.g., knowing how to add, subtract, multiply, or divide) but also provide some contact with everyday situations in which that subject matter is used.

Because of their complexity, performance formats require specific bases for evaluation. Rubrics appear to provide a useful basis for communicating expectations regarding the criteria by which performance is to be rated. For example, in setting up a laboratory experiment, it is necessary to make certain that the order of mixing acid and water is correct, that glass tubing is correctly bent so as not to obstruct the passage of gases, and so on. Pick a sport (tennis, golf, bowling, and so on) of your choice and write down a few "musts" (in holding a golf club, in a backhand in tennis, in making a strike in bowling) and you will be on your way in understanding just what makes up a rubric. In addition, the student can be made aware of where he or she stands at present in the performance and where he or she will be at the end of the lesson. The characteristics conveyed by the rubrics thus can be developed by both students and teachers, thereby reducing the ambiguity and taking the mystery out of the grading systems used. As important, however, the characteristics provide useful statements of lesson objectives, helping keep the teacher on track regarding student expectations. Through carefully stated rubrics the performance criteria are made public so that all participants and stakeholders—parents, students, administrators, community members—know how the nature and quality of the performance were defined, what standards were used in judging students' excellence in performance, and what was necessary for the student to achieve success in a subject matter area (Arter & McTighe, 2001). They provide the basis for judging improvement made in progressing toward the educational objective by the student, whether the strategies of the teacher were working efficiently, and, if not, what instructional repair strategies were necessary.

Alternative assessments that are authentic have distinct advantages because they are mini-versions of real-life situations and, as such, do not have as much at stake. They prevent or anticipate the ineffective outcomes that might occur in real life, avoiding any damaging outcomes that might occur if the mistake was made in real life. Merely selecting performance assessments because they seem authentic isn't a sufficient reason for using them. Such assessments should be selected, as with any other assessment, because they are related to informing students and teachers of the progress they are making in learning. The situations and the criteria for performance should be closely linked to standards-based educational objectives. Teachers will want to make certain that they implement learning targets that are closely linked to what they want students to know and learn in specific subject matter areas.

Exercise 5.1

Go on the World Wide Web to Rubistar.com (http://rubistar .4teachers.org/index.php). This website provides assistance in automating the creation of rubrics. Choose one for either science or math. Note that while the program will provide cut-points and descriptions of what they mean, it is ultimately up to the teacher to incorporate these "as is" or to modify them in a way that will ultimately make sense when sharing them with students or others (e.g., parents).

Exercise 5.2

Plan a portfolio that you might create to best display to a prospective employer your qualifications for teaching your subject-matter area (or grade level) to increase your prospects for a job. What categories (such as volunteer teaching) of things (pictures, letters, publicity, community work, news articles, and so on) would you include? What categories would be less relevant (e.g., some kinds of part-time work) and possibly add clutter to the portfolio?

■ References

Arter, J., & McTighe, J. (2001). *Scoring rubrics in the classroom.* Thousand Oaks, CA: Corwin Press.

Bloom, B. S., Krathwohl, D., & Masia, B. B. (1973). *Taxonomy of educational objectives: Handbook II. Affective Domain.* New York: David McKay.

Carl, K., & Rosen, M. (1992). Using alternative assessment with English Language Learners [EAC East resource list compiled by Carl & Rosen]. Retrieved April 1, 2008, from www.gwu.edu/~eaceast/ reslist/alter.htm.

Clark, D. R. (2004). Instructional system design concept map. Retrieved January 25, 2010, from http://nwlink.com/~donclark/ hrd/ahold/isd.html.

Collins, A. (1992). Portfolios for science education: Issues in purpose, structure, and authenticity. *Science Education, 76,* 451–463.

Dave, R. (1967). *Psychomotor domain.* Berlin: International Conference of Educational Testing.

Dewey, J. (1923). *Democracy and education: An introduction to the philosophy of education*. New York: MacMillan.

Haney, W., & Madaus, G. (1989). Searching for alternatives to standardized tests: Why's, what's, and whither's. *Phi Delta Kappan*, *70*, 683–687.

Harrow, A. (1972). *A taxonomy of psychomotor domain: A guide for developing behavioral objectives*. New York: David McKay.

Herman, J. L. (1992). What research tells us about god assessment. *Educational Leadership*, *49*(8), 74–78.

Mager, R. F. (1976). *Preparing instructional objectives* (2nd ed.). San Francisco: Fearon.

Neill, D. M., & Medina, N. J. (1989). Standardized testing: Harmful to educational health. *Phi Delta Kappan*, *70*, 688–697.

O'Neil, J. (1992). Putting performance assessment to the test. *Educational Leadership*, *49*(8), 14–19.

Pierce, L. V., & O'Malley, J. M. (1992). *Performance and portfolio assessment for language minority students (Program Information Guide Series 9)*. Washington, DC: National Clearinghouse for Bilingual Education, Office of Bilingual Education and Minority Languages (Education) Affairs.

Simpson, E. J. (1972). *The classification of educational objectives in the psychomotor domain*. Washington, DC: Gryphon House.

Stiggins, R. J. (1987). The design and development of performance assessments. *Educational Measurement: Issues and Practice*, *6*, 33–42.

Tierney, R., Carter, M., & Desai, L. (1991). *Portfolio assessment in the reading and writing classroom*. Norwood, MA: Christopher Gordon.

Wiggins, G. (1989). Teaching to the authentic test. *Educational Leadership*, *46*(7), 41–47.

CHAPTER 6

Developing Objective Tests

POPULAR TEST FORMATS include multiple choice, true-false, matching, fill-in-the-blank, short answer, and essay. The first four of these formats, often known as *objective tests*, are covered in this chapter. Short-answer and essay formats are discussed in Chapter 7 on subjective tests. The other leading assessment format, performance assessment, is treated in Chapter 5.

■ Considerations in Choosing a Test Format

The choice of an assessment format involves consideration of a number of different factors, most of which relate to the objectives of the instructional unit or the course and how that format affects student processing. Formats used by most teachers for assessment in their classrooms fall into the four categories described in this chapter: true-false, multiple choice, matching, and completion (Janson, 2002). The principles for constructing these tests apply not only to test construction by teachers but are the same principles guiding specialists in test construction. Knowing these principles also provides a basis for selecting or evaluating tests, whether they are informal or formal tests and whether or not the tests are standardized.

As you learn about any one format, know that it is simply one from among many that you will learn about. Knowing these different formats provides you with choices when making decisions about evaluations at different points in time, the purposes for which the evaluations are to be used, and the convenience in constructing or using them. All have a common concern for maximizing reliability and validity, and they have overlapping potential for measuring student understanding, transfer, and application, although some may be more effective than others in doing so. In this chapter we have attempted to use examples that illustrate the potential of multiple-choice items for measuring understanding when the characteristics of such items are understood (Downing & Haladyna, 2006).

Advantages of Objective Test Formats

An advantage of these formats, and especially of the multiple-choice format, is the ability to cover a wide range of content material in a relatively short period of administration time. Many topics can be covered in a 90-minute end-of-term examination (Burnstein & Lederman, 2007). Classroom teachers, using formative assessment, can use the same formats advantageously for shorter examinations administered more frequently to monitor student progress and the effectiveness of instructional methods.

Limitations of Objective Formats

Nevertheless, the multiple-choice or true-false formats do have limitations for some instructional objectives, such as determining how well a student can reason in problem-solving situations or how articulately students can write (Burnstein & Lederman, 2007). To achieve these objectives by the use of the objective format may require considerable effort and thought, and so for interim measures of such objectives an assessment based on essay or performance measures may be more feasible.

In terms of the amount of time it takes to create and grade an assessment, most testing formats eventually sum to the same (or similar) investments of effort. It's a trade-off of time in developing an efficient test versus time required to score the test. An essay exam question is relatively easy to construct, but the grading of the questions may take a while. A multiple-choice test can be graded very quickly (often by a machine scanner) but usually requires a long time to compose each item with effective stems and alternatives.

Using Available Item Banks

In addition to constructing your own tests, you will find item pools that are readily available from other sources. In particular, teachers at all grade levels and in all subject matter areas have relied heavily on the packages of test items that came with their textbook (Janson, 2002).

It is common to find textbooks supplemented with item banks of test questions. When the items are well constructed and properly classified they can facilitate test construction for chapter assignments. But we caution the necessity of evaluating each test question thoroughly to ensure that it correctly targets your instructional objective, whether it is the attainment of factual knowledge or the engagement of the learning in complex problem solving. It is well documented that item banks do not represent chapter or curricular objectives well (Frisbie, Miranda, & Baker, 1993). Out of convenience, items in textbook banks are often constructed by matching item phrases with the textbook sentences or phrases. As a result, the majority of items fail to measure more than mere factual knowledge and fail to tap the higher-level cognitive objectives such as understanding. If used frequently, students quickly note that the strategy for good performance is to memorize the textbook.

The Importance of Aligning Item and Curricular Content

There is nothing more frustrating to a student than to encounter a test question tangential to the material that was presented in class or discussed in the text. This is not to say that items can't reflect unique or new situations (by definition they must be new in order to be considered at the application level in Bloom's taxonomy). But if you say that the test will cover "a, b, and c," and then test on "d, e, and f," you can expect some complaints. The point is that although item banks can be helpful, their use requires judgment based on a comparison of item content both with (a) the content of the text and classroom discussion and with (b) instructional objectives. It would not be wise to use intact tests from textbook item banks for classroom assessment. A part of the criteria for evaluating textbooks and their assessment packages for classroom use should be based on their alignment with curricular objectives and with state standards. It is important that the test items provide a sampling of the instructional objectives, the expectations for student performance, and the work studied in meeting the objectives in order to combat the practice of pulling item content directly from curricular materials, mainly assessing recall of basic facts (Boyd, 2008).

Lines of Validity Evidence

Test formats are not all good or all bad. The question here is whether the evaluation procedure really samples the objectives intended. This point is often described in terms of the extent to which the test (or item) is aligned with objectives (whether classroom objectives, content area standards, or state standards). Each format has its advantages in providing certain degrees of evidence over other formats. Even with classroom assessment conducted with teacher-made tests, the degree to which the tests are aligned with state proficiency tests is a concern—assuming, of course, that state standards represent the content and constructs acceptable to the local community. Locally constructed measures often include additional standards as well. The basic premise in statewide assessment, as in all assessment, is that aligning classroom tests with standards (note that alignment is with standards; it is *not* with items in state tests) is the proper way of implementing instruction that also improves student performance in meeting those standards.

The feedback from assessment outcomes influences improvements in the curriculum, instruction, and learning. Teachers making frequent classroom assessments are sensitive to the necessity for using good item construction principles, whether in developing their own assessment measures or selecting items from item banks. In doing so, they avoid the weaknesses that often characterize unstandardized assessments— such weaknesses as (a) containing items assessing low-level cognitive function (e.g., rote memory of simple facts, emphasis on textbook statements, and so on); (b) a predominance of low-level multiple-choice items (i.e., those requiring simple recall of information); and (c) a lack of concern for different lines of validity evidence (AERA, APA, & NCME, 1999).

In making classroom tests, teachers are concerned with making certain that the test items are good work-sample representations of objectives, that the objectives are aligned with known professional standards, and that they correspond to local needs and demands of their community. If the test meets these requirements and samples situations that will be met in the future (applications) then the test will have some degree of validity, known as face or content validity. We can also obtain some notion of the validity of teacher-made test if we ask the question, "Are we aware of what the test measures?" This somewhat more subjective notion of validity illustrates that classroom tests, without opportunities for more detailed analysis, can be thoughtfully scrutinized for validity rather than simply constructing items on the basis of such overly simplistic rules as lifting phrases from the textbook. But even so, validation is a never-ending process requiring the test constructor to be ever vigilant about the uses to which the assessment is being put (Swaffield, 2008).

The *Standards for Educational and Psychological Testing* (1999, pp. 11–16) outline ways of judging validity that are useful considerations in constructing tests within any of the formats, however informal (teacher-made tests) or formal (statewide or standardized tests) the test may be. The lines of validity are:

- *Content.* Does the test content correspond to the content specified as an outcome of instruction? (e.g., if alignment with state proficiency tests is intended, do the items reflect that intention?)
- *Internal structure.* Do the items function consistently with or at variance with the purpose for which the test is to be used? (e.g., if the test is alleged to measure the general principle of a construct such as democracy, are the items sufficiently consistent to provide evidence that the construct has been mastered at the level intended?)
- *Response processes.* Is there a correspondence or fit between the stated purposes of the test and the required processing in taking the test? (e.g., if you intend to measure understanding of an idea, are students taking the test demonstrating understanding or simply parroting teacher or textbook explanations?)

"Teachers teach what they test" implies the need for serious consideration of validity evidence in constructing tests. One format may be more effective than another for assessing certain objectives. An integration of the lines of validity evidence can be achieved by consideration of the advantages and limitations of a format in the effective construction of measures. "Teachers teach what they test" doesn't mean that one should teach test items. The phrase has a different meaning, which we reiterate: Assessments should be functionally related to standards and objectives if they are to have a positive influence on instructional improvement and learning. Assessments aimed at facilitating achievement of the standards of understanding and application are far more effective in facilitating learning than those simply aimed at the student's ability to do well on a test item.

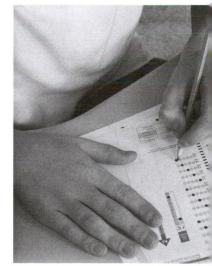

■ True-False Tests

The *true-false* test format consists of a statement which the student judges to be true or false. The premise underlying true-false (T/F) questions is that there are important propositions that can be classified as either true or false, and knowledgeable students should be able to discern the difference. Here is one example of a true-false item:

T/F   1. According to FBI statistics for the year 2008, the city of Chicago had the highest murder rate in the United States of America.

While at first it may seem easy enough to compile true-false statements, writing such sentences can be quite challenging. In the example above, the sentence is associated with four qualifiers: (1) "according to FBI statistics," (2) "for the year 2008," (3) "the city of Chicago," and (4) "in the United States of America." The student is faced with the problem of determining whether the item is true because of the source of the statistics, the year in which the statistics were obtained, the city for which the murder rate is reported, or the country with which it is being compared. The grammatical complexity created by the four qualifiers contributes to the ambiguity of items. Even knowledgeable students may make errors if they depend on an unintended qualifier to cue their answer because changing any one of these four qualifiers might change this sentence from true to false.

A general difficulty associated with the construction of items is the temptation to lift sentences directly out of a textbook or other source, making minor changes in wording or not to modify the claims originally made. This creates a source of invalidity almost immediately because it raises the question of whether the student is responding to the fact that the premise in the statement is true or false or whether the student is responding to the fact that the statement was the one made in the textbook or something different. In addition, it raises the question of whether or not the cultural context is taken into account (Stobart, 2008). Additionally, the probability of obtaining higher scores by guessing is 50 percent, which is sufficient to encourage guessing. Sometimes guessing is believed to be discouraged by invoking penalties such as doubling the score for wrong answers. Nevertheless, true-false tests, carefully constructed, can be useful measures of the ability of the student to recognize a correct fact, association, cause-effect relation, or broad range of situations to which a principle applies.

Truth or Falsity of Items

In useful true-false items, the statement should be 100 percent true, or at the least, it should be 100 percent true according to a respected source; otherwise it is false. Items should not represent opinion, unless the opinion is part of an invoked authority. If it is, then you should be prepared to defend the credentials of the authority. The following item is an example of a judgment made without showing the source:

T/F   2. President Abraham Lincoln's Gettysburg Address is more important for where it was given than what was actually said.

This statement may or may not be true. The question is, "On what basis is the importance determined?" The truth in this case is a matter of debate or interpretation; it is simply an opinion, and for that reason the item is not appropriate for a true-false test. Here is another example:

T/F   3. Vermont has the best winter ski resorts in the USA.

If you hail from the state of Colorado, you may well disagree. In order for the statement to be demonstrably true, you would have to attribute the opinion to an authority on ski resorts:

T/F   4. According to the 2009 SkiMaster Guide, Vermont has the best winter ski resorts in the USA.

Relation of Statements to Learning Objectives

In writing items, it is important that a student should know the information represented by a test item; that is, the material being tested should have been studied, is relevant to objectives, and is not simply trivial knowledge that has little or no bearing on the intended acquisition of curricular objectives. In example 4, the information might be important for a course in tourism, but it would be a bit of trivia in eighth-grade geography. It is all too easy to write true-false statements that get at unimportant or narrowly construed factual information:

T/F   5. Stop signs in the USA have an octagonal shape.

This statement is true, measures a single idea, and would have some relevance in a driver's education class, but it is a relatively minor fact as it stands.

The Effect of Qualifiers

Some qualifiers tend to make a statement false. For example, if a true-false statement contains the word *always* or *never*, then it is likely to be false. If the statement contains the words *sometimes* or *usually*, the statement is likely to be true. The testwise person will pick up on these tendencies and increase the probability of guessing correctly. Take this item for example:

T/F   6. Housing starts usually coincide with reductions in the prime lending rate.

This is not a good test question. The smart test taker will guess that it is true because of the modifier *usually*.

A good general rule is that a true-false statement should present only one idea. It is sometimes tempting to make an item more complex in an attempt to increase the difficulty, but often it results in making the item more obscure and ambiguous. Take this item, for example:

T/F   7. The baseball diamond is not a diamond but is a square.

The item is obviously composed of two propositions (ideas); the first is "the diamond is not a diamond," which would make the item false, and the second is "the diamond is a square," which is true. By containing two propositions the item is neither completely true or false. It can be revised to:

T/F   8. The baseball diamond is also a square.

The reasoning is that a diamond is a rhombus. The definition of a rhombus is that the sides are parallel. Thus, a square has sides that are parallel. It is a parallelogram. However, the definition of a parallelogram doesn't say anything about the size of the angles; whereas the definition of a square does—the angles must be 90 degrees each. So a square is a parallelogram; however, not all parallelograms are squares.

Summary: Guidelines for Constructing True-False Statements

The guidelines for formulating true-false statements are summed up in Text Box 6.1. The main advantage of using the true-false format is that one can cover factual information from a variety of vantage points in a very short period of time. If an item covers a clearly defined point, then performance on the item will show precisely where strengths or needs for remediation lie. If the student answers an item incorrectly it becomes a reason for further diagnosing "why" in order to help in further assignments.

Text Box 6.1 Guidelines for Writing True-False Test Items

1. Each statement has to be clearly true or false.
2. If a statement's veracity depends on some authority, then reference the authority from which it is drawn. The statement should not be a matter of opinion.
3. The statement has to be important.
4. The statement should be unambiguous; it should be based on a single idea.
5. The statement should minimize the use of qualifiers.
6. Avoid the use of absolute terms such as *always*, *never*, *all*, or *none*.
7. Avoid the use of modifiers such as *usually* or *sometimes*.

The principal drawback of true-false items is that generating a significant statement that is either true or false, without exceptions, is a challenging task. Most important truths are validated by their exceptions. Another drawback is that, for some students, the format encourages guessing. The chance of guessing the correct answer for any individual statement is 50 percent; on that basis it is possible to get a number of items right by guessing. The difficulty with the true-false format is that you cannot be certain that the student knows the material simply because he or she answered the item correctly—he or she may simply have made a good guess.

■ Multiple-Choice Tests

The *multiple-choice* format presents the test taker with a statement or question and a series of possible responses. Each question in its entirety is called an item. Each item is typically composed of a *stem* portion, which states the general problem to be answered, and a set of *alternatives* that contains one *correct answer* and two or more incorrect answers, called *distractors*. The following is an example of a multiple-choice item with the parts labeled.

(Item) 1.	*(Stem)* Which of the following was the main cause of the dust bowl phenomenon in Kansas and neighboring states in the 1930s?
	(Alternatives)
(distractor)	a. exodus of farmers to urban jobs
(distractor)	b. technical advances in farm machinery
(correct answer)	c. agricultural practices of plowing and planting
(distractor)	d. seasonal variations in wind and rain

The initial portion, known as the stem, can be either a statement or a question, but it is usually easier for the test taker to comprehend if in question format. Here is the stem in the preceding example rewritten as a statement:

1. The main cause of the dust bowl phenomenon in Kansas and neighboring states during the 1930s was:

The response alternatives are choices that have the potential for completing the stem. They are intended to represent a series of plausible answers, one of which is the correct or best answer. As is the case with true-false questions, the correct response alternatives should be unambiguously correct or clearly the best answer. The distractors should be plausible enough to attract those unfamiliar with the content, but clearly wrong.

Advantages to Using Multiple-Choice Format

The multiple-choice format has several advantages in terms of the amount of effort, the efficiency of assessment (scope of material covered relative to time required to administer), and the assessment objectives. Some of these are:

- Many aspects of an objective or construct can be measured in a relatively short period of time.
- The format is easy to score.
- With continued use in classes, the format lends itself to improvement through the use of item analysis. A difficulty index can be obtained by simply calculating the percent of students who answered items correctly. To determine whether alternatives are functioning properly, which are nonfunctional and which are dysfunctional, the ratio of achievers to nonachievers who select the alternative can be used—achievers more than nonachievers should select the correct alternative, whereas more nonachievers than achievers should select the distractors (see Chapter 10, "Improving Tests").
- Multiple-choice items allow options with varying degree of correctness, avoiding the absolute judgments found in true-false tests (Curran, DeAyala, & Koch, 1985; Jacobs & Chase, 1992).

Using Multiple-Choice Formats Based on Cognitive Response Processes

It is well worth the time and effort to write good multiple-choice items. Properly constructed, their use is not limited to measures of acquisition of facts. They can be used for identifying where instruction is succeeding and working efficiently and where it needs revision and/or remediation. As importantly, multiple-choice tests can be used to diagnose student difficulties, such as misconceptions, in any content area, and to assess student ability outcomes that are similar to those classified in typical taxonomies (Burton, Sudweeks, Merrill, & Wood, 1991). To name but a few outcomes, multiple-choice tests can be used to measure student ability in:

- *Analysis* (e.g., of the stages of maturation in insects and mammals)
- *Application* of principles (e.g., the application of the Bernoullian principle to flight or of Archimedes' principle to flotation of ships)
- *Comprehension* (of such concepts as compounds, solutions, and mixtures)
- *Discrimination* (e.g., among the functions of the executive, judicial, and legislative branches of government)
- *Interpretation* (e.g., of charts and graphs showing population trends or physiological growth patterns in the stages of human development)
- *Solving problems* (e.g., from balancing budgets to ways of reducing crime rates)
- *Cause-effect* (e.g., the relation of fuel consumption to global warming)

Limitations of the Multiple-Choice Format

As indicated earlier, any given format is not all good or all bad. Each format has its potential for being effective, but simultaneously, there are situations in which it is much less effective or not at all effective when compared to other formats. The limitations of the multiple-choice format (as well as true-false tests) are primarily due to the restriction that the alternatives are provided rather than generated by the student. By providing alternative responses and eliminating the need to generate potential responses, the multiple-choice test is not adaptable (or, at least, less adaptable) to assessing such outcomes as the ability to:

- Generate explanations (e.g., of an author's intent or of the effects of evaporation on water levels and temperature)
- Elaborate (e.g., students' understanding of democracy in its various forms)

- Describe personal thoughts about how problems were solved (e.g., strategies used)
- Produce different organizations of the content (e.g., organize compounds into organic and inorganic as well as in terms of states at various temperatures)
- Produce original ideas or new examples (e.g., to show how credit and debit worksheets can be used in budgeting, tracking checkbook balances, and reporting corporate finances)
- Perform (e.g., any skill such as debating, evaluating, demonstrating) (Burton et al., 1991)

These limitations suggest that other methods of assessment are more effective for some uses. Illustrations include *modified multiple choice* (e.g., writing an explanation of why an alternative was selected as an answer), *constructed response* (e.g., completion of a sentence with the correct concept), *essay* (e.g., to assess writing or oratory skills or for reporting on thought processes), or *performance* (e.g., map reading).

Construction of Multiple-Choice Items for Measuring Understanding

There are several considerations in constructing valid multiple-choice items, making the process both challenging and time-consuming. Difficulties arise both in constructing the stem and in constructing the alternatives to achieve tests that are at the appropriate level of difficulty while simultaneously differentiating the achiever from the nonachiever.

The Stem

Though the stem of the multiple-choice question can require the test taker to synthesize multiple concepts, "window dressing" or enhancements to the stem that do not contribute to the question should be avoided. For example:

Officer Smith pulled over a speeding driver who was going 55 miles per hour in a posted 45-mile-per-hour zone. State law imposes a fine of $7.50 for every mile over the speed limit. What is the amount of the fine the driver paid?

If the teacher wanted only to assess the student's knowledge of arithmetic operations, the lengthy word problem could be reduced to:

What is 10×7.50?

The elaborated word problem may help provide some face validity, especially if the test is being administered to police officer candidates. Or it may be that what you are really trying to determine is whether the examinee can apply arithmetic operations within the context of word problems. However, if the objective is to determine whether the student can multiply a decimal by a whole number, the less elaborated stem would be better.

Similarly, though the question may ask for the synthesis of multiple concepts, it should still be based on a single learning objective or domain. Figure 6.1 is an example of one that might be used in a beginning geometry class:

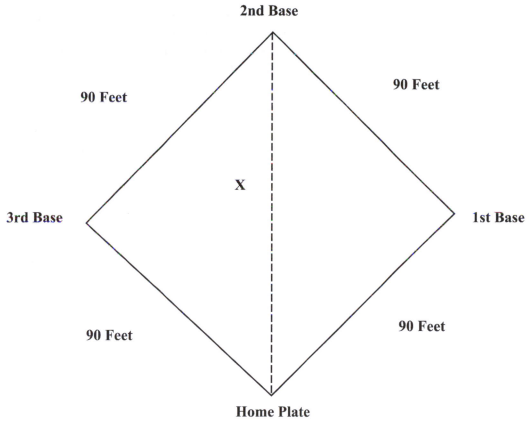

Figure 6.1. A schematic of a baseball diamond.

In the figure of the baseball diamond above, how many feet (within 3 or 4 inches) is it between first and third base?
  a. 107
  b. 117
  c. 127
  d. 137

As the problem stands, the reader can see that the teacher's objective in constructing this item is to examine the student's understanding and use of the Pythagorean theorem. The problem can be a perplexing one for the uninformed student or the student who approaches it without careful analysis. In order to solve the problem without guessing, the student needs to make such analyses and syntheses as these: First, baseball diamonds are square, although because of the perspective of their layouts they intuitively look more like parallelograms. Second, because they are square, a diagonal can be constructed by connecting opposite corners—in this case, bases (home plate with second base; first base with third base). Third, one set of connecting opposites results in the formation of two triangles within the figure; the lines connecting each base with the next are the sides of a triangle, and the diagonal is the hypotenuse. Fourth, because the diamond is, in fact, a square, the triangles are right triangles. And, finally, the geometry student knows that the diagonals of a square are equal. Given this knowledge base, the Pythagorean theorem $a^2 + b^2 = c^2$ can be applied. By substitution of the given numbers of feet between bases, the calculations $(90 \times 90) + (90 \times 90) = 16200$ and $\sqrt{16200} = 127.28$ yields the correct answer for the number of feet between the first and third base. Each alternative may seem reasonable if the student is not calculating the answer or using the theorem, but rather is guessing or making an estimation of the correct answer. To avoid dependence on extraneous cues, the answers are not only thematically similar (homogeneous or parallel) but are placed in ascending order (one way of avoiding cues from the position of the alternative).

Note that this item might also serve as an application item by modifying the stem as follows:

Modification: "If the third baseman catches the ball, how far must he throw it to get it to the first baseman?"

Of course, a number of other contexts might be appropriate, such as designing a house or planning the planting of crops on a square acre of farm land. The student must still make the same analysis as in the original; however, as in any application the student must transfer the abstract principle to the situation at hand; that is, the student must see the relation between the situation and the principles that are to be applied. Note, too, that the stem of an item does not need to be restricted to a verbal format, but can be accompanied by an appropriate display, as in this example in which the layout of the baseball diamond is shown as a figure.

The Alternatives

A problem that departs from asking simply for the recall of information or a definition is illustrated below. Here it can be seen that the alternatives all provide a basis for measuring important conceptual distinctions such as physical and chemical changes. In providing for the measurement of such understanding the alternatives are constructed parallel to one another in the sense that they all represent change by different processes (evaporation, freezing, burning, and melting) that result in some change in materials. Each alternative is related to the stem, but only one is related to the kind of change denoted.

Which of the following is a chemical change?
  a. Evaporation of alcohol
  b. Freezing of water
  c. Burning of oil
  d. Melting of wax

As you can see, each alternative in this example represents some sort of change in a substance: for example, the melting of wax is a change from a solid to a liquid, the evaporation of alcohol is a change from a liquid to a gas, and the freezing of water is a change from a liquid to a solid. The selection of the correct response might be made on a purely associative basis if the alternatives were lifted from a textbook. However, assuming they were *not* taken directly from the text, the alternatives are effectively distinctive because each process is associated with a different kind of change, only one of which is a chemical change that occurs when material (in this case oil) is burned. To answer this item correctly the student must understand the difference between physical and chemical changes and that burning an object results in chemical changes.

Other ways the item could be worded to keep it equally effective are shown in the revised item below. The words on the left of the list are general processes that change the form of the material, but only one of which results in a chemical change of any material. The words in parentheses are all related to water, consistent with the rule that the alternatives should be parallel to each other and at the same time consistent with the stem.

Which of the following will result in a chemical change?
  a. Evaporation (of water)
  b. Freezing (of water)
  c. Electrolysis (of water)
  d. Sublimation (of snow)
  e. Melting (of snow or ice)

Although this is not a perfect model of an item, it is an example of an item that meets most requirements well. If the alternatives were constructed of processes only (without qualification in the parentheses) the selection of the correct answer requires understanding how the process changes the chemical structure of *any* material. However, putting in a qualifier (e.g., burning *of oil* or electrolysis *of water*) on which the process acts provides a possible cue to the correct answer, which is not only irrelevant to measuring what the student knows about chemical change but is useful in showing how well the student can apply the principle within a specific context, perhaps different from the one in which it was learned. Dealing only with water in one form or another may help to avoid providing cues to a greater extent than if burning of wood was also mentioned. A testwise student who did not study the lesson still might select electrolysis or sublimation because they are less commonly experienced and are therefore unique and obviously different from the more common processes.

Construction of Alternatives

Although we most often think of test items and assessments in general as measures of correct responses (of what the student has learned correctly) they are also measures of what the student is capable of doing. As often, we fail to recognize the vast amount of information in knowing what the student has not learned, has learned incorrectly, or has otherwise failed to acquire a level of understanding commensurate with curricular objectives. It is just as important, then, to understand where students fail to see the distinctions which they are capable of making (e.g., democracy vs. democratic monarchies), where they have misconceptions (e.g., that all small, crawly things are insects), where they have incorrect metacognitions (e.g., "I only need to learn enough to pass a test"), and so on. The alternatives to multiple-choice questions can be viewed as providing that opportunity. Rather than posing alternatives simply as distractors, as obviously wrong alternatives, they can be used to serve diagnostic purposes—to show not only that the student is correct, but the ways in which he or she is correct; not only is the student making mistakes, but what kind of mistake is being made. Items can be developed to require students to retrieve one kind of information over another or to construct responses (e.g., through the use of analogy, application, or other strategy) rather than to simply find the correct answer (some examples in this chapter are the items on the Pythagorean theorem and the ones on chemical change).

In meeting these requirements, response alternatives should be plausible. To help assure that students are making judgments based on an understanding of the knowledge involved in the test content and not on irrelevant factors such as length or position of the alternatives, adhering to a few rules will help in making useful alternatives: they should (a) be thematically homogeneous (deal with variations of the same idea), (b) be of about the same length, (c) represent a logical order when taken together (e.g., serially or chronologically), and (d) be randomly positioned in the set.

An example of an item that provides a basis for understanding how precisely an elementary school student is defining a concept (in this case the concept of "bird") might be as follows:

Which of the following is the defining feature that taxonomically separates birds from other animals?
   a. Beak
   b. Claws
   c. Eggs
   d. Feathers
   e. Nest

Criteria for Evaluating Item Alternatives

You can evaluate the potential effectiveness of the previous item by checking the extent to which these criteria have been met:

- *Is the stem sufficiently brief?* Is it clear? Could parts be left out?
- *Would selection of any distractor (incorrect alternative) provide information of how or what the student learned?* For instance, if Rosa selected "beak" or "claws" she might have based her answer on what she already knew rather than on the classroom lesson. And, of course, other animals are hatched from eggs external to the mother and have a hatching period.
- *Is there an advantage to having the student identify the distinguishing characteristic of the category of birds, rather than the characteristic features of birds?* For instance, would the student's answer, based on any of the alternatives, help you to diagnose student learning, to understand what the student

knows and does not know about classification or about birds—if he or she were able to name all of the characteristics of birds? What is added by requiring the student to identify the defining feature of birds?

- *Are the alternatives thematically homogeneous?* Do they deal with a main theme like features or characteristics (another theme might have included activities such as bird calls, nesting habits, flight, migration, caring for the young, and so on)?
- *Are cues to the answer held at a minimum?* For example, are the alternatives the same length? Is there something about the position of the correct answer that gives the answer away?

Consider this example:

Correlating a new test with some already well-established test is an example of:
    a. Predictive validity
    b. Concurrent validity
    c. Test-retest reliability
    d. Internal consistency reliability

The correct answer is b, "concurrent validity." A testwise individual will evaluate the question, and if he or she can somehow determine that it is one of validity, then the individual can reduce the probability of guessing correctly from one-in-four to one-in-two by eliminating the answers having to do with reliability (c and d).

A parallel item illustrates how this difficulty may also be present in an elementary school test:

Buyers are unwilling to pay the price a seller is charging for telephones. According to the rules of supply and demand, which of the following is *most likely* to happen?
    a. Buyers will make their own telephones.
    b. Buyers will attempt to barter for telephones.
    c. The seller will lower the price of telephones.
    d. The seller will increase the production of telephones.

Avoid Providing Irrelevant Cues; Do Require Discrimination among Alternatives

Using the same reasoning as in the previous example, we can see that a testwise individual will evaluate the question and determine that it is one involving buying or selling; then the individual can reduce the probability of guessing correctly from one-in-four to one-in-two by eliminating the answers having to do with buying, because that is an implication of the buyer being unwilling to pay the price demanded by the company (a and b). Furthermore, the demand and supply are associated with price and production, respectively, not with making telephones or with barter exchange. A modification of the question to offset these problems might be as follows:

According to the economic principle of supply and demand, which one of the following factors is *most likely* to be taken into consideration by a corporation to increase demand?
   a. Price of service
   b. Number of services
   c. Level of service
   d. Quality of service

As you can see, the alternatives all deal with service, requiring discrimination among the kinds of service. This example further illustrates the construction of selected-response test items that require problem solving based on real-life situations. Their use need not be limited to recall of facts or to contexts provided during instruction.

There are other ways in which cues to the correct answer may be provided when simple format problems are often ignored. For example, changes in the complexity, length, or language of an alternative may provide cues to the correct answer. Examine the following items. Can you identify a possible cue to the correct answer that has nothing to do with the student's knowledge of the subject matter being tested?

The primary function of an aptitude test is to:
   a. Select a job.
   b. Select applicants for an organization.
   c. Recommend courses.
   d. Ascertain if the examinee has the capacity to benefit from certain kinds of instruction.

In this case, of course, the correct answer is d. We have made it longer purposefully to show how a testwise student might have selected this alternative even if he or she didn't know the correct answer. The test-taking strategy is, simply, "pick the response that is longer than any of the others." In most multiple-choice tests, a longer, more precise answer has a far greater chance of being correct than a brief or generalized answer (often simply due to the fact that a correct answer is difficult to construct without providing specific details).

Which is the missing concept in the diagram below (Figure 6.2)?

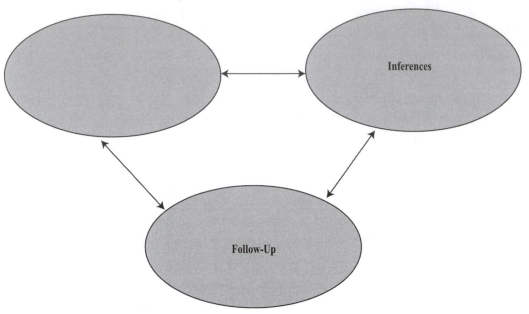

Figure 6.2. A multiple-choice test item figure.

    a. Criteria
    b. Observations*
    c. Standards
    d. Capacity

Summary: Constructing Multiple-Choice Tests

Text Box 6.2 offers some guidelines for developing good multiple-choice items.

■ Fill-in-the-Blank (Completion) Tests

The *fill-in-the-blank* format is a popular format, especially in elementary and secondary grades. Characterized as a free-response test, the student supplies missing information to make a sentence meaningful, to complete an idea, or solve a problem. It is most often constructed to be answered with a single word, but can be usefully framed to require an established order of events (e.g., a chronological order such as the sequence in the development of insects from egg to adult), a procedure (e.g., the

Text Box 6.2 Guidelines for Writing Multiple-Choice Test Items

Item as a Unit
- Each item should be based on a single idea or objective.
- Items should have correct grammar, spelling, and punctuation.
- Verify the helpfulness of any items used previously in your course.
- The overall layout of the test should be clear and consistent; for instance, in using the hanging indentation, the stems of all items are at the margins and numbered, whereas the alternatives are indented and either numbered or alphabetized.

Stems
- The stem should be based on a specific, clearly stated problem.
- It should clearly represent a sample of the targeted objectives.
- It should be concise and avoid irrelevant material.
- It should be stated in positive form.

Alternatives and Distractors
- Include three to five options for each item.
- Alternatives should be mutually exclusive; avoid redundancy, repetitive phrases, or overlap among alternatives.
- The content of the alternatives should be similar (dates, concepts, and so on).
- There should be no grammatical, syntactical, semantic, or mechanical (length or number of words) cues to the correct answer.
- Avoid excessive use of negatives and/or double negatives.
- The use of *all of the above* and *none of the above* should be limited or avoided altogether.
- Distractors should be functional; students who did not learn the content should select the alternative more frequently than those who did.
- Distractors should be more than incorrect selections; if selected they should provide diagnostic information regarding misconceptualizations or processes used, showing where further learning is needed.

Alternatives: Answer
- The position of the correct answer should vary randomly from item to item.
- The length of the response options should be about the same within each item.
- There should be a single correct answer to each item or, at least, a clear best answer.
- The correct answer should be randomly placed from item to item.

Source: Adapted from Burton et al. (1991); Curran et al. (1985).

steps in conducting an experiment), a list of the components of a concept (e.g., the characteristics of birds), and so on. Unlike the selected-response formats of true-false, multiple-choice, or matching tests, the completion or fill-in-the-blank test requires the retrieval from long-term memory of potentially correct answers based on the requirements of the problem. Sometimes alternatives must be generated from several sources of information. Once those alternatives have been identified, they are then evaluated for their value in answering the question or filling in the blanks correctly, in making the final selection.

This format is very similar to the short-answer question (discussed in a later chapter), but it solicits a very specific response. For example, one declarative form might be:

_____ gas is produced when mixing zinc and hydrochloric acid.

The answer here is "hydrogen." No other answer is correct.

In order to reduce disruption in interpreting the question raised by the statement, it is usually better to put the blank at the end of the sentence. In the example above, a better declarative statement might be the following:

A mixture of zinc and hydrochloric acid will produce _____ gas.

By placing the blank at the end, the statement provides continuity to the idea. By first providing the two compounds, the chemistry student is signaled that the statement refers to a cause-effect relation. A source of irrelevant variance is removed by reducing the amount of processing time because the student does not have to reread the sentence in order to understand what response is required. The interruption of the cue-based grammatical order interferes with comprehension so that a second reading is required.

Variations in the Basic Completion Item Format

Another useful technique is to transform a statement into a question:

What gas is produced by mixing zinc and hydrochloric acid? _____

Note as well the possibility of requiring the respondent to generate answers from a wider knowledge base. For example:

What is the outcome of adding zinc to hydrochloric acid?

_____

To answer this question requires the student to do more thinking, that is, to retrieve from his or her knowledge base the information that (a) the combination will cause a chemical reaction (not merely a solution or mixture), (b) the outcome will be a gas (e.g., not a precipitate) and some heat, and (c) the gas will be hydrogen (e.g., not oxygen or other gas).

Although fill-in-the-blanks tests usually require only a single answer, there are occasions when multiple responses may be required, as in these examples:

Question format: What were the last names of the presidents of the United States who also had sons who later became presidents?

Fill-in-the-blank format: The last names of the presidents of the United States who also had sons who later became presidents were (a)_____, (b) _____, and (c) _____.

Advantages of Fill-in-the-Blank Tests

Fill-in-the-blank tests have these advantages:

- They are relatively easy to construct.
- They reduce the amount of guessing because the student must recall the answer rather than simply choosing it from a list.
- Properly constructed, fill-in-the-blank items can measure the extent to which the student understands the content; for instance, in the chemistry example, the answer can be generated from knowledge of how a metal and acid react to produce hydrogen and zinc chloride.
- They generally take less time than multiple-choice tests to construct by the teacher and less time to complete by the student.

Limitations

As with other item formats, the fill-in-the-blank format has its limitations. Fortunately, they can be avoided by attending to principles of item construction.

First, the format may encourage construction of a test item by simply deleting key words from textbook sentences. If such items are used frequently, the practice encourages meta-cognitions in some students that rote memorization of the text rather than using the material in applications requiring higher-order cognitive skills is related to their performance. However, this point is true for any test format, as we have pointed out earlier. For example, if the constructor of an essay test were to use such prompts as, "List the three events that led to World War II," students would quickly learn (acquire the metacognition) that such lists could have been answered from reading the textbook. By answering items written directly from textbook presentations without modification or concern for validity, students soon learn to study by memorizing lists of facts in anticipation of the test they are to take.

Second, items with only one correct answer may sometimes be tricky to construct and may require careful attention to qualifiers, as in the following example:

Original: A _____ is less than a quarter of a dollar. (correct answers could be *penny*, *nickel*, or *dime* in U.S. currency).

Better: A _____ is worth one-fifth of a quarter. (correct answer: *nickel*)

Third, a potential trap of using fill-in-the-blank questions is the tendency to create blanks that solicit trivial or relatively unimportant pieces of information—items that require only simple recall of facts without conceptual understanding, as in the following example:

A _____ of zinc and hydrochloric acid will produce hydrogen. (correct answer: mixture)

Summary

Text Box 6.3 lists some things to keep in mind as you put together fill-in-the-blank or completion-type items.

■ Matching Tests

The *matching* format is used to assess student knowledge regarding characteristics associated with homogeneous sets of ideas, terms, concepts, events, and the like (Mandernach, 2003). There are two parts or item clusters presented in two lists or columns. The first is referred to as the *premises*; it may include concepts, events, theorists, or taxonomic or other categories. The second cluster, in a similar format, is referred to as the *alternatives* or

---

Text Box 6.3 Guidelines for Writing Fill-in-the-Blank Test Items

1. Items should require a single-word answer or a brief and definite statement.
2. Avoid statements that are so indefinite that they may be answered equally well by several terms.
3. Avoid grammatical clues. For example: the central core of an _____ is the nucleus. Either write the item as "the central core of a(n) _____ is the nucleus" or as "the central core of an atom is the _____."
4. A direct question is often more desirable than an incomplete statement.
5. Blank spaces should usually occur at or near the end of the sentence following the problem, rather than at the beginning or in the middle.
6. Avoid omission of less important or irrelevant information (e.g., "the central _____ of an atom is the nucleus" versus "the central core of an atom is the _____."
7. Be sure that the required answer is factually correct.
8. Omit only key words; don't eliminate so many elements that the meaning or main point of the item is disrupted or lost.
9. If the problem requires a numerical answer, indicate the units in which it is to be expressed.
10. Avoid lifting statements directly from sources the student has studied, whether text, reference, lecture, or any other source.

---

response choices and is a list of ideas or characteristics associated with the premises.

As in other objective formats, the student's task is to identify, select, or recognize the alternative(s) associated with each event (premise). The selection may be based simply on knowledge of factual associations or may require a logical understanding of the relation between the two. The format enables assessing processes of discrimination, classification, or comparison among ideas as well as simple associations. Depending upon the objectives of the test, more than one alternative may be appropriately selected for any premise. On occasions, the response requirement may be to rank the alternatives. Whatever the response requirement may be, the instructions should clearly specify how the selection is to be recorded.

Consider the example shown in Table 6.1. In this matching problem, the goal is to match the state (premise) with its official bird (alternatives); the response requirement is to select a factual association, a lower-order cognitive task. As this example illustrates, the basis for matching should be explicitly stated and should encompass one general idea.

Table 6.1. Example of a Matching Problem

Directions: Match the state with its official bird. Write the letter of the bird you selected in the blank beside the state to which the bird belongs.

State	Bird
___1. California	a. *Parus atricapillus*
___2. Maine	b. Quail
___3. Florida	c. Western Meadowlark
___4. Montana	d. Mockingbird
___5. Nebraska	e. Hermit Thrush
___6. Vermont	f. Golden Poppy
	g. Cardinal
	h. Yellowhammer

There are a few characteristics in this problem format to be noticed:

- The premises are numbered, and alternatives are usually identified by a letter of the alphabet.
- The number of alternatives should be longer than the number of premises. Why? Because if you have an equal number of both, the last selection is automatic once the next-to-last decision is made.
- The premises should be homogeneous in the sense that they are conceptually consistent, in this case they are all states. In other cases, they might be all authors, all theorists, all taxonomic categories, and so on.
- The alternatives, too, should be homogeneous; in this case they should all be common bird names. In Table 6.1, alternative f is not a bird but rather a state flower (California's) and should not be in the mix. Alternative a (*Parus atricapillus*) is in fact a bird, but it is the Latin name for the chicadee (Maine's state bird). It is not homogeneous in that the other names in the list are common English names.
- The matching should be one to one. In Table 6.1, premises 4 and 5 are problematic because the correct alternative for both is Western Meadowlark (alternative c). If you include such items, you may have to indicate whether an alternative can be used more than once.
- In situations where there is a difference in the length of the stimuli, longer phrases should be used as premises and alternatives should remain fairly short. So, for instance, if we were matching quotes with their authors, the quotes would be part of the premise and the authors would be listed as alternatives.
- Finally, take care that you don't give any unintentional clues by making some premises and responses plural and some singular.

There are several advantages in using matching items. The format is simple to construct and score and is a straightforward measure of association among facts. In comparison to multiple-choice items, it does reduce the effects of guessing. The major drawback in this format is the tendency to trivialize information and to emphasize memorization (Curran et al., 1985).

■ The Challenge of Assessing Higher-Order Thinking

All testing formats have the capacity to address all levels of Bloom's taxonomy, but with objective tests it can be difficult to assess higher-order thinking. Consider the following example (Bloom, Hastings, & Madaus, 1971):

A measurement is to be made of the heat evolved in the complete combustion of a certain type of coal. The sample of coal is placed in a thin metal capsule, oxygen is admitted, and the capsule is sealed. The capsule is immersed in water contained in an insulated vessel and the contents are ignited by means of an electric spark. The amount of heat evolved in the capsule is determined from the rise of the temperature of the surrounding water.

Directions: Keeping in mind the purpose of the determination described above, choose the *one* best alternative for each of the following items and *blacken* the corresponding answer space.

1. The weight of the coal sample
   a. must be known accurately.
   b. need only be known approximately, that is, to about 50 percent.
   c. need not be known, but must at least equal the weight of water.
   d. is entirely immaterial.
2. The amount of the water in the vessel
   a. must be known accurately.
   b. must be known only well enough to permit addition of water to balance evaporation.
   c. is immaterial as long as it covers the capsule completely.
   d. is immaterial but should not cover the capsule completely.

The correct answers are _____.

This item is interesting in two ways. First, it illustrates that it is possible to construct a multiple-choice item at the analysis and synthesis levels of Bloom's taxonomy. Second, the response alternatives were created to illustrate common misperceptions of the concepts involved. In that sense, they might have diagnostic utility. The major drawback is that one can never be sure if the analysis or synthesis that took place was a function of true analytic thinking, simply recognizing the best answer, or mere guessing.

Because of this limitation in objective tests, teachers often use subjective formats for assessing the kinds of processes associated with reasoning and higher-order cognitions. We examine subjective tests in the next chapter.

Exercise 6.1

You have learned many characteristics of items that contribute to both their effectiveness and ineffectiveness. Below is an item deliberately constructed to contain many item faults that typically are associated with objective test items, especially when they are thoughtlessly or hastily thrown together. How many difficulties can you identify in the example?

Item: Technical advances in computers; (a) encourage communication because fewer people live near each other anymore; (b) increase the cost of living; (c) revolutionized the electronics industry; (d) always occurs rapidly; (e) none of the above

Now revise the item so that it eliminates the difficulties and meets the criteria for an effective item. Your main task will be to construct alternatives, the responses to which will be useful in understanding what the student has learned and in diagnosing gaps in his or her learning. You may want to start with a stem such as the following or rewrite your own. Some phrases that might be helpful in constructing alternatives are provided as a start in writing alternatives. They are not in themselves the alternatives but phrases around which alternatives might be constructed.

Stem: Which of the following is the best explanation of why technical advances in computers led to an increase in communication?

Phrases for Alternatives: grammatical and spelling checks; many word processing programs; numerous communication channels; national and international boundaries eliminated; tools for communication

■ Summary

Objective tests gained popularity because they seemed easy to construct, were consistent from one time period to another, and were less prone to the weakness of scorer bias than, for example, such tests as essay tests. The utility of the scores based on well-constructed objective tests is documented in their ability to predict success in school settings. The SAT scores, for example, predict first-year college success almost as well as the four-year high school grades. The statistical characteristics could be examined meticulously by psychometricians (e.g., Haladyna, Downing, & Rodriguez, 2002). As a result objective tests became the standard formats for widely used standardized tests at the state and national level. Because they seemed to be relatively easy to construct and grade, they also became the favorites of teachers for classroom use.

As with the delivery of subject matter content, it is possible to emphasize the handing over (testing) of subject matter delivered to the student as sheer listings of factual knowledge, rather than teaching or testing of subject matter with understanding (Black & Wiliam, 2006). More recently, as we have shown throughout this chapter, objective formats have been increasingly used for a variety of outcomes related to thinking, comprehension, understanding, and other higher cognitive processes, including problem solving and critical thinking. As importantly, they can be used in conjunction with other forms of assessment as part of an assessment system for providing feedback directed at regulating and managing learning that goes on in the classroom, to be used by teacher and students alike.

Exercise 6.2

Describe a specific objective for a class at the grade level you intend to teach. The objective should be closely linked to a standard in the content area (science, language, reading, social studies, etc.). To make this exercise as useful as possible, keep in mind that the items should be sufficiently useful to you that you will retain them for later use in your teaching, whether in supervised practice or in your position as a teacher. You and your instructor may agree on a modification of this exercise in terms of numbers or orientation of items, on how your work will be evaluated, and on the feedback to be provided for improving the items. The exercise is as follows: Following the principles described in this chapter,

- Write five true-false items each related to different facets of the objective.

- Write five multiple-choice items with four alternatives.
- Write 10 completion items, two for measuring factual information and two each for measuring four different facets of the objective (understanding, problem solving) or contexts (situations) in which the learning would apply.

Exercise 6.3

At a PTA meeting, the parents of one of your students adamantly argue that the multiple-choice tests you are using are not useful for measuring what their child, who consistently earns poor scores on the tests in your class, knows. They believe that the student's poor scores are due to the format of the tests and essentially demand that you desist using any objective tests in the future.

What are some scenarios that would take into account how you would engage them in constructive dialogue regarding the use of these tests? What would you say that would be helpful in understanding the use of these tests and the changes, if any, you might make in your assessment?

■ References

American Educational Research Association (AERA), American Psychological Association (APA), & National Council Measurement in Education (NCME). (1999). *Standards for educational and psychological testing.* Washington, DC: American Educational Research Association.

Black, P., & Wiliam, D. (2006). Developing a theory of formative assessment. In J. Gardner (Ed.), *Assessment and learning* (pp. 81–100). Thousand Oaks, CA: Sage.

Bloom, B. S., Hastings, J. T., & Madaus, G. F. (1971). *Handbook on formative and summative evaluation of student learning.* New York: McGraw-Hill.

Boyd, B. T. (2008). Effects of state tests on classroom test items in mathematics. Retrieved February 17, 2009, from www.accessmy library.com/coms2/browse_JJ.

Burnstein, R. A., & Lederman, L. M. (2007). Wireless keypads: A new classroom technology using enhanced multiple-choice questions. *Physics Education, 24*(3), 189–196.

Burton, S. J., Sudweeks, R. R., Merrill, P. F., & Wood, B. (1991). *How to prepare better multiple-choice items: Guidelines for university faculty.* Brigham Young University Testing Services and the Department of Instructional Science.

Curran, L. T., DeAyala, R. J., & Koch, W. R. (1985). *Developing effective examinations.* Austin, TX: Measurement and Evaluation Center, The University of Texas at Austin.

Downing, S., & Haladyna, T. (Eds.). (2006). *Handbook of test development*. Mahwah, NJ: Lawrence Erlbaum Associates.

Frisbie, D. A., Miranda, D. U., & Baker, K. K. (1993). An evaluation of elementary textbook tests as classroom assessment tools. *Applied Measurement in Education*, 6(1), 21–36.

Haladyna, T. M., Downing, S. M., Rodriguez, & M. C. (2002). A review of multiple-choice item-writing guidelines for classroom assessment. *Applied Measurement in Education*, 15(3), 309–334.

Jacobs, L. C., & Chase, C. I. (1992). *Developing and using tests effectively*. San Francisco: Jossey-Bass.

Janson, D. C. (2002). *Assessment practices of third and fifth grade science teachers: A comparison of the style/format, process, and content of Ohio's Proficiency Tests*. Ph.D. Dissertation, University of Cincinnati (ED 478989).

Mandernach, B. J. (2003). Writing matching items. *Park University Faculty Development Quick Tips*. Retrieved September 10, 2007, from www.park.edu/cetl/quicktips/matching.html#top.

Stobart, G. (2008). *Testing times: The uses and abuses of assessment*. London: Routledge.

Swaffield, S. (Ed.). (2008). *Unlocking assessment*. Oxford: Routledge.

CHAPTER 7

Developing Subjective Tests

I N THIS CHAPTER we focus on short-answer and essay tests. These assessments are often called *subjective tests* because they do not call for predetermined, fixed answers. Rather, they ask the student to write a more extended response in his or her own words. The scoring is subjective in the sense that the score for a particular response may not be obvious; two teachers may even disagree in their scoring. Yet there are definite standards for scoring these tests—and for constructing them, as you will discover.

■ Constructed-Response Tests

The term *subjective* relates primarily to the fact that scoring standards are often related to biases and idiosyncrasies of the scorers. It is more useful to base our classification of these tests on the way they are constructed or the function(s) they serve. Accordingly, a more accurate name for subjective tests is the constructed-response test, which describes the format for responding to the test question or items. Although items in this format are easier to construct than selected-response (or limited-response) items, they should not be constructed casually or hastily, with little regard for purpose, as they might be when a teacher, on the spur of the moment, constructs an item because he or she feels it would be an opportune time to give a test. Essay questions, one of the formats in this category, can and do serve unique functions in measuring higher cognitive processes. However, the findings are that, as typically used, they assess little more than the sheer acquisition of facts in such questions as, "Describe the details of Columbus' voyage to discover America" (Janson, 2002).

From Selection to Construction

The unique feature of the constructed-response tests is, as the term states, that the answers are constructed or generated around a framework prompted by the question, rather than selected, as in the selected- or limited-response formats. Although, as we have noted in the previous chapter, selected-response formats can require the student to use critical thinking processes, students more often treat the selected-response format as though selection requires only the recognition of the correct response from the set of provided alternatives.

There is some validity to the conclusion that if the student can't recognize the correct answer, there is a high probability that that answer can't be generated. However, in answering constructed-response questions, the assumed cognitive processes involve:

1. Interpreting the problem
2. Identifying, from one's knowledge structures, material that is seen to be related to the problem as it has been interpreted
3. Deciding which of the retrieved material is relevant to the answer
4. Selecting the material that answers the problem
5. Organizing it appropriately in terms of the demands made by the problem statement

From the answer based on careful thought, there are many outcomes that the teacher scoring the paper can identify: how well the problem is understood, what material the student considers relevant, the approach taken (which material is retrieved first), the order in which the material is retrieved, any misconceptualizations, the ability to reason and communicate ideas, or other factors affecting the response positively or negatively. With such diagnostic feedback, students are provided with knowledge of their strengths as well as the areas in which they need to improve. They are provided with the knowledge that they can improve as well as ways for improving their learning. Tests that tell what needs to be learned next, what should be reviewed further, or what learning processes require remediation provide students with constructive evidence for keeping them involved and on task in their work.

These considerations support the unique quality of essay tests, that is, their potential for engaging cognitive processes involved in the communication of ideas to an extent that multiple-choice items cannot. They can measure the integration of information to an extent that, if multiple-choice items were to be used, could only be achieved with complex item formats and with a large number of items.

Writing Questions for the Constructed-Response Test

Items of any type, but especially those for a constructed-response test, seem on the surface to be so easy to prepare that teachers forget their possibilities for measuring more complex learning. Keep in mind that selected-response or constructed-response tests need not be limited to measuring recall of facts or conceptual details. Think of writing the questions for a constructed-response test as a statement about the task to be performed by the student, a task in which success depends upon the construction of an answer. The less trustworthy generic prompts *who*, *what*, *when*, *describe*, or *list*, often found in hastily constructed essay tests, limit responses to recall of factual information. In their place you might easily use *why*, *explain*, *compare*, *relate*, *contrast*, *interpret*, *analyze*, *criticize*, and *evaluate* as prompts to evoke complex processing for arriving at relevant answers. To avoid the tendency of students to study by rote memory to the neglect of main ideas and critical thinking, consider writing questions that require analysis of a process, comparison of ideas (perhaps through analogy), construction of a system by integration of its components (e.g., of the heart, valves, arteries, and veins), or relating a principle (e.g., from organic chemistry) to a current concern (e.g., sustainability). Of course, which terms are used depends upon the specific behavior described in the learning outcome to be measured.

A general concern in writing essay questions is the degree to which the content is sampled. Domain sampling is an important attribute related to reliability and content validity of a test. At the time the test is constructed you may wish to consider that the more general type of question—such as this one, based on content in the example under the heading "The Assessment Triangle":

Item: Critically examine linear versus stage theories.

—will take more time to answer than more specific questions, cover only a limited range of understanding taught, and, due to its global generality, be subject to a variety of interpretations, all of which make scoring unreliable. If you use more questions with clearly specified intents and requiring shorter answers, you

have the opportunity of increasing the range of topics taught.
For example:

- What is the major difference between stage and linear theories
  of development?
- Compare a stage theory in intellectual development with a
  stage theory of computer operation.
- Link the concepts of stage and linear theories to descriptions
  of insect and arachnid or crustacean development.

At the time of scoring there are other considerations. Scoring
rubrics for more global questions need to be extended in order to
cover the topics appearing in the variety of answers expected. The
answers to shorter questions are more specific and can be rated
more consistently (e.g., from rater to rater) than the answers to
more global questions. There is also more assurance that underlying processes will be measured with prompts to shorter questions than with prompts to questions in the more open format.
For example, shorter questions can focus on such requirements as
analogical understanding, observing a relation between or among
ideas, or applying content to another topic or problem.

The Assessment Triangle in Assessment by Constructed-Response Measures

Returning to previous discussions of the three-factor triangle,
we turn to its use in understanding formative assessment via
constructed assessment. Here such formats as the essay assessment can effectively capture the student's cognitive representations following a lesson such as the following:

Stage and linear theories of development can be seen in natural
occurrences ranging from the development of insects to cognitive development. Development theorized to occur in *stages*
emphasizes changes in *structures*, as illustrated by the egg, lar-
val, pupal, and adult stages of insect development and by the
Piagetian stages in cognitive ability—sensorimotor, concrete
operations, and formal operations. *Linear* theories, on the other
hand, focus on *accretion* of existing components, for instance,
an insect might be supposed to begin growth as a tiny representation of the adult with changes in size of body parts corresponding to the age of the organism. (A linear theory of a cognitive ability such as intelligence would make similar assumptions; in this case attributes of intelligence such as vocabulary
simply become larger with increases in chronological age).

To some students, this instruction might appear to require sheer memorization of facts. But our intent was to require students to *link* the facts taught to other facts they might know about, to *organize* them around ideas in other content areas (e.g., they might see that the three facets of the memory structure and components of computer memory are analogous), or to *represent* the facts as patterns present in a number of situations (e.g., stage and linear descriptions).

With clear statements of your intent, the corresponding assessments should permit you to identify any discrepancy between the students' perceptions and your intent. The processing required in answering the prompts to constructed-response measures can provide the opportunity to evoke responses related to any level of knowledge representation. The observed responses can then be scored not simply as a number right or wrong but as interpretations about what the student has achieved. A scoring key with accompanying rubrics is essential. Although we will discuss the use of rubrics for reliable scoring of acceptable answers, for the present we suggest that answers to a short-answer or essay test can be scored by using a scoring key comprised of a list of statements, facts, ideas, or processes that should be in the answer to receive credit. Alternative phrasing for answers to receive partial credit might also be listed. The key could be used effectively to achieve consistent results by anyone informed of its use, including students.

Student Participation in Assessment

Involving the students in understanding the purpose of testing is as important in administering constructed-response tests as it is for any other format. Teachers understand that assessments will be used by students to modify their learning practices; students should as well. Under the right tutelage students will understand that assessments not only provide a measure of performance (in terms of a number) but are a way of providing feedback on some aspect of outcomes represented in the standards of the content area, providing specific information about their strengths and weaknesses in learning and what they know. For example, the teacher of social studies needs to know that a student possesses more knowledge than the simple fact that the United States is a democratic government. If students fail to understand the concept of a democratic government, teachers want to know the details of where misunderstandings occur. In such cases they look for details, in responses to questions, of where and when confusions occur or what misconceptions there are about democracies in other countries such as Britain or India. Any questions would be aligned to an examination of the student's conceptual understanding of such characteristics as the branches of government, the separation of power, checks and balances in the separation of power, the differences between parliamentary ministers and presidents, and the type of elections, whether by proportional representation or plurality elections.

By sharing in the construction of tests targeting learning goals and standards and receiving the feedback from these assessments, students, too, can use these tests for diagnostic purposes. They can learn several things:

- Skills or knowledge they need to refine
- Resources to use for extending their knowledge
- Misconceptualizations they possess
- Processes that effectively reach curricular objectives
- Which of their own learning processes need to be monitored
- Repair processes to make effective adjustments in learning and comprehension

As a reminder, as in the use of any assessment, teaching to the test is not an alternative. Rather, if there is a need for preparation for tests, the task may be appropriately accomplished by teaching to the standards of the content area represented.

■ Short-Answer Questions

A short-answer question is typically in open-ended form and solicits a brief response from the writer. The objective is to determine if examinees can formulate an answer in their own words. Because a list of responses is not provided, the short-answer format cuts down on the random guessing that often occurs in true-false and multiple-choice tests. This very basic form of the constructed-response format takes advantage of the potential for measuring responses based on student processing.

Here is a typical short-answer question:

1. What are the three main parts of any behavioral objective? (Answer: conditions under which the behavior will occur, an observable behavior, and a performance criterion.)

Let's look closely at this question. First, there is a correct response, but it is broken up into three parts. Examinees might get some parts correct but not other parts. There may also be some variability in how closely the students' responses match the desired answer. For example, for the second part of the answer, students may write just "behavior" rather than "observable behavior." The teacher then must know whether the word *observable* is important. (It is.) So even within an answer segment, there may be responses that are partially correct. Finally, the answer to the question is based on Robert Mager's (1997) definition of a good behavioral objective. If an examinee had prior exposure to other authors who defined behavioral objectives, there might be other possible correct answers.

Here is another example:

Maria has reported the following clinical symptoms: loss of appetite, inability to sleep, feeling "blue," lethargy followed by periods of high activity, feelings of isolation, and suicidal ideation. According to the *DSM-IV*, what would be her likely clinical diagnosis? Explain your answer.

This question is interesting insofar as there probably is only a *best* answer, not necessarily a *correct* one. The reasoning associated with justifying a particular diagnostic category is probably just as important as identifying the category itself.

Text Box 7.1 offers some tips for writing good short-answer questions.

Text Box 7.1 Guidelines for Writing Short-Answer Questions

1. Ask about important concepts.
2. If the answer is based on an authority, specify that authority ("According to Burstein [2003], what are . . .").
3. If you are looking for a particular type of reasoning, indicate what that is ("Put your response in the context of Plato's five forms of government").
4. Specify the form of the desired response (bullet points, phrases, sentences, or paragraphs) and approximately how long the response should be.
5. Indicate the relative scores for partial responses ("You will receive one point for identifying the protagonist of the story, one point for identifying the antagonist," etc.).
6. Ensure that the relative time spent on short-answer questions is commensurate with the time spent on other test format types. For example, if you have multiple-choice items that take one minute apiece, and each item counts for one point, then a five-point short-answer question should take about five minutes.
7. For items that may receive partial credit, prepare a scoring guide that provides a rationale for the point allocations.

■ Essay Questions

We have explained previously that when the instructional objective is to measure knowledge outcomes such as specific facts or terminology, the objective formats are effective because any one of them, whether true-false, multiple choice, or fill in the blank, is capable of good sampling, representative sampling, and ease in scoring. Further, their psychometric characteristics, such as difficulty or discriminability, can be easily computed for refinement or elimination of alternatives that are not working effectively. In large-scale use, norms can be produced for the general population or for subsamples (disaggregated norms) taking the test. However, when the objective is to provide a measure of higher-level cognitive processes such as those required in reasoning, translating, interpreting, formulating conclusions, or any other process that involves the use of knowledge acquired, then the essay test has distinctive advantages. Typical questions here might be "Evaluate the President's speech in terms of the content in the Joint Chief of Staff's report on the war" or, "Plan the operations that would be involved in setting up a useful household budget in view of limited financial resources."

Student Use of Assessment by Essay Tests

There are several advantages to using essay test questions. Their use should be explained to students to help them develop metacognitions (knowing about knowing) that acquired knowledge is useful beyond its storage and regurgitation and can be transferred to applications in other settings than the immediate classroom.

With this understanding, the use of the essay test format gives the student opportunity to practice using the higher-order skills, to understand that comparison, contrast, translation, and interpretation can and should be applied in making decisions in everyday or career situations—or, simply, that information they have acquired is useful beyond "knowing the textbook."

Teachers often use essay tests because they can be hastily put together at the last moment, but that use is a wasted effort. It ordinarily results in getting measures of objectives that are best suited by use of the objective format. Or, conversely, they can require such complicated answers that scoring them with a sufficient degree of reliability would be virtually impossible.

Moreover, the essay examination is a helpful device in giving students the opportunity to express and communicate ideas, pro and con arguments where appropriate, reasoning involved in answering the question, comparison with other ideas, and creative solutions or applications.

Characteristics of Essay Examinations

When you intend to evaluate how well students reason or when you want to gauge their ability to communicate effectively, then the essay format is a good choice. But it needs to be done carefully, keeping the questions close to the standards they are to represent. The lines of validity (discussed in Chapter 6 on the selected-response formats) apply to both the objective and the subjective formats alike, although they may be more difficult to achieve in the subjective format because of scoring requirements. Nevertheless, with careful planning, both in the construction of the items and in the development and application of scoring keys and rubrics, this difficulty can be reduced. Because of their flexibility, essay questions can more easily be constructed to tap higher-order thinking skills.

There are, however, some disadvantages in using this assessment format:

- Because essays generally require more time to complete than other testing formats, the domains of assessment are likely to be restricted—you will have fewer questions for a specific testing period, so you may not be able to test for everything you might want to assess.
- Students will spend most of their time *writing* an essay. This may not be a bad thing if you are evaluating the ability to communicate effectively, but it may be problematic if you are trying to assess knowledge of broader domains. In fact, it can be argued that writing ability may even mask true abilities in these other domains.
- Scoring of essays is difficult and sometimes unreliable unless one takes great pains to create a comprehensive scoring guide and establish a routine that helps promote consistency of scoring.
- Finally, grading of essays generally takes a long time even when guides and routines are in place.

Preparing Students for Essay Examinations

In preparing students for an essay exam, some instructors provide students a list of potential essay questions and specify that the actual test questions will be drawn from the list. This is essentially a form of test blueprint. This practice is fine as long as all students answer the *same* subset of test questions. Your evaluation will be difficult if you must try to evaluate fairly across all potential questions. Also, there is some evidence that when left to choose a subset of questions, weaker students will choose harder questions and stronger students will choose easier questions. Why? The stronger students are likely to be more metacognitively aware—that is, they know the results of a thorough search of what they know, they can anticipate the consequences of incorrect selections, and they are aware of the relevance of the information they select to the question to be answered. Self-awareness of knowing about knowing is the essence of metacognitive thinking (see an example in Theory to Practice Box 7.3, later in the chapter, illustrating two students' ways of thinking about taking a test and answering questions).

Writing the Question Statement for Essay Formats

The essay format is especially useful for finding out how students organize their ideas in problem solving and decision making. The inadequacy of the essay test for sampling of information and for undependability in scoring has already been mentioned. Avoid vague questions such as "What were the causes of the recession in the early 21st century?" You would be confronted with as many answers as there are students. One student believes the question requires a listing of facts. Another thinks of the strategy of giving a few examples of causes; for example, he or she develops the difficulty encountered by financial institutions lending for subprime mortgages. Another thinks of his or her own circumstances and indicates the rate of unemployment creeping toward 10 percent. A student in other circumstances might indicate something about the collapse of the stock market, in which many high-flying stocks achieved penny-stock status. One student thinks the question deals with the immediate causes, while another thinks it is necessary to go back to the 1990s. Obviously, the papers are virtually impossible to compare. There are as many different answers and perspectives as there are students in the class. Essay questions need clear statements of what is required and should target significant types of understanding and reasoning.

As an example of how the responses to essay or other constructed-response assessments provide data regarding the cognitive processes underlying understanding, thinking, and reasoning, let's return to the baseball-field problem in the previous chapter. Several ways of questioning, each with different outcomes, might be constructed to test the student's ability regarding the use of the Pythagorean principle. Each has its own outcomes. Some illustrations of questioning student understanding of the principle are provided below with a series of increasing question complexity and corresponding processing requirements.

- "What is the Pythagorean formula?" This question would provide an answer that shows essentially whether the student has acquired a fact. It can be answered by simply writing the equation.
- "If the lengths of the side and base of a right triangle are 3 and 4 units, respectively, what would be the length of the hypotenuse?" This question requires recall of the formula as relevant to the problem and shows that the student knows how to substitute the numbers for the symbols but little else. A limitation of this problem is that if the student recalled the simple mnemonic that the sides of a right triangle are 3, 4, and 5, the answer could be obtained without calculation.
- "If you know the two sides of a rectangle are 6 and 9, respectively, what is the length of the diagonal? Explain your answer." This question tells what information the student considers important (rectangles and right angles), the information he or she has organized around the theorem (diagonals and right triangles; *diagonal* and *hypotenuse* are the same), and the ability to relate the theory to solving the problem.
- "If the distance from home base to first base is 60 feet, how far would the third baseman have to throw the ball to first base?" To the unwary student, this question appears to have insufficient information for answering it intelligently. To the more informed student, who approaches the question with understanding of the underlying principles, the answer to this question will demonstrate a number of processes in ability to apply a textbook understanding of the geometry theorem to an external situation: the rotation of the diamond, which looks like a parallelogram rather than a square, so that the apex of the diamond now takes on the form of the corners of the square; the understanding of the relation between squares and parallelograms; the analysis of squares into triangles with phantom hypotenuses; the relation between the diagonal of the square and the hypotenuse of the triangles composing it; the fact that throwing the ball from third to first base is along the line of one of the diagonals; the fact that throwing the ball

from third base to first base would be the same distance as throwing it from home base to second base; and so on.

Guidelines for Writing Essay Questions

The guidelines for writing essay questions (Text Box 7.2) are similar to those for short-answer items. The instructions and scoring system, however, are usually more elaborate for essays than for short-answer tests.

Theory to Practice Box 7.1 shows an example of instructions for an essay exam. Notice that the instructions indicate how the questions are to be treated (with "an organizing mechanism")

Text Box 7.2 Guidelines for Writing Essay Questions

1. Design the questions to tap important concepts, objectives, and standards.
2. Consider the utility of introducing a new context other than the one in which the information was learned.
3. Consider using a different process than the one used in learning. Emphasize understanding rather than sheer memory; for example, "List three conditions . . ." can be answered without understanding. In the place of questions tapping sheer recall, ask questions such as, "What conditions leading to the recession were not considered in the text?"
4. Depending on the background of the student, appropriate questions might begin with "What are three possible explanations for [a case study or outcome]?" "Explain three procedures that would be used effectively to solve the problem [in a vignette, a case study, etc.]?" or "How would an [expert, novice, informed layperson] be expected to change the situation [a current event, an organizational problem, etc.]?" Students with backgrounds in economics might be asked, "How would a financial expert handle this problem compared to an economist?" Or, they might be given a weekly report of the state of the economy and asked, "What additional information would you need to decide how to handle the weakening job market?" or "What reasons are implied for the failure of governmental assistance to financial institutions?"
5. In writing the questions, decide whether your questions are worded such that the answers provide you with the information you intended in terms of meeting your objectives and standards. You might want to see whether the students organized the material in certain ways, whether the students made sound suggestions, whether the students retained a misconceptualization, or whether subscores were feasible or desirable.
6. For a classroom test, make certain that the questions provide answers that will have the potential of providing a guide that is definite enough to be fair and reliable for all students and that the answers have the potential of informing the student just how his or her performance compares with an acceptable response.

Theory to Practice Box 7.1
EXAMPLE OF INSTRUCTIONS FOR AN ESSAY TEST

The following is a vignette that consists of four parts. Each part is worth four points, and four additional points will be awarded for the mechanics of the essay including organization, grammar, syntax, and style. Make sure that you have an integrated response that uses the questions primarily as an organizing mechanism. I'm interested in how well you express yourself as well as your knowledge level. It would be unresponsive to simply answer the questions.

and the kinds of things the instructor is looking for (and what the instructor does not want to see).

Appropriate weighting of the scores is an important element of the process. Notice that the instructions in Theory to Practice Box 7.1 indicate that each part of the essay will have a maximum score of four points, with an additional four points allocated for writing mechanics. In contrast, consider the following example:

Discuss the causes of (5 points) and name three major battles in (5 points) the U.S. Civil War.

This is really two questions—an essay on the causes of the Civil War and a short-answer question about the battles. The point allocation here is suspect. Is listing three major battles of the Civil War equivalent to a detailed account of its causes? Probably not. Also note that the essay topic is ambiguous: Is the test author looking for economic, geographical, or political causes?

Theory to Practice Box 7.2 continues the example from Theory to Practice Box 7.1. Here you see one of the vignettes that might form the heart of this essay test. In this case the vignette

Theory to Practice Box 7.2
EXAMPLE OF INSTRUCTIONS FOR AN ESSAY TEST BASED ON A VIGNETTE

You have always believed in the rights of free speech and assembly, but get concerned when you find out that a so-called hate group is organizing a rally at your high school. Should the group be allowed to meet? Provide a 125-word essay defending your point of view with a particular emphasis on freedoms and responsibilities discussed in the U.S. Constitution and its amendments.

describes a kind of conflict that students do not necessarily face on a daily basis. To write an appropriate essay, students have to recognize that a possible ethical conflict exists and then identify what that conflict might be. To narrow down the task, students are given further instructions about the length of the essay and the points they should emphasize.

■ Evaluating Essays

Scoring Provides Information for Formative Assessment

Different formats of measures provide opportunities for unique observations. Each has its own advantages and some limitations. As we have shown in several places, multiple-choice items can be used at some levels more easily than at others. Essay test items provide the opportunity for measuring complex learning outcomes such as applications and metacognitions. Obviously, if the test item was not made in consideration of the cognitive representation you intended, it is unlikely that the item will be capable of providing the interpretation you want. For example, look at the very interesting reasons given for answering the open-ended question shown in the Theory to Practice Box 7.3.

Had the question been stated in a multiple-choice format, Student A's response would be graded as correct whereas Student B's response have been graded as incorrect or regarded as partially correct. Neither interpretation alone provides the opportunity for interpreting how well the student understands the event. Simply selecting an alternative tells nothing about either the representations students hold of the material they have learned or of their metacognitions regarding how the material was studied, how progress was monitored, how lack of progress toward goals was repaired, or how study strategies were improved, if at all. And, from the teacher's viewpoint, a right-or-wrong score provides little feedback that will help for improving instruction in any arena—student representations, student strategies, or student metacognitions. The interpretation of a score, as a datum point, might be simply that instruction was going all well and good; for sheer memorization of facts such was the case for Student A. However, the interview reveals another important finding—although Student A knows the correct answer, the quality of that knowledge is so poor that it may be described as completely inert knowledge (devoid of understanding or comprehension); rather than facilitating later learning it has the potential for hindering later progress in using that information. By itself, the answer of "yes" or "no" provides little or no guidance, for either the student

Theory to Practice Box 7.3
RETHINKING THE BEST WAYS TO ASSESS COMPETENCE

Consider the following two assessment situations:

Assessment of Student A

Teacher: What was the date of the battle of the Spanish Armada?

Student: 1588. [correct]

Teacher: What can you tell me about what this meant?

Student: Not much. It was one of the dates I memorized for the exam. Want to hear the others?

Assessment of Student B

Teacher: What was the date of the battle of the Spanish Armada?

Student: It must have been around 1590.

Teacher: Why do you say that?

Student: I know the English began to settle in Virginia just after 1600, not sure of the exact date. They wouldn't have dared start overseas explorations if Spain still had control of the seas. It would take a little while to get expeditions organized, so England must have gained naval supremacy somewhere in the late 1500s.

Most people would agree that the second student showed a better understanding of the Age of Colonization than the first, but too many examinations would assign the first student a better score. When assessing knowledge, one needs to understand how the student connects pieces of knowledge to one another. Once this is known, the teacher may want to improve the connections, showing the student how to expand his or her knowledge.

Source: Pellegrino, Chudowsky, & Glaser (2001).

or teacher, regarding the advisability of remedial instruction for Student A. The student might need to learn strategies for understanding, but that possibility would not be offered by the scoring procedure. The student is left with no other alternative than continuing the use of the unfortunate strategy he or she had been using—nothing less than a devastating mistake.

On the other hand, Student B's response reveals the more efficient strategies he or she used for arriving at an answer, what information he or she deemed was important to answering the question, and the knowledge structures engaged in estimating the approximate date of the event. For the teacher, the student's response provides rich information regarding the student's acquisition of the material, how he or she thinks or reasons in finding answers to problems, and how his or her information is organized, all of which goes much beyond the simple acquisition of a single fact.

Scoring Guides: Rubrics and Keys

You can get an idea of the content validity of your items when you reach the point of scoring it. If at the time you constructed the test questions you intended to measure some outcome, you should ask, "Can the answers be scored to represent those outcomes? Can I identify the outcome from the information retrieved by the student in his or her answer? Can I identify the organizational level I intended the student to use? Will I be able to identify the strategies the students use to suggest how students interpreted instruction and instructional assignments? Does the form of the question enable me to identify misconceptualizations that tend to occur in this subject-matter domain?"

Scoring of essays is either accomplished holistically or analytically. A *holistic score* is based on a rating of the global quality of the answer. The score represents an overall decision, often an impression, that this item or paper is an A or B response, for example. In one sense holistic scoring is easy because it requires only a summary judgment. The challenge is in attempting to justify the scores assigned to student answers. When grading a number of papers, the grader may change or shift standards so that the bases for grading the first papers are different from those used in grading the last papers.

Analytic scores are generated either through a comparison with a scoring guide or by using a rubric. Theory to Practice Box 7.4 shows a scoring guide for the essay question in Theory to Practice Box 7.2. The guide specifies all of the key elements of the desired response. It can be further refined by stating how one achieves the threshold for point allocations. For example, you might allocate a certain number of points for recognizing the conflict, for making a decision, and for providing a justification for the decision.

A scoring guide is especially important because of the subjective nature of essay scoring. These devices will help increase the reliability of your scoring and will be useful when you discuss the basis of your scoring with students. Students may not fully appreciate (or agree with) the score they obtain on an essay, but if you have a scoring guide in place, the general

Theory to Practice Box 7.4
EXAMPLE OF A GENERAL RUBRIC FOR SCORING

The basic question here is, to what degree do we support groups or individuals who might overthrow the government or marginalize the citizenry that allows them to assemble in the first place? The writer should be able to identify this conflict or a strongly related one (e.g., tolerating intolerance) and then provide a rationale as whether he or she would support the meeting or not. For example, banning the meeting because of the risk of violence to innocent bystanders may be one rationale. Allowing the meeting, but restricting the time or location so that active conflict can be avoided, is another rationale. A recommendation based only on bureaucratic rules (e.g., the high school does not permit assemblies of any kind) can receive a maximum of 50 percent credit.

perception will be that the process was fairer than if you gave a holistic assessment. It will also have been useful to consider the basis for scoring when you constructed the test (see Text Box 7.2). Students typically want to know what they lost points for, being unsatisfied with a score that represents an overall impression of how you liked their work. A scoring guide will let you point to missing or weak elements of the essay.

Another way of generating an analytic score is by allocating scores with a rubric. You might think of a rubric as a standardized scoring guide, one that might be used across a number of different writing topics, with the potential of specific feedback to the student. The rubric generally includes examples of answers that are rated on a scale of 1 to 3 or 1 to 4. For example, to score answers to a question on the causes of a crime wave, one possibility for a rubric might be:

3 = Causes and their origin are clearly identified. Roots of the causes are related to legal, economic, or governmental concerns.

2 = Causes and origins are identified, but roots of the causes are poorly organized and too general.

1 = Description of causes and origins are either vague or unsupported by evidence. They appear to be generated from general limited experience and impression rather than from sound evidence.

A well-constructed rubric can be used successfully by a variety of raters, including elementary and high school students. In professional situations such as administering a nationwide test, becoming a rater requires training in the rubric's use. When used with care, rubrics result in high levels of interrater reliability (consistency in scoring among different raters).

For grading the dimension of writing, the 6+1 Traits™ scoring rubric (Northwest Educational Research Laboratories, 1999) might be used to grade an extended essay. This rubric encompasses the following traits or writing characteristics: *ideas, organization, voice, word choice, sentence fluency,* and *conventions.* (The "+1" trait of *presentation* is optional). Table 7.1 describes these traits in detail. For each trait the student's performance is rated on a 1-to-5 scale, ranging from "Not Yet" to "Strong." Theory to Practice Box 7.5 displays a sample that would rate a score of 3 ("Developing") on all the traits.

Grading Tips

One of the big concerns in evaluating essay responses centers on maintaining high reliability in scoring. There are a few steps that can help in this regard:

1. Grade each student's answer to a particular question before proceeding to the next question. In this way, you can more easily monitor any drift that might be present in the way you are grading. Drift may manifest itself in a number of ways. You may start off grading in a lenient fashion, but as you continue through the stack of papers, you unconsciously raise the bar in the way you assign scores. The opposite may also occur—you may start off grading responses in strict accord with some preconceived answer, but as you proceed in grading, you become more lenient. The trick here is to be able to monitor any drift in the bases for scoring, a not-uncommon occurrence.

2. Students' identities should remain anonymous while the test is being graded. As raters we often like to think that we are fair and impartial while grading, but in fact we are all prone to some sort of halo bias. That is, our perceptions of how students perform on one aspect of class performance may influence our expectations on some other dimension of performance—for instance, "Pedro's paper isn't a really good answer. But, he is a good student. Maybe he had an off day. I'll give him the benefit of the doubt and give him a few more points. He deserves a higher score. I'll add a few points to his grade." It would not be unusual to reason that a student who is articulate in class discussions might also express that facility in a written essay. The bias created in such thinking

Table 7.1. The 6+1 Traits™ Defined

Trait	Definition
Ideas	*The Ideas are the heart of the message, the content of the piece, the main theme, together with all the details that enrich and develop that theme.* The ideas are strong when the message is clear, not garbled. The writer chooses details that are interesting, important, and informative—often the kinds of details the reader would not normally anticipate or predict. Successful writers do not tell readers things they already know; e.g., "It was a sunny day, and the sky was blue, the clouds were fluffy white. . . ." They notice what others overlook, seek out the extraordinary, the unusual, the bits and pieces of life that others might not see.
Organization	*Organization is the internal structure of a piece of writing, the thread of central meaning, the pattern, so long as it fits the central idea.* Organizational structure can be based on comparison-contrast, deductive logic, point-by-point analysis, development of a central theme, chronological history of an event, or any of a dozen other identifiable patterns. When the organization is strong, the piece begins meaningfully and creates in the reader a sense of anticipation that is, ultimately, systematically fulfilled. Events proceed logically; information is given to the reader in the right doses at the right times so that the reader never loses interest. Connections are strong, which is another way of saying that bridges from one idea to the next hold up. The piece closes with a sense of resolution, tying up loose ends, bringing things to closure, answering important questions, while still leaving the reader something to think about.
Voice	*The Voice is the writer coming through the words, the sense that a real person is speaking to us and cares about the message.* It is the heart and soul of the writing, the magic, the wit, the feeling, the life and breath. When the writer is engaged personally with the topic, he or she imparts a personal tone and flavor to the piece that is unmistakably his or hers alone. And it is that individual something—different from the mark of all other writers—that we call voice.
Word Choice	*Word Choice is the use of rich, colorful, precise language that communicates not just in a functional way, but in a way that moves and enlightens the reader.* In good descriptive writing, strong word choice clarifies and expands ideas. In persuasive writing, careful word choice moves the reader to a new vision of things. Strong word choice is characterized not so much by an exceptional vocabulary that impresses the reader, but more by the skill to use everyday words well.
Sentence Fluency	*Sentence Fluency is the rhythm and flow of the language, the sound of word patterns, the way in which the writing plays to the ear, not just to the eye.* How does it sound when read aloud? That's the test. Fluent writing has cadence, power, rhythm, and movement. It is free of awkward word patterns that slow the reader's progress. Sentences vary in length and style and are so well crafted that the writer moves through the piece with ease.
Conventions	*Conventions are the mechanical correctness of the piece—spelling, grammar and usage, paragraphing (indenting at the appropriate spots), use of capitals, and*

(continued)

Table 7.1. (*continued*)

Trait	Definition
	punctuation. Writing that is strong in conventions has been proofread and edited with care. Handwriting and neatness are not part of this trait. Since this trait has so many pieces to it, it's almost a holistic trait within an analytic system. As you assess a piece for convention, ask yourself: "How much work would a copy editor need to do to prepare the piece for publication?" This will keep all of the elements in conventions equally in play. Conventions is the only trait where we make specific grade level accommodations.
Presentation	*Presentation combines both visual and verbal elements. It is the way we "exhibit" our message on paper.* Even if our ideas, words, and sentences are vivid, precise, and well constructed, the piece will not be inviting to read unless the guidelines of presentation are present. Think about examples of text and presentation in your environment. Which signs and billboards attract your attention? Why do you reach for one CD over another? All great writers are aware of the necessity of presentation, particularly technical writers who must include graphs, maps, and visual instructions along with their text.

Source: Northwest Educational Research Labs (Northwest Educational Research Laboratories, 1999).

Theory to Practice Box 7.5
AN EXAMPLE OF A PAPER WRITTEN AT THE "3" LEVEL ACROSS ALL TRAITS OF THE 6+1 TRAITS™ RUBRIC

Paper Title: My Best Thing

Grade: Middle School (6–8)

My Best Thing:
The thing I am best at is science. And the way I learned it is through hard work, concentration, studing, and the ability to think hard. It takes a lot of reserch and observation to truly make it stay in your mind. You also have to be patient for this kind of activity, because no one gets an experiment right on the first time. So that means test after test until you get it right. When you get into science you have got to keep the bad things in mind such as: all the stress, taking your job home, the sleepless nights, and the chances of dying from your own experiment. I think that science is the best job field to get into, because it is high paying, interesting and filled with entertainment. In this job field there is always something new to do. One day I'll be in the science field, and I'll be famous.

Source: Northwest Regional Educational Laboratory, www.nwrel.org/assessment/scoring practice.php?odelay=3&d=1&search=1&t=0&s=3&g=5&p=10.

is the difference between that expectation and what actually occurs. In the same vein, you should keep scores of answers to previously read items out of sight. The purpose here is to make certain that the rater is rating the papers on the basis of clearly specified criteria and is not influenced by the answers of other students in scoring any given paper.

3. On occasion you may get a response that is simply off target. This may occur for either legitimate or illegitimate reasons; perhaps the question was misinterpreted, or perhaps the student is trying to bluff. You should think about a policy (e.g., retaking the examination, using a follow-up interview, or a similar procedure) for addressing legitimately off-target incorrect, irrelevant, or in some cases, illegible answers.

4. Students like feedback, but only up to a point. Our discussions with students suggest that a comprehensive markup (corrective marginal comments) of the essay is probably counterproductive. Rather, highlight the first and second occurrence of a problem and indicate that it repeats itself throughout the essay. Also consider highlighting something that was well done. In a short summary at the end of the essay, indicate patterns of expression that you liked or didn't like. Suggest an alternative. If points were deducted because the response did not match the scoring guide or ideal answer, then refer to the discrepancy in a short but descriptive sentence.

Exercise 7.1: Write An Essay Question

Below are some examples, taken from a more extensive list, of expectations (standards) in the use of English by nonnative speakers of English as a result of instruction. The list provides (a) descriptors of the way the standard is represented in student learning, and (b) the progress indicators, that is, the tasks that students might perform to enable observation of the progress they have made.

Task

Using the principles described in the section on essays, write a well-constructed essay item that will reflect the progress the ELL students have made in being able to use the English language in your subject matter area. (Your instructor may choose to assign you the task of constructing two sets of items: a global or holistic item *and* a series of three items that would measure specific facets represented in the global item. The set of three items should be expected to take the student the same amount of time to answer as would the global item.) Restrict your question to the standard, descriptors, and indicators presented below (under "The Framework") for your guidance. Your question will be based on selected items from the list, not from all of the items.

The Framework
Standard
- To use English language by English language users with sufficient skill to achieve academically in all content areas.
- Students will use English to obtain, process, construct, and provide subject-matter information in spoken and written form.

Descriptors
- Listening to, speaking, reading, and writing about subject-matter information.
- Retelling information, knowing, using, and understanding the language of the technical area (content area).
- Generating and asking questions.
- Gathering information, selecting, connecting, and explaining information.
- Formulating and asking questions.

Sample of Potentially Useful Progress Indicators
- *Identify* and associate written symbols with words, such as the symbol for numbers, the compass directional symbols, chemical symbols, or symbols on a computer toolbar with appropriate technical words.
- Read a story and *relate* the sequence of events that took place to another person according to the genre represented (e.g., a detective story, historical sequence, logical sequence).
- *Explain* change (e.g., developmental process, seasonal changes, characters in literature, genetic changes).
- *Edit and revise* written assignments.
- *Use contextual cues.*
- *Consult* resources and *locate* reference materials for studying a concept (e.g., conservation or sustainability).

Abstracted from Elmore, R. F. & Rothman, R. (Eds.). (1999). *Testing, teaching, and learning: A guide for states and school districts* (p. 38, Figure 3-2, Standards and an annotated classroom vignette illustrating English as a second language standards for grades pre-K-3). Washington, DC: National Academy Press.

■ Summary

Essay tests have an important place in the overall measurement of educational achievement. They are part of a balanced assessment in satisfying the need for attainment of performance objectives (Arter & McTighe, 2001). With reliable judgments of response quality, essay tests provide ways of measuring behaviors related to understanding, comprehension, and application, going beyond the simple rote memorization and recognition of inert knowledge.

Essay tests are subjective mainly in the sense that questions can be variously interpreted by students (but so can multiple-choice stems). More importantly, the major source of subjectivity is the effect of rater bias in scoring, sometimes to the extent that an answer rated as excellent by one teacher might be rated as a failure by another teacher.

■ References

Arter, J., & McTighe, J. (2001). *Scoring rubrics in the classroom.* Thousand Oaks, CA: Corwin Press.

Elmore, R. E., & Rothman, R. (1999). *Testing, teaching, and learning: A guide for states and school districts.* Washington, DC: National Academy Press.

Janson, D. C. (2002). *Assessment practices of third and fifth grade science teachers: A comparison to the style/format, process, and content of Ohio's Proficiency Tests.* Ph.D. Dissertation, University of Cincinnati (ED 478989).

Mager, R. F. (1997). *Preparing instructional objectives* (3rd ed.). Atlanta, GA: The Center for Effective Performance.

Northwest Educational Research Laboratories (1999). 6+1 traits of writing rubric. Retrieved December, 1999, from www.nwrel.org/eval/pdfs/6plus1traits.pdf.

Pelligrino, J. W., Chudowsky, N., & Glaser, R. (2001). *Knowing what students know: The science and design of educational assessment.* Washington, DC: National Academy Press.

CHAPTER 8

Selecting Standardized Tests

I N LEARNING ABOUT the construction of tests you now understand much about how good tests are constructed and the purposes to which test results can be applied. For most assessment activities in the classroom, and for periodic assessments related to instructional feedback for both teacher and students, well-constructed teacher-made tests will be the way to go. However, there will be situations where existing formal measures, tests, or item banks are available for specialized purposes. By using them with little or no modifications, you will be able to produce assessments that become a part of an assessment system that meets both your needs and the needs of the broader educational community.

Your need to understand that knowing about the selection of tests is an essential preparation in classroom instruction. Teachers, at one time or another, will be involved at some level in test selection for planning interventions, improving curricula, responding to community inquiries, or communicating outcomes related to accountability issues. Of course, you may also select them independently of others for specific purposes in your classroom—to understand how student achievement compares with externally constructed tests based on professional standards or when you want to learn about students' processing, including their misconceptualizations, learning strategies, or working styles. Such information has important implications for instructional improvement. More frequently, however, you will be working cooperatively with other professionals, such as educational counselors or school psychologists, in selecting tests to aid planning the placement of students, interventions, or remedial programs. You will certainly need to understand tests selected by others such as policy makers who have jurisdiction over statewide tests or tests dictated by legislation, tests that are summative evaluations of student progress and are used for accountability. Finally, you can count on the fact that parents of your students will ask you to provide an interpretation of a test that you may know little about.

■ Objectives

Your primary objective in learning about the selection of tests is to learn:

- The *process* of selecting formal or standardized tests
- The *advantages* and *limitations* in using whatever test you have selected
- The use of any test, whether formal or informal, whether teacher-made or commercial, as a facet of a *system of assessment* rather than the simple addition of another test to the armamentarium of tests used by a school
- How the standardized test fits in with the overall assessment process
- The resources available for making decisions about the right test to use for achieving instructional and educational goals
- The unique characteristics of scoring and norming used in standardized tests, steps ordinarily done by external sources such as commercial companies and increasingly with the use of technology
- Scoring of tests that require special procedures such as the use of rubrics in scoring of the composition or other performance outcomes measured by sections of the test—procedures for authentic assessments which are increasingly being demanded by the school and community
- Limits on the way test results can be used; the inferences and the implications for educational purposes including instruction, placement of students in special classes, the design of interventions, and similar purposes
- How the results are disseminated at various levels by the administrator of tests that serve to comply with policy; explanations and interpretations must be communicated to the general public, parents, and students in meaningful ways
- Engagement of students in taking the test and understanding the outcomes for themselves
- What test selections and their results imply for instruction, intervention, and the development of future testing plans

It is critical for teachers to know and understand the bases for any choice or use of standardized tests. This chapter is devoted to the bases by which measures potentially useful to you are identified and chosen. They are important for helping you make decisions in the process of selecting tests, should you be engaged directly in that process. Knowing the bases of test selection will help you understand and evaluate the wisdom of choices made by others such as district or state educational office who may have mandated the use of a test for accountability purposes. Understanding the bases for selecting a test is also part of a knowledgeable explanation of assessment outcomes and interpretation that might be communicated to the community (parents, boards of education, school administrators). You will see that the principles guiding the development and use of standardized tests are essentially the same as those you would consider, perhaps somewhat more flexibly, in the development and use of classroom tests. As such they are an extension of the principles of classroom assessment in practice, as you can see from the review in Text Box 8.1.

The use of standardized testing resources should make your life easier for most phases of assessment such as the comparison of your class's performance with others similar to yours that are represented in disaggregated norms. However, this will be true only if the resources are readily identifiable, accessible, and align well with the learning objectives for the segment that you are teaching.

The varieties of available formal assessment measures serve many purposes. They are used by school psychologists and special education teachers to diagnose students with learning disabilities or to determine placement in special classes. They are used for summative evaluations in making policy decisions regarding accountability. Although some standardized tests must be administered by certified school personnel, the classroom teacher is certain to be involved at some point in selecting and administering the tests, interpreting the results, and using the results in planning curricular activities and programs for individual students.

■ Principles for Selecting Standardized Tests

The steps in selecting and using formal standardized tests are similar to those employed in determining the adequacy of any measure. You can see that they parallel the objectives outlined above. They are:

- Identify the purpose for using the test.
- Identify the adequacy of the test for the purpose intended.
- Know the test's relation to other tests.

Text Box 8.1 A Review of the Basics Relevant to Test Selection

The principles discussed up to this point in the text come together in selecting tests to help you to use tests wisely and responsibly. The technical knowledge obtained through your education and professional development is also an essential element in the process. As you investigate the extent to which a test is relevant for your purposes, you will become knowledgeable and conversant through reviews, manuals, and observations about the following basic aspects of a test in order for you to become proficient in test selection or use:

• *Reliability of Test Results.* You have come across the term *reliability* on a number of occasions. It is the extent to which the test yields consistent (similar) results on separate occasions. An estimate of test reliability might be obtained by (a) correlating test scores at separate times (called test-retest); (b) by correlating one part of the test with another (such as a score based on all even items with a score based on all odd-numbered items, called internal consistency); or (c) by correlating two forms of a test (called parallel or equivalent forms). In the case of an essay test scored by two different raters, the reliability would be obtained by correlating the raters' scores (called interrater reliability). Which method is used to calculate and estimate reliability depends on the purpose for which the test is used.

• *Validity of Test Results.* Does the test measure what it is intended to measure? Look for evidence that supports whatever interpretation is intended. For instance, is it to be interpreted as a measure of progress? As a summative measure of the student's status? As a measure of the school's achievement? As a predictor for success in college? As a characteristic of how well a test achieves its goals, recognize that it may have different validity for different purposes. For example, the test may be highly predictive of reading ability, but may have less predictability for first-year grades in college. Look for evidence of potential differences in validity. The validity of a test for instructional purposes needs to be understood in terms of its alignment to objectives, whether state standards, professional content area standards, or classroom instructional objectives.

• *Scores for Test Results.* Know and identify the basic differences between different kinds of scores. Only tests that accurately report the types of scores and use accurate scoring procedures should be used. You may recall, for example, our earlier concern with the terms *norm-referenced* and *criterion-referenced*; they refer to differences in the ways the scores were interpreted, not to differences in tests. Evidence for these differences may be found in reviews. When reviewing test characteristics, ask yourself whether the scores are criterion- or norm-referenced and how the interpretations are related to the intended use of the test. You will find other kinds of scores referred to in evaluative reports of tests or in test manuals, including *part* scores; scores based on the *kinds* of content (facts, concepts, problem solving); and scores based on *processes*—for example, in reading you might find scores related to reading rate, recall, or comprehension. In other situations you will need to discriminate among raw scores, percentage correct, percentile scores, and so on.

- *Variability of Test Results.* You have come across the idea of incidental or random influences on test results in journalistic reports of poll results. For example, a TV journalist might say something like the following, "In a recent poll, 40 percent of one group responded favorably while 43 percent of another group responded favorably; as such, the difference was too close to say that one group was more favorably disposed than the other." The idea here is that you don't want test results to vary too much, but some variability is to be expected due to extenuating circumstances and must be considered when interpreting the scores. Such differences can occur because of influences unrelated to the "true" achievement or attitudes of the student; these may include differences due to motivation, interpretations of the questions, or perspectives. These factors contribute to *measurement errors* or *error of measurement*; estimations of the error of measurement are reported in reviews and should be considered when interpreting scores to support informed decisions.

- *Norms for Test Results.* Examine carefully the way the test scores were normed. You should be able to determine from the reviews whether a norm group for comparing with the local group is available or defensible for the appropriate interpretation of scores. For example, how large were the samples of respondents? Were the norms based on respondents from a diversity of settings (schools, districts, and so on) or from one school or setting? If you are to make comparisons with your classes, how representative of your class or school was the sample from the standpoints of their grade level, the instruction they might have received, the characteristics of your school district, and so on. On occasion you might find normative data for the performance of all students who took the test (called aggregated scores) or you might find the normative data separated according to specific groups such as areas of the country, state, ethnicity, grade level, and so on (called disaggregated scores).

- Make reasonable interpretations of the test, limiting your interpretations to the data provided by the test norms and test characteristics.

As you follow these steps, you should use whatever sources are available for learning about a test's development, the ways it has been used, and its desirable and undesirable characteristics. Later in this chapter we describe major sources of such information. By pulling together all the available facts, you should be able to answer questions like the following:

- *For what purposes was the test designed?* Look for clear evidence of what the test is intended to accomplish, for instance, testing of persons with disabilities; program evaluation; or testing of educational progress for purposes of accountability.

- *Ask yourself how well the test's aims suit your own purposes.* As an initial caveat do not depend upon the title (name) given to the test. A test cannot be selected solely on the name given to it. For example, a test may be given the title "A Test of Reading." It is necessary to look for other evidence regarding exactly what is being measured. The specific items could be inspected: Do the items deal with vocabulary? With simple comprehension? With comprehension requiring inferences? Do they deal with simple recall of words in a passage, or with recall of inferences? and so on. Important in the selection of tests are such reviews as those in the *Mental Measurements Yearbook*, which we describe later in this chapter. The *Yearbook* provides expert reviews based on evidence regarding the quality of the test (its psychometric characteristics) as well as the appropriate uses of the tests.

- *What exactly should the test do?* Look for evidence regarding the adequacy of the test for diagnosing strengths or weaknesses, identifying some important characteristic such as anxiety or motivation, differentiating the performance of some group relative to another, conveying data to reflect student progress in achievement—all, of course, depending on what your purposes are.

- *What particular outcomes are being measured by the test?* The test *review* or *manual* will specify what is being measured, along with supporting validity data. Some specific measures that are available will be found under the topics of literacy (use of language reception as in reading or language production as in speaking), problem solving (in everyday situations or in specific content areas like math), perceptual-motor skills, achievement (in specified subject-matter areas), learning styles and strategies, and emotional-motivational tendencies (anxiety, self-esteem, classroom motivation).

- *What is the typical response type and mode used in the test?* Characteristically, responses will be specified as objective or essay; verbal or nonverbal; oral or written. The test taker's response might be as simple as a check mark or as complex as an essay.

- *How is the test administered?* Tests may be administered individually or in groups. Depending on assumptions about language ability, the test may be delivered in oral or written form, and it may be either timed or self-paced. The conditions vary with the test, and they are important because they affect the norms. If, for example, you wanted to extend your class's test-taking time, you would want to know whether the test was normed on the basis of time restrictions.

- *In what form is the score?* You may receive raw scores, standard scores, or percentiles; you may get a total score for each student or a collection of subscores.
- *What are the norms used in standardization?* Norms describe the populations against which performances are judged. They may include all the students who ever took the test (aggregated norms) or they may be subgroups (disaggregated norms) based on chronological age, grade level, district (local, state, or national), or demographic characteristics (socioeconomic status, gender, cultural diversity, ethnicity, linguistic diversity, first and second language). In addition to looking for limiting characteristics of the normative population, look for the recency of norming. The importance of this criterion is supported in Theory to Practice Box 8.1, which includes illustrations of how considerations of prior experience in diverse environments affect the utility of test results.
- *How adequate are the psychometric characteristics of the test?* Look for evidence of adequate reliability (test-retest stability; homogeneity of items and internal consistency; inter-rater agreement). Look for the bases of the test's claim to the validity of test scores. You may want to refer back to Text Box 8.1 for a review of the characteristics of well-constructed tests.
- *What do users or reviewers say about the test's adequacy and usefulness?* Look for reviewers' comments on the test's fairness, the adequacy of its revisions, its supporting documentation, and its overall strengths and weaknesses.

Remember that, however impressive a test may look outwardly, single scores alone should not be used for making sweeping decisions about individuals—for example, in such decisions as those involved in grade retention, placement in special classes, or graduation. The American Psychological Association's (2001) statement on test policy includes the following caution:

> Any decision about a student's continued education, such as retention, tracking, or graduation, should not be based on the results of a single test, but should include other relevant and valid information.

Virtually any test should be part of system in which it is supplemented by other sources of information. Standardized

Theory to Practice Box 8.1
EXAMPLE OF HOW PRIOR EXPERIENCES AFFECT STANDARDIZED TESTS RESULTS

A test constructed in one era might not be appropriately used in another era without being revised. Tests frequently become outmoded because of changes in the experiences that affect the scores of respondents, when test items are based on those experiences. Such differences are due to experiences in unique populations (cohorts) or subgroups based on locality, culture, ethnicity, or other variables. Students from a culture that is aligned with the instruction and assessment will perform more adequately on the assessment than students from another culture not aligned with that in which the instruction and assessment are based. One such examination was a recent revision of the widely used Stanford Binet Intelligence Test, which had been invented in the early part of the 20th century, but in which some of the items became out of date late in the century.

The cultural adequacy of a test might be invalidated due to the poor representation of the norms that are used for interpretation of the scores. For example, norms based on student performance in one locality, such as an urban area, might not be useful for interpreting student performance in another locality, such as a rural area. Similarly, a test might be invalidated because the test is biased (unfair) to one group or another due to cultural, age, or other differences. Scores based on responses to items in which the characteristics of groups were ignored can lead to discrepancies in interpretations regarding achievement level of students in a program. You can see, for example, that groups composed of your counterparts in the prespace era (older cohort) undoubtedly had different definitions than you have had (recent cohorts). Your cohort has had considerable everyday experiences with such terms as *countdown*, *rap*, *e-mail*, *spacewalk*, *cool*, *word processor*, *digital*, *gigabyte*, and *nanosecond*. Put these content-specific terms into standardized test items and a younger cohort will probably perform well on them. A much older cohort will undoubtedly have more difficulty with the items; their aggregate norms for scores are certain to be much lower. On the other hand, the older cohort will have more knowledge about such events as the pop music, economics, and politics associated with their day; their understanding of *swing music*, *pony express*, *depression*, *isolationism*, *gold standard*, or *typewriter* (even possibly substituting *ram* for *RAM*) will undoubtedly be richly associated with meanings that will seem to evade the younger cohort. Thus, an item in which the response was based on the meaning of these terms might not only be elusive to younger cohorts, but might actually be unknown to them. Each cohort has a better working knowledge of the terms associated with their respective experiences in understanding events. As a result, their scores of the two cohorts would differ considerably on any items in which these terms and their contexts were central. The lesson to be learned here for the selection of tests is that the available norms have to be carefully evaluated for their value in making interpretations of the scores obtained.

tests are typically developed for assessing behavioral outcomes beyond the local classroom, for instance, they may have been developed out of standards agreed upon by the profession, irrespective of local needs. Having been developed for specific purposes, they are likely to be based on different content than that assigned and studied in a particular class, so they must be scrutinized carefully from several vantage points (grade level, norms, age group, locality) before they are considered for grading purposes, if at all.

The procedures described are reflections of a more formal statement of the qualities to look for in selecting tests, as summarized by the American Psychological Association. A summary of the portion of that statement dealing with test selection is presented in Text Box 8.2.

Text Box 8.2 Considerations in Selection of Tests

Test users should select tests that meet the intended purpose and that are appropriate for the intended test takers.

1. Define the purpose for testing, the content and skills to be tested, and the intended test takers. Select and use the most appropriate test based on a thorough review of available information.
2. Review and select tests based on the appropriateness of test content, skills tested, and content coverage for the intended purpose of testing.
3. Review materials provided by test developers and select tests for which clear, accurate, and complete information is provided.
4. Select tests through a process that includes persons with appropriate knowledge, skills, and training.
5. Evaluate evidence of the technical quality of the test provided by the test developer and any independent reviewers.
6. Evaluate representative samples of test questions or practice tests, directions, answer sheets, manuals, and score reports before selecting a test.
7. Evaluate procedures and materials used by test developers, as well as the resulting test, to ensure that potentially offensive content or language is avoided.
8. Select tests with appropriately modified forms or administration procedures for test takers with disabilities who need special accommodations.
9. Evaluate the available evidence on the performance of test takers of diverse subgroups. Determine to the extent feasible which performance differences may have been caused by factors unrelated to the skills being assessed.

Source: Adapted from Joint Committee on Testing Practices (2007).

■ Sources to Guide Selection of Standardized Tests

This rest of this chapter is devoted to sources of assessment information that can be used to help as you develop lesson plans and as you serve on committees that deal with educational decisions, as you certainly will in such tasks as developing Individual Education Plans (IEPs) for special education students under provisions of inclusion in general classes.

Initially, we will present examples of resources that you can consult to learn more about a test, a type of test, or a testing topic. Then we present the current standards by which tests are judged. The hope is that you will not only know where to go to get test information, but also be able to judge the quality of a test based on formal testing parameters such as validity and reliability. Finally, we want to reiterate the caveat that merely because a test is printed or has a label attached to it, it is not automatically a valid measure.

■ Buros Mental Measurements Yearbook and Tests in Print

The Mental Measurements Yearbook (MMY) is an important resource for learning about virtually every test that has been published. The volumes are published by the Buros Institute of Mental Measurements at the University of Nebraska–Lincoln and are a most extensive source of information about available formal tests. The *MMY* contains reviews and descriptions of commercially published tests in the English language. Though not published annually, it is updated every few years.

The *MMY* series is cumulative; later volumes do not replace earlier ones. An adjunct document, *Tests in Print (TIP)*, consists of descriptive listings, without reviews, of commercially published tests in print. *TIP* is also a comprehensive document where the contents of previously published *Mental Measurements Yearbooks* are indexed.

There are three basic ways to search for an appropriate test in *MMY*. You can search by (a) the *title* of the test (such as Slosson Test of Reading Readiness); (b) the *type* or category of test content that you need (for instance, reading); or (c) an *author's name*. In this last category, you can find the author of (a) a test, (b) a review, or (c) a referenced article in which the test is discussed. Each of these searches is described in more detail below.

Text Box 8.3 Guiding Selection of Standardized Tests: Using Test Reviews

Specialized personnel, teacher-educators, and community members who are qualified users of tests understand the principles of measurement; the derivation of scores and norms; the conduct of the administration of the test according to prescribed procedures; the underlying necessities for accurate scoring; the informed interpretation of test scores for individuals and groups; and the knowledgeable and productive applications of the results.

The reviews that you will find in the Buros *Mental Measurements Yearbook* or in technical journals will contain much of that information. Nevertheless, reviews will vary in the extent to which information about these characteristics appear. Although the list below provides some information that will appear in such reviews, some may add or modify the information as required. To help you use the reviews effectively the checklist will help you avoid overlooking any important information that might be contained in the review and identify information that might be absent in the review.

Information Related to Test Administration

Test administration necessarily requires following standard procedures so that the test is used in the manner specified by the test developers. Sometimes this requires qualified users certified to administer the tests, for example, those professional educators trained in administering the Stanford Binet Intelligence test. In many instances, test administrators are expected to ensure that test takers work within conditions that maximize opportunity for optimum performance. All who are involved in the various aspects of selecting tests will give attention to:

- The extent to which test administration is conducted by informed personnel who are adequately trained in the standard testing procedures
- The extent to which test administrators follow the instructions in the test manual; demonstrate verbal clarity; use verbatim directions; adhere to verbatim directions; follow exact sequence and timing; and use materials that are identical to those specified by the test publisher
- The extent to which reports are made of factors that may invalidate test performance and results, such as deviations from prescribed test administration procedures, including information on problems, irregularities, and accommodations that may have occurred

Information Related to Test Scoring

It may appear on the surface that test scores are absolute. However, even the most objective scores are subject to errors. For example, there can be careless construction of

(continued)

Text Box 8.3 *(Continued)*

scoring keys. If scored by hand there can be errors in reading the answers. If scored by machine, the answers may not have been recorded by the proper pencils. Essays can be subject to greater bias if scored without rubrics than with rubrics. But rubrics are also subject to error if they do not carefully define the criteria required for different levels of performance. Accurate measurement necessitates adequate procedures for scoring the responses of test takers. Examine reviews for the information they provide on:

- The provision, implementation and monitoring of standard scoring procedures
- The presence of rubrics that clearly specify the criteria for scoring; scoring consistency should be constantly monitored
- How scores can be defended when they are challenged for quality concerns by end users

Information Related to the Norms

The characteristics of those taking the test—those students' scores on which the norms were based—will help determine whether the characteristics of the test norms are appropriate for the intended audience and are of sufficient technical quality for the purpose at hand. Some areas to consider include:

- What were the test takers like? Technical information should be reviewed to determine if the test characteristics are appropriate for the test taker (e.g., age, grade level, language, cultural background).
- Were accommodations employed for special groups? If so, what modifications were made? Were individuals with disabilities considered? How? For instance, were alternative measures found and used? Were accommodations in test-taking procedures employed? How did any change in procedure affect interpretations?
- Were characteristics related to test fairness considered? Care should be taken to make certain that the test is fair, that is, that the test does not bias the results for special-needs students. Some characteristics of situations may be unrelated (e.g., age, ethnic background, existence of cheating) to what is being measured but nevertheless may bias results so that they convey invalid information. In instructional situation, fairness also relates to whether or not the student has had an opportunity to learn or has had unequal availability of test-preparation programs.

Information Related to Test Interpretation

Whatever role one might play in the use of standardized tests, they must be interpreted responsibly. Interpretation requires knowledge about and experience with the test, the scores, and the decisions to be made. Interpretation of scores on any test should not take place without a thorough knowledge of the technical aspects of the test, the test results, and their limitations. Many factors can impact the valid and useful interpretations of test scores. Reviews will contain some consideration of these factors, which can be grouped into several categories including test characteristics, knowledge of the respondents (test takers), and the situations in which the test is given.

- *The Test and Its Characteristics.* The factors described in Text Box 8.1 are important when interpreting test results. These basic characteristics of a test should be known, as should the way each impacts the scores and the interpretation of test results.
- *The Characteristics of the Test Takers.* We have touched on the test taker in a number of sections of this book as well as in the foregoing sections of this Text Box. If you know that the test requires special interpretation for special needs or similar requirements, then look in the review for group memberships (different curricula, special needs, different aims) and how that membership may impact the results of the test. It is a critical factor in the interpretation of test results to know that the test norms are based on vocational students rather than college-oriented students; that they are based on ethnic groups with a language other than English as their first language rather than one in which English is the first language; or that the test is a measure of a content-area standard rather than a local standard. Specifically, you will want to interpret test results by the evidence regarding the impact of gender, age, ethnicity, race, socioeconomic status, and so forth.
- *The Characteristics of the Situation.* This feature takes into account that the results on any test will be uniquely affected by the local context. Test results will reflect the local instructional program, opportunity to learn, quality of the educational program, work and home environment, and other factors. Find as much information about the test as possible to assist you in understanding the limitations in interpreting test results. For example, a test that is not aligned to curriculum standards and how those standards are taught in the classroom will likely provide limited useful information or, at the least, will limit the extent to which they can be interpreted correctly.

Information about Communicating Test Results

Informed communication of test results rests on a foundation of understanding the basics of measurement and assessment, an informed foundation of test construction and interpretation, and an understanding of a particular test selected or used. This foundation can be provided in part by the test manual and supplemented by such resources as the Buros *Mental Measurements Yearbook* or by reviews of tests in professional and technical journals.

Ultimately, test results and their interpretations must be conveyed in a language that end users, whether students, parents, teachers, community members, legislators,

(*continued*)

Text Box 8.3 (Continued)

or the general public can understand. The language used is a key element in helping others understand the meaning of the test results. It is essential, then, in the selection of tests to make certain that the test selected is sufficiently well understood that it can be interpreted in a manner that will be useful to all concerned. Some supplementation with background information can help explain the results with cautions about misinterpretations. Reviews will help the test user make decisions about the extent to which the communication can be made by indicating how the test results can be and should not be interpreted.

Source: Based on American Counseling Association (2003); Joint Committee on Testing Practices (2007); and Wall, Augustin, Eberly, Erford, Lundberg, & Vansickle (2003).

Searching by the Title of the Test

Use the Index of Titles, which lists all the titles included in the volume. It includes cross-references for tests with superseded or alternative titles. (The Index of Acronyms is an alternative index. It lists tests sometimes better known by their acronyms than their full titles; SAT and MAT are examples.)

When you find the test title in the index, the numbers immediately following the title refer to entry numbers, not page numbers. Turn to that numbered item and you will find the information available on that test. Often, too, you will find a letter notation following the name of the test: (N) indicates a new, recently published test; (R) means that it has been revised or supplemented since its last appearance in an *MMY*.

Here is an example from the *MMY*'s Index of Titles:

Slosson Test of Reading Readiness, 360 (N)
Social Behavior Assessment Inventory, 361 (R)
Social Climate Scales, see *Family Environment Scale, Second Ed.*, 151
Social Skills Rating System, 362 (N)
Softball Skills Test, 363 (N)

Searching by the Type of Test

Use the Classified Subject Index to locate various categories of tests, such as achievement, intelligence, and personality tests. This index organizes all tests into 18 major content area categories; tests appear alphabetically within each category. As you can see in the following example, the population for which the test is intended is also listed. Again keep in mind that citation numbers refer to entry numbers, not to page numbers.

Diagnostic Assessments of Reading, Grades 1–12, see 115

Gray Oral Reading Tests, Third Edition, Ages 7–0 to 18–11, see 166

Group Diagnostic Reading Aptitude and Achievement Tests, Intermediate Form, Grades 3–9, see 170

Group Reading Test, Third Edition, Ages 6–4 to 11–11 and 8–0 to 11–11—below average, see 171

Johnston Informal Reading Inventory, Grades 7–12, see 202

Searching by the Name of a Test Author or Reviewer

Here you will use the Index of Names. Following each name, this index tells you what kind of material is involved: "test" refers to a test author, "rev" to a review author, and "ref" to the author of a referenced article. Again, note that numbers refer to entry numbers. You may also find numbers in parentheses. These refer to another numbered test in the volume that you can turn to if you wish. An "r," on the other hand, indicates there is a reference cited by the reviewer, but it is not a numbered reference in the volume. Here is a sample from the Index of Names:

Dewey, D.: ref, 353(16)
Dewey, M. E.: ref, 159(75)
DeZolt, D. M.: rev, 68
Diack, H.: ref, 277r
Diaferia, G.: ref, 343(78)
Dial, J. G.: test, 284
Diamond, E. E.: rev, 258, 328
Diamond, F.: ref, 36r
Diamond, R.: ref, 343(138)
Dick, H.: ref, 343(193)

Using the Buros Institute Website

In addition to the printed *MMY*, you can obtain information from the Buros Institute website (www.unl.edu/buros/). A section called Test Reviews Online links to both an alphabetical list of test names and a list of tests by category. This page also allows you to search by keywords. For example, the keyword search "stress response" finds, among other entries, the *Stress*

BUROS INSTITUTE | Buros Institute of Mental Measurements / Test Reviews Online / www.unl.edu/buros

Title: Stress Response Scale
Author: Chandler, Louis A.; Shermis, Mark D.
Purpose: A measure of children's emotional status "designed for children referred for possible emotional adjustment problems or behavior problems."
Acronym: SRS
Note: Test was reviewed in The Eleventh Mental Measurements Yearbook (1992). As of January 2002, publisher advises test is now out of print.
Publisher: Psychological Assessment Resources, Inc.
Publisher address: Psychological Assessment Resources, Inc., 16204 N. Florida Avenue, Lutz, FL 33549-8119; Telephone: 800-331-8378; FAX: 800-727-9329; E-mail: custsupp@parinc.com; Web: www.parinc.com
Reviewed In: Kramer, J. J., & Conoley, J. C. (Eds.). (1992). The eleventh mental measurements yearbook. Lincoln, NE: Buros Institute of Mental Measurements. To purchase this review, click on "Add Review to Shopping Cart."

[View Shopping Cart] [Add Review to Shopping Cart] [Continue Searching]

Figure 8.1. Description of the *Stress Response Scale* from the Buros Institute website. Used by permission.

Response Scale, a measure of children's emotional status developed by Louis A. Chandler.

When you find a test on the website, click on the name to see a brief description of it, as shown in Figure 8.1. From this screen, you can order a full review for a small fee. As noted in Text Box 8.4, the web is a useful, but not exclusive, resource when searching for information about tests.

Text Box 8.4 Why Not Rely on Web Searches?

As our discussion of the Buros and ETS websites indicates, you can find a lot of excellent information about formal assessment measures online. In fact, if you were to ask undergraduate students how they might get information regarding tests and assessments (or most anything else for that matter), they would most likely say they would search online with a search engine such as Google (www.google.com/) or Yahoo! (www.yahoo.com/). Why shouldn't you get all your information that way? Why bother going to the Buros database or any other standard site for educational assessment?

Although there is nothing wrong with online searches, the problem is that ordinary search engines are not subject to formal or informal reviews, which means that you have to serve as the in-house expert when reviewing the material. And, because some search engines take advertising budgets in return for the way websites display search results, the hits you view may be a function of how advertising dollars are spent.

As an example, we did a search for "psychic powers test" on Google (a site containing an index of billions of web-based documents). In 130 milliseconds, we obtained information on 76,800 documents! One of our hits was the site Bella Online (www.bellaonline.com) which offers a *Psychic Test and Quiz*. Whether you believe in psychic powers or not, you might think this is a genuine attempt to test for such powers. Upon further investigation, though, you will find, buried in the website, an acknowledgement that the test is a humorous prank. If you failed to scrutinize the material carefully, you might have believed that the test had some foundation to it.

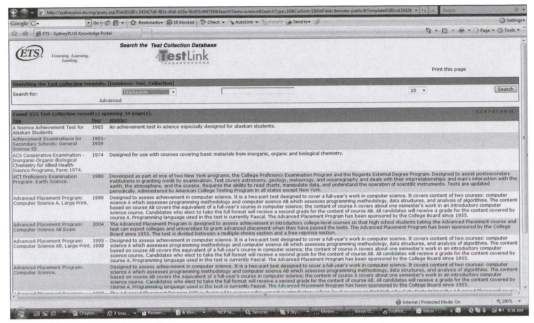

Figure 8.2. A partial listing of the results of the keyword search "science" in the ETS TestLink database.

■ The ETS Test Collection

The ETS Test Collection is a database of over 20,000 tests and assessment instruments from throughout the English-speaking world. The collection is less formal than that listed in the *MMY* because many of the assessments have not been published or formally reviewed. A limited number of the tests can actually be downloaded from the ETS website for a modest fee.

To use this test collection, go online to the ETS TestLink homepage (www.ets.org/testcoll/index.html), click on the search button, and choose the type of search you want. Usually you will want to search by title, by author, or by descriptor (keyword). Figure 8.2 shows a partial listing of the search results obtained with the descriptor "science." When your search results appear, you can click on the name of a test to learn more about it.

■ ERIC

The Educational Resources Information Center (ERIC®) is a national information system designed to provide ready access to an extensive body of education-related literature. ERIC, established in 1966, is organized by topical areas. It provides an index of major educationally related journals and serves as a repository for academic monographs, reports, and papers. ERIC also commissions internally generated reports on topics of interest to educators.

Of particular interest in this chapter, is the *ERICAE.net* test locator database, which will help you locate assessments that were incorporated as part of a journal article or were appended to selected research reports.

To illustrate its use, let's assume you wanted to find a test on math anxiety. You would first go to the address www.eric.gov. Then go to Advanced Search. Enter the keyword "math anxiety," and under Publication Types, click on "tests/questionnaires." You would then view a screen similar to that shown in Figure 8.3.

The search will produce several options, as shown in Figure 8.4.

From the search result, you can obtain a citation or, for more recent entries, the full pdf text of the article or instrument.

■ Standards for Educational and Psychological Testing

The Standards for Educational and Psychological Testing (AERA, APA, & NCME, 1999) is a synthesis of the efforts of several groups to govern the use of tests in education and psychology. The guidelines were developed mainly by three

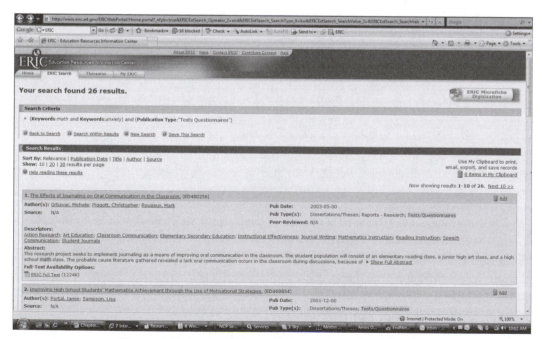

Figure 8.3. A search for "math anxiety" using ERIC.

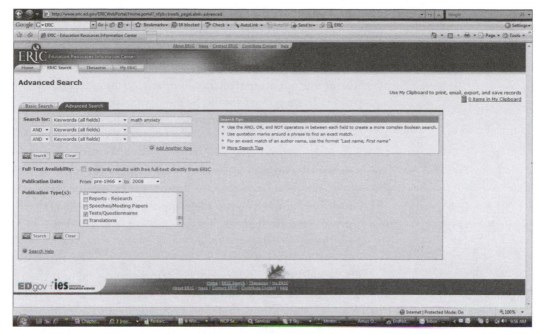

Figure 8.4. The search result.

organizations: the American Educational Research Association (AERA), the American Psychological Association (APA), and the National Council on Measurement in Education (NCME). In addition, more than 60 other organizations were involved in reviewing the *Standards* for the 1999 edition. The *Standards* evolved over a 50-year period. It is quite likely that they will continue to be modified in response to changing mores and sensitivities.

With the number of institutions involved in both development and review, it is obvious that the *Standards* reaches a wide audience. Nevertheless, it is unlikely that any participants in that audience, whether large testing companies or individual teachers, can be 100 percent faithful to each and every guideline. Even with tests that have been published for a number of years, the accumulation of evidence is a never-ending process. A study conducted in 1986, for example, may need to be replicated in the 2000s to determine whether changes in population demographics affect the norms or other characteristics of the test.

Still, the importance of the *Standards* lies in the criteria they offer for judging the usefulness of a test for given purposes. The *Standards* discuss the importance of evidence regarding reliability and objectivity, for example. They also cover topics such as test development and revision, methods of test administration and scoring, and the rights and responsibilities of test takers.

As a demonstration of the way the *Standards'* criteria are applied, consider the following two standards from Part I: Test Construction, Evaluation, and Documentation:

Norms that are presented should refer to clearly described groups. These groups should be the ones with whom users of the test will ordinarily wish to compare the people who are tested. (p. 33)

Reports of norming studies should include the year in which normative data were collected, provide descriptive statistics, and describe the sampling design and participation rates in sufficient detail so that the study can be evaluated for appropriateness. (p. 33)

The application of the first criterion prompted a revision of the widely used *Peabody Picture Vocabulary Test (PPVT)*. The *PPVT*, ostensibly a non-oral (nonvocal) measure of intelligence, was originally designed for developmentally delayed U.S. children. The measure had been standardized (normed) on 2,000 white children from rural Kentucky. Because of its ease in administration, however, the instrument became very popular as an assessment for immigrant children during the late 1970s and early 1980s. But comparing the scores of immigrant children, such as Vietnamese refugees, with those of a normative group of students in Kentucky clearly failed to comply with the provision that the normative groups should be a good match for the actual test takers.

In response to such criticisms, the test publishers collected additional data with the assessment, using a more diverse sample to ensure greater alignment between the norms and the populations to whom the test was being administered. The publishers' report also complied with the second standard quoted above; it described the sampling and norming process in detail so that users could make an informed judgment about the test's usefulness. The standards for educational and psychological tests are illustrated in Text Box 8.5. As you study the illustrations you will see the implementation of important test characteristics. Please visit the source if you wish to see the complete document. It provides a guide for test constructors and test publishers alike, and is a useful guide for the selection of tests.

Text Box 8.5 An Example from
The Standards for Educational and Psychological Testing

Note that this is currently being revised.

Testing Individuals of Diverse Linguistic Backgrounds

Standard 9.1

Testing practice should be designed to reduce threats to the reliability and validity of test score inferences that may arise from language differences.

Standard 9.2

When credible research evidence reports that test scores differ in meaning across subgroups of linguistically diverse test takers, then to the extent feasible, test developers should collect for each linguistic subgroup studied the same form of validity evidence collected for the examinee population as a whole.

Standard 9.3

When testing an examinee proficient in two or more languages for which the test is available, the examinee's relative language proficiencies should be determined. The test generally should be administered in the test taker's most proficient language, unless proficiency in the less proficient language is part of the assessment.

Standard 9.4

Linguistic modifications recommended by test publishers, as well as the rational for the modifications, should be described in detail in the test manual.

Standard 9.5

When there is credible evidence of score comparability across regular and modified tests or administrations, no flag should be attached to a score. When such evidence is lacking, specific information about the nature of the modifications should be provided, if permitted by law, to assist test users properly to interpret and act on test scores.

Standard 9.6

When a test is recommended for use with linguistically diverse test takers, test developers and publishers should provide the information necessary for appropriate test use and interpretation.

Standard 9.7

When a test is translated from one language to another, the methods used in establishing the adequacy of the translation should be described, and empirical and logical evidence should be provided for score reliability and the validity of the translated test's score inferences for the uses intended in the linguistic groups to be tested.

(continued)

Standard 9.8

In employment and credentialing testing, the proficiency level required in the language of the test should not exceed that appropriate to the relevant occupation or profession.

Standard 9.9

When multiple language versions of a test are intended to be comparable, test developers should report evidence of test comparability.

Standard 9.10

Inferences about test takers' general language proficiency should be based on tests that measure a range of language features, and not on a single linguistic skill.

Standard 9.11

When an interpreter is used in testing, the interpreter should be fluent in both the language of the test and the examinee's native language, should have expertise in translating, and should have a basic understanding of the assessment process.

Source: American Educational Research Association et al. (1999).

■ Standardized Tests and Classroom Assessments

Standardized tests are important as one source of assessment data. However, they do not ordinarily substitute for the teacher-made classroom test. Using formal tests for instructional purposes can create problems of interpretation (Elmore & Rothman, 1999). Even if a test is modified for particular instructional use in a classroom, the test score might be misinterpreted as representing what *had actually been taught* in the classroom, with the consequent potential for errors in its implications for designing instruction or interventions.

In keeping with general practices advocated throughout this text, we reiterate this point: No single source of information, no single test, can provide the complete picture of students that may be required for diagnostic, curriculum-planning, or other classroom purposes. Supplements include teacher-made tests, observations, formal tests, and accountability tests, all of which contribute to a holistic picture of student performance.

Based on poorly informed decisions, formal standardized tests are sometimes selected for the purpose of preparing students who will be taking similarly formatted tests. The procedure is known as teaching to the test. Although the evidence is mixed regarding the extent to which teachers or schools engage in this practice, it is not uncommon for schools to select existing, publicly available test banks in preparing students for taking statewide tests, commonly referred to as high-stakes tests, used for accountability. The practice of teaching to the test cannot be judged as anything other than a poor one. It is unanimously understood as well as empirically supported that teaching to specific test items limits learning, encourages memorization of items, and may interfere with transfer of conceptual information; practice on specific items does enhance test scores if identical items appear on a test, but does not enhance the educationally relevant outcomes of understanding and application. The positive outcomes (if enhancing test scores without enhancing understanding can be called positive) are achieved by demonstrating to students the type of item on which they are to be tested and the kind of response called for in answering the test item, perhaps even calling their attention to memorizing a specific fact or term to be memorized for later recognition if it appears on the test to be taken. Instruction based on available measures may be acceptable, if the teacher is cautious in using the item as a guide for identifying the underlying standards, skills, or knowledge of a domain represented in the test rather than on the assumed similarity of the item structure and specific content (fact). It must be understood that a test item is a mere representation of some skill or knowledge in a domain. And, further, it is only one sample of the representation of that skill or knowledge.

It is important here to remind our readers of the importance of engaging students in self- and peer-assessment in focusing on targets for learning. Such feedback informs students about the goals of learning and the quality criteria that apply to their work. As a result, students learn to identify learning goals for which they initially lacked confidence and in which they needed help; they acquire metacognitions related to the requirements for their own learning—requirements of which they were initially unaware. Such orientations in the use of standardized tests keep the interdependency of assessment and learning intact rather than treating them as separately compartmentalized activities.

Exercise 8.1: Selecting Tests

Section A. This exercise is intended to help you learn about the actual results of a search for information you might use in test selection. For an initial attempt:

1. Identify a test that is commonly used, such as the California Achievement Test (CAT) or the Stanford Achievement

Test (SAT). Your instructor may wish to have you search for information about another test.

2. If there is a test library at your school, look at the test and manual so that you become familiar with its construction.

3. Begin a review for your evaluation by going to the Buros *Mental Measurement Yearbook*, which is probably available through your library (most libraries house this in their reference collection).

4. Follow up with other sources for finding out about the test.

In your own words, write an evaluation of the test:

1. Begin with a statement of objectives that would be served by the test. You might want to use the material in the boxes (e.g., Text Box 8.1 or Text Box 8.4) as a guide for your report.

2. Summarize the extent to which the test meets good test standards.

3. Be certain to mention any limitations that might have been noted by the reviewers.

4. Summarize reasons for using or not using the test as well as the purposes that might be served and under what circumstances it would be useful.

Section B. Now that you have become familiar with how to use the sources:

1. Identify an instructional objective that would be important in your own teaching for which a standardized test might be appropriate (e.g., you might want to learn about the reading comprehension level of your class before or after instruction, or you might want to learn how your students in your class compare with those in other schools in the state in meeting standards for mastery of basic arithmetic facts and operations).

2. Search the Buros *MMY* volumes for available tests.

3. Identify tests that seem appropriate. Keep in mind that your search might be extended to additional or different tests as you progress through your review.

4. Go to additional sources (e.g., online searches) for information, if it seems necessary.

5. In a written report summarize the comparisons you made (see also the last paragraph under Section A above).

6. Include in your report the reasons why you made the selection out of all the tests you initially selected.

■ Summary

There are good reasons for attending to the technical concerns in the selection of tests. You will be doing much that involves tests selected from outside sources. They are readily available and used for a variety of purposes serving instructional needs within the classroom, but, additionally, such tests are generally available for (a) student selection, (b) diagnostic purposes, (c) intervention program planning, (d) summative evaluation of student status, and (e) accountability purposes by policymakers. Attending to the technical details outlined in this chapter will make your final selection from the myriad of choices more appropriate for your purposes.

Teachers may be involved directly in the selection of standardized tests when they want to supplement data from informal measures. The Stanford Achievement Tests, for example, can be used for assessing progress in reading, science, or mathematics.

Most teachers in the elementary grades, at least, will be involved in making recommendations regarding the selection of appropriate measures to be used in Individualized Educational Plans. Or they may be involved with measures for which they provide no direct or indirect guidance in selection, but that are policy requirements that affect evaluations of accountability and for which they regularly participate in preparing students to take the tests. These and similar situations require professionally informed decisions. Contrary to the opinion of some, using and interpreting standardized tests are a critical part of the normal activities of teaching.

Formally developed measures go beyond the assessment of ability and achievement. A teacher in reading may wish to use a test of metacognitions regarding reading, a teacher in science may wish to use a test of misconceptualizations in science, or any teacher might wish to evaluate the personality and motivational characteristics of their students by measures that are available either from commercial sources or from the literature. A selection of such measures, from whatever source, necessitates a well-informed knowledge base regarding the process.

In general, the teacher's roles may include taking part in the proper administration of formal group tests (e.g., the statewide comprehension tests) to assure that performance is being measured accurately (i.e., under standardized conditions). Teachers engage in the selection of tests related to a particular field and serve on committees that engage in the selection for guidance purposes (preparation of individual educational programs, remediation, or enrichment placement), all of which require an understanding of the bases for test selection.

In these situations the role of teachers may include the interpretation of test results that are stored and retrieved for their use. They communicate their understanding of tests, test scores, and functions served by tests to the public through interaction with parents, school boards, and groups such as the parent-teacher association. Increasingly, the information provided by standardized test results are employed for use by trained personnel such as teachers responsible for the education of children with special needs or by school psychologists and guidance counselors for placement of children in remedial or enrichment classes. Many of the more formal tests, such as those for diagnostic purposes, must be administered by trained personnel.

The characteristics by which available tests are to be selected are central to informed decisions. To arrive at valid interpretations or inferences regarding student progress in understanding and thinking, teachers must use a variety of assessments, both formal and informal. To achieve the purposes intended in the use of standardized tests, the technical quality of the assessment, the items selected, and their characteristics must be explicit. A test is judged not by its label or by what the author intended the test to measure. It is judged on the basis of its items, the content they tap, the standards they represent, the extent to which the subject matter is sampled, and the underlying processes tapped. The items comprising the test must be examined for what they are measuring and the extent to which those assessments sample the range of knowledge, understanding, and skills intended. The overall test and the items on which it is based must be sensitive to language and cultural differences as well as the needs of students with special disabilities who are the potential examinees. Standardized assessment measures, like instructional assignments, are expected to be challenging, not frustrating or unimportant performance tasks.

In summary, the bases for selection of tests are the following:

- *Purpose.* Know the purpose for which the test is being selected—accountability, diagnosis, or the alignment with standards.
- *Measure.* Know the characteristics of the test—whether it is capable of providing information useful to the purpose intended.
- *Conditions.* Know the conditions under which administration of the test is appropriate.
- *Student examinees.* Know the appropriateness of the test for diversity characteristics, whether cultural, age, grade level, or other individual difference. Know the norms available.

- *Scoring.* Know the basis for the scoring of the measures, their accuracy, and the norms available for their interpretation.

When selecting tests carefully inspect the alignment between what is tested and the instructional objectives (i.e., what is taught) if you intend to use the test results for your instruction. It is important that the selection be based on consideration of information about the educational program and students to provide a rounded body of information if it is to be useful for recommendations about curricular changes or remedial programs for students.

The selection of tests to be employed in standardized fashion involves considerations regarding the administration of the test. Are there special provisions for certification of the administrator of the tests? What special training, if any, is required of the administrator of the measure? Are the conditions for meeting standard administration requirements detailed for the administrator of the measure to follow? Can the test be administered appropriately by the personnel available? (For example, some intelligence tests require administration by trained school psychologists.)

The characteristics of students to whom the test is being administered must be addressed. Consider whether the test is to be used with students with special disabilities, students from different cultures, students whose primary language is other than English, or even students who have different experiences due to education in different but adjoining localities or districts. Age, grade level, and socioeconomic status are all considerations as well.

Scoring procedures must be clear; they should yield consistent and accurate scores for interpretation. When the scores are to be used in normative comparisons, the appropriate norm should be available regarding special groups being tested (disaggregated norms) in order to avoid misclassification of students in these groups. They should be useful in identifying students who can profit from the interventions available.

In view of fairness considerations (covered in Chapter 16 on test accommodations) it is important to consider whether the test or its administration can be modified for special-needs students or whether there are alternative forms or measures that have been validated against the original forms. When selecting the test consider whether instruction and the curriculum have provided the opportunity for learning to the standards being measured in the test.

After you are satisfied that the test is generally oriented toward your purpose, examine its supporting data. For example, if you want the test for selection of students who will succeed in the second-level algebra course, is the data such that it supports predictive validity? That is, do the scores on the test correlate with success in the second course? A standardized achievement test for one content area can't be used for making predictions about success in another content area if that was the intended purpose; examine the data to determine how the predictions were made. Any item or entire test has to be evaluated against reliability and validity criteria.

If you are attempting to use standardized test results for your own teaching, the concern is the extent to which the measure serves the function of formative assessment; that is, the interpretation of test results should have implications for influencing instruction positively, both in content and instructional methods. Fortunately, the easily accessible reviews by experts, such as those in the *Mental Measurements Yearbooks* (Buros Institute of Mental Measurements, 2000), provide useful resources for teachers involved at any level in the selection of tests for specific outcomes and purposes.

■ References

American Counseling Association. (2003). *Standards for qualifications of test users*. Alexandria, VA: Author.

American Educational Research Association (AERA), American Psychological Association (APA), & National Council Measurement in Education (NCME). (1999). *Standards for educational and psychological testing*. Washington, DC: American Educational Research Association.

American Psychological Association. (2001). Appropriate use of high-stakes testing in our nation's schools. *APA Online Public Affairs*. Retrieved March 15, 2009, from www.apa.org/pubinfo/testing.htm.

Buros Institute of Mental Measurements. (2000). *Mental measurements yearbook*. Lincoln, NE: Buros Institute of Mental Measurements.

Elmore, R. F., & Rothman, R. (1999). *Testing, teaching, and learning: A guide for states and school districts*. Washington, DC: National Academy Press.

Joint Committee on Testing Practices. (2007). Testing and assessment: Code of fair testing practices in education. Retrieved September 25, 2007, from www.apa.org/science/fairtestcode.html.

Marshall, P. (2002). *Cultural diversity in our schools*. Belmont, CA: Wadsworth/Thomson Learning.

Wall, J., Augustin, J., Eberly, C., Erford, B., Lundberg, D., & Vansickle, T. (2003). *Responsibilities of users of standardized tests (RUST)*. Association for Assessment in Counseling (AAC).

CHAPTER 9

Technology in Assessment

THE PURPOSE OF applying technology in classroom assessment is threefold: to collect information with greater reliability and validity, to collect it more efficiently, and to provide a mechanism to feed into instructional efforts resulting from the assessment. One of the advantages of using computer-based technologies is that they, unlike large-scale standardized tests, are easily amenable to classroom adaptation. The challenge is simply trying to keep abreast of all of the innovations that can help you perform assessments. In this chapter we will survey assessment technology aids that might be used in the classroom. In particular we will provide an example of one technology that it becoming more commonplace—automated essay scoring, or the ability of a computer to evaluate written essays (Shermis, Burstein, & Leacock, 2006). This technology works well in the classroom and provides sufficient feedback to be used in instructional settings.

Other applications that foretell future possibilities include automated speech scoring, automated scoring of short written answers, and the development of broadly defined summative assessments corresponding as much to new thinking in assessment as to traditional assessment. The targeting of specific cognitive skills aligned with subject-matter standards hold the promise for critical guidance in instructional improvement (Board of Testing and Assessment/National Research Council, 2002).

■ Technological Formats for Instruction: Emergence of Formative Assessment

The concern with elements of formative assessment—alignment with subject matter standards, data regarding student

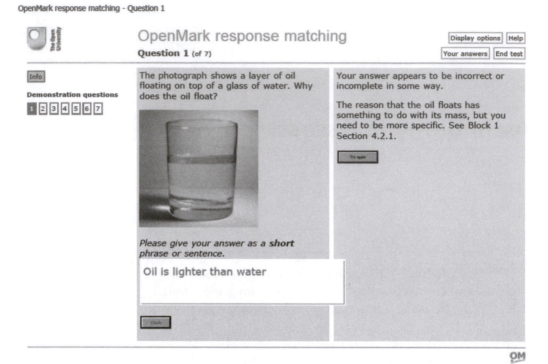

Figure 9.1. An example of an OpenMark free text question.

performance, feedback, and interpretations of feedback for both learners and instructors—has been facilitated by developments in technology. Instructional developments that run the gamut from linear programming of instruction to complex branching instructional programs within instructional environments were made possible by technological developments. In the later stages of development they became known as computer-assisted instruction or CAI (Hunka, 1977).

Each stage in development contained elements that contributed to the essence of formative assessment, providing for the integration of instruction and assessment such that the two were virtually indistinguishable. Each, in its own way, provided for delivery and spiraling of instruction toward student achievement of well-defined objectives, individual responses, immediate feedback, and continuation of instruction or changes in instruction based on assessment of student progress toward achieving standards-based objectives. Although these developments have become increasingly integrated with instruction, they do not displace the delivery and management of traditional assessments by emerging technology-based assessment in instruction but, rather, suggest the need to merge the two.

An example here is the OpenMark system, developed by the Open University in the United Kingdom as a mechanism for administering formative assessments via the Internet (Butcher, 2008). In the example in Figure 9.1, the initial short response was given in the space provided on the left and evaluated on the right-hand side. The software provides a hint, and the student is referred to a section in the instructional materials for more information on the topic. The assessment author can specify how many times a student may try to correctly answer the question.

Programmed Instruction

Although a detailed analysis would yield many technological developments in which assessment and instruction have been integrated, a few have been selected to illustrate some events that, at the time of their appearance, attracted much attention and interest of both researchers and educators. Each selected event has contributed to the evolution of current emphases in assessment and instruction by their contributions to student understanding and thinking rather than simply to the acquisition of facts.

An early innovation, which included many elements of formative assessment, was programmed instruction (Glaser, 1965). It was empirically based on the principles of operant learning (Skinner, 1954, 1968). The technology associated with programmed learning was a rather crude device, by today's standards, known as the teaching machine (sometimes presented in a textbook format (Lumsdaine & Glaser, 1960). The general principle underlying instruction by this method was that the instruction was programmed, that is, the student was taught bits of information and then responded to questions using that information. Each step in the instruction brought the student closer to the instructional objectives. The small steps were presented in the form of frames (corresponding to formats of test items) to present new information, followed by requests for student responses. The responses were either selected from a set of responses, as in a multiple-choice format, or constructed, as in a fill-in-the-blank format. Students were then informed immediately whether the response was correct or incorrect (the basis for the feedback was whether the response matched a correct one built into the program). If correct, the student went to the next frame of information, followed by the same sequence of responding and feedback. If incorrect, the student would be presented the same information and questions.

In the early development of this device, programming was linear, that is, learning was guided by progressive steps to achieving the objective. Small steps were used in an attempt to achieve approximations to errorless learning. However, errors did occur, so a technological advancement provided branching opportunities. Multiple-choice alternatives for responding provided opportunities for the program to identify where responses were wrong and what information the student neglected. Thus, if the response was incorrect the student was guided to a subprogram to learn the information required. (Within today's environment, the student might be directed to some address on the Internet for more information.) Once it was learned, he or she returned to the original program. Overall, the basics of formative assessment were present: (a) the sequence was predetermined by the programmer (instructor); (b) the student was presented information (instruction); (c) the student responded; (d) the response was evaluated (assessed); and (e) further progression (instruction) was guided by the assessment. Within this framework, new information, whether in a linear or branched sequence, is not guided by what the student wanted but is guided by being a small step toward acquisition of the subject matter defining the objective.

The Responsive Reading Environment

Another technological event consisted of an apparatus for teaching reading, known as the Responsive Reading Environment (RRE) (Moore, 1964). It was based not on one learning theory, as was programmed instruction, but on principles of learning from several theories, including Skinner's description of operant learning and Piaget's (1955) theory of child development. As can be seen from the inclusion of *environment* in the title, it is illustrative of the move from the preset programmed learning to somewhat more flexible situations in which students learn through activities of their own choosing, a framework more closely related to formative assessment than that of programmed learning.

The RRE was popularly known as the "talking typewriter" (Moore, 1980), and consisted of a keyboard coupled with an audio device for providing feedback. It was used to teach children as young as two or three. Upon introduction to the device the child's fingernails were color-coded to match the keys with which they were associated. Thus, for example, the left forefinger might be colored red to match the keys *f*, *r*, *t*, *v*, *b*, and *g*, which were also red. In this way the child also learned the touch typing system. The system was programmed to verbally instruct the child about the letters to be typed; for example, the instruction might be "t." The child typed the letter and was then informed whether it was correct or not by the device saying the letter that was actually typed. The procedure contains the elements of an environment, rather than a program, for learning because it was an interactive system in which the child can make his or her own discoveries and progresses toward the objective by using his or her own procedures, whether for typing a letter, writing a word, or writing a paragraph about a historical event.

In parallel with the other developments, the talking typewriter, as instructor, permitted changes in instruction based on the assessment of learner progress. Unlike the linearity of programmed learning, the requirements were more flexible, allowing students to discover their own opportunities; for example, they could type a letter more than once, typing letters or words other than those programmed into the instruction; they could use newly learned words in written products of their own choosing. Instruction was modified according to assessments.

Logo: Microworlds for Mathematics Instruction

Still more flexibility in instruction was introduced by the interactive environment of a computer-based environment. The environment was produced by a programming method known as Logo and described in a book titled *Mindstorms* (Papert, 1980). Papert was concerned with Piaget's (1955) premise that understanding emerged from whatever construction was made by the cognitive activity of the learner. Instruction, then, was the establishment of environments that permitted the emergence of discovery and invention. Within this framework and manipulating a "turtle" (corresponding to a cursor) that had properties such as drawing a continuous line, the student through pointing and clicking and using symbols could create interactive simulations allowing the exploration and invention of arithmetic and mathematical ideas such as the requirements for forming rectangles or squares. The essence of the program was that students could explore and test their ideas within an exploratory, experimental, and imaginative environment. The instruction was in the framework of a progressively developing environment. The assessment came through the individual testing of the validity of ideas; for example, did the drawing of lines produce a square (i.e., a closed figure with four equal sides and angles) or something else (such as an open figure)? Rather than emphasizing coverage of the material to be learned, the intent was to develop the child's understanding through becoming conversant with underlying principles and discovering, in his or her own language, the principles of mathematics and writing (Papert, 1993).

Thinker Tools, Virtual Environments, and Emerging Assessments

Current programs are a considerable departure from the earlier instructional assessment characteristic of the era of teaching machines (Pelligrino, Chudowsky, & Glaser, 2001; White & Frederiksen, 2000). Current programs for K–12 instruction assess problem solving central to professions within both the physical sciences and the social-cultural arenas. Both require access to a vast amount of information that underlies the environments related to decision making within their respective professions and information related to problem-solving skills in the problem-solving domain. Access to the Internet, for example, enables the search for evidence related to such diverse authentic events as planning an airplane trip to rescue a wounded bird to understanding the extinction of a biological species (e.g., dinosaurs), the evidence for the validity of differing claims about an event (such as the effect of a drug upon the genetic characteristics of the offspring of people taking the drug), and the equally important evidence opposing such claims. The programs provide opportunities for interaction within these contexts. The student must use cognitive tools central to the problem such as manipulating variables to enable evaluation of the effects of these variables on outcomes for collecting data (Cognition and Technology Group at Vanderbilt, 2000). Assessments are intrinsic to the task—goals are clearly specified, good problem-solving strategies are made salient to students during the course of arriving at the answer by feedback, and efficient problem solving is marked by successful solutions (e.g., planning the course taken by an airplane without running out of gas, but still bringing the wounded bird to safety).

In contemplating these new developments it can be seen that the collection of data streams themselves provide data about student thinking on each step of their engagement in learning activities—a source of assessment data that because of its complexity has been virtually untouched before the advent of the computer (White & Frederiksen, 1998). It becomes possible to identify such points of interest as selection of information, establishing subgoals, evaluating strategies for goal (comprehension, understanding) attainment, and the implementation of repair strategies when the achievement of the goal is being hindered. It is noteworthy that as students progress toward solutions they provide evidence regarding the ways (processes and strategies) they approach and pursue solution paths as opposed to the traditional method of simply evaluating the outcome, problem solution, or product.

Students working with these programs in virtual environments on problem-solving tasks can identify their metacognitions by cross-checking their procedures with criteria such as standards, goals, or objectives (White & Frederiksen, 1998). Thinker Tools, for example, is such a a program. It encourages students to propose and test their own as well as other's theories in science by such devices as proposing opposing theories, carrying out experiments to test these theories, and reaching a consensus about the best theory (Pelligrino et al., 2001). They are enabled to carry out experiments by adding or subtracting variables (e.g., those that turn friction on or off) and see for themselves the effects associated with principles of science. They can examine the impact of temperature, utility resources, water management, food resources, population growth, and energy use in emerging countries on conservation and sustainability of resources. None of these activities would be easily implemented, if at all, within traditional classroom instruction. Feedback about the correctness or appropriateness of student thinking or reasoning is a critical component of the assessments embedded within the instructional system.

■ Technology and Assessment

Although oral and written tests are in no immediate danger of disappearing, new technologies are supplementing and replacing the more traditional forms of assessment. Computer-based technologies provide the opportunity for:

- Item generation and test production with precise psychometric and content qualities, dramatically altering the technology of test production and alternative assessment tools
- Enabling the administration and presentation of these new tools through complex, multistep problems that may incorporate varied contextual environments, use multimodal presentations, require alternative paths to reach a solution, or have multiple correct solutions
- Advancing scoring procedures by linking these attributes to the computer's ability to record the details of the student responses reflected in the processes and paths explored while solving problems or constructing solutions

These capabilities provide opportunities to learn about students' knowledge with on-the-spot diagnoses of conceptual understanding and cognitive development. Scoring of complex products such as those produced in essays, concept mapping of conceptual areas, portfolios, or other alternative assessments can be accomplished in ways that would be difficult to achieve with earlier testing technology.

To illustrate one aspect of these potential contributions of emerging technology, we will discuss the use of the LXR*Test 6.0 software package. This comprehensive software package can be used to create and administer tests in multiple formats. We will also discuss the use of automated essay scoring as a technology to both instruct and evaluate writing performance. Many of these technologies hold the promise of being embedded and so well integrated in the development and delivery of curricular content that the line between instruction and assessment is blurred, becoming virtually indistinguishable as it is expected to be in formative assessment. As importantly, the technological applications allow for assessments to be administered in different locations and at any time of the day; both attributes would be particularly important for such applications as distance learning and open university settings. Finally, this chapter will review some of the key technology applications in assessment with a view towards possible implications for teachers. We will start, however, with a section on the role of the Internet in helping to shape future practices.

The Internet

The Internet is an expansive and fast-growing resource for teachers who are interested in issues of educational assessment, one that is constantly evolving through both formal and informal standards of development. The Internet began in the 1960s when the U.S. government created it in order to promote the sharing of supercomputers among researchers in the United States. It has since grown into a vast network that connects many independent networks spanning over 170 countries. It links clusters of commercial companies, private individuals, educational institutions, and many other types of organizations to one another through routing paths. Stated simply, the Internet is composed of millions of computers linked by a high-speed backbone (Shermis & Daniels, 2002). As of this writing, North American Internet usage is about 251 million people for the United States, Canada, and Mexico, or an overall penetration of about 73.9 percent. The amount of information and the

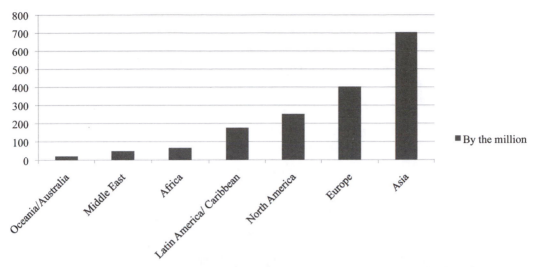

Figure 9.2. Internet users in the world (in millions) by geographical region.

speed with which it can be accessed is an advantageous resource for both instruction and assessment at any grade level. Figure 9.2 shows Internet users in the world by geographical region.

Adults in the United States spend approximately 27 hours per month on their home computers (women Internet users in the United States number more than men) looking at web pages, and a whopping 78 hours per month at work. In a typical month, home Internet users visit about 54 web domains, and those at work visit an average of 104 different web domains. The attention span of web surfers is short, with individuals spending about 1 minute for each web page visited (www.clickz.com/).

The growth rate of the traffic on the public Internet is about 106 percent a year in North American and 311 percent a year in the Mideast. While a higher proportion of women in the United States use the Internet (52 percent versus 48 percent of men, which mirrors U.S. adult demographics), it turns out that men on average spend slightly more money per year shopping on the web ($648 versus $606).

The backbone of the Internet is the property of commercial communications corporations and the federal government. For example, the federal government has underwritten significant costs in implementing Internet 2, a superset of connection points that permits the high-speed delivery of multimedia and other high-bandwidth operations. Figure 9.3 shows the hub connections for Internet 2.

A recent search of the Internet using Google revealed 341 million hits with the keyword "assessment." A search for "assessment" that simply lists or indicates a definition of the term

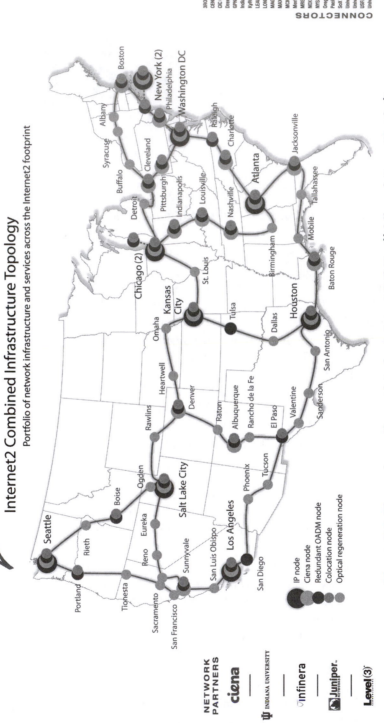

Figure 9.3. The main routing points for Internet 2 (http://abilene.internet2.edu/).

received 174 million hits. We were able to narrow down the number of hits to 32 million with the modifier "classroom," as in "classroom assessment." This begs the question as to how useful and reliable the information is when collected via the Internet through search engines. It certainly is convenient, though there is reason to be skeptical with the results one is provided.

While it is inviting to believe that Internet search engines provide the consumer with the most relevant matches to an inquiry (some even estimate their relevance based on search criteria), the fact is that many search engines prioritize their search result listings based on contractual arrangements with vendors rather than on scientific merit alone. A vendor pays for product placement in the same way that advertisers pay for product highlighting in movies or TV shows. This is one way in which the search engine companies make their money.

Moreover, information from the Internet suffers from a lack of critical review. Take a look at Figure 9.4, which was a result of a search based on the keywords "psychic test." As we reported in the previous chapter, the website that provided a so-called test and a wealth of information on the topic turned out to be constructed as a practical joke.

In contrast to web-based search engines, academic journals and books typically go through an editorial review process that challenges the authors to remain current, accurate, and balanced in their presentation. These three qualities are not necessarily guaranteed, but they are more likely to occur than if the information was simply posted on a website, which anybody with Internet access and some spare disk space can do.

Tests

Probably the most common assessment of student learning involves the use of tests. Over the past several years software

How to tell if you are psychic: take this test. Predict which card will appear. After going through ten rounds, you will find out how psychic you are!

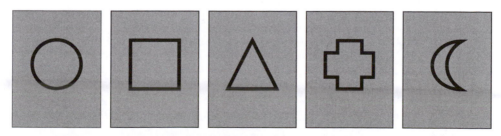

Figure 9.4. An example "test item" drawn from a psychic website.

vendors have transformed their desktop testing software to web-based delivery systems that typically include a server-administrator and test creation software. Creation and administration via the web have a number of advantages, including greater flexibility in testing configurations, reduced costs, instantaneous feedback for students, and the ability of faculty to collaborate on item banks or test construction (Shermis & Daniels, 2002). Multiple testing formats are supported, including multiple-choice, true-false, fill-in-the-blank, short answer, and essay tests. Most programs provide the capability to automatically grade all of the formats with the exception of essay tests. However, many programs allow the test administrator to view an extended response and then assign points to it from within the testing package. Figure 9.5 illustrates an example of a multiple-choice test item administered through a web-based platform.

One of the primary methods for generating tests is to draw the questions from large item banks. Most assessment software enables the test author to construct a personal item bank or to adopt one that is provided by a textbook publisher. Often, instructors have accumulated many test questions over

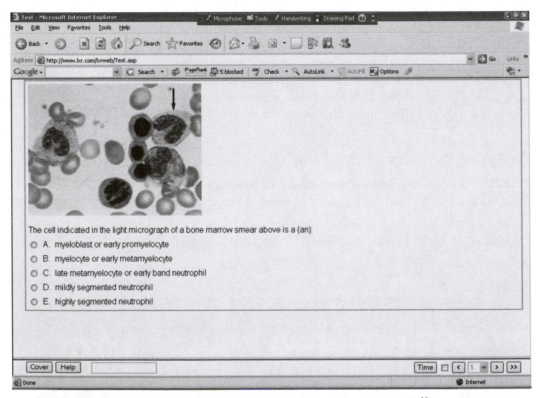

Figure 9.5. An example of a web-based test item. Source: http://www.lxr.com.

the years and already have a large question bank from which to draw subsets of questions. Most item banks can be accessed by their relationship to book chapters, topic areas, goals, behavioral objectives, taxonomic level (e.g., Bloom's taxonomy), or other organizing mechanisms.

It is quite popular these days to organize primary and secondary teachers by teams. Most often the team is created around a grade level or a particular cohort of students. So for example, there might be a team consisting of the five first-grade teachers in an elementary school. These teachers can choose to collaborate on common lessons and assessments. If there is an upcoming math assessment, the team of five teachers might assign each instructor to create 10 items for a 50-item test.

Using a product like LXR*Test, each teacher can log on to a common test-item database and enter in their 10-item contribution. Alternatively, the task may be to update or revise items given in a previous year. The team leader can then assemble the test and add any finishing touches such as instructions.

■ Some Available Testing Software

Perception—Question Mark Computing

Perception, offered by Question Mark Computing (www.qmark.com), enables the user to make questions and tests or surveys. It consists of two Windows applications and three web-based applications. The two Windows applications include the Question Manager and the Session Manager. The web-based applications include the Perception Server, the Security Manager, and the Enterprise Reporter.

Question Manager allows one to create questions and store them in hierarchically organized topics. It also scores the questions and creates feedback for right or wrong answers. Questions can either be customized or chosen from nine predesigned questions, including multiple choice, multiple response, text match, fill in the blank, numeric, selection, matrix, hotspot, or explanation. Within this application, questions and blocks can be tried out in advance, and a multimedia wizard is available to help include multimedia within the test. The application also allows for the storage of hundreds of thousands of questions and the organization of these questions into hierarchical topic databases.

Session Manager organizes the questions created in Question Manager into tests or surveys, called sessions. Questions can be selected individually, from a topic as a group, or randomly from one or more topics. Links can also be created to another location in the test or survey (or another test or survey) based on individual questions or scores.

The Perception Server is the web server application. It consists of the software that delivers the session to participants, the Security Manager, and the Enterprise Reporter. It enables one to present questions to participants one at a time, rather than all on the same page, and allows for the handling of thousands of participants.

Security Manager gives one control over who takes the sessions and who has user rights to use Enterprise Reporter as well as gain access to the software. It enables one to enter a participant's name and password into the system, arrange participants into groups, set up user rights to the Security Manager and Enterprise Reporter, and schedule groups or individuals to take the assessment.

Enterprise Reporter allows for one to conduct online reporting from anywhere in the world. It runs on the web and enables analysis of responses to the surveys or tests in an easily accessible fashion. The questions, answers, scores, and other statistics are stored in databases. Customized web reports can be created and then saved for repeated use.

Assessment by Technologically Based Surveys

The World Wide Web (WWW or web) is a medium that allows quick and easy collection of survey data. Web documents have the advantage of offering display forms. Respondents simply click, in small circles or boxes, their selection of an option, or they may be required to type responses into a box. After the participant submits a response, data are automatically sent to the survey creators (investigators) for compiling and processing information the respondents have provided. Due to the form feature and time savings, the medium appears to have advantages over traditional paper-and-pencil methods. These forms are convenient, simple to complete, and available to multiple users. Respondent and data-entry errors are virtually eliminated, and costs are considerably reduced because the need for paper, envelopes, and stamps are eliminated (Petit, 1999).

Conducting surveys via the web has some technical limitations. Several browsers do not support advanced HTML programming; therefore, it is important to use simple HTML code that most browsers will be able to read. Additionally, not every browser is able to read Java and Javascript programming language, so its use may be limited. Finally, it is also very important to consider that the web is accessible to all audiences, even children. Due to this fact, one needs to ensure that the measures selected for the survey are sensitive to age and maturity factors so as not to be offensive to younger populations.

Survey Monkey

Survey Monkey (www.surveymonkey.com) is a website that allows you to create, administer, and analyze simple surveys without cost; the generation of more complex surveys for web-based administration is available at a modest cost. The website contains templates for a number of different topics to get you started, and helpful manuals provide some guidance on the general principles of survey construction. Those who subscribe to the fee-based service can get additional help from the service's experts. If your target sample can be reached via the Internet, then this option may be the more desirable one for your purposes. Figure 9.6 shows what a set of survey questions might look like as displayed on the web.

SurveyWiz

SurveyWiz is a website that facilitates easy placement of surveys and questionnaires on the web (Birnbaum, 2001). This program (http://psych.fullerton.edu/mbirnbaum/programs/surveyWiz .htm) allows the user to add questions with either text boxes for input or scales composed of a series of radio buttons, the numbers and endpoint labels of which can be specified (Birnbaum, 2001). The survey must be given both a descriptive name (used for the title of the page and heading for the file) and a short name for reference. After the names are written, the Start Form button is pressed to begin survey construction. After the questions have been written, the type of response required selected, and the labels for the radio button scale composed (if applicable), the Demographic button is pressed. This button provides preset demographic questions that can be added to the beginning, middle, or end of the form. The Finish the Form button is then pressed, and one can type instructions within the HTML code in the area titled "(put your instructions here)." As a final step, the HTML text is copied and pasted into a text editor and the file loaded to the intended browser.

Other examples of web-based survey applications include Zoomerang (www.zoomerang.com), which is a division of MarketTools. It allows one to conduct surveys, obtain prompt responses to questions, and view data in real time. Also available

1.) How many school age children do you have (K − 12)?

○ 1

○ 2

○ 3

○ 4

○ 5 +

2.) Which elementary school is in your district?

```
[                                              ]
```

3.) What school(s) do your children attend?

1 `[                                              ]`

2 `[                                              ]`

3 `[                                              ]`

4.) My child/children attend(s)

○ Public school

○ Non-local public school

○ Charter school

○ Private School

○ Does not attend school yet

○ Graduated

○ Other (please specify) `[                              ]`

5.) What is your impression of the public school in your district?

○ Positive impression, my child/children are, will be attending this school

○ Negative impression, my child/children are, will be attending another public school

○ Negative impression, my child/children are, will be attending a private school

○ Undecided

Figure 9.6. An example of a public school survey.

is HostedSurvey.com (www.hostedsurvey.com) by Hosted-ware Corporation. It is entirely web based and standardized, so one's survey is compatible with all browsers on any PC, Macintosh, or other platform. Clients of HostedSurvey.com include those in academics, businesses, and nonprofit organizations. One final example is Qstation (www.qstation.com) by Atypica, Inc. Qstation is a self-service website where one can set up (or arrange to have set up) web-based structured data-gathering forms such as surveys.

■ Measurement and Reports of Problem Solving

A frequently cited criticism of objective tests is that they may lack authenticity (validity) or may only tangentially tap higher-order thinking skills. Two factors may explain why this occurs: Reporting thinking-process data is expensive, labor intensive, and consumes a lot of time; and higher-order thinking is often described in abstract terms, making it very difficult to measure concretely (Schacter, Herl, Chung, Dennis, & O'Neil, 1999). Broad definitions of problem solving have allowed standardized test developers to develop tests to assess a construct, even though such problems may seem trivial and do not represent the thinking processes (Shermis & Daniels, 2002). However, in the future, computer-based performance assessments will be able to assess such thinking processes for the same cost as standardized tests. They can be administered, scored, and reported online. Relational databases that capture student processes, backed by cognitive models of optimal thinking processes and performance, will allow the reporting of outcome and process variables (Schacter et al., 1999).

A study by Schacter and colleagues (1999) was conducted in which problem solving was assessed in informational environments through networked technology. Students were supposed to construct computer-based "knowledge maps" about environmental topics. The problem-solving processes and performance were assessed with CRESST's (National Center for Research on Evaluation, Standards, and Student Testing) Java Mapper, a simulated World Wide Web environment, a bookmarking applet, and outcome feedback. The Java Mapper was employed so that students could select concepts and link them to other concepts. The simulated World Wide Web consisted of over 200 web pages pertaining to environmental science and other topic areas, and the bookmarking applet allowed students to send web pages found during the search directly to concepts in their knowledge maps. While the students were searching for information and constructing their knowledge maps, they could access immediate outcome feedback concerning whether the links in their concept maps were correct and what additional work was needed.

The feedback was based on comparing student map performance to the map performance of experts. Besides reporting to students about performance on the outcome measures, feedback was given about which thinking processes contributed to or detracted from their performance. Those students who searched the web, browsed the pages to find relevant information, and accessed feedback were told the frequencies with which they employed these problem-solving processes. It was found that the students' scores on the knowledge mapping after this experiment (posttest) improved from the scores before the experiment (pretest). This kind of technology records students' thinking processes and gives them feedback on how well they engage in these processes. Using software and assessments such as this, teachers could benefit from the detailed record of student process data.

Technology-Based Science Assessment Environments

The study described in the foregoing section illustrates the opportunity for assessment provided by current technology but, as Quellmalz and Haertel (2000) indicate, there is still the emphasis in assessment on the extent to which content—the traditional declarative and procedural knowledges that guide most classroom instruction—has been mastered. Large-scale assessments tend to neglect deep subject matter understanding, inquiry strategies, communication, metacognitive and self-monitoring strategies, and collaboration.

Their position is that currently available assessments are only weakly aligned with the National Science Education Standards (NSES) and the National Council of Teachers of Mathematics (NCTM) standards. The weaknesses of traditional measures of such standards as formulating scientific explanations or communicating scientific understanding can be offset by the potential for development of technology-based assessments. Their illustrations of improvements that could be made in the areas of physical science, life science, and knowledge about ecosystems prove to be illuminating for any subject matter and any grade level.

Physical Sciences

Students' understanding of the ways that heat, light, mechanical motion, and electricity behave during nuclear reactions could be readily assessed in a computer simulation, but depicting the complexity of such dynamic interactions is too difficult for a paper-and-pencil, multiple-choice format and too dangerous for hands-on experiments.

Life Sciences

In the life sciences, understanding the multiple ways that cells interact to sustain life, or the passage of hereditary information through processes such as meiosis, gene alteration, or crossover, can be depicted best by using dynamic models that demonstrate the effects of changes at one biological level (e.g., DNA, chromosome) on other levels of life. Again, technology-based assessment tasks that take advantage of simulations developed for curriculum programs are well suited to assess knowledge of these highly interrelated systems.

Ecosystems

The effects of the rock cycle, patterns of atmospheric movement, and the impacts of natural and biological hazards on species can be more appropriately measured by using technology-based assessments. Such assessments can represent natural or artificial phenomena, systems, substances, or tools that are too large, too small, too dynamic, too complex, or too dangerous to be adequately represented in a paper-and-pencil test or a performance test format (Quellmalz, 1987). Quellmaz and Haertel's (2000) analysis of the ways in which technology based assessments differ from traditional assessments is shown in Table 9.1.

Within this framework, technology shows much promise for implementing formative assessment in its most desirable form. Ongoing assessments can be conducted within curriculum units designed to be aligned with standards. Contextual variations will be easily implemented to vary relevant learning environments consistent with those standards. Student responses can be continuously collected in digital formats for ready retrieval and analysis. Interpretations of data obtained by various forms of automated categorical scoring will support qualitative and quantitative summaries of performance, diagnosis of student difficulties, and recommendations for improvement of instruction, whether to individuals or classrooms. Concomitantly, electronic portfolios and case libraries will collect and display student work and digitally link work to standards (Quellmalz & Haertel, 2000).

Table 9.1. Contrast of Task/Item Designs in Traditional Tests with Technology-Supported Assessments of Scientific Inquiry

Scientific Inquiry Components	Traditional Testing Practice	Technology-Supported Assessments
Contexts and problems	• Decontextualized content • Discrete, brief problems	• Rich environments • Extensive web-based resources • Access to remote experts • Extended, authentic problems • Scaffolded/adapted tasks and sequences
Collaboration	• Typically prohibited	• Directly assessed in ongoing documentation
Planning and design	• Seldom tested, then with brief responses	• Documented and appraised iteratively
Conducting investigations, collecting data	• Infrequently tested • In performance tasks, limited to safe, economical, accessible equipment	• Addressed in web searches, hands-on tasks, simulations, and probeware
Analyzing and interpreting	• Typically limited to small data sets and hand calculations	• Possible to handle massive data sets, visualizations • Conduct complex multivariate analyses and display with spreadsheets, graphing tools
Communication and presenting	• Occasionally, brief, written conclusions, reports	• Support and documentation for ongoing informal communication, multimedia reports, and presentations
Monitoring, evaluating, reflecting, extending	• Typically not tested; if so, in brief written format	• Documented and scaffolded by electronic notebooks, portfolios, online multimedia case libraries of student work rated according to rubrics with annotated commentary

Source: Quellmalz & Haertel (2000).

■ Expansion of Computer-Based Assessment Technology

Delivery Through Multimedia

Computerized assessments can be expanded to include multimedia. Types of multimedia might include actual motion footage of an event, firsthand radio reports, and animations. Including these types of multimedia permits the presentation of tasks that are more like those actually encountered in academic and work settings. The ability to present these tasks may aid the measurement of problem-solving and other cognitive performances that were previously omitted due to impracticality or the impossibility of assessment with paper-and-pencil instruments. For example, in the discipline of science, an assessment could contain the multimedia aspects of a static electrocardiogram strip, a dynamic trace from a heart monitor (that moves left to right), and a heart sound keyed to the monitor display. The student has to use this information to diagnose the patient's condition correctly. For the assessment, making the correct diagnosis depends on the audio information, a skill that could not be tested easily in paper-and-pencil format (Bennett et al., 1999). By using such technology and including multimedia in online assessments, students can be assessed in situations that are more applicable to real life.

However, there are important issues to consider before incorporating multimedia in tests, including measurement, test development, test delivery, and concerns about cost. For example, it is important to ascertain exactly what the multimedia is supposed to elicit. Construct distortion and introduction of irrelevant factors can creep into the measurement equation if the multimedia is not appropriate. In reference to test development, one needs to determine if the tasks can be mass produced and whether normal development tools and processes should be changed. After considering development, delivery is also an important consideration. Can test centers or testing sites support technology, and what new hardware and software will be required? Security issues have to be addressed, and it must be determined how to prepare test takers for new technology (Shermis & Averitt, 2002). Finally, the cost to implement multimedia must be weighed to assess if the benefits of such technology justify its incorporation. After these concerns have been resolved, multimedia can be applied, giving test takers a more realistic type of assessment experience.

Scoring: Automated Essay Scoring

Automated Essay Scoring (AES) is the evaluation of written work via computers. Initial research restricted AES to English, but has recently extended to Japanese (Kawate-Mierzejewska, 2003), Hebrew (Vantage Learning, n.d.), Bahasa (Vantage Learning, 2002), and other languages. The interfaces are predominantly Internet-based, though there are some implementations that use CD-ROMs.

Most packages place documents within an electronic portfolio. They provide a holistic assessment of the writing, which can be supplemented by trait scores based on an established rubric and may provide qualitative critiques through discourse analysis. Most use ratings from humans as the criterion for determining accuracy of performance, though some of the packages will permit validation against other sources of information (e.g., large informational databases).

Obviously, computers don't understand written messages in the same way that humans do, a point that may be unnerving until one reflects on ways alternative technologies achieve similar results. Thus, cooking was once associated primarily with convection heating, a form of heating external to the food. But thinking outside the box, it can be seen that the same outcome can be achieved by a technology not based on convection, but on molecular activity within the uncooked items (i.e., the microwave oven) (Shermis et al., 2006).

The computer scores essays according to models of what human raters consider desirable and undesirable writing elements. Collections of these elements are referred to as traits; the intrinsic characteristics of writing are called trins (Page & Petersen, 1995); and the specific elements are called proxies or proxes (Page & Petersen, 1995).

Work on this technology has been underway for over 40 years, but only during the past 8 years has it become commercially available. There are four main automated essay scoring vendors: ETS (Criterion), Vantage Learning (Intellimetric), Pearson Knowledge Technologies (Intelligent Essay Assessor), and Measurement Incorporated (PEG).

Shermis, Mzumara, Olson, and Harrington (2001) conducted a study exploring the feasibility of using Project Essay Grade (PEG) software to evaluate web-based student essays serving as placement tests at a large Midwestern university. The students' essays were evaluated by six raters drawn from a pool of 15 instructional faculty and then evaluated by the PEG software. An inter-judge correlation among the human raters of $r = .62$ and a comparative statistic of $r = .71$ for the computer provided evidence that the computer model outperformed the multiple human judges in terms of producing consistent ratings.

Another study, conducted by Shermis, Koch, Page, Keith, and Harrington (2002), used PEG to evaluate essays, both holistically and with the rating of traits (i.e., content, organization, style, mechanics, and creativity). Results of two combined experiments were reported, with the first using the essays of 807 students to create statistical predictions for the essay grading software. The second experiment used the ratings from a

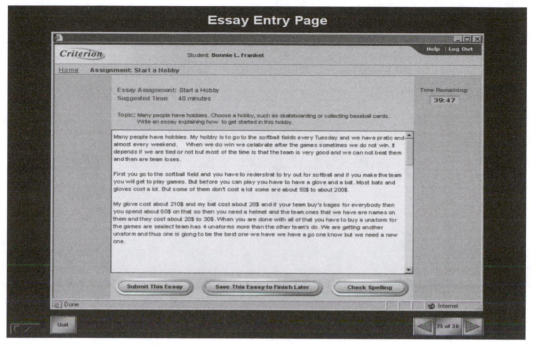

Figure 9.7. The essay entry page in Criterion(SM).

separate, random sample of 386 essays to compare the ratings of six human judges against those generated by the computer. The automated essay grading technique achieved significantly higher interrater reliability ($r = .83$) than human raters ($r = .71$) on an overall holistic assessment of writing. Similar results were obtained from the trait ratings as well.

Figure 9.7 shows an example of the Criterion(SM) automated essay scoring program by the Educational Testing Service. Criterion works as both an electronic portfolio (discussed below) and AES system. In Figure 9.7, the student types in an essay for grading. Essay prompts are provided by the program and have been precalibrated by human raters for grading. The selection in Figure 9.8 illustrates the manner in which the software provides feedback to the student. Criterion can provide both quantitative scores and feedback in the form of discourse analysis. With discourse analysis, the computer summarizes what it has formulated as the intent of the writer's essay. It will typically identify the writer's main theme, supporting points, and conclusions. If these do not match the writer's intent, then the writer can modify the essay until the computer's summary provides a better match.

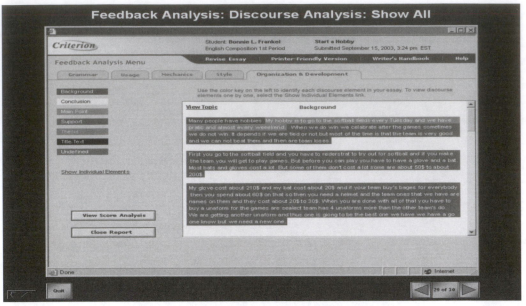

Figure 9.8. Criterion(SM)'s feedback page.

Alternative Assessments: Electronic Portfolios

What are electronic portfolios? As you know from earlier reading, portfolios are purposeful organizations of learner-selected evidence of school and non-school accomplishments. An *electronic* portfolio is similarly defined except that the evidence is contained on electronic media such as a flash drive, CD-ROM, or the web. Usually the work contained in a portfolio represents the best example of what the learner is capable of doing for a particular class of products. The selection of works to include in the portfolio is made by the student, which means that the student has to develop criteria and expertise to evaluate his or her own work.

Six major premises underlie the use of electronic portfolios. The electronic portfolio is:

1. Learner-centered and learner-directed
2. A developmental tool to help the learner set goals and expectations for performance
3. An instrument that provides a means for the learner to become self-aware and capable of gathering stronger evidence of skills
4. A basis for documenting and planning lifelong learning
5. An integration of career planning, counseling, curriculum, instruction, and assessment activity
6. Inclusive of the entire program (Stemmer, 1993)

The sixth premise relates to the fact that some selections may come from outside the formal curriculum (nonwork accomplishments relating to major field of interest).

Pros and Cons of Electronic Portfolios

Electronic portfolios have advantages over nonelectronic portfolios in that they typically stimulate greater acceptance from both teachers and students and are useful for other purposes such as job interviews or applications for higher education. Also, they apply to both individual and program evaluations and historically have correlated well with other outcome measures in disciplines where they have been used (Hatfield, 1997).

Electronic portfolios are not without disadvantages, however. There is a significant time investment for teachers and students, especially during the startup activities, and faculty and students may not have sophisticated knowledge of the software and hardware needed. Also, electronic portfolios require technical support, and there are varying levels of acceptance from other potential consumers. Figure 9.9 shows a screen shot of an electronic portfolio cover page.

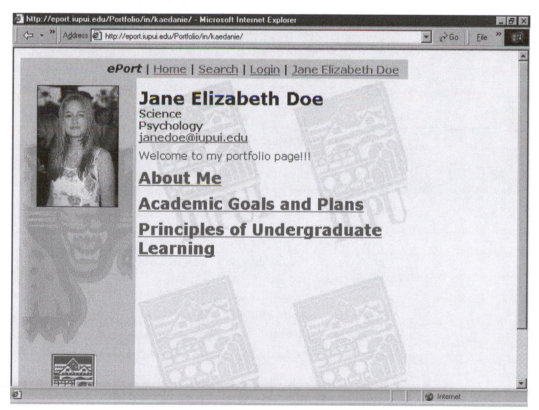

Figure 9.9. Example of an electronic portfolio.

Websites for Electronic Portfolios

Some academic websites provide additional examples of electronic portfolios. One is the portfolio page for Indiana University-Purdue University Indianapolis (https://oncourse .iu.edu/osp-portal/site/!eportfoliogateway). From this web page, students can log in and revise their portfolios, or visitors may search for a portfolio by typing in a student's last name or ID number. Another electronic portfolio site is www .essdack.org/port, presented by Soderstrom Elementary School in Kansas. This site gives tips for creating electronic portfolios as well as providing examples of elementary students' portfolios. Two additional sites include Helen Barrett's online publications (http://transition.alaska.edu/www/port folios.html) and the Kalamazoo Portfolio Project (www.idc .ufl.edu/resources/Electronic_Portfolios).

■ Observations

Peer Review

Peer and self-assessment have proven useful for formative evaluation. An advantage of self-assessment is that student motivation often improves when students are respected and involved in the learning process. An advantage of peer assessment is that feedback from an instructor may not necessarily be interpreted appropriately from the student's standpoint. Similarly, feedback from another student may have a larger impact than feedback from a teacher. There are also benefits to the peer assessors in that assessing other students' work forces the learners to think about the attributes of good work, gives them more of an incentive to learn material, and enables them to see the strengths and weaknesses of their own work compared to that of peers (Robinson, 1999).

Problems arise with peer reviewing when used as a part of summative assessment. Some peer reviewers may be trained to employ specific criteria in reviewing documents of low complexity. But for many students and for more complex documents, it is very difficult to teach the means of reviewing a document against rubrics. Therefore, a review from a single student may not be sufficient to produce a revision that meets the instructor's standards. An additional concern is that peer reviewers may not review a friend as critically as they would another student. These concerns can be addressed by employing anonymous and multiple peer reviews.

Multiple peer reviews protect against subjective judgments and increase the credibility of the evaluation of a document. If reviews are anonymous, biases toward friends may be alleviated and more objective evaluations can be made. One drawback in using this process is the burden that results from the accretion of multiple copies of reviews and revisions contributed by students. When conducted electronically, the paperwork is eliminated or at least lessened considerably.

To facilitate electronic self- and peer reviews a database network or web-based system is required. Students produce their documents in digital form and submit the form electronically so that it can be channeled into a database and stored. Multiple reviews of the documents can also be submitted electronically and then sorted with the documents to which they pertain. This web-based database system permits a double-blind system in which reviewers do not know whose document they are reviewing.

Advantages of a computer-based anonymous peer review system include ease of reviewing and rewriting before a grade is assigned to student performance. Also, the system can allow for team-based writing projects in which the instructor is no longer viewed as a grader, but as a facilitator who helps students help one another. Finally, systems can be set up in which students first write and outline a proposal, then exchange comments with peers before writing their papers. This stimulates thought about the process of writing and makes it harder to plagiarize from the large number of documents in electronic circulation.

Automated Data Collectors for Indirect Observation

Hedden (1997) has evaluated an apparatus that allows subjects to collect data on their own experiences. He uses the apparatus to study subject interaction with computer games, but believes it can be used for research on practically any type of human-computer interaction. In such studies intrinsic motivation is important; people learn better when they are motivated by interest in the content or process of learning (Hedden, 1997).

Intrinsic motivation can be fostered by a sense that one is in control and acting on one's own will. Hedden found that to create these feelings of autonomy, there should be no limits on the students' choice of what to do or how long to keep trying. In addition, the investigator should not be present during the study. To comply with these conditions, Hedden removed the experimenter and allowed students to collect and record data interacting with a computer. Hedden's apparatus can be referred to as a computer-within-a-computer. The outer computer represents an observer of the student while interacting with the software that runs on the inner computer. This represents an attempt to ensure intrinsic motivation by forming a context that is supportive of the student's autonomy.

For this system to work, it must have a single switch operation in which students begin and end each session by manipulating a single switch. It is also recommended that a single source, platform-independent transcoded S-VHS output to a VCR be used. This allows for recording at the slowest speed, so that students will not have to change tapes as often, and allows for quicker fast-forward and rewind scans. Additionally, an audio mixer is needed so that the student's voice is blended with the audio from the target software. This is required so that the sound effects from the software (if any) do not overpower the sound of the student's voice. The operating system must also be able to support multiple tasks and the software should be able to handle all aspects of the programming. Finally, a number of ports should be available for a variety of data output and transformation.

After the system is operational, but before data collection begins, students need to be trained on the apparatus. They should understand the experimental procedures as well as the target software and task. It is also highly recommended that students practice on the apparatus and view a test recording of their performance with the investigator present. After these precautions are taken, both the system and student should be prepared for data collection.

■ Summary

The field of web-based assessment is vast, and this chapter provides only a sampling of the evolving technology. We have described several emerging technical frameworks, some principal data collection procedures, and a few popular sites offering software to implement such procedures. Space does not permit a comprehensive coverage of all the software, and for any given reader a selection of a few sites would be all that is necessary. Accordingly, we provide an appendix to this chapter with a listing of websites pertaining to assessment that would be helpful to review on a continuing basis. These sites can provide the reader a sense in emerging web-based assessment as it continues to evolve in the future.

It should be evident from the contents of this chapter that within the context of introducing alternative forms of assessment into the classroom, the new technologies associated with computer delivery have considerable potential for technology-based assessments in the use of portfolios, surveys, distributed learning, learning communities, and learning environments. Technologically based assessments are driven by active problem solution, frequent probing of student progress in understanding and use of strategies, and feedback. Feedback can be provided interactively by teachers and other students or functionally by the observation of outcomes achieved by following different strategic paths.

In brief, as summarized by Pelligrino and colleagues (2001), technology (computer)-supported assessments have the potential for:

- Providing virtual learning contexts. They create rich environments capable of targeting domain-specific objectives through examination of (or experiment with) variations embedded in cognitions about the relations in the subject matter, including organization, conceptualizations, or cause-effect.
- Making use of distributed learning experiences among students. By linking clusters of computers, each of which is used by a student interactively with other students, technology is capable of collecting data to be used for assessments of the contributions of each student and group on attaining instructional objectives.
- Tracking student use of metacognitive strategies. As noted elsewhere, this is a continually emerging trend in understanding student learning; technology can be used to compare student thinking patterns with the way experts initiate and monitor their reasoning and strategies as problems are initiated, attempted, solved, reflected on, and repaired in moving toward instructional goals.
- Providing instructors with sensitive feedback for suggesting alternative ways for engaging students in performance tasks and for responding to assessment tasks.
- Detailed, empirically supported feedback on the kind of content selected, on the relevance of information used for given problem types, and on processing strategies associated with finding solutions in decision making or problem solving.
- Automated scoring of complex responses reliably and validly where the scoring by human raters, in achieving reliable and valid scores for essays, concept maps, portfolios, or

performance, would be difficult at best within a reasonable amount of time.

- Introducing standardized variations and current developments in instructional aids with known positive effects on learning; they can be developed to parallel the kind of assessments needed to track student progress; for declaring what information is needed for implementing student thinking; for identifying sources of information for easy accessibility; and for determining the processing of the material, consistent with learning objectives, that ought to be considered.
- Connecting to the immense corpus of information, bibliographic collections, and current thinking available at the multitude of sources and locations on the Internet, all of which would be virtually impossible using only library resources.
- Following up instructional practice in terms of detailed assessments of process-paths as well as the traditional assessments of outcomes, thereby incorporating important requirements for use of formative assessment in facilitating instructional adaptation to student progress.

■ Appendix: Resource List of Websites Pertaining to Assessment

- AERA
  www.aera.net
- AERA Division D Measurement and Research Methodology
  www.aera.net/divisions/d
- AERA SIG Rasch Measurements Special Interest Group
  http://209.41.24.153/rmt/index.htm
- American Evaluation Association
  www.eval.org
- Aptitudes
  http://members.aol.com/jocrf19/index.html
- Applied Measurement Professionals, Inc.
  www.applmeapro.com
- AskERIC:
  http://ericir.syr.edu
- Assessment and Evaluation on the Internet
  http://ericae.net/intbod.stm
- Assessment Links
  http://cresst96.cse.ucla.edu/index.htm
- Assessment Projects
  www.mcrel.org/products/assessment/index.asp

- Sustainable Standards-Based Assessment System homepage
  www.mcrel.org/products/assessment/designing.asp
- Assessment Systems
  www.assess.com
- Association for Institutional Research
  www.fsu.edu/~air/home.htm
- Buros Institute of Mental Measurements
  www.unl.edu/buros/
- College Board
  www.collegeboard.org/
- Comprehensive Adult Student Assessment System
  www.casas.org/
- CourseMetric
  www.coursemetric.com
- Educational Testing Service
  www.ets.org
- ERIC Clearinghouse on Assessment and Evaluation
  http://ericae.net
- ERIC Test Locator
  http://ericae.net/testcol.htm
- GMAT
  www.gmac.com
- GRE Online
  www.gre.org/
- Instructional Assessment System (IAS) at the University of Washington
  www.washington.edu/oea/ias1.htm
- Journal of Psychoeducational Assessment
  www.psychoeducational.com
- Kaplan
  www.kaplan.com
- Law School Admission Service
  www.lsas.org
- MCAT
  www.aamc.org/stuapps/admiss/mcat/start.htm
- AERA SIGS
  www.aera.net/sigs/
- Multiple Choice Test Demonstration
  www.nott.ac.uk/cal/mathtest/demon.htm
- National Association of Test Directors
  www.natd.org
- National Council on Measurement in Education (NCME)
  www.ncme.org/
- NCS
  www.ncs.com

- Question Mark (QM)
  www.qmark.com/
- Reporting Assessment Results
  www.ncrel.org/sdrs/areas/issues/methods/assment/as600.htm
- Scanning Systems
  www.scantron.com
- Search ERIC Wizard
  http://ericae.net/scripts/ewiz
- Student Evaluation of Educational Quality (SEEQ) at Pennsylvania State University
  www.psu.edu/celt/SEEQ.html
- Undergraduate Outcomes Assessment of the University of Colorado at Boulder
  www.colorado.edu/pba/outcomes
- Web-Based Assessment Tools
  http://ist-socrates.berkeley.edu:7521/wbi-tools/assessment-tools.html

University Testing Services

- BYU Testing Services
  testing.byu.edu/testinghome
- Indiana University Purdue University Indianapolis
  http://assessment.iupui.edu/testing/
- Michigan State University
  www.couns.msu.edu/testing/
- Northern Arizona University
  www.nau.edu/~ctc/
- Oklahoma State University Testing and Evaluation Service
  www.okstate.edu/ed/extension/testing/testeval.htm
- Old Dominion University
  http://web.odu.edu/webroot/orgs/STU/stuserv.nsf/pages/test_ctr
- San Francisco State University
  www.sfsu.edu/~testing
- Texas A&M University
  www.tamu.edu/marshome
- Tulsa Community College
  www.tulsa.cc.ok.us/catalog/general/stuserv.html#p6_0
- University of Alabama in Huntsville
  http://info.uah.edu/admissions/tstsrv/test.html
- University of Alaska–Anchorage
  www.uaa.alaska.edu/advise/home.html

- University of South Alabama
  www.southalabama.edu/counseling/testing1.htm
- University of Texas–Austin
  www.utexas.edu/academic/mec

■ References

Bennett, R. E., Goodman, M., Hessinger, J., Kahn, H., Ligget, J., Marshall, G., et al. (1999). Using mulitmedia in large-scale computer-based testing programs. *Computers in Human Behavior, 15*(3–4), 283–294.

Birnbaum, M. H. (2001). *Introduction to behavioral research on the internet.* Englewood Cliffs, NJ: Prentice Hall.

Board of Testing and Assessment/National Research Council. (2002). *Technology and assessment: Thinking ahead—proceedings from a workshop.* Washington, DC: The National Academy Press.

Butcher, P. G. (2008, July). *Online assessment at the Open University using open source software.* Paper presented at the CAA Conference, Loughborough, UK.

Cognition and Technology Group at Vanderbilt. (2000). Adventures in anchored instruction: Lessons from beyond the ivory tower. In R. Glaser (Ed.), *Advances in instructional psychology: Vol. 5. Educational design and cognitive science* (pp. 35–99). Mahwah, NJ: Erlbaum.

Glaser, R. (1965). *Teaching machines and programmed learning, II: Data and directions.* Washington, DC: National Education Association of the United States.

Hatfield, S. (1997). *Assessment in the major: Tools and tips for getting started.* Paper presented at the 1997 Assessment Conference, Indianapolis, IN.

Hedden, C. (1997). An automated data collector for study of human-computer interaction. *Computers in Human Behavior, 13*(2), 205–227.

Hunka, S. M. (1977). *Eight years of computer-assisted instruction: Now what?* (No. RIR-77-6). Edmonton, AB: University of Alberta, Division of Educational Research Services.

Kawate-Mierzejewska, M. (2003, March). *E-rater software.* Paper presented at the Japanese Association for Language Teaching, Tokyo, Japan.

Lumsdaine, A. A., & Glaser, R. (1960). *Teaching machines and programmed learning: A source book.* Washington, DC: National Education Association of the United States.

Moore, O. K. (1964). *Autotelic response environments and exceptional children: Special children in century 21.* Seattle, WA: Special Child Publications.

Moore, O. K. (1980). About talking typewriters, folk models, and discontinuities: A progress report on twenty years of research, development and application. *Educational Technology*, *20*(2), 15–27.

Page, E. B., & Petersen, N. S. (1995). The computer moves into essay grading: Updating the ancient test. *Phi Delta Kappan*, *76*(7), 561–565.

Papert, S. (1980). *Mindstorms: Children, computers, and powerful ideas*. New York: Basic Books.

Papert, S. (1993). *The children's machine: Rethinking school in the age of the computer*. New York: Basic Books.

Pelligrino, J. W., Chudowsky, N., & Glaser, R. (2001). *Knowing what students know: The science and design of educational assessment*. Washington, DC: National Academy Press.

Petit, F. A. (1999). Exploring the use of the World Wide Web as a psychology data collection tool. *Computers in Human Behavior*, *15*, 67–71.

Piaget, J. (1955). *The child's construction of reality*. London: Routledge.

Quellmalz, E. S. (1987). Developing reasoning skill. In J. R. Baron & R. J. Sternberg (Eds.), *Teaching thinking skills: Theory and practice*. New York: Freedman Press.

Quellmalz, E. S., & Haertel, G. D. (2000). Breaking the mold: Technology-based science assessment in the 21st century. Retrieved February 19, 2008, from http://pals.sri.com/papers/21stC/21stcentury.htm.

Robinson, J. M. (1999). Computer-assisted peer review. In S. Brown, P. Race, & J. Bull (Eds.), *Computer-assisted assessment in higher education*. London: Kogan Page Limited.

Schacter, J., Herl, H. E., Chung, G. K. W. K., Dennis, R. A., & O'Neil, H. F., Jr. (1999). Computer-based performance assessments: A solution to the narrow measurment and reporting of problem-solving. *Computers in Human Behavior*, *15*(3–4), 403–418.

Shermis, M. D., & Averitt, J. (2002). Where did all the data go? Internet security for web-based assessments. *Educational Measurement: Issues and Practice*, *21*(2), 20–25.

Shermis, M. D., Burstein, J., & Leacock, C. (2006). Applications of computers in assessment and analysis of writing. In C. A. MacArthur, S. Graham, & J. Fitzgerald (Eds.), *Handbook of writing research* (pp. 403–416). New York: Guilford Publications.

Shermis, M. D., & Daniels, K. E. (2002). Web applications in assessment. In T. Banta & Associates (Eds.), *Building a scholarship of assessment* (pp. 148–166). San Francisco: Jossey-Bass.

Shermis, M. D., Koch, C. M., Page, E. B., Keith, T., & Harrington, S. (2002). Trait ratings for automated essay grading. *Educational and Psychological Measurement*, *62*(1), 5–18.

Shermis, M. D., Mzumara, H. R., Olson, J., & Harrington, S. (2001). On-line grading of student essays: PEG goes on the web at IUPUI. *Assessment and Evaluation in Higher Education*, *26*(3), 247–259.

Skinner, B. F. (1954). The science of learning and the art of teaching. *Harvard Educational Review*, *24*(2), 86–97.

Skinner, B. F. (1968). *The technology of teaching, 1968.* New York: Appleton-Century-Crofts.

Stemmer, P. (1993). *Electronic portfolios: Are they going to be the very next craze?* Paper presented at the Michigan School Testing Conference, Ann Arbor, MI.

Vantage Learning. (2002). *A study of IntelliMetric™ scoring for responses written in Bahasa Malay* (No. RB-735). Newtown, PA: Vantage Learning.

Vantage Learning. (n.d.). *A preliminary study of the efficacy of IntelliMetric™ for use in scoring Hebrew assessments.* Newtown, PA: Vantage Learning.

White, B. Y., & Frederiksen, J. R. (1998). Inquiry, modeling, and metacognition: Making science accessible to all students. *Cognition and Instruction, 16*(1), 3–118.

White, B. Y., & Frederiksen, J. R. (2000). Metacognitive facilitation: An approach to making scientific inquiry accessible to all. In J. Minstrell & van Zee, E. (Eds.), *Teaching in the inquiry-based science classroom.* Washington, DC: American Association for the Advancement of Science.

CHAPTER 10

Improving Tests

I T IS HARD TO KNOW exactly what is meant when a student says your test was fair or when a standardized test is claimed to be inappropriate. What does *fair* or *inappropriate* mean? Is it fair or appropriate because it seems to reach idiosyncratic academic goals or because it satisfies the intended goals of the test constructor? Because achieving a high score is challenging but attainable, or because it should be within the grasp of anyone having taken a course? Because the test effectively separates those who studied the hardest from those who did not study or because we all should achieve the same grade? Or, simply, is it fair or appropriate because those who achieved a passing grade think it was fair?

Initially, it may seem that reaching the level of a good test for either formative or summative evaluation is a challenging endeavor. However, meeting the challenge simply requires constant attention to the alignment of measures to standards, improving reliability of the measures, improving the extent to which the test measures what it is intended to measure, improving the ability of the test to discriminate those who have learned from those who haven't learned, and, of course, improving the ability of the test to provide information about what and how students have learned.

■ The Context of Test Improvement

Schools and classrooms are increasingly subjected to testing from a variety of sources, including standardized tests used by counselors or school psychologists for specialized purposes in individuals, by legislators concerned with meeting NCLB requirements, and by states that participate by their development of comprehensive examinations. These assessments supplement both the formal and informal assessments employed by classroom teachers for assessing the progress of their classrooms. On occasion the functions of these two sets of assessments appear to be in opposition, rather than supplementary, to one another in terms of their utility.

Current views of classroom assessment strongly suggest that the most meaningful measures for facilitating learning should be those given by classroom teachers. In doing so, as Shepard has cautioned,

> Good teaching and assessment constantly asks about old understandings in new ways, calls for new applications, and draws new connections. (Shepard, 1997, p. 27)

and,

> We should not . . . agree to a contract with our student which says that the only fair test is one with familiar and well-rehearsed problems [that inevitably lead to rote memorization]. The assessment system (should) provide a basis for developing a metacognitive awareness of what are important characteristics of [good thinking], addressing not only the product one is trying to achieve, but also the process of achieving it. (Wiggins, 1989, p. 30, as quoted in Shepard, 2000, p. 62)

Theory to Practice Box 10.1 outlines the questions raised as guidance for developing such a system. A similar plan regarding what principals should know is outlined in Emberger (2007).

Principles of Test Construction

Any measure, for whatever function it is to serve, must be well constructed to achieve clear-cut academic purposes (goals or standards). The professional assessment community, engaged in establishing frameworks for effective assessment, does adhere to stringent standards of test development. The assessment practitioner's theories and practices involve care in making certain that test characteristics satisfactorily lead to effective measurement. Furthermore, there is the recognition that effective assessments are not achieved on a single trial but require continual administration, analysis, and revision in attempts to meet acceptable criteria for suitable measures of educational progress.

Theory to Practice Box 10.1
THINKING LIKE AN ASSESSMENT SPECIALIST

1. What is the learning goal for which the test or assessment is to be used? Is this measure designed on the basis of what I want students to know? Was it designed before instruction was planned so that it is contiguous with my instructional plan? Is it a continuing measure or is it simply a stop-gap, one-time measure of the end result of my teaching of a unit?

2. I know a number of testing modes and techniques, their functions and limitations. Which one among the many alternatives would provide me with the information I need?

3. Within the technique that I have selected for a trial attempt, what will be the best way to apply it? Should I use a paper-and-pencil test? Have I considered the possibility of using computerized testing, data collection, storage of items in an item bank, analyses, and so on?

4. Will I construct test items of a limited-response type? Should I have students write an essay to describe the conduct of an experiment? Or should I have the students perform a skill and then measure them by use of rubrics?

5. When I gather the scores on the examination will I be able to analyze them in language that students and parents will understand? Will I be able to use the scores for feedback both to me for improving instruction and to students for improving their learning? Or does the test I propose simply provide a score of performance at the end of a unit?

6. How will I use the data I have gathered for improving the measure? How will I use the psychometric measures to inform me that the test item or rubrics are working satisfactorily? How will I evaluate the measure, items, or rubric as good ones for the purpose of assessing the student performance? Will I be able to evaluate the reliability and validity effectively? Will the test differentiate students on important factors such as knowledge, understanding, comprehension, or problem solving? Will it differentiate successful from less successful students (on the total test, component parts, or specific items)?

7. Have I made the necessary preparations for using the test or test components in future classes? For example, in what form will the test be stored—as a unit or as test items or components? For limited-response tests, will I know how the alternatives functioned (too easy, too difficult) on which to base revisions? For performance tests, will I have the scoring bases in a form that can be retrieved and revised?

Continual activity, beginning with the planning of a test, underlies revisions (often multiple revisions) based on awareness of (a) *standards*, (b) available *procedures* for effective attainment of measures of those standards, (c) *monitoring* the effectiveness of those procedures for reaching those standards, and (d) *repair strategies* for assessment measures that are only partially (or not at all) effective for reaching those standards. In particular, careful revision is made of measures according to:

- The *content specialists'* standards for the *content of assessment* devices
- The *psychometrician's* (measurement specialist) principles of test construction (psychometrics) regarding *test and item characteristics* known to be related to precise measurement

These principles are also those that belong to you, one of the most important users of assessment tools. The underlying principles of good assessments are employed by informed teachers, perhaps less formally than by the professional content specialist or the psychometrician, but nevertheless taken into consideration in the development of assessment plans. Awareness of the roles of both the content specialists and the test professionals in producing effective measures will provide a more informed knowledge base for improving assessments. It also serves us in understanding how other measures, such as standardized measures (which are sometimes believed to be thoughtlessly imposed on the school), undergo continuous improvement for effectively serving instruction and learning.

Effective Classroom Assessment

In the forefront of instructional considerations, current evidence demonstrates that assessment, particularly formative assessment practices, are influential in producing significant gains in achievement (Black & Wiliam, 1998). However, simply designed assessments, without attention given to the characteristics of good test construction, whether formative or summative, don't automatically produce gains (Shepard, 2000). To produce acceleration of learning through effective instructional practice, teachers must interpret or otherwise act upon the data that is produced by the assessment and is assumed to be precise and accurate. Also, the data must be understood for its implications by the teacher or other user of the information. In other words, the teacher, in concert with other stakeholders using the test data, must know:

- *What* the test is intended to do
- *That* the test is doing its job
- *What* the test or test items represent
- *How* the test relates to instructional methods

- The *relevance* of scores for different phases of instruction (diagnosis of entering knowledge or behavior, ongoing instruction, or end products)
- The *relation* of the scores to the identification of strategies or styles students use for learning

To understand requirements for improving tests also involves understanding that tests represent underlying curriculum models. For example, a curriculum model might be based on *mastery of content*; if so, students might emphasize the acquisition of precise individual performance regardless of the performance of others. The related assessments would be challenging, but attainable. On the other hand, a curriculum model based on *sorting students* from excellent to poor along some ability dimension would suggest a comparison with others (more or less excellent); student perceptions might emphasize that "those who studied the hardest got the best score." An *assessment-centered classroom* (Donovan & Bransford, 2005) would emphasize formative assessment. Students would be expected to be able to assess the quality of their thinking; the adequacy of their language; the scientific, linguistic, or mathematic tools they use in solving problems; and the effectiveness of the outcomes of their thinking. These assessments provide opportunity for feedback on how to revise students' thinking or behaviors that enter into the effectiveness of their efforts rather than simply deriving a score and then going on to the next unit (Donovan & Bransford, 2005, pp. 45–46). These descriptions of classrooms, of course, are limited illustrations. There are many other alternative emphases and perceptions for these or other examples of curriculum models; which one is used depends on your own curricular objectives.

■ Item Improvement

A common perception that should be abandoned is that educational measures are simply compilations of questions in a given format such as true-false, multiple choice, open ended, and so on. Tests and test items are carefully and technically developed measures. As such they have characteristics that can be useful in differentiating students according to their achievement of different classroom objectives. By using these characteristics with confidence, tests can be used appropriately to achieve classroom purposes, whether formative or summative, whether in biology or language, whether acquisition of facts or development of concepts, or any other focus.

The goal of test improvement may appear to imply a concern with improving teacher-made tests alone. Although this is an important focus, you will also see that the procedures to be discussed apply to development of tests where banks of test items accompany text books, from which you make selections for testing students at given points in instruction.

The procedures for improving tests are the ones used by expert specialists in assessment who are employed as professional test constructors—procedures with which you, too, should become familiar. Understanding the properties of tests and test items within the context of improving tests is certainly a concern when you make decisions to select or evaluate standardized tests, whether for diagnosis, determination of student status on personality characteristics (learning style, motivation), or accountability. We should not neglect to note that the underlying concepts regarding test improvement apply equally to other aspects of measurement such as the use of rubrics employed in scoring essays and performance measures. They also extend to other forms of measurement such as inventories (e.g., interest inventories), surveys (e.g., surveys of student motivations), or rating scales (e.g., evaluations of an oral report).

Placement of Students in a Distribution of Test Scores

Among the many purposes of assessments is their use in classification of students according to some underlying ability or performance. These assessments might be obtained for placing students in special classes for remedial work, for enrichment, or for curricular interests. The technical question here is "Are the resulting scores mostly at one end or the other, or are they in the middle (mean, median) of a distribution of scores?" A related question is "Are the scores bunched together, or are they dispersed around the mean?" For more accurate use, the scores should be so distributed that they discriminate the test takers in terms of the ability or achievement criteria on which the purpose of classification depends.

A primary characteristic of this function of measurement is that the test should distinguish or separate out the most successful (the high scorers) from the least successful (the low scorers); for instance, you may want to determine who the best reader is, the second-best reader, and so on. You might want to sort students on other bases; for example, will the test results provide information that will allow you to identify students who are using flexible versus rigid processes or strategies in solving problems? With appropriately designed tests, the scoring of items will result in a distribution of test scores, allowing us to make reliable classifications.

Assessments that sort students will distribute student scores according to a normal or approximately normal distribution provided the test is composed of items that are working well. You are probably already familiar with the representation of this distribution as a bell-shaped curve. You will most likely meet it frequently in other courses or in everyday reading such as events in the news.

The statistical properties of the normal curve permit norm-referenced interpretation of student performance on a test. For example, the middle of the distribution corresponds to the 50th percentile—the midpoint below and above which are 50 percent of the distribution of all people who took the test. In a bell-shaped normal curve, it is also the mean or average. By using the psychometric characteristics of test items, we have the potential for evaluating the value of the item for understanding not only the achievement of a student but also the implications of the scores for instructional improvement.

Characteristics of Items: Item Analysis

An initial (and primary) concern in any educational assessment, whether formal or informal, is the alignment of the test items

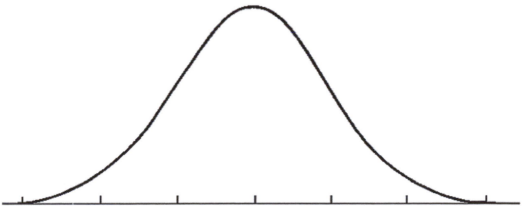

Figure 10.1. A normal curve.

with standards. You know whether the test is aligned by the extent to which the content of the test items matches the content (topics and skills) in the standards; each test item should correspond to an objective in the standards, and key ideas in the standards should appear, proportionately, on the tests.

Item analysis is geared to identifying problems that might have been encountered in constructing a test. How difficult is the item? That is, how many students answered the item correctly? Did the item separate the high from the low scorers? Were the test scores normally distributed? Was the score on an item (correct or incorrect) correlated with the total score? Which items were too easy? Which too difficult? Are there items to be replaced? Are there items that work well, but will work more efficiently if revised? If two items seem to be equally effective in measuring a given objective, is there reason for using both or can one be selected over the other?

In order to determine whether or not an item is working well—whether it is a good item to be retained or a bad item to be discarded—two aspects of the responses to that item are determined: *difficulty* and *discrimination*.

The Difficulty Index

Difficulty takes into consideration the number of respondents who answer an item correctly; for instance, if 95 percent of students answer an item correctly, the item is easy. An interpretation of an item answered correctly by most or all students might be that it is not effectively identifying where difficulties in learning or instruction have occurred. Moreover, we might question the validity of the item as it might have been answered on the basis of sources of information other than instruction—for instance, selected from prior knowledge or selected as the only possible answer from a poorly constructed set of alternatives (distractors). Such interpretations lessen the utility of an item for diagnosing the reasons for adequate student achievement or lack thereof.

If items have been developed to differentiate students according to achievement and understanding related to instructional processes, then the item will be diagnostically useful for feedback to teachers and students alike. An appropriate level of difficulty is one that is challenging, that is a measure of student progress, and that is a step up from entering levels of learning. If the distractors represent those answers that can be identified with memorizing information, understanding information, or transferring conceptual understandings, then the item will be diagnostically useful—it will have been strategically answered according to the functional utility of the information acquired by the student.

The difficulty of an item is calculated by determining the proportion of individuals who answered the item correctly (in the case of multiple-choice tests, it is the percentage of students who selected the correct alternative). Converting the score to percentages provides the desired measure of difficulty, technically labeled p (associate the letter with *percentage*).

If one had a class of 30 students, and 21 students answered the item correctly, the item difficulty, represented by p, would be

$$p = 21/30 = .72$$

A p of .72 represents the percentage (72 percent) of the class responding correctly to the item. An interpretation of this p-value is that the item is moderately easy. An item that has a difficulty index of 100 percent, in addition to being easy, might mean that the answer is obvious to all, that there was a giveaway in the item noticed by testwise students who may otherwise have had no knowledge of the item content, or that instruction reached all students so efficiently regarding the item content that all got the item correct. Conversely, a very low difficulty index, representing the fact that a majority of the students failed the item, could be interpreted as being due to ambiguous alternatives, students' lack of understanding, or poor instruction. If a multiple-choice item had four alternatives, and students answered the question by sheer guessing (chance), the difficulty index would be $p = .25$.

An item that is too easy or too difficult may be thought to disclose little or nothing about the student's performance and, accordingly, may be discarded or in need of significant revision. In general, difficulty levels between .50 and .65 provide optimal bases for reliability and validity (the range .50–.65 is a function of the number of alternatives in an objective question). You can demonstrate this point for yourself by considering an item at the extremes, say with 100 percent of the class responding correctly to the item. However you group the respondents, the average difficulty index would be the same for each group—100 percent—and therefore the item failed to yield scores that differentiated the groups. It does not provide opportunity to discriminate high- from low-achieving students. Nevertheless, in classroom practice, it is desirable to have some moderately easy (higher than $p = .50$) or difficult (less that $p = .50$) items to constrain the range between $p = .25$ and $p = .75$; if nothing more, the mix of items would provide varying degrees of motivation, challenge, and success.

To avoid premature decisions to discard an item with a very high or very low difficulty index but that may otherwise be useful, the discrimination index provides another source of useful information—an index of the degree to which the item, regardless of its difficulty, differentiates the high from the low performers on the overall test.

The Discrimination Index

Determining whether an item is good or bad can be enhanced by understanding how well response alternatives discriminate successful from less-successful students. Constructing good multiple-choice questions is not simply a matter of providing one correct and a few incorrect answers, however *correctness* is defined. Poorly constructed distractors are almost certainly going to make your questions less worthwhile than they might be.

First, we can assume the overall test score is a basis for identifying good and poor students. Then, it can be determined that the extent to which the responses to an item for each group differentiates students who perform well (those who get high scores on the total test) from those who perform poorly (those who get low scores on the total test).

Secondly, the functioning of the distractors of each item can be determined by similar comparisons. Thus, differential performance of high- and low-performing students on item correct answers and distractors enables an understanding of the item's ability to differentiate high-performing from low-performing students. (Note that the same principle applies to the use of a given rubric in scoring performance.) Thus, for an item constructed to measure transferability of a principle in science, it should be found that those who have achieved this understanding will answer the item(s) correctly (i.e., select the correct alternative) more often than those who do not. Similarly, those who have not achieved this understanding will make errors represented in the selection of the distractors (i.e., they select the incorrect alternatives, the distractors).

The differentiation between groups is described as the *discrimination index* for an item. Regardless of an item's difficulty, the discrimination index represents the extent to which the high scorers on the total test answer the item correctly compared to the extent to which the low scorers on the total test answer the item correctly. In that case the item is said to have a positive value; for example, it might be stated as +.65. If the opposite is true (i.e., poorer students do better than good students), we say the item is a negative discriminator. The statistic D can take on a range from −1 to +1. The better the items in a test discriminate good students from poor students, the more reliable the test will be.

How is D calculated? Let's say we have another class of 30 students. Rank order the test scores from highest to lowest. Then put the top 15 scores above the median score in the high group and the bottom 15 scores below the median score in the low group. You have probably noted that the base number or denominator is 15. Now calculate the p (remember, this is the difficulty index) on our hypothetical item for each of the groups—the high and the low group.

Assuming that 12 of the 15 students with high scores responded correctly to the item, the p for the high group is calculated as follows:

$$p = 12/15 = .8$$

Assuming that nine of the low-performing students responded correctly to the item, we would calculate the p for the low group as follows:

$$p = 9/15 = .6$$

The discrimination index, or D, is calculated by subtracting one difficulty index from the other, as follows:

$$D = .8 \text{ (the } p \text{ for the high group)} - .6 \text{ (the } p \text{ for the low group)} = +.2$$

This item seems to be working reasonably well. That is, 70 percent $[(.8 + .6)/2]$ of the total group is answering the item correctly, and it is doing a reasonable job in discriminating the better students from the poorer students.

The Relationship between *p* and *D*

At the extremes it is easy to visualize the relationship between *p* and *D*. If *p* is 0 (no one in the group gets the item correct), then *D* would also be 0. Also, when *p* is 1, then *D* would be 0. We would say that items at these extremes are nondiscriminating and do not contribute anything to our ability to sort students from highest to lowest. From a test-construction perspective, you could discard these items without serious consequences. We note in passing that *p* values in the middle (near or at .5) tend to have higher positive discrimination values. In the case where the item can be influenced by guessing, the optimal value of *p* is offset by the number of response alternatives available to the examinee. So for instance, when taking a true-false test, the optimal value of *p* would be .5, but for a four-response multiple-choice test, the optimal value would be .65.

Indices for Alternatives: An Example of Improving Test Items

Let's analyze a typical test item to see how difficulty and discrimination might help in providing useful information for revising the test. The illustration is shown in Figure 10.2, where

---

Test Item Example

You are interested in marketing your newly constructed PPTI (a Paper-and-Pencil Test designed to measure Intelligence). You wish to convince potential customers that the test was measuring the same thing as measured by individually administered intelligence tests. As a way of meeting this requirement you administered the WISC-IV (an individually administered children's version of a widely used intelligence test) to a group of 30 children. After a short break, you administered your new paper-and-pencil test to those very same children. You then correlated the scores from the two tests. What characteristic of the test are you trying to demonstrate?

1. Test-retest reliability
2. Internal consistency reliability
3. Predictive validity
4. Concurrent validity*

*d is the correct answer

Figure 10.2. An example of an item from a test of student knowledge about test construction.

A "Poor" Distribution of Selections for Test Item Alternatives of the Test Item Shown in Figure 10.2

a. .00
b. .00
c. .32
d. .68*

*correct answer
$p=.68$

Figure 10.3. "Poor" distribution of alternative selections.

an example of a test item that you might see in a course on psychological test construction is presented.

Figure 10.3 displays the percentage of students who selected each alternative, which can also be interpreted as the distributions of responses among alternatives. For multiple-choice tests, in addition to looking at the difficulty and discrimination of test items, we would also be interested in showing the distribution of the selections made to each response alternative. As you can see, alternatives a and b were not selected by any student—implying that they are not differentiating among student responses and should be revised.

The good news is that 68 percent of the examinees got the item correct (or $p = .68$). In this table, we aren't providing the D value, so we don't know how well the item discriminates, but the distribution of response alternative selections indicates that the item isn't functioning as we would like it to—no one chose either response alternative a or b.

Assume that this item is the same as in the previous example, but on this second administration, perhaps of a revised item or the same item to another class, the response distribution for the incorrect alternatives is similar, which probably means that examinees are randomly guessing across the incorrect response alternatives. The alternatives in the example shown in Figure 10.4 are working as we would like them to: Most people select the correct answer, and equal percentages of people select the other alternatives.

Now the question is how teachers improve items where the percentages of responses are similar to those shown in Figure 10.3. First, note that if any guessing has taken place it was between response alternatives c (where 32 percent chose the alternative) and d (where 68 percent chose the alternative). No

A "Better" Selection of Test Item Alternatives for the Test Item Shown in Figure 10.2

a. .10
b. .11
c. .11
d. .68*

*correct answer

Figure 10.4. An illustration of an item with "better" distribution of selections of alternatives.

one chose the other alternatives, a and b; they have no functional utility. Because the first two alternatives were not selected by anyone and because most people chose the last two alternatives, the item has for all practical purposes become a two-choice rather than a four-response alternative multiple-choice item. Some of its full potential for usefulness as a measure has been lost. If you want to retain a four-choice alternative format, then this item needs to be improved.

Sometimes only very small changes are necessary to make items more or less dependent on cognitive demands. In this case we might attempt a revision in which the distractors might be as shown in Figure 10.5.

You are interested in marketing your newly constructed PPTI (a Paper-and-Pencil Test designed to measure Intelligence). You wish to convince potential customers that the test was measuring the same thing as measured by individually administered intelligence tests. As a way of meeting this requirement you administered the WISC-IV (an individually administered children's version of a widely used intelligence test) to a group of 30 children. You are interested in the concurrent validity of the test. What is the general procedure you would use?

To determine the concurrent validity of the newly constructed PPTI you would

a. perform a content analysis of the WISC-IV test
b. factor analyze the PPTI scores
c. correlate a test score with a criterion measure collected six months later
d. correlate a test score with a criterion measure collected simultaneously*

Figure 10.5. A revised version of the item.

The new alternatives require more discrimination because all items were based on a comparison of two measures, rather than some based on a concept label and others based on what was correlated; the alternatives required more demand on thinking because the outcomes of the correlations had to be identified, the alternatives were of equal length, and so on.

The item in Figure 10.5 shows another improvement in the item by reducing the attractiveness of response alternative c and/or making alternatives a and b more attractive. In reviewing the earlier version of the item, notice that *two of the response alternatives are based on validity while the other two address reliability issues*. If the student infers from the stem that measuring what a test measures is a validity concern, then the word *reliability* indicates those two alternatives don't fit—they are throw-aways. The next step in the decision is simply to eliminate responses addressing reliability and choose between the other two. Note how this decision-making process for the test-wise student drastically reduces the difficulty of an item where alternatives can be categorized.

Based on this understanding of test taking, the test constructor then will develop alternatives (distractors) that require more discrimination among them. The way this might be done is illustrated in Figure 10.6 where the reworked alternatives now require discrimination among forms of validity rather than between reliability and validity.

Improving the Usefulness of Alternatives in Test Items

Suppose you were interested in marketing a paper-and-pencil test designed to measure intelligence. As a way to convince potential customers that the test was measuring the same thing as measured by individually administered intelligence tests, you took a group of 30 children and administered the WISC-III, took a short break, and administered your new paper-and-pencil test to those very same children. You then correlated the scores from the two tests. What characteristic of the test are you trying to demonstrate?

a. Content validity
b. Construct validity
c. Predictive validity
d. Concurrent validity*

Figure 10.6. A possible revision of test alternatives to make them more equally appealing and requiring more discriminating thought in selecting the correct alternative.

Exercise 10.1 will give you some practice on making response alternatives more (or less) attractive.

Exercise 10.1: Revising Response Alternatives

1. Can you make a set of alternatives based on the data from Figures 10.2 and 10.3 without emphasizing validity or allowing distinctions among groups of items that make the correct answer obvious?
2. Write a multiple-choice item in your own field of interest with alternatives that make the correct answer an easy choice for the majority of students. Then write a revision of the same item with a set of alternatives that you feel would require more understanding of the subject matter in order to discriminate the correct answer from among the four and has the potential of yielding data, more like that shown in Figure 10.4.

Answers to items that work well should have moderate to high correlations with total scores. If they are negatively correlated, look for reasons why students picked the incorrect answers. Was it because they misunderstood the concept that was taught? Were there omissions in teaching the concept? Or, as is often the case, was the answer keyed incorrectly? When analysis of item distractors show that a distractor is not chosen by any examinees, then that distractor should be revised, replaced, or eliminated. It does not contribute to the measurement potential of the test, that is, its ability to discriminate the good students from the poor students. Any poorly performing distractor should be inspected for what it is measuring. It is not expected that each distractor would be chosen by the same number of students because it is reasonable to expect that some distractors will be chosen more often than others as well as for different reasons, which may be unique to individual students. But if a distractor is functioning poorly for a majority of the students, it may be measuring something other than the intended criteria of achievement or performance.

Summary

Specialists examine items to determine the extent to which they satisfy test blueprint rules. Items are reviewed for face and content validity. Items are assembled to be psychometrically similar, especially for the construction of different forms of a test. Because some items will not have survived the evaluation of psychometric characteristics, additional items are often found to be needed to satisfy requirements of the assessment. Then they will be subjected to field testing and item analysis. Although you will probably not be as detailed in your use of these processes, your awareness of these possibilities will assist you in the development of well-constructed items for use in current and future classes.

■ Testing for Mastery

Much, if not most of the time, you will be testing for mastery. Because in testing for mastery a cut-off score (e.g., 80 percent or 90 percent correct) is ordinarily put in place, you would expect the test and items to function equally well; a student's performance would be efficiently measured. But if all students achieved mastery or nearly so, the conundrum is that if they actually have achieved mastery, the item difficulty level values would be high (i.e., easy) and the discrimination levels minimal (most students would have scores within a very narrow range). This factor would result in unacceptably low reliability; that is, the variation in scores would be more influenced by chance or random factors than by real differences in performance.

One way to work around this problem is to generate items in a range of moderate difficulty and then define mastery as performing to a certain level, standard, or cut-off. Choosing items with a range of difficulty of, say, .60 to .75 will permit the generation of a reliable test, and a defensible cut-off can then be chosen to define mastery. On this basis it would seem that a score of 70 to 75 percent would usefully define higher-level performance for such matters as state- or district-wide assessments. Note that, in this example, the apparently low cut-off values that define mastery may be more of a reflection of the difficulty level for the items composing the test rather than a true definition of what mastery might be (performance at, say, 95 percent). This is a compromise between two opposing goals: creating a test in which everyone responds to the items correctly (demonstrating mastery) and a test that demonstrates high statistical reliability (virtually impossible with a preponderance of easy items). It can be argued, for example, that a test in which all items had very high p values (difficulty indexes), consequently being too easy, is doing little more than measuring some lower-than-mastery level of performance.

If the task requirements can be clearly specified, as they are for some types of performance assessments, a 100 percent mastery requirement would be defensible. This could be a possibility, for example, for certifying airline pilots, where standards of mastery can be clearly defined in detail. For high-stakes assessments, there are formal procedures for setting cut-off scores (scores that delineate high from low scorers) (Jaeger & Mills, 2001), which employ a combination of both (a) empirical outcomes (defined by item difficulty and discrimination) and (b) a series of judgments by content experts.

Pretesting

It would be ideal to be able to try out (pretest) a set of items on a sample of participants similar to those that you anticipate working with in a real assessment or test situation. However, the more usual circumstance for teachers is that the first class to which the test is given can be used as a basis for collecting data on which revisions are based; that is, consider your current or first class in which the test is used as a pretest group for the later development of a measure. The analysis of the achievement test results is a continual process in which you examine the results to determine whether there might be a problem with a test item or with alternatives by examining the distribution, difficulty, and discriminability of test responses.

Additionally, an examination would be made of the total configuration of the context in which the test is administered that may be hindering or facilitating students' ability to perform a task. For example, you would consider:

- How clearly the directions were for students at this level
- Whether vocabulary was appropriate for this level of development or achievement, and whether there was a common frame of reference (the course, assignment, and so on)
- The affectivity of questions (were they threatening? hostile? derogatory?)
- The sequence of questions (appropriate? misleading? or some unusual sequence such as difficult to easy or vice versa that might affect student responses?)

To reiterate our earlier discussions, the first step in developing a test is to plan the test by using a blueprint for defining what your measure is intended to do. This need not be elaborate for a classroom test, but should be carefully prepared in line with attention to details that might also be used for a standardized test. You would employ a matrix of items by objectives that would allow you to determine the number of items for each objective and the kinds of items, as well as the total length of the test.

Once the test constructor is satisfied with the initial construction of sets of items, the pretesting begins. The initial step is to examine the items for content or construct validity. Each item you construct should match the content in the standards (classroom objectives, state standards, professional standards, or other criteria). Items should correspond to objectives. Key ideas (not simply specific facts or words) in the standards should be well represented in the items as well as the content (topics and skills). The range or breadth of the objectives, both in content and level, should be represented in the test. Tests are *not* aligned well when there is a preponderance of items that reflect one or only a few objectives or when the range of understanding is underrepresented.

Before any formal pretest is accomplished, much information can be obtained by your (or the test constructor's) professional judgment and examination. The statistics from the administration of a pretest to a group with similar characteristics to those of the group to whom the test is to be administered will provide additional information about the appropriate level of the test, help to identify candidates for item difficulties before the test is administered, and help to make certain that all that can be done is done to provide reasonable assurance that the test will tap the abilities and achievements intended.

Because it is more difficult to produce tests that challenge higher-order thinking, it is common for test constructors to fall back on the easier alternative of producing test items that measure only the recall of factual information. This behavior results in tests that are not as well aligned with standards as they might be; instead of measuring, for example, the creative use of principles of geometry (as in civil engineering) the resulting test might measure only the simple recall of theorems.

The focus on less challenging objectives is not uncommon in initial attempts at constructing a test or when the blueprint is not followed precisely. Upon perusing the first attempt at constructing items it may be found that some, if not most, items measure lower-order thinking—represented in requirements to recognize, list, recall, identify, or use—when the plan shows that the items should have been written to require the student to use higher-order thinking. Items to measure higher-order thinking would contain in their stems such requirements as drawing conclusions based on the citation of supporting evidence, developing logical arguments for alternative explanations of phenomena, or applying concepts for critically analyzing problems in order to arrive at useful solutions.

Once the test constructor is satisfied that the test provides a matched representation of the standards (objectives) in the blueprint or plan, the test is then pretested on a sample of students with characteristics similar to the general population of students to whom the test will be administered. Simply put, the test is tried out to see that the items function properly. In the technical development of a standardized test, the trial group is one that will not be included in the group to be tested.

This procedure implies that teachers won't always have the opportunity to try out a test on students who are in the class in which the test is to be used. If possible they may take the test themselves or administer the test to other teachers or to students in other classes. But, in practice, teachers will rely on the use of a carefully prepared test without pretesting when it is administered the first time. However, by keeping an item bank with each item coded and revised, each administration of a test amounts to a pretest for the next time it is to be used.

Exercise 10.2: Analyzing Test Items

These examples are based on items that might be used for measuring second- or third-grade pupils' understanding of arithmetic number facts and arithmetic operations.

Item Example A. What number of yards would be the next largest figure than any of these: (a) 23 inches, (b) 30 inches, (c) 37 inches, (d) ___?

What processes will be required for answering this question? Does the response require mainly selection, choice, or generation of a new alternative? On what number facts does it depend? Which arithmetic operations?

Below are presented some variations of questions at the second- or third-grade level. Answer the same questions as in the previous example. Even though the questions below are multiple choice and the one above is completion, is the one above easier or more difficult than the ones below? Are fewer or more learning processes required? Which processes? What differences are there in the standards or objectives targeted by each?

Item Example B. Jim has made two unusual rulers. They are not like the ones we are used to. One of the rulers he has made is 10 inches long and the other is 14 inches long. If you put the rulers he has made end to end, how long will they be?
   a. One foot ($D = .25$; picked if 10 and 14 are added and divided by 2, the number of rulers)
   b. 14 inches ($D = .15$; picked if student picks the largest of the two rulers)

c. Two feet (D = .50; the right answer, obtained by adding the two together)

d. One yard (D = .10; picked if the student guesses, tries to select the odd answer, or thinks the longest is the answer)

This item requires the second- or third-grade student to use number sense, self-regulation in thinking, imposing meaning, and effort in numbers. It requires recall information about the relation of inches to feet and to yards (Anderson, Morgan, Greaney, & Kellaghan, 2008; Grouws, 2006). It requires imaging of the two rulers. Examining the D for each alternative, the teacher probably would feel this item worked reasonably well. The data provided a basis for identifying "bugs" in the students' processing of information.

Note that this items could also be stated in a open-ended format, as either:

Item Example C:
10 + 14 =

If one ruler is 10 inches and the other is 14 inches long, their total length end to end would be ___.

These alternative formats provide different kinds of information about the students' learning; for instance, conversions would not be necessary; keeping information in mind for problem solving is not required; and the questions could be answered as facts from memory.

Item Example D. Which of these children is the tallest?
  a. Annie is two and a half feet tall (might be chosen if the student has a tendency to pick the first answer as the correct one or selects an answer that sounds right)
  b. Bill is 1 yard and four inches tall (the right answer; would be chosen if the some facts about yards, feet, and inches were known and the student remembered and compared answers for all alternatives on a common denominator of inches)
  c. Sally is three feet tall (being able to convert inches or feet to yards helps in making a choice)
  d. Pete is 39 inches tall (this too is a simple measure that might be mistaken as the correct one if considered simply as being longer than a yard)

This item appears to be similar to the previous one, but looking more closely it involves a comparison among objects rather than finding a sum when two lengths are known. The interpretations involve the ability to make conversions, hold converted data in memory, arrange the data from high to low, and choose the largest number for finding the tallest student.

General Exercise

Your instructor may require some modifications to the instructions for this exercise, but the general procedure will be somewhat as follows:

Following a sequence similar to the above examples, construct an item or a few items that might be used for a unit in a class you may be teaching or intend to teach in the future. Write the item initially such that it measures mere recall of facts. Informally analyze each item for (a) the extent to which it is aligned with standards, (b) the learning processes required for answering the item, and (c) the extent to which it corresponds to the instruction received.

If you have the opportunity, administer the test items to a group of children (these could be in a classroom or selected from family or neighborhood children). You will need about 10 respondents in all. When you have 10 or more completed tests, analyze the items for p and D as described above. In terms of that data, rewrite the items in ways that you believe will increase their alignment with objectives that will achieve favorable p and D statistics. Analyze them, as shown above, for processes that are engaged when answering each item. Remember that your items will be measuring different processes than those involved above, so your comments will not follow the same points.

Summary

When a pretest is conducted, the question asked is, "Are the results what you expected?" You will examine the distribution of scores for the range of scores obtained, perhaps looking to see that they are similar to a normal distribution. You will examine what kinds of feedback are possible about the difficulty of the test (was the test too easy? too difficult? about right?). The test results will also help you to identify the problems students had in learning (were the items focusing on details rather than applications? Were there differences in the item conceptualizations you intended from the ones perceived by the students? and so on.) Also, the test results can be examined to help you determine what score represents a good grade requiring student enrichment and what is a poorer grade requiring different instructional emphases by the teacher or more effective learning strategies by the student. At this point, the instruction you used can be reviewed for the degree to which the objectives were reached by the methods you used or whether some change is necessary.

A worthwhile procedure is to keep a record of tests and items as they are used. An item bank helps in storing the test items. Keeping notes with a copy of the test helps in recalling your satisfaction with the test or test item for future use. In addition to knowing about items that can be retained intact or with revisions, you can record any student responses or outcomes that were unanticipated.

■ Keep an Item Bank or Item Pool: Putting It All Together

Consider storing psychometric information on each of the items you use from the first test you construct for given objectives. In keeping a record of how students perform on given items or your use of a rubric, you have a basis for continual improvement of that item or rubric. It will not only facilitate your ability to make good tests, but also to use those tests efficiently and to follow good testing procedures; in the long run you can draw on the items in the bank, saving you time in constructing useful tests of specific outcomes in the future. Most teachers, including the authors of this text, have used or are using test item banks in constructing tests for middle and high school as well as in college instruction.

The standard procedure is to print each item on a card just as it would appear on the test. In an earlier era this meant typing it directly on a 3" × 5" or 5" × 8" card. After the test has been administered the item characteristics are recorded on the card, along with data describing the class (grade level, semester, and so on). Information would be recorded in coded form (for easy sorting in the future) stating the objective being tested by the item. If obtained, any statistical data such as the difficulty of the item or alternatives or the correlation between item scores and the total test score would be recorded (see a sample of some records in Figures 10.2 to 10.4). Whatever revisions were necessary might be noted on the card. The card then is stored in a file box.

Currently, there are software programs available for developing test item banks. They reduce the effort expended and make retrieval of items for given objectives easy. Whether index cards or computer software is used, the general procedure is as follows:

- Type the item into a file segment as a separate entity that can be pooled with other items used on another occasion for the same course, selected for a new test according to curricular objectives, documented with class response data, moved from one conceptual category to another that might be deemed more appropriate conceptually, or revised according to data about responses to items or alternatives. Similar records could be used for rubrics associated with essay questions.
- Code the item in any ways that you think would be useful to you. For example, an item could be coded according to characteristics of the class in which it was used: grade level, age level, content topic, outcome level (memory of fact, definition of term, understanding concept, solving problem, application to similar problem, synthesis of information, and so on), or other characteristic such as year.
- Identify the correct answer (keyed as correct) by an asterisk.
- Enter item characteristics to summarize data regarding administration to a class. You might include the number of students in the class to which the test had been administered, the number of the item in the test, the number of correct responses, the number of responses made by high- and low-performing students to each of the alternatives, a calculated difficulty index for the item, and the discrimination index.
- Review the data for each item separately. Identify those for which data suggests improvement is needed; for instance, items with difficulty indexes higher than .75 or lower than .25 need to be inspected for possible revision. Then review those items for discrimination indexes that are out of the normal range. Look for distractors that did not work well—those which had too many or too few selections.
- Identify the possible causes such as ambiguity, wording, phrasing, and the like in both the stem and the alternatives, including the correct alternative. Sometimes items that are keyed incorrectly are identified in this process (e.g., the majority of a class—say 75 percent—selected another alternative as correct).

- Revise the item stem or distractors and make whatever changes appear to be important for the purposes to be served.

Making improvements frequently and adding items to the pool over time will, in a very short period of time, provide you with a basis for selecting items according to content, outcome, or other variables in making new tests. Constructing future tests on the basis of their item characteristics will provide you with a better test than you might have made up on the spur of the moment. With an increasingly larger pool of items, each coded according to content, assignment or other criteria, you can make up different forms of a test that will be comparable for different purposes, such as testing before and after an instructional unit, comparing classes, or comparing groups based on demographic characteristics.

Selection of items based on discrimination and difficulty indexes provide a basis for developing test forms that will function equally well in terms of difficulty and discrimination—provided the characteristics of the students remain the same (e.g., grade level, age, experience). Whenever items are selected to make equivalent forms, it is always advisable to include some of the same items with known characteristics on all forms to determine whether a new form of the test is functioning the same as an earlier one.

A Software Program for Item Analysis

Although items can be copied, coded, and stored on 3" × 5" cards, for many teachers it would be more convenient and more practical to store them on a computer in a 3" × 5" or other format of their choice. This could be accomplished with a variety of formats based on commonly used programs for word and data processing. There are also programs available for purposes of item analysis, one of which is described in Text Box 10.1.

■ Some General Guidelines for Improving Test Items

Make use of criteria for considering the content (using some base such as a taxonomy), difficulty indexes, and discrimination indexes in reviewing and revising items. Don't make decisions on the basis of one of these alone.

Examine both the stem and the distractors for consistency. Make certain that irrelevant cues, not part of the intended

Text Box 10.1 Item Analysis in LXR*Test

It is possible to obtain software support for assessment item analysis. LXR*Test builds in test-performance historical information with each class that takes your classroom-based tests. For example, you can score a test by using the scoring feature of LXR*Test with one of many popular mark-sense readers. LXR*Test will generate a file that contains the performance of each student on both the overall test score and each item of your test. That file can be imported into an electronic gradebook, and you can update LXR*Test's question bank. In addition, the score file will contain some basic test information that you can report back to your students.

Based on the item statistics, you may choose to eliminate the item, revise it, or keep it as is. The question bank will show you the difficulty level, p, the r_{pb} or discrimination level, the response distribution for multiple-choice items, and the last time the item was used. The next time you construct a test, you can use this information to determine whether to use the item again, whether to revise the stem and/or the alternatives, or whether to use it as in previous years. You might even do nothing more than to change the order of the alternatives to provide a different configuration (grouping). Figure 10.7 shows a screenshot of a physics item and the corresponding item statistics. These can be stored for handy reference at a later time. As they are accumulated, they can be categorized according to topic or objective. From this pool of items a selection can be made so that the same items are not included on the test year after year. By selecting items according to their statistical characteristics you can maintain the difficulty of the test, the overall level of performance to reach mastery, and so on, provided—and this is a *big* provision—that the characteristics of the students (ability, effort, motivation, achievement level) in the earlier and present classes are similar.

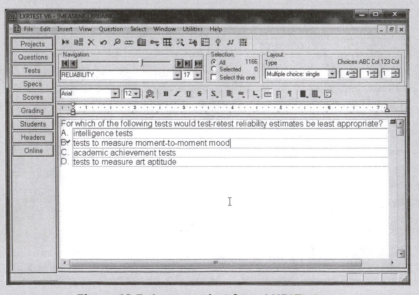

Figure 10.7. A screenshot from LXR*Test.

purpose or objective of the item, are eliminated (grammatical cues indicating animate objects, numbers of objects, appearance, and so on).

Tests in which most items have a difficulty index of 50 percent work best in optimizing psychometric characteristics of discrimination, reliability, and validity.

Items with extreme p values may be superficially interpreted as easy or difficult for the respondent. However, extreme values may also be indicative of shortcomings or faults (imperfections) in the way the item is constructed. Examine item stems, correct alternatives, and distractors for such faults as ambiguities that might lead to very low correct responses, grammatical cues such as stems asking for animate objects and all but one distractor (the correct answer) referring to inanimate objects, or lack of clarity in wording that again may lead to unreliability of the measure.

On occasion the test constructor will find a negative discrimination index; that is, more low scorers respond correctly to the item than did high scorers. Most often, this is simply the result of an inadvertent error in keying the test. However, sometimes more low achievers will respond to the correct item (keyed as correct) because low scores attend to a feature of the stem or of the distractors that was not intended to be relevant to the answer. For example, test constructors short-cut the construction of alternatives by making one of the distractors "all of the above" or "none of the above." The nondiscriminating student, who scores low on the entire test, may simply be taking the easy way out. There is little evidence to indicate some general reason for negative discrimination. What is clear is that the item should be scrutinized carefully for points that may appear in need of improvement.

Distractors function best when the responses are equally distributed among the three alternatives (in a four-alternative multiple-choice item).

Make distractors effective by carrying a common theme across them but making them similar on all other characteristics, thereby requiring discrimination of the critical characteristics. According to this rule, the following is a poor item:

Which of the following is not a mammal? (a) elephant, (b) rhinoceros, (c) giraffe, and (d) crocodile

There are too many bases for selecting the correct answer unrelated to the definition of mammal, including differences in configuration (legs, body segments), skin covering (hair), habitat (water) and so on. A better item would be one in which the alternatives share conceptual similarities:

Which of the following is not a mammal? (a) shark, (b) walrus, (c) platypus, (d) whale

The test constructor would consider other alternatives for distractors, such as (e) seal and (f) manatee. Also, this is a type of item where the following would be effective distractors as well: (g) none of the above and (h) all of the above.

Avoid ambiguities sometimes introduced by deliberately composing distractors with two ideas that require students to make a decision about which one is to be attended to. Similarly, avoid adding "all of the above" or "a and b but not c" as distractors in the belief that it increases the difficulty of the test.

If the indexes are based on small numbers of respondents, as they are certain to be in initial administrations of the test in classrooms, evaluate the role of guessing as a chance contributor to the unreliability of the item. In addition, the fact that each item makes a small contribution to a total score for a small base of respondents leads to questions about the reliability of the item for diagnosing weaknesses in student performance (lack of content knowledge, failure to meet levels of objectives, and so on). As shown throughout this text, the more evidence (increases in number of items, use of several kinds of data, use of data from several sources or over several time periods) increases the confidence we can have in the reasons for the test results—another reason for keeping a track record of item functioning in item banks.

■ Summary

Tests are components of an integrated system of education within which classroom assessment is an integral part. Although often misunderstood, classroom assessment is not something done to the school and classroom, but an *enabling* component contributing to the effectiveness of school and classroom performance. The popular view too often compartmentalizes assessment and instruction. It is often said, and believed, that we instruct on the one hand and we measure what the student has learned on the other hand—the traditional view being that the two are separate components, serving different goals without a common bond. In particular, the view is that on the one hand we teach—the teacher's job—and on the other the student learns—the student's job. In this separation, it is often the case that testing and reporting grades are independent of their implication for instruction. It is as though the only consideration was whether students achieved what they were taught—not how they got there or what we did to help them progress (or not, as the case may be).

Instruction and reporting in this view are two separate entities. In opposition to this view, the current view, represented in the term *classroom assessment*, is that all assessments have explicit and recognizable roles in enabling the school and classroom to perform their educational functions more effectively. But, to achieve this goal, tests are under continual improvement through revisions based on the known characteristics of worthwhile assessment—(a) they must have clearly stated purposes (goals); (b) the purposes must be represented in the scores they yield (validity); (c) the tests must yield consistent results (reliability); and (d) the test results must have validity for instruction, learning, and accountability.

Improving tests is part of a continual process in test development, whether in multiple-choice or alternative assessments, whether formal or informal. Improvement of measures or criteria (rubrics) to be used in measuring is necessary for good quality (precise) assessments. In turn, such assessments also have potential usefulness for feedback on instruction. Whatever the concern, test improvement facilitates the interpretation of scores and therefore their utility for the purposes they are to serve.

There are several features of tests that undergo improvement from one administration of the test to the next, whether the procedure is a standardized test of an ability or achievement in a subject matter area, a personality test, an alternative assessment measure, or a survey of attitudes toward school (see for example Anderson et al., 2008). Illustrations of attempts at improving tests may be seen by comparing yearly reports of specific tests in the Buros *Mental Measurements Yearbook*, in professional journals, and so on. These revisions are often in response to concerns about the validity of a test.

The specific features of tests targeted for improvement or revision are the following:

- *Items* and their psychometric characteristics (the manner in which they differentiate achievers from nonachievers)
- *Purpose* of the test as implied in the professional standards and as judged by professional content specialists
- *Functions* of the test, whether diagnostic, summative, or formative
- *Interpretations* that can be made regarding instruction and learning from the data provided

- *Feedback* the test data provide; that is, are you using the assessment merely as a score, or can you interpret the score for implications regarding the improvement of learning and instruction

Despite the need for employing alternative assessment judiciously and wisely, the multiple-choice format remains a flexible format for use in either formative (classroom assessment) or summative (e.g., statewide standardized comprehensive) assessment. It can be used alone or as one of many approaches to assessment. Nevertheless, assessment methods and measures, whether traditional or alternative, should not be viewed as having an all-or-none quality, that is to say, one format is not universally better or worse than another. Each has its unique advantages and disadvantages when judged against standards or functional use. What is of concern is that, whatever their format, they measure what they are supposed to measure, function in the way they are expected to function, and enable effective implications and interpretations.

When undergoing revision, it is assumed that the first use of a test will not function as well as it might. Accordingly, test items, item alternatives, rubrics (in the case of performance measures), and so on are continually evaluated for their psychometric characteristics, including discrimination and difficulty, associated with their capability for providing useful data about student progress and instructional feedback.

Discrimination is indexed by the extent to which a test alternative separates high from low scorers.

Difficulty is examined by the percentage of examinees (students) answering the item correctly. In the case of rubrics, the concern is whether the rubric is an essential characteristic of the performance (e.g., would posture be a criterion for a well-organized oral presentation?) and whether a number of raters use the same ratings on a set of papers or performances.

Achievement of purpose is examined by the correlation of scores (right or wrong, achieved or not achieved) on a given item (or rubric) with the total score (high or low). Note that the last criterion (the correlation of the item with the total score) is based on the assumption that an item (or rubric) is but one contributor to the total score.

As a consequence of revision, the test, test item, or rubric will be improved regarding its ability to "do the job" intended. The expectation is that the outcome of the measurement, the data, can be understood and interpreted in terms of the demands of classroom instruction and learning regarding the following:

- *Student outcomes.* The test measures level of achievement and quality of outcome (e.g., rote memory of facts, understanding, problem solving, transferability). It enables differentiation among learners of these qualities as they are related to learning outcomes.

- *Instructional effectiveness.* The test items reflect the extent to which the item (stem, correct answer, and alternatives) represents some desired quality or qualities of the instructional procedure (e.g., consideration of the entering level of the student, emphasis on breadth of content, use of context to enable transfer, emphasis on conceptualization, relating content to other areas) intended to produce qualitatively different outcomes. Do the test items measure the curricular content (and instruction) or are they measuring something else? If the test is to be used for examining the effect of a particular curriculum or instructional method on student achievement, it is important to sort out what the student already knows (prior knowledge) as it differs from what the student has acquired as a result of the curriculum.

■ References

Anderson, P., Morgan, G., Greaney, V., & Kellaghan, T. (Eds.). (2008). *Developing tests and questionnaires for a National Assessment of Educational Achievement* (Vols. 1–2). Washington, DC: World Bank Publications.

Black, P., & Wiliam, D. (1998). Assessment and classroom learning. *Assessment in Education: Principles, Policy, and Practice, 5*(1), 7–74.

Donovan, M. S., & Bransford, J. D. (Eds.). (2005). *How students learn: Science in the classroom.* Washington, DC: National Academy of Science, National Academies Press.

Emberger, M. (2007). Helping teachers improve classroom assessments. *Principal Leadership, 7*(9), 24–29.

Grouws, D. A. (2006). *Handbook of research on mathematics: Teaching and learning.* Charlotte, NC: Information Age Publishing.

Jaeger, R. M., & Mills, C. N. (2001). An integrated judgment procedure for setting standards on complex, large-scale assessments. In G. J. Cizek (Ed.), *Setting performance standards: Concepts, methods, and perspectives* (pp. 313–338). Mahwah, NJ: Lawrence Erlbaum Associates.

Shepard, L. A. (1997). *Measuring achievement: What does it mean to test for robust understanding?* Princeton, NJ: Educational Testing Service, Policy Information Center.

Shepard, L. A. (2000). The role of assessment in a learning culture. *Educational Research, 29*(7), 4–14.

Wiggins, G. (1989). A true test: Toward more authentic and equitable assessment. *Phi Delta Kappan 70*(9), 703–713.

CHAPTER 11

Domain-Specific Assessment and Learning

MUCH OF YOUR classroom assessment will be related to learning in subject-matter domains. Your assessments will be designed to check how well your students understand the history material, the science principles, or the math concepts central to your objectives. Then you will interpret and translate the results of your assessment into instructional practices matched to the needs of your students as revealed in the assessment (Heritage, 2007).

This chapter will give you a framework for approaching such assessment tasks. Although each subject-matter area has its own unique set of opportunities for assessment, we will only offer some general solutions to assessment across content areas. The focus is on formative rather than on summative assessment, but most of what you learn about formative measures can also be applied to summative assessment at the end of your instructional unit should you choose to do so. We will also again address preassessment—assessment you do even before the formal instruction begins.

Current emphases on content and performance standards provide sets of goals to be achieved within subject-matter areas—that is, instruction is standards based, both as to content and performance. *Content standards* emphasize the specific knowledge to be learned and its organization. *Performance standards* emphasize what the students can do with the content they have acquired in the expectation that learning will be useable beyond the present instructional setting. Both are adjusted to developmental levels represented in the grade level you teach.

A major aim of instruction is to facilitate student ability to transfer knowledge to new situations. Students should be able to *use* their knowledge in the workplace, in social interactions, and in community affairs. For that reason, today's subject-matter assessments often include authentic tasks that ask students to apply their learning to realistic tasks or solve everyday problems. However, decisions in everyday teaching are also informed by other assessments of student status regarding (a) *what students know*, (b) what their expectations are regarding *what they are to learn*, (c) *how* they are to reach the objectives of assignments and lessons, and (d) *awareness* of what they have accomplished (Pelligrino, Chudowsky, & Glaser, 2001). To help you understand how instruction is influenced by these assessments we begin with a brief look at traditional theories of assessment and learning as they are related to current approaches to assessment for the classroom.

■ Perspectives on Subject-Matter Instruction and Assessment

Earlier theories of teaching tended to be based on the belief that everything taught was new to the student. The student was believed to know nothing about the topic and accordingly would learn the material by copying it from instruction onto a mental "blank slate." Learning was viewed as the accretion of isolated bits of knowledge, a belief rooted in behaviorist theories of learning. This view was the guide for most teaching, and testing emphasized recall of facts, the isolated bits of knowledge. The more recent approaches focus on student processing of information. Rather than emphasizing accretion of facts the emphasis is now on developing understanding and applications.

Early Perspectives

Historically (Shepard 1997, 2000) the early theory of instruction was simple: The teacher was the authority in both the subject matter and the instructional method (it was not unusual to find students to say, "It must be right, the teacher [or the book] said so"). The model for grade levels (first grade, second grade, etc.) across schools, districts, and communities was stable: The instructional model was to tell the student the facts, give seatwork drills and exercises that required repetitive use of those facts, follow up with homework assignments using more repetitive drills and exercises, and then test for the amount the student had acquired (Shepard, 2000).

The implication for assessment within that framework was equally simple: The student had to learn important facts. The important measure was a test of the student's ability to repeat the material as it had been presented. When they appeared on the scene, the objective tests appeared to offer an excellent avenue for making these measurements; the multiple-choice or true-false formats were easily adapted to serve as measures of recognition and recall. A student who failed to perform at a given level (a passing grade) might be given more assignments and then tested again until the percentage of correct answers reached the passing level. Some schools adopted the practice of retention in the same grade until a passing grade was achieved.

Unlike current views, assessment and instruction were seen, characteristically, as separated events in both time and purpose. They were separate in time because instruction came first and testing came at the end of the unit. They were different in purpose because instruction was intended to help students learn and testing was designed as a basis for reporting on their success or failure (Graue, 1993). Teacher-made tests and measures were soon to evolve as emulations of the standardized test.

This earlier view assumed such characteristics of learning and instruction as the following (based on Shepard [2000]):

- Instruction was sequenced in small steps, from the simple to the more complex, because that was believed to be the way students learned.
- Teachers provided applications specifically for given situations; the theory of transfer via identical elements in the original and new learning situations was supported by a classic study on thousands of students in New York City schools (Thorndike, 1924).
- Sorting and classifying students according to ability levels (as inferred from test scores) was an important aid to teaching; students could be grouped, for example, in order that teaching could be adapted to the respective capability levels.
- The assignment of grades was believed to induce motivation by rewarding (or punishing) accomplishment (or lack of accomplishment). Extrinsic rewards (of which grades were one) were believed to facilitate disciplined or well-managed classrooms. Intrinsic rewards were neglected in their considerations.

In this building-block approach, assessment focused on the degree of mastery of small steps in student achievement. With the identification of the objective-type tests holding promise for impartiality, uniformity, and standardization of testing advocated by the experts of the day. Instruction and assessment remained as separate events but still tended to support the notion that the student's task was the rote recall of details (Verschaffel, Greer, & De Corte, 2000).

Theories of learning have changed greatly in recent years, as the next section shows. Yet old beliefs, similar to those described above, persist in stakeholders and educators alike, hampering the development of modern approaches that would emphasize the link between assessment and instruction. As the relation among learning, instruction, cognitive processing, and assessment becomes increasingly apparent in theories of learning, several unique methods particularly useful for formative assessment emerge.

Constructivist Approaches to Learning and Instruction

The constructivist approach dominates thinking about teaching, learning, and assessment. Its key position is that education is not a series of isolated or independent events, but an integration of curriculum, instruction, learning, and assessment—a radical change from the earlier position emphasizing small steps. The current position is guided by such principles as the following (Pelligrino et al., 2001; Siegler, 1998):

- *Knowledge and understandings are constructed by the learner.* The earlier position seemed to focus on the accretion of unrelated simple units or facts, sometimes seeming more unrelated than conceptually linked. Current positions suggest that new learning is constructed. The product is formed by the synthesis of new learning with the knowledge already acquired by the learner. It is the result of the way the learner synthesizes ideas and fits the pieces together. You can see that this feature of learning, alone, can result in a multitude of outcomes among learners.

  During the course of learning, the instructional content is interpreted by the learner in terms of his or her prior knowledge. Thus, the new learning is integrated in varying degrees with the old learning; the result is a new product, a new construction. Any one test fails to capture all of what has been learned or the reasons why learning from one student to another often differs so much. The richness of the products of learning events are not easily measured in a single test, which probably only captures the tip of the iceberg of learning. Because of the difficulty of incorporating into a test such variables as how much previous knowledge goes into the new learning, how the student arrives at an answer or perceives the new learning, or how the test situations is perceived typically cannot be obtained on a single test or performance.

- *Prior knowledge and its organization.* Although content is an important part of the knowledge base, the organization of that content is equally important. Together, they comprise the *cognitive structure* of the learner. Organization can have profound effects on the relations among ideas in the mind of the learner, thereby affecting the *accessibility* of the content (information, topics, etc.), the *availability* of the content in answering questions, and the *retrievability* (ability to recall, remember, or retrieve) of information in response to specific prompts, cues, or other contexts, particularly in unique thinking such as problem solving or creativity. All earlier experiences with a topic, whether learned in school or experienced out of school, and the way those experiences are organized and incorporated into the cognitive structure (prior knowledge) enter into the construction of "new" knowledge.

  When teachers want to learn about the ways students have organized the material in a lesson, assessment measures paralleling the organization of content might be used. Some examples are displayed later in this and other chapters, and are seen in measures based on cognitive maps, graphic organizers, webs, and so on. (Also see additional examples on websites. One URL with many examples is given at the end of this chapter.)

- *Metacognitive knowledge.* This seemingly complex term conveys a valuable understanding of processing by the learner. It says that what the learner knows about his or her own learning is central to all aspects of learning, whether the acquisition of facts, the transfer of learning to new situations, or the response to assessment tasks. An illustration of how metacognitive activities are applied to reading is shown in Theory to Practice Box 11.1. The examples in the Theory to Practice Box illustrate the use of an inventory used in assessment for helping students report such activities as how they study, what they do when studying, and what procedures work best for them when studying school subjects such as math, reading, social studies, writing, or other content areas. The items shown in the box illustrate one format for construction of questionnaires, surveys, or inventories, showing the need for teachers and students to carefully state (a) the objectives of assignments and of assessments, (b) the relation of the item

Theory to Practice Box 11.1
DEVELOPING AN INVENTORY

Inventories are useful devices for self-reports of behaviors that are not easily observed or tested in other ways. This box briefly describes some steps in developing an inventory for measuring metacognitive skills in reading (e.g., Mokhtari & Reichard, 2002).

Plan the inventory. The development of the assessment (in this case, the inventory) begins with setting objectives, such as "develop a scale to measure metacognitions related to good or poor reading." The planning of the inventory is initiated with a definition or statement of the evidence-based knowledge related to this objective, for instance, of the strategies and activities that contribute to effective reading.

Specify the contents of the inventory. The categories represented in the inventory are (a) *domain-general reading strategies* that are typical of readers in general; (b) *higher-level reading strategies* that are useful for meeting the challenge of comprehending difficult reading tasks such as those required in reading material requiring unique organizations for solving problems, making decisions, or reaching other higher-level goals; and (c) *strategies for effective reading* such as making certain that the reader is concentrating and attending or that they use repair strategies when comprehension fails.

Develop individual items for each category. The items are comprised of stems representing the category and selecting one of several commonly used scales for making responses to the item. In this illustration we use scales for obtaining student's rough estimates of the frequency with which a strategy or reading activity is used. Different numbers (usually three, five, or seven) of scalar units can be used to record responses; in this illustration we use a five-point bipolar scale in which

1 means, "I *never or almost never* do this."
5 means, "I *always or almost always* do this."

Summary. The considerations in developing such inventories are identifying categories of the concept to be measured; developing definitions and defining examples of the category; developing specific items (stems) contributing to the category score; and deciding upon a response mode (bipolar scales). These steps are illustrated below with representative examples of items for the category.

Domain-General Reading Strategies

Examples of *the stems for domain-general reading strategies or activities* might include determining why one is reading, determining what information one has that can be used to help reading, surveying chapter headings to determine what the text is about, skimming to note text characteristics, making decisions about what is to be emphasized (facts, generalities) in reading, using context and text structure to fine-tune reading (e.g., reading dependent upon genre or subject-matter domain).

Items:

I think about what I know about the subject matter to help me comprehend the reading.
Circle the number which best represents how often you use the strategy: 1 2 3 4 5

I base my reading strategies on my objectives for reading (i.e., "why I am reading").
Circle the number which best represents how often you use the strategy: 1 2 3 4 5

Higher-Level Reading Strategies

Examples of *higher-level reading strategies* include reading at a pace, or with sufficient pauses, to permit thought processes such as reflection, organization, or integration of ideas to be used; changing reading rate according to difficulty (slower for difficult passages, faster for easy passages), and/or making deliberate attempts to attend and concentrate.

Items:

I make decisions during reading about what content to read closely and what to ignore.
Circle the number which best represents how often you use the strategy: 1 2 3 4 5

I change the pace of my reading when understanding a passage becomes difficult.
Circle the number which best represents how often you use the strategy: 1 2 3 4 5

Strategies for Quality Reading

These are activities that achieve effective comprehension for reaching reading goals. Such activities include making notes while reading, paraphrasing ideas, rereading, self-questioning, using the dictionary for the meanings of words, summarization, and so on.

Items:

I make notes in the margins of the text for important ideas.
Circle the number which best represents how often you use the strategy: 1 2 3 4 5

(continued)

Theory to Practice Box 11.1
(Continued)

I put ideas in the text into my own words while thinking about what I am reading.
Circle the number which best represents how often you use the strategy: 1 2 3 4 5

I go to supplementary sources for information to help me understand what I am
   reading.
Circle the number which best represents how often you use the strategy: 1 2 3 4 5

The category items and descriptions in each category illustrate the overall process of constructing an inventory. The planning of the inventory is based on (a)
specifying the objectives to be achieved by its use, (b) the kinds of scores that
might be obtained, and (c) sample items that might be developed for each category together with the response mode. Some descriptions parallel those used
in currently developed scales such as the MARSI (VERSION 1)

Source: Adapted from Mokhtari and Reichard (2002).

statements to the objectives, and (c) the method of responding to the measure.

• *Students' attitudes, beliefs, and dispositions.* These were at
one time omitted in considerations of classroom assessment. However, these behaviors are important behavioral
elements related to attention, interest, and effort directed
at learning tasks. They are also of considerable importance
in considering classroom management. In general, these
behaviors are measured by inventories, of which the *Motivation for Studying and Learning Questionnaire* (Pintrich &
De Groot, 1990; Pintrich & Schrauben, 1992) is an example.
It is a frequently used measure of motivation and its subcategories of motivation *for* learning, self-regulation *of* learning, and anxiety *about* learning. Examples of items related to
motivation are:

Please rate the following items based on your behavior in this
   class. For each item *circle the number* which best represents
   your feelings on a seven-point scale where *1 = not at all true
   of me* to *7 = very true of me.*

1. I prefer class work that is challenging so I can learn new things. 1 2 3 4 5 6 7
2. It is important for me to learn what is being taught in this class. 1 2 3 4 5 6 7
3. I like what I am learning in this class. 1 2 3 4 5 6 7

To help you construct items of this type, note the features of inventory items. They have (a) *item stems*—simple declarative statements that represent some aspect of motivation; (b) a *response mode*—a scale for the kind of response; (c) *scale values*—a seven-point scale for level of agreement; and (d) bipolar *anchors* for the ends of the scale, "not at all true of me" to "very true of me."

This example is simply one of many different formats used in inventories; it is presented merely to distinguish formats for inventories from measures for cognitive behaviors and performance of skills. There are other formats (variations of the features) as well, including using smiling or frowning faces rather than a numbered rating scale for indicating degree of agreement (especially useful for very young students); selecting bipolar anchors from a variety of alternatives, such as agree-disagree; always-never; or good-bad, and using a different number of scalar points such as three or five, rather than seven as in the example.

■ Constructivism in Assessment

We have identified several features of the constructivist position as it appears in assessment. It is apparent that higher-order thinking and genuine understanding are clearly emphasized over mere factual recall in the constructivist approach. Nevertheless, factual information is neither ignored nor neglected because much of initial learning is necessarily based on the acquisition of facts, so they are necessary for efficient higher-order learning and understanding.

Even at this level, however, the constructivist position targets the measurement of understanding and level of product rather than amount of sheer recall of facts (Sadler, 1998). In the course of these achievements, students should be actively involved in framing their expectations and in evaluating their own work beyond the mere acquisition of what the textbook or the teacher says. As importantly, teachers should recognize the relevance of student processing of learning outcomes, as well as their students' ability to learn and what the students have learned, when teaching methods are being assessed. Outcomes are strongly colored by teachers' perceptions of teaching and learning. We continue to be surprised at the differences in teachers' personal theories about how students learn and the best ways for teaching them as we supervise their teaching or discuss these matters in roundtable discussions of such matters.

Constructivist principles are clearly relevant to assessment. Figure 11.1 offers an excellent, much-cited example in which Shepard (2000) shows how an idea in math is translated into a set of problems. Notice the complexity of the set of items. Shepard has based the items on visual properties that help students see the part-whole relationship. The questions require students to consider what they know, what information would be most useful, and what solution paths are available to help solve the problem. Such problems require thinking skills rather than mere demonstrations of mechanical arithmetic skills. Responses to items constructed in this way are as useful for instructional feedback as they are for summative assessment.

Student Cognitions

Cognitions resulting from instruction are reflected in knowledge representations (e.g., facts student *know* versus their organization and use in reasoning). These representations, in turn, affect all aspects of behavior including student perceptions and understanding. The ultimate network of ideas and facts, their organization resulting from schooling and personal experiences of knowledge representations, constitutes *prior learning* or the *cognitive structure*.

Assessment of Representations

To illustrate cognitive representations as they appear in teaching as well as in the knowledge structure, basic arithmetic operations can be represented in a number of ways. For example, $8 \times 4 = 32$ can be represented simply as two numbers separated (or mediated) by an $\times$ (multiplier). Or they can be represented as 8 groups of 4 objects or 4 groups of 8 objects. Representations include the level of organization involved in sequencing; for example knowing the names of 20 birds and arranging them in alphabetic order according to their names is not as good a measure of understanding as ordering the 20 birds in terms of the taxonomic categories they represent, such as land or water fowl, predators, hunters, and so on. Creative works of art, inventions, and scientific theories are typically founded on new configurations or combinations of commonly known ideas—that is, on new representations.

Grade 4 Mathematics Problem Set

(Mathematics Sciences Education Board, 1993)

All of the bridges in this part are built with yellow rods for spans and red rods for supports, like the one shown here. This is a 2 span bridge like the one you just built. Note that the yellow rods are 5 cm long.

Yellow

Red

1. Now build a 3-span bridge.
    a. How many yellow rods did you use? _____
    b. How long is your bridge? _____
    c. How many red rods did you use? _____
    d. How many rods did you use all together? _____

2. Try to answer these questions without building a 5-span bridge.
    a. How many yellow rods would you need for a 5-span bridge? _____
    b. How long would your bridge be? _____
    c. How many red rods would you need? _____
    d. How many rods would you need all together? _____

3. Without building a 12-span bridge, answer the following questions.
    a. How many yellow rods would you need for a 12-span bridge? _____
    b. How long would your bridge be? _____
    c. How many red rods would you need? _____
    d. How many rods would you need all together? _____

4. How many yellow rods and red rods would you need to build a 28-span bridge?
    _____ yellow rods and _____ red rods. Explain your answer.

5. Write a rule for figuring out a total number of rods you would need to build a bridge if you knew how many spans the bridge had.

6. How many yellow rods and red rods would you need to build a bridge that is 185 cm long?
    _____ yellow rods and _____ red rods. Explain your answer.

Figure 11.1. Example of a mathematics assessment consistent with constructivist principles. Source: Shepard, 2000.

The assessment of representations differs from the assessment of mere factual retention. The student brings into the solution of the problem a number of ideas from several sources but also must integrate these around the central focus (the problem). Assessment of cognitive skills for using that knowledge can and should be assessed. It is one thing, for example, to know the icons, the cursor, and the clicks on the computer's mouse, but it is quite another matter to use these in particular sequences, on demand, for specific outcomes, and with expertise in the rapidity with which they are used.

Assessment of Procedural Knowledge

Cognitive skills used in thinking, problem solving, and so on are sometimes referred to as *procedural knowledge*. They include appropriate use of strategies for solving problems; analyzing problems; and synthesizing ideas, explanations, and methods of assembling objects from instructions. Many of these can be found in the problems illustrated in Figure 11.1. As part of the knowledge representations, they can be assessed by observing performance directly, for instance, in such activities as engaging in a debate or observing how the student solves a surveyor's problem. Or you can establish situations in which a procedure is required as part of an answer; for example mathematics teachers may require students to turn in their worksheets along with test papers to show the procedures used for arriving at an answer (students often arrive at the correct answer by an inefficient or even incorrect procedure, or they may be using the correct procedure but a careless error yields an incorrect answer). In a reading assignment, teachers may learn about the student's strategies for comprehension (comprehension metacognitions) by seeing whether students have detected anomalies in a reading passage.

Procedural knowledge is often emphasized in school settings as learning strategies, for instance by using analogies to understand scientific principles (the clock and the rotation of the earth), making comparisons of conceptual distinctions among forms of governments (such as the distinctions among monarchies, democracies, and dictatorships), or pairing objects (e.g., a butterfly and moth) to compare the two in placing them in a taxononmy.

Assessment of student cognitions and procedural knowledge requires an understanding of how learning in the subject matter of that domain proceeds developmentally (Roth, 1990; Siegler, 1998). In some assignments, students can reach reasonable levels of understanding building on or extending what they already know. At other times, they must modify their existing knowledge if it is incomplete, contains misconceptions, or is not compatible with the new information. At other times they must learn new procedures—ways of integrating and organizing information.

Assessment Contexts

When any observations are made for purposes of assessment, the teacher's intent is to interpret them in terms of the student's cognitions and achievement. But the opportunity for making such observations in everyday situations is not always available. Much of education is directed toward use in future or out-of-school situations. Furthermore, information, understanding, or skills taught in school settings are used infrequently or sporadically in everyday situations, restricted to appropriate situations in which they apply. Such behaviors as making change for a purchase may be done more frequently than verifying a balance in a checking account, but still most behaviors are performed only on select occasions. A civil engineer will use some trigonometric functions more often than others, but again there may be long delays between uses. A researcher will select research methods, theories, or methods of analyses according to purpose, but these too are employed only at opportune times in all that researchers do.

Functionality of Behaviors Observed

As with contexts in which behaviors occur, educational outcomes are intended to have functionality in everyday life. But, in actuality, the use of any behavior can be sporadic; all educational benefits are not used with the same frequency and occasions—whether one is teaching children or adults. Recognizing such demands, teachers and test makers (psychometricians) prepare test tasks that will make certain infrequently used behaviors have the opportunity to be evoked—enter tests and other performance measures. As in our example in Theory to Practice Box 11.2, it is highly unlikely that all the creatures depicted will ever be seen simultaneously—so we establish standard settings, artificially created to enable the use of higher-order comparison and contrast learning.

In the absence of establishing such settings, teachers will still want to identify situations where the behaviors are more likely to be evoked (i.e., used more frequently), thereby providing the opportunity for observation (such as observing the way a student approaches reading a new chapter in a study

Theory to Practice Box 11.2
ASSESSING REPRESENTATIONS

Higher-order thinking can be evaluated by the student's ability to discriminate taxonomic categories. The categories are based on perceived distinctive features (defining and characteristic features) of the class of organisms called *Insecta*. Such measures have the potential of identifying what students attend to, the ways students make differentiations, and the level of their understanding through comparisons and contrasts to identify the concept represented.

A display might be presented either as a printed set of drawings as shown here or as a demonstration in which real objects are displayed on a table or other location. A number of questions might be asked. However, assume your interest is in identifying whether students have knowledge of the classes of organisms within the phylum *Arthropoda* and can use that knowledge in making discriminations among members of that phylum. There are many characteristics to be learned and in different combinations—leg joints and number, respiration, reproduction, body segments, skeletons—but we'll merely use a few to illustrate a few more ways of assessing different cognitive levels.

Among the questions that might be asked are:

Item 1: List three different insects. _____ _____ _____
Item 2: Which of the following is an insect?
   a. Bee
   b. Spider
   c. Snail
   d. Earthworm

Although these might be typical examples of a hastily constructed assessment, we might ask whether item 1 and item 2 are measuring much more than the retrieval of information from a lecture or textbook. With a little extra consideration we might develop a better item to meet the objective: Students should know the defining and differentiating features of insects that separate them from other classes in the taxonomic hierarchy.

Accordingly, a teacher might decide to employ a format in which the student would differentiate insects from noninsects. He or she might use the procedure displayed in the following question:

Which of the objects below have characteristics of (belong to) the class *Insecta* (phylum *Arthropoda*) and which are not insects? Use the following codes for your answer in the blanks following each name: I = example of an insect. NI = example of a noninsect.

Caterpillar ____   Bee ____   Ant ____   Pupa ____

Spider ____   Butterfly ____   Earthworm ____   Dragonfly ____   Snail ____

Crab ____   Walking Stick ____   Centipede ____

Figure 11.2. A multiple-choice test item figure.

You will notice that the display requires discrimination on the basis of many characteristics: insects with and without wings; small animals with legs, with six legs, with eight legs; and without legs; a representation of the life cycles. Understanding the systematic combination of these characteristics enters into the appraisal of the student's ability to make applications of their learning and into the teacher's ability to analyze aspects of the student's learning and under-standing. Overall, the question emphasizes the dependence on domain-specific knowledge in correctly analyzing and interpreting test results.

Before you read further, interrupt your reading to answer these questions: What interpretations can you make of students' correct and incorrect answers to each of the small creatures? Are there some things that would be desirable to measure for improving your teaching but that can't be measured? What would make a better test (using other items) than this one alone? Make a written list of your interpretations of student errors in terms of what was learned and what might be done to improve learning of such classifications. After doing so, read on to see some possible interpretations and compare them with yours.

(continued)

**Theory to Practice Box 11.2
(*Continued*)**

Some interpretations of responses might be as follows: Some students will indicate the crab is an insect; if so, they may not recognize the class of crustaceans, which belong in the phylum *Arthropoda*. Those who might have selected the centipede probably did not recognize the absence of body parts. The selection of the snail as an insect probably results from a complete lack of knowledge of the characteristics of insects; the student thinks only that insects are small. These responses suggest that the respondent considers crabs and centipedes as "bugs" or simply as small, crawly things. Similarly, a respondent who selects the spider may have learned that insects have three body parts, or may have failed to recognized the discriminating features of spiders as having two body parts (fused head and thorax) and eight (rather than six) legs. Students who didn't select the walking stick may have considered that large, sticklike organisms are not the prototypical "bugs"; the absence of wings may also have played a part in incorrect classifications. If they failed to select the cocoon or larva they may have considered only the adult stage and had no awareness of the life stages in the metamorphosis of insects. Failing to select the ant suggests the possible representation that insects have wings (some ants, of course, do have wings, and those that seem to be without wings have vestigial wings). When insects are lumped into a category characterized as "tiny things with legs" even a newborn mouse (not shown) might have been included as an insect.

Note that you don't have to make tests with drawings or be limited to biology to assess such comparisons. In this exercise, the teacher could have used actual insects spread out on a laboratory table. A chemistry teacher has a wealth of potential set-ups for laboratory displays of objects such as iron, brass, water, oxygen tanks, and so on asking the question, "Which are elements and compounds?" or "Which of the following are compounds, mixtures, or solutions?" using a rusty nail, a syrup, a mixture of sand and salt, and so on. In a language class one could present lists of words to be sorted into categories: verbs, nouns, and adjectives. In geography, with drawings or simply verbal labels, ask, "Which are continents, subcontinents, islands, or peninsulas?" (using Google Earth would provide excellent displays for comparison), or, "Which are ponds, lakes, bays, gulfs, oceans, or seas?" In social studies, with or without diagrams showing leaders, followers, constituencies, and communication lines, ask, "Which are monarchies, democracies, or dictatorships?" These are but a few illustrations. Any number of conceptualizations within any subject-matter area and any level (expert or novice) of a subject-matter area provide this opportunity.

You will have noticed that this format could also be used as a test item or as an exercise in seat work. As a test item, it could be passed or failed, based on a response that might be retrieved as a fact from memory—for instance, for each object in the above example, you might have asked, "Is this an insect? Yes or No?" But by requiring comparisons and by using wrong examples, the student must keep a number of characteristics in mind: the life stages for each class, the discriminating features, and the prototypical representations (e.g., the most typical "picture" of a concept—in the case of an insect, it is probably most typically characterized as an ant or grasshopper).

Of course, the exercise could have been extended by questioning the life stages and adding a few more pictures for life stages of insects and arachnids or other members of *Arthropoda*. Such items are capable of assessing procedural knowledge, in this case the procedures used for identifying, sorting, and classifying an object as an insect rather than an arachnid. An alternative question, such as, "Which of the following belong to the arachnids (or the crustaceans)?" would have the potential for identifying ways the student arrives at the distinctions among various classes of the phylum *Arthropoda*. Follow-up questions provide opportunities to identify or infer related metacognitions that influence either instruction or learning strategies. Such questions might be: "Which of the figures are insects?" "How do you know?" "What general procedure did you use to come up with the answer?" and "Explain your decision about each of the figures." For complete development of a concept, students must be able to identify which examples are excluded as well as those that are included.

Awareness of the functions of assessment is critical to its effective use in understanding how the learning outcomes were achieved either through instruction or by the processes the learner used. As you can see in these examples, the teacher's working knowledge of the subject-matter domain is essential and critically important to the success of any analysis of an assessment (Heritage, 2007). Without a deep understanding of domain-specific knowledge there is certain to be only surface analysis at the expense of the higher levels of understanding. When student responses or behaviors are incorrectly or only superficially analyzed, the students' instructional needs will not be met.

Thus, illustrations such as that shown in this box are not simply illustrations of potential items for specific class units. Rather, the reader should be aware of the reasons for constructing the test items in given formats. Awareness of the potential of tests and test items for showing what students know about the subject matter beyond the sheer recall of facts is a critical consideration. At some point in every grade level, assessments must enable interpretations of student responses in terms of identifiable emerging higher-level conceptual understandings, misconceptions, and ability to apply the knowledge in new ways.

hall, observing the way a student interacts with others on the playground, simulating bartering in a stock exchange through instruction in economics, going on a shopping trip to evaluate the nutrients on packaged foods, or participating in debates to simulate political challenges of candidates for state or national positions). These examples are not based on the premise that infrequently used behaviors provide better clues to students' cognitions. Rather they illustrate the need for finding situations where these behaviors can be observed. In the absence of finding such situations, establish test situations where learned concepts must be used to enable observation of them.

Making Observations Meaningful

Though perhaps an obvious observation, if you know the components of good problemsolving, understanding, or comprehension, where to look for their various manifestations, and how they will appear in certain situations, your assessments (and your instruction) will be more accurate than they would be in the absence of this knowledge. Obviously, without such knowledge you won't know what to look for, you won't know where to look for the behaviors, and, consequently, you won't be able to make useful observations for assessment.

The following checklist provides a guide for developing tasks that will provide useful assessments:

- Find tasks or situations in their subject-matter area target cognitions, procedural knowledge, or learning strategies. These are often common parts of subject-matter areas such as debating, setting up laboratory situations, holding class discussions around a dilemma in a current event, or figuring out when to use a past participle in Spanish.
- Learn from observation the different ways the performance or behaviors will be manifested in different situations. We have noted that the use of any knowledge is highly dependent on the student's prior knowledge. Because perceptions vary as a consequence, it is logical to recognize that students vary in the way they approach problems.
- Relate performance to standards, that is, to targeted knowledge, understanding, and skills. What knowledge does a student bring to a situation such as making change for a shopping spree? We know of a person who claimed to know how to hook up cables to jump start a dead battery. Claiming knowledge of how to do it, when the task was approached the cables were attached in reverse order to that recommended

(i.e., the first clamp was attached to the positive terminal of the live battery; the second clamp was attached to the negative terminal of the same battery).

- It is desirable, for ease of learning and teaching, to break down learning into small steps. See the battery example. Another example might be an operational analysis of some computer function such as copy and paste.

- We have illustrated several ways in which the assessment format can be manipulated to reveal specific information about the targeted objectives. The format has implications for assessing the quality of the performance, for instance, identifying that the student is missing a step in a laboratory procedure such as forgetting that acid is added slowly to the water rather than the reverse, or the student who continually leaves out a syllable in speaking Spanish. What are the implications of such omissions for instruction?

Assessment tasks are carefully linked to, or aligned with, the cognitions or procedures to be measured. If you are aiming at formative assessment it is important that your assessments support accurate inferences about students' understanding. The example of identifying insects (see Theory to Practice Box 11.2) shows the construction of an item designed to reveal the *targeted cognition* of *comparison and contrast*, thereby achieving the ability to test conceptual differentiation. In constructing a test of this form, think through the inferences that could be made when certain items are selected—for instance, when the spider is selected as an insect the response reveals the possibility that the student doesn't know or hasn't perceived that insects have three body segments or that the arachnid has two body segments. It might also be inferred that the student fails to make the differentiation because he or she is unable to use the knowledge because he or she fails to perceive the number of body segments in the examples of either category. Without employing that understanding, teachers could erroneously view a poorly designed assessment task as acceptable on the surface, as simply informing him or her that the student knows or doesn't know the answer when, in fact, the teacher isn't taking full advantage of the feedback provided in the wrong (or correct) answers.

Interpretation

In considering the assessment of learning, knowledge, understanding, and procedural knowledge, it is important to recognize that the mere fact of data gathering, whether by observation or tests, never stands alone. The data must be interpreted. The interpretations must answer the question, "What does the evidence show?" Drawing inferences about student acquisition from observations requires comparisons of student performance against content standards. In classroom situations, interpretations can also be made against a framework of informed intuitive or qualitative judgments of what constitutes good performance. Such judgments are often tied to assumptions regarding the characteristics of experts who presumably have deep understanding of both domain-specific and domain-general knowledge. They employ underlying principles in making judgments rather than relying on superficial characteristics.

■ Assessment at Instructional Phases

The functions of assessment differ according to the phase of instruction. Instruction is sometimes viewed as a single event. It goes on for a class period or continues over many weeks as an ongoing event. However, more current views analyze instruction in terms of phases or stages, each phase with it own demands for instruction, student participation, and assessment. These stages, as we have described them in earlier chapters, are simply *before*, *during*, and *after* instruction.

Three Phases of Instruction

The instructional phases may have been initially represented in reading, but for our purposes here, we have extended their importance to understanding instructional phases in any subject-matter area. In parallel to the phases, the questions are represented in a memory device known as KWL: Before learning, what do students *Know* about the topic? During learning, what do they *Want* to know? After learning, what have they *Learned* about the topic? To personalize the questions from the students' view point, the phases appear as Before instruction, what do I *Know* about the topic? During instruction, what do I *Want* (or need) to know about the topic? After instruction, what did I *Learn* about the topic?

The KWL procedure (Ogle, 1986) was originally developed within the framework of reading instruction. Nevertheless, it is a useful way of thinking about assessment in virtually any subject-matter area. Engaging student participation within this framework enables the gathering of evidence useful for both teachers and students to:

• Establish existing levels of knowledge (prior knowledge) about the topic being studied

- Set the purpose or objectives for an instructional unit
- Monitor student learning
- Learn how to repair difficulties that occur while learning; for example, how to know when one isn't comprehending a passage being read and how to go about repairing the poor comprehension, that is, how to use repair strategies when subgoals aren't being achieved
- Making applications of learning or extending learning beyond assignments
- Providing feedback on what was achieved

The record of the student responses, for use by the teacher, can be made on a form similar to the illustration in Theory to Practice Box 11.3 of a student record for his or her knowledge about gravity before reading an assignment. It is based on the use of the KWL procedure as illustrated by Conner (2006).

Theory to Practice Box 11.3
AN ILLUSTRATION OF HOW THE KWL PROCEDURE MIGHT BE USED IN TEACHING ABOUT GRAVITY

K: What I KNOW (*Before* instruction)	W: What I WANT to Know (*During* Instruction)	L: What I LEARNED (*After* Instruction)
Without it things would float around just as they do in a spaceship.	How do we define gravity? Is there more than one definition?	We speak of gravitational pull. It is the force that pulls all objects towards Earth and makes them fall—stalled airplanes, seeds from plants, jumping off a roof, or dropping a pencil.
Because of gravity apples fall to the ground.	Why is there less gravity on some extraterrestial bodies than others? What about the gravitational pull on the Moon? On Mars? How would you find out, if you didn't know?	Gravity in extraterrestrial bodies depends on their masses. The moon is a lot less massive than the Earth, so there is less gravity on the moon than there is on Earth.
Some stellar bodies have no gravity and you can take giant steps or lift heavy objects.		
Someone, I can't remember who, discovered gravity. It was a physicist.	Can we make conditions on Earth that have no gravity? How did Newton discover gravity? What determines how fast something will fall to the ground? *(teacher question)*	All objects fall at the same rate. It seems that some fall faster than others, when they produce more or less air resistance. Air resistance determines how fast something will fall to the ground.

Source: Adapted from Conner (2006).

Assessments before Learning

Assessment before instruction, sometimes called *preassessment*, is often useful for later comparisons with assessments of performance after instruction to measure student progress. But assessments before instruction can also be used for diagnosis of learning difficulties, placement within remedial or enrichment classes, and planning of instructional programs. Initial assessments are valued for the information they provide about diverse groups, their language ability, the cultural experiences they bring to the classroom, and any affective behaviors (attitudes, interests, motivation, or opinions) that may impact instructional effectiveness and so must be considered in adapting instruction to individual differences.

However, there is another important but frequently ignored reason for assessing students before instruction begins. Preassessment is useful for helping make teaching decisions through information about:

- How prepared the students are for teaching at the level you intended (whether you judged accurately how much the students already know about the topic on which your lesson plans were based)
- Time you and the students will need for instruction and learning
- Misconceptions that you did not anticipate but have identified; you now can consider steps to remove those misconceptions
- How concerned the student is with making applications of prior knowledge to new situations (see Theory to Practice Box 11.3 for an example)

Preassessment begins with instructional targets or objectives for a given unit. Then ask questions such as, "Where do the students stand in relation to those objectives?" "What is their ability to learn at the level I intended to teach this unit?" "Do they know more (or less) than I initially thought?" "What is required in instruction to fill the gap?" "What is the best method by which to do this?" and "Can I jump ahead in my teaching?"

The information obtained about what students know at the beginning of instruction can help to identify misconceptions that often hinder progress of student achievement. Illustrations include:

- "We will be studying insect eating plants. What do you know already about insect eating plants?"

- "Today (in music appreciation class) we will be studying important forms of percussion. Do you know which instruments are percussion instruments? Which, if any of the following are percussion instruments—violin, cello, trumpet, piano, tambourine, cymbals, kettle drum, triangle? What are the common characteristics of those that are percussion instruments? What are the commonalities of the roles percussion instruments play in such diverse settings as symphonic orchestras, marching bands, or rock-and-roll bands? Are there any trends in musical forms that make more use of percussion instruments than other forms?"

Without some understanding of where students stand at the beginning of instruction, whether in the elementary or high school grades, you will probably be using inefficient methods with unreliable outcomes. Of course, you gain important information about your students simply by knowing their background: age, parentage, parents' occupation, socioeconomic status, ethnicity, and so on. But preassessment of knowledge gives you more specific information about students' entering behaviors that contribute to readiness for learning the subject matter you teach.

You can sample what students know from tests you construct, but you can also ask students informal questions about the subject matter (Roth, 1990). Questioning is a useful assessment device for gathering such information. When you do so, don't look mainly for right or wrong answers, but for students' ability to summarize, organize, elaborate, and explain, as we have said earlier in this chapter. This type of information helps you determine where to begin your instruction.

Students' prior knowledge comes in many forms. Sometimes it is a sound foundation for what you intend to teach and only needs extension. For example, students may know that a pendulum comes to rest at the same place, but may not see that the resting place is analogous to a spring at rest or a ball at the bottom of an inclined plane. At other times, students' prior knowledge takes the form of naïve theories of the world. For instance, young students may think the moon is like a pancake rather than like a sphere. Slightly older students may see spiders and grasshoppers as belonging to the same group ("small bugs") rather than to the separate groups of insects and arachnids (which differ not only in bodily structure but also in methods of reproduction) or miss the distinction between sucking and chewing insects (a fact important in determining sprays for controlling insects). In these cases, the student will need to change his or her views of the moon's shape or of what comprises the classes of creatures in the phylum *Arthropoda*. Preconceptions are such an important concern in new learning that we consider their assessment at length in the next section.

Assessment of Preconceptions

All students enter every learning situation with prior knowledge or beliefs that are certain to affect their learning. Even preschool children arrive at the learning scene with prior knowledge. They have a world theory, made up of ideas about how things work, and these ideas affect the way they approach new learning. Some of that prior knowledge, in virtually every content area of instruction, consists of what adults perceive as misrepresentations or misconceptions. (This is not to say that college undergraduate and graduate students and other adult learners are not without misconceptions; they have many and some of those they have can interfere significantly with their new learning.)

Children's naïve views are not wrong; they are often part of development. For teachers they can be stepping stones to becoming increasingly defined with instruction and experience. As such, they are called developing representations or alternative representations. For example, noticing that a feather falls more slowly than a ball is a first step in understanding gravity, despite its being a misconception when it takes the form of a belief.

Characteristics of Preconceptions

A common intuition of preschool children is that their shadow follows them (Ogle, 1986; Piaget & Inhelder, 1973). This very simple idea, based on perceptual experience, is tested out in performance—the toddler may turn around quickly to step on the shadow or to chase it away. At some point of development, some toddlers may believe the shadow has tangible properties. They may be unable to explain why the shadow disappears on a cloudy day. These, too, are examples of developing misrepresentations.

Other kinds of misrepresentations include the common belief that many inanimate objects are alive (Carey, 2000). A rolling rock may be thought to be alive simply because it moves. Examples of other common beliefs are shown in Table 11.1.

Table 11.1. Some Preconceptions of Common Topics That Interfere with New Learning

Object or Event	Common Belief
The Sun	Alive, solid, and mainly made of yellow and orange light.
Water	Found only in lakes, ponds, rain, and snow, not in the air. Water molecules are equidistant and constant in liquid, gas, or solid states.
Genetics	Changes in characteristics of living organisms, whether in physiology or behavior, that occur due to environmental circumstances can be transmitted to offspring.

Source: Although these kinds of beliefs are likely to be common to many of us, these particular items and beliefs about them have been selected and modified from a list assembled by Woloshyn, Paivio, and Pressley (1994).

Persistence of Misconceptions

We have noted that current thinking considers conceptions like the ones listed in Table 11.1 as developmental, emerging with maturity toward more complete or scientific understandings. But clearly instruction plays a major role in this change. For example, initially young students might believe that the sun is composed of solid matter. However, when we teach students that the sun's surface is gaseous, we expect that knowing that will translate into the belief that it is not solid, although we may never mention that fact (that the sun's surface is gaseous). Confronted with facts such as these may create conflicts in students' understanding when early misrepresentations clash with their new learning, but these conflicts are critical to new learning—old ideas require changing previous knowledge to accommodate the new information. Such accommodation contributes to the learning of complex ideas (Piaget, 1969).

When preconceptions linger indefinitely, even after instruction, they have a continual effect on understanding. The display in Theory to Practice Box 11.4 provides examples of lingering preconceptions and the difficulties they may cause in college (Anderson, Sheldon, & Dubay, 1990). This is another demonstration that adult learning and behavior is prone to some of the same difficulties as those of children. A pervasive inhibitor of change, preconceptions can interfere in new learning, whether of children, college students, or older adults.

As demonstrated in such examples as that shown in Theory to Practice Box 11.4, the understanding of a concept requires the abandonment of old ideas to accommodate the new ones.

Theory to Practice Box 11.4
ASSESSMENT IN IDENTIFYING THE PERSISTENCE OF PRECONCEPTIONS

The effect of preconceptions on thinking is shown in a striking finding of a study of students who were learning about photosynthesis (Anderson, Sheldon, & Dubay, 1990), based on a description in Pressley and McCormick (1995). In this study, college students were able to give fairly reasonable definitions of photosynthesis after instruction, but they showed little ability to apply the new information. When presented with a real-world question, the students reverted to their preconceptions. The conceptual understanding of these students was superficial, lacking in depth of understanding the complexity of photosynthesis—most knew that light was involved, but few understood the transfer and storage of solar energy or the role of water in making food. Despite their level of education the students were not conversant with the roles of carbon dioxide, oxygen, water uptake, and respiration.

After being taught about photosynthesis (a process by which sunlight and carbon dioxide are converted to food by chlorophyll in the leaves) the students were asked to define photosynthesis. They did so using terms that captured the "manufacturing" or "conversion into energy" components, albeit somewhat imprecisely. The students gave answers such as:

- "Plants change carbon dioxide into oxygen."
- "They turn sunlight and carbon dioxide into chlorophyll."
- "Chlorophyll manufactures food for the plants."

Students also came up with ideas analogous to the way humans ingest food for nutrition. They thought in terms of plants ingesting minerals and water from the earth and sunlight from the sun (Roth & Anderson, 1987).

The teachers expected that this learning would have some utility beyond the classroom. So, to test the students' ability to use the new learning, a delayed test was administered, asking, "How does a plant on the window sill get its food?" At this point, students' answers contained *no mention of photosynthesis* or of the plant's ability to manufacture its own food. Answers were mainly of this type, based on the students' preconceptions:

- "They were fertilized and watered."
- "They take the fertilizer and water through their roots."

These are typical responses of children in elementary grades as well. The implication of these studies for formative assessment (Roth & Anderson, 1987) is that the teacher can identify the extent to which student learning in class instruction results in conceptual understanding or in the acquisition of inert knowledge (inert knowledge is knowledge that can be recalled on a test but is not, or cannot be, applied readily to other situations).

Source: This is a modification of a description in Pressley and McCormick (1995) combined with other basic science information on photosynthesis.

Educators agree that the key to facilitating accommodation is to provide the new material to be learned in contexts appropriate to the child's level of intellectual development (Piaget, 1969). These extended or supplementary contexts have the potential of moving the child from naïve conceptualizations to conceptualizations with more depth and complexity as the child progresses through school.

The assessment of prior knowledge is generally considered essential in this developmental process (Resnick, 1987; Von Glasserfeld, 1989), suggesting the importance of assessing students' prior knowledge before instruction particularly to understand what knowledge is available and to build on that knowledge with instruction. Additionally, assessment at this phase of instruction serves to increase student awareness of instructional objectives, thereby making certain that the students' objectives are the same as the instructor's objectives.

Resistance to Change

When we identify the misconceptions through testing and other measures, the objective becomes changing them to evidence-based conceptions. Further testing may show that even with instruction, they have not changed. Why are some preconceptions or misconceptualizations so difficult to change? Misconceptions formed early become associated with a wide range of situations (Pressley & McCormick, 1995). They have utility for everyday explanations. They continue to be used because they are, in their own way, functional in the child's life and are right much of the time (e.g., feathers do fall more slowly than many other objects; the moon does seem to move as you walk).

However, these preconceptions present a problem for teachers because, upon being tested, they are found not to be easily replaceable in new learning. As can be seen in Box 11.4, the early ideas of photosynthesis can persist into the college years. A number of reasons can be given for this persistence: We look for evidence that confirms what we already know or believe to be important; we select events that confirm our prior knowledge; we avoid evidence that fails to confirm our expectations. All of this may be unintentional. We can easily see how we try to use preconceptions as excuses for biased responses; students will say "I already knew that" or "That's what I meant" and then give an explanation that corresponds to their earlier conceptions rather than to the new material. This characteristic can have unseen effects on studying: When students tag information as already known, they may not study the information for understanding; it is thought to support what they already know and warrants no further attention. As a result the student may learn that material superficially or may focus instead on other information, which may even be less relevant, perhaps to the extent of memorizing it by rote. By doing so, they develop knowledge that can be repeated back correctly, but at the expense of genuine understanding. Certainly, the new information has not been learned.

What do these examples of misrepresentation imply for assessment? You can assess students' existing misrepresentations either by teacher-made tests or by discussion. The identification, via preassessment, gives you a chance to confront and correct these ideas. If you find, through your assessments, that preconceptions will interfere or hinder the acquisition of new knowledge, you can set up learning situations that challenge the students' thinking and guide them to modify their ideas accordingly. The delivery of subject-matter content can be made in different contexts (see examples in this chapter) requiring the use of the subject matter in different ways (e.g., in settings where the information is used in different applications).

During Learning

The purpose of assessment *during* learning is to provide data that will be useful in monitoring students' progress and, in doing so, inform teaching effectiveness. If students are found, through assessments, to be struggling with one or more aspects of the lesson, the instructional plan can be modified. Although understanding may be targeted in the assessments you make, other objectives may be of importance, including such objectives as the development of *attitudes* toward the scientific method, music or art *appreciation*, and the development of motor *skills* whether in dancing, playing a sport, using a computer, or drawing. These, too, may be judged to be of sufficient importance to be assessed. For example, you might want to know how successful your teaching was in changing attitudes toward the scientific method or toward conservation and sustainability.

Assessment of Content (Declarative Knowledge)

Declarative knowledge consists of understanding both the facts related to the subject matter and the way these facts are organized and explained. Declarative knowledge is typically represented in the subject-matter content of a domain such as science, math, language, or social studies. It represents more than simple facts, however. It also includes concepts and the ways these concepts can be selected and organized. These characteristics are of critical importance when content is to be retrieved in alternative ways in creative or problem-solving situations. When measuring declarative knowledge, you will look for acquisition of facts, but you will also want to use tasks within contexts that emphasize classifications, combinations of concrete and abstract concepts, organizations of concepts, critical examination of the material, and how these knowledges can be extended to alternative, imaginative, and creative solutions.

For example, if you were teaching a social studies unit about the U.S. invasion of Iraq in 2003, in addition to such facts as dates when troops arrived there, you might ask a question like this:

What were the major causes of the Iraqi conflict? Why did the initial phase of the war end quickly compared to the endurance of the later phases?

Answering questions like these requires more than a miscellany of facts. You will want students to demonstrate the way they have conceptualized the material and the relevance of the information they may have used. If the students' responses meet your criteria, you can continue instruction as planned. But if students' achievement falls short of your criteria, you can modify your instruction accordingly. Many of the boxes in this chapter provide illustrations of the development of student understanding of declarative knowledge.

Assessment of Performance (Procedural Knowledge)

Procedural knowledge refers to the how and what of learning: how the students explain phenomena and what explanations are used, how they select their strategies and methods of learning and what methods or strategies are used, how they sequence their procedures and what procedures are used, and so on. Many conceptualizations in science, for example, lean heavily on research evidence drawn from scientific inquiry, which involves collecting data relevant to making decisions and forming judgments. For many types of higher-order thinking, the procedures (processes) engaged for solving problems or finding solutions may be equally as important as the basic information in arriving at a feasible solution.

As you can see, an important part of a student's knowledge base consists of procedures used for organizing information in a subject-matter (content) domain. Music appreciation, for example, requires an understanding of unique technical information and concepts such as pitch, rhythm, intervals, scales, and key signatures; historical composers of music; and groupings of instruments. These can be taught as declarative knowledge, and music theory is an important underlying component. However, associated with each is what to look for and how to perceive or observe such characteristics of music as pitch, rhythm, intervals, and scales. In addition, for music appreciation objectives, the student may be required to learn how and what to listen for in live or recorded concert performances. As a performer the student learns to play a musical instrument with a standard of proficiency that includes the dynamics of the performance. Procedures for organizing and thinking can be seen in other areas such as taxonomic hierarchies in biology, Venn diagrams to represent relations in math, or flow charts used for computer programming.

To assess knowledge and procedures learned in a unit, say, on the scientific method, you will want to plan your measures around such targets as what the student perceives (believes) to be important, what questions are asked, whether a testable hypothesis has been formed, and what explanations are offered. Simple changes in format can make major differences in the kinds of inferences that can be made from the results. For example, upon performing a laboratory exercise in which two chemicals are combined, you might ask the question, "Did you see the blue and white precipitate when the two compounds were mixed?" This often-asked question in laboratory exercise manuals has little potential for helping you understand much more than the ability of the student to answer the leading question. The answer simply requires answering *yes* or *no* to whether or not he or she saw a precipitate.

On the other hand, you might ask, *before* conducting the experiment, "What do you expect will happen when these [two] chemicals are combined?" This question would assess the availability (or access) of the content knowledge related to the problem and the ability to form testable hypotheses. Then there is an additional question that might be asked after the experiment was performed, "What actually happened when the two chemicals were combined? Did it confirm your hypothesis? Why or why not?" This question provides the opportunity to assess whether perception was sufficient to see the blue and white precipitate and whether the student could communicate a sufficient explanation of the event, including evidence for or against his or her hypothesis. Obviously, different aspects of student acquisition are revealed by the wording of questions asked in assessments.

After Learning

Much of what we have said regarding assessment during learning applies to assessment after learning. However, assessment after learning is looking back at what was learned, how learning progressed, and what was or was not achieved. Hopefully, any assessment after learning will show progress—grades, inferences, and ability to transfer should show improvement from the initial testing.

The Priority of Prior Knowledge in Responding to Tests

Assessment after learning, for example, might examine the influence of learning strategies used by students on learning outcomes, as shown in an interpretation of a study by Roth (1990) as described by Gagne, Yekovich, and Yekovich (1993, p. 413). This description also contains implications for alternative ways of assessing student achievement and provides some bases for drawing inferences from student responses to measures used. The finding from this study is striking: After a unit of instruction, students made little change in the old ways they preserved their prior knowledge despite instruction.

Students in the study read an assigned science text about plants and then responded to questions from an interviewer. The students were asked to give the main ideas from the reading, and then they were probed to determine whether their ideas had changed as a result of exposure to these ideas. Some questions were aimed at determining whether the reader depended on prior knowledge or on text-based knowledge (that is, knowledge gained from the reading).

A description that follows provides a basis for assessing the strategies students in your class were using and the extent to which their strategies were based on prior knowledge (knowledge they already knew before instruction) or on understanding the text (understandings acquired as a result of instruction). Several ineffective strategies were identified in the Roth study:

- *Prior knowledge took precedence over new information.* Some students used prior knowledge exclusively for answering questions, whether they were text-based or real-world questions. They believed that prior knowledge could help answer questions and that it was proper to use prior knowledge to help finish the assignment.
- *When studying, students emphasized unique words in the text improperly as cues for later retrieval or other use.* They might have based their selection of a word on whether it

was an unusual word, a big word, or some such basis; the idea of course was they thought such words, because they were unique, were important and would help in completing a school task such as retrieving the word for a test. Perhaps they thought, "Teachers often ask for definitions of such words; perhaps, this teacher will, too."

- *It is not unusual for students to use prior knowledge to the exclusion of new learning.* When students combine what they know (prior knowledge) with new ideas presented in the instruction or in the text, they draw on both sources to answer text-based and real-world questions. However, prior knowledge often dominates. While learning, the instructional content was selected to achieve confirmation or support for what they already knew, a weakness in learners of which the teacher should be aware. The students' essential attitude was, "I already knew that."

Following these assessments, after completing the interviews with students, the teachers in this study deliberately taught a strategy for new approaches to the assignment. They demonstrated ways of searching for knowledge from the text not merely to answer questions on the text, but also to understand real-world situations. Students were made aware of the inefficient strategies they might be using. This focus on learning strategy, stimulated by the results of the assessment, led students to revise their reading strategies targeting improvement in conceptual understanding.

Assessments of procedural knowledge thus can provide a basis for revising instructional procedures or implementing new instructional procedures. In general, when you suspect that students have gaps or "bugs" (errors or mistakes that prevent arrival at a correct answer) in their procedural knowledge, assessments by questioning to reveal the procedures or processes being used can be helpful to guide remedial instruction.

Metacognitions and Transfer

Metacognition is critical not only to initial learning but to effective applications and transfer of learning to new situations. Metacognitions, awareness of how they learn or knowing about how they learn, and factors that influence their learning such as misconceptions, biases, and opinions—all the issues we have discussed up to this point in the chapter—all have powerful effects on the degree to which the content is accepted, whether it is understood, and whether it is relatable to other subject-matter areas or is simply limited to passing the next test or the specific course or class in which it is taught.

Metacognitive Awareness

Current teaching methods aim to promote a greater ability to transfer. Using varied examples such as those shown in Theory to Practice Box 11.2 on discriminating insects from other classes of arthropods is only one way. Assessments will suggest when students must learn to differentiate characteristics for classifications, what they are to gain from comparison and contrast, and how to retrieve information on the basis of problem statements. But such metacognitions must always begin with the *awareness of what one (the learner) knows*, how one's knowledge base affects learning and transfer, the basis of the differentiations in a specific task, available alternative perspectives for viewing similarities and differences, and awareness of expectations regarding outcomes to be achieved. Questionnaires and inventories aimed at measuring metacognitions can be useful supplements to regular tests for gathering data on metacognitions. The development and use of questionnaires for measuring such variables as metacognitions are described in the final section of this chapter.

Importance of Metacognition in Transfer

Assessments of declarative knowledge (knowing "that") and procedural knowledge (knowing "how") should be combined with measures of understanding to demonstrate the relation of both to acquiring the ability to transfer.

Teaching for the transfer of knowledge, that is, for application to other situations than the classroom, means instruction specifically designed to make the knowledge available in a number of contextual settings. The assessments must focus on more than mere recall. They must be robust and authentic; they must call on student competence "to draw on understandings in new ways, new applications and new connections" (Shepard, 1997, p. 27, as cited in Shepard, 2000, p. 11). In this regard, accompanying metacognitions are imperative, raising such questions as the following for teachers:

• Do my students know that what they have learned can help to solve the new problem?
• Are they aware of the different ways to view the principle (e.g., can they extend Bernoulli's principle to explain the increase of air speed over an airplane wing)?

- Do they know some study or learning strategies that will help them to recall information under different circumstances?
- Are they aware of the differences between storing information to be recalled later and accessing and recalling information stored?

For example, suppose your students were studying the concept of osmosis. You might simply ask for a definition of osmosis. Or you might have them describe a laboratory experiment (using an egg or other membrane material) that involves osmosis. Either test would do little more than provide evidence that the students could repeat some material in the assignment. A more effective assessment would be one in which the students applied the principle to plant and animal physiology, water purification, or waste disposal.

Similarly, following a unit on metals in which students learned concepts like melting points and molecular weights, we might assess whether students can relate the characteristics of metals to consequences for recycling, for delaying corrosion, and for combining one metal with another. By a careful construction of test items we can assess student ability to predict such things as the physiological consequences when metals such as lead and mercury are ingested (e.g., do these molecules pass through membranes? Which membranes? Where are they stored in the body?). We might also predict that students would learn such other processes as plasmolysis and osmotic pressure more easily had they learned these with an understanding of osmosis rather than the simple facts underlying it.

Alternative Measures

As important as such measures are, alternative measures provide useful supplements for formative assessment at any phase of instruction. We have illustrated the use of questionnaires for informing us about student metacognitions and affective dispositions, which can be important information for evaluating the effectiveness of ongoing day-to-day instruction. We now turn to a short discussion of how these alternative measures are constructed.

■ Constructing and Using Questionnaires to Measure Dispositions, Metacognitions, and Affect

Questionnaires and inventories are useful techniques for student reactions to study materials. Results on these measures provide feedback for instructional remediation that would be difficult to obtain through achievement tests alone. In fact, like tests, the questionnaire should be considered as important a part of testing within instructional method as any other part of instruction. Questionnaires have useful potential for feedback to both student and teachers. The feedback they provide should be immediate, constructive, and nonthreatening.

By following a few relatively simple rules you can construct questionnaires or surveys that have utility for assessing cognitive and affect factors contributing to student learning. Such information is often obtained indirectly or informally by asking individual students questions regarding what they know, what they have learned, and so on. Or the information may be obtained by implication or inference from traditional test measures. The planned use of inventories, surveys, or questionnaires (including focus groups and interviews) enables you to gather information from an entire class on significant factors that affect student learning.

Construction of Questionnaires

Construction of surveys, as with test construction, is initiated with a plan or objective. Many such objectives appear in examples used in the previous sections. These questions can then be paraphrased as declarative statements followed by a rating scale. The following review of previous sections will serve as a guide to developing measures that might supplement other measures. Refer to examples in previous sections, where necessary. We caution that the current discussion focuses mainly on scales that measure student awareness at different phases of instruction. Our aim is simply to demonstrate how questionnaires and similar measures can be used in subject-matter areas.

In general, the use of subjective reports (reports of how the respondent feels) can be helpful in informing you of student metacognitions, attitudes, and expectations that will affect how you implement instruction.

Begin with measuring *student awareness of what they know at the beginning of a lesson*. Raising questions about a topic before learning provides a basis for increasing student awareness of what they have already learned about a topic (e.g., Conner, 2006; Graesser, Cai, Louwerse, & Daniel, 2006). However, it is preferable to provide feedback to actively guide students in *recognizing* their level of learning, such as what facts they have learned, the depth of their understanding, the use of particular strategies, or how to apply the knowledge base, rather than to assume that scores on assignments or questions will automatically raise awareness of whatever self-correction of learning processes are needed. As indicated earlier, you can also identify from such measures the student's overreliance on prior knowledge in the acquisition of new understandings.

Questionnaire Topics

Questionnaire scales provide ready ways of learning what knowledge students retrieve (access) from memory of previous learning and, perhaps, the way the information was organized. As importantly, questions with such scales can focus on the awareness of what students know about a topic, whether a topic is or is not entirely new to them, and whether they can retrieve or access what they learned by rote or by understanding the topics of a lesson.

Measure what students think they need to learn to acquire facts, to understand, or to transfer. Questions organized around this topic are a valuable source of information targeting awareness of goals and objectives. Whatever their awareness, whether of prior knowledge or of text assignments, that awareness dramatically affects what is learned. In discussions with some elementary students, we have heard successful students say, "I do all the exercises and I get good marks on all of them, but I never know why I am doing them (the exercises) or what I am supposed to learn from them." Clearly, those students have no awareness of the objectives of an exercise, so they have no way of knowing what to learn. A lack of awareness and metacognitions (regarding objectives, kinds of information that can be acquired, or learning processes important for such goals as understanding and application) are forerunners of inert knowledge. Such questions as the following are useful to counteract this result:

- "What more could you learn about insect-eating plants? What would you want to learn about them?"
- "What can we learn, in addition to what you already know, about percussion instruments?

Often students are not aware of what applications can be made of such topics as geometry or algebra. Teaching often stops at the point of telling the information. A case in point is a comment by one of our mathematics professors, who said, "I really don't think understanding fractals (parts that repeat the pattern of the whole—e.g., parts of the fern leaf have characteristics of the whole leaf) has much use in everyday life." This comment neglects the findings that once the characteristics of fractals are understood, their applications are many. Fractal patterns, for example, appear in such varied applications as art appreciation, architectural design, computer design of games, and medical classifications, to name but a few.

Use these measures (scales, questionnaire items, inventory items, and so on) to get information on student beliefs about what was learned, how it was learned, and the potential uses and transferability of what was learned (Stobart, 2008). By focusing on marks or grades, the simple expedient of reporting test scores makes us prone to the incorrect assumption that students know how to use the grade as feedback for facilitating their progress (e.g., where the methods of studying and learning were successful or where they went awry). By transferring the responsibility for improving achievement to the student we override the possibility that instructional procedures and emphases might have some effect on student acquisition.

We should not be left with the expectation that because it was taught students will be aware of what they have learned, how they learned it, or how well they understand (or comprehend) the content learned. Questionnaire data can be useful for class discussions of content to be reviewed, identification and sharing of potential learning strategies, corrections to errors in achievement (repair strategies), awareness of achievement, and how well student achievement corresponded to instructional goals. Such questions might be:

- "Tell the things you learned in this lesson on osmosis."
- "How do you think you changed in understanding how osmosis can be used in understanding plant and animal physiology, water purification, waste disposal, and so on?"

Survey student use of study strategies. Such measures can be useful in helping students become aware of strategies, reporting strategies that they use, and the effective use of strategies. There are several study-habits questionnaires available on the Internet and from commercial companies that might be selected rather than constructing a new one. They include items such as:

- How frequently do you try to use a memory aid such as a jingle in studying? (Often–Not at All)
- I find that repetition of material is essential for me to learn the material. (Agree–Disagree)
- When I have difficulty with an assignment, I search for reasons why I don't comprehend it. (Agree–Disagree)

Some measures can be constructed to obtain feedback regarding affective components of learning (for the use of questions in this arena, see Graesser, Bowers, Olde, & Pomeroy, 1999) *rather than leaving assumptions about them to chance.* Teachers frequently comment that they want their students to have the same passion for the subject matter (e.g., literature, science, math) as they have or, conversely, they comment, "I don't know why the students seem so disinterested" and, in between, teachers comment, "I gave a splendid presentation (on conservation, political controversy, growth of the economy, etc.) in this morning's class and we had a fine discussion. Everyone learned a lot." Rather than leaving such commentary undocumented, it would be worthwhile to determine just how effective the teaching was for achieving affective outcomes.

Use questionnaires for obtaining judgments, attitudes, and opinions regarding such objectives as appreciation for a subject (e.g., music appreciation or appreciation of the scientific method); amount of time spent (too much time or too little time) on the topic; opinions (e.g., regarding ability to use the information, ways of assessing their performance) dispositions in using a procedure (e.g., using the scientific method or a learning strategy); or dispositions for selecting one activity over another (e.g., reading detective versus historical novels or playing tennis versus playing chess). Examples of item statements that can be used for attitudinal ratings, using a three-, five-, or seven-point scale are:

- When I go to the library I look for manuals on how to play (a video game, a sport, a card game). (Agree-Disagree)
- I would rather read a detective story than a historical novel. (Agree-Disagree)
- I look for the sounds of the different musical instruments when I listen to a symphony orchestra. (Agree-Disagree)
- I think that learning ability is inherited. (Agree-Disagree)
- I would judge the quality of a new product by scientific rather than anecdotal evidence. (Agree-Disagree)

■ Summary

In traditional behavioristic views, learning meant acquiring isolated bits of information in small steps, and the accompanying tests focused on the acquisition of that detailed knowledge. More recent approaches for assessing acquisition in subject-matter areas are based on constructivist views that emphasize deeper understanding and higher-order thinking. Prior knowledge is an important component of constructed knowledge that plays an important role in student achievement. The ultimate goal, in the constructivist position, is understanding and positive transfer of knowledge to real-life situations.

The construction of assessment tasks has developed from an initial behavioral base to an emphasis on useful knowledge. Today, assessment of student acquisition is focused on student cognitions and learning processes, including the way students organize learning, the incorporation of prior knowledge with new text-based knowledge, the broader conceptualization of the content beyond the rote memory of isolated facts, the strategies used for studying, and how knowledge and understandings are acquired and used in authentic settings (Wiggins, 1992). These are important bases for the feedback on instruction that characterizes formative assessment.

A useful way of considering assessment methods and the deployment of assessment results to achieve instructional effectiveness is to understand how assessment appears in the instructional requirements at different phases of instruction, a view implicit in the KWL procedure. Within this view, each phase of instruction is seen to emphasize unique instructional and assessment requirements. The first phase (before learning) is a diagnostic phase to determine student status, in all its forms, regarding the topic to be learned. It is also a phase during which background knowledge related to lesson objectives is activated.

The next phase (during learning) is devoted to student understanding of questions to be answered as learning and instruction are taking place. We might focus on things that aren't completely understood, linking what we know to new learning, organizing the material into meaningful patterns like hierarchies or Venn diagrams, finding applications in authentic settings, or metacognitive awareness of different approaches to the topic being studied. Students are encouraged during this phase to actively look for confirmation of hypotheses or inferences, applications and use of the information, and what still remains unanswered or yet to be discovered.

The last phase (after learning) is looking back at what was learned, the progress made, how progress was facilitated, new applications or methods of organization, and new questions for further study.

Surveys, inventories, and questionnaires are useful alternative ways of measuring student progress during these phases of instruction. Questions and scales are not only valuable for assessment, but play useful roles in formative assessment for instruction as well (e.g., see the use of questions in reading by

Cooper, 2000). The general procedures for developing questions and questionnaires are illustrated in the examples in this chapter. There are a number of variations, typically referred to as inventories, surveys, rating scales, checklists, or questionnaires. They don't *look* like tests, so their value in formative assessment may be overlooked. They are ordinarily planned according to specifications by the teacher, by the professional field, or by adaptation from existing scales. In many cases, adequate questionnaires are available on the Internet or from commercial or research sources. (A helpful source for developing survey questions may be found in Graesser et al., 2006.)

Underlying the procedures for constructing questionnaires are interrogative statements that target a judgment, interest, opinion, or feeling about a given topic. Sometimes the question is translated into a declarative statement accompanied by a scale for a rating response to the statement. The responses can then be summarized as averages of either the entire scale or subcategories. These averages then provide the general sentiment of the entire class as well as that of individual students.

The reliability and validity of items in questionnaires and surveys certainly should be carefully considered. However, when they are used for everyday feedback, these measures will not stand up to the rigorous demands for reliability and validity required when they are used for research purposes.

The topics targeted by questionnaires are on such topics as estimates of time spent on, or use of study habits; reports that permit inferences about some aspect of motivation; personality variables such as self-concepts and self-esteem; affective variables such as anxiety; appreciation of art, music, or science; or agreement with policies such as conservation or sustainability of resources. They are important parts of informal assessments as they may be used to answer questions of importance to a particular classroom by supplementing information from the traditional subject-matter tests and by framing them for the unique purposes of individual classes. Further, these are not replacements for standardized measures or summative measures of achievement. Rather they are among the many assessment procedures teachers have available to monitor students' growth and development within instructional settings.

■ Helpful Readings

For illustrations of a variety of graphic organizers see the website for edhelper.com: www.edhelper.com/teachers/General_graphic_organizers.htm. The site displays illustrations of a number of different graphic organizers for special areas such as graphing, math, and reading as well as for the time of learning, such as before, during, and after reading—the familiar K (what do I Know?), W (what do I Want to find out?), and L (what did I Learn?).

■ References

Anderson, C. W., Sheldon, T. H., & Dubay, J. (1990). The effects of instruction on college nonmajors' conceptions of respiration and photosynthesis. *Journal of Research in Science Teaching, 27*(8), 761–776.

Carey, S. (2000). Science education as conceptual change. *Journal of Applied Developmental Psychology, 21*, 13–19.

Conner, J. (2006). Instructional reading strategy: KWL (Know, Want to know, Learned). Retrieved November 23, 2007, from www.indiana.edu/~l517/KWL.htm.

Cooper, J. D. (2000). *Literacy: Helping children construct meaning* (4th ed.). Boston: Houghton Mifflin.

Gagne, E. D., Yekovich, C. W., & Yekovich, F. R. (1993). *The cognitive psychology of school learning* (2nd ed.). New York: Harper Collins.

Graesser, A. C., Bowers, C., Olde, B., & Pomeroy, V. (1999). Who said what? Source memory for narrator and character agents in literary short stories. *Journal of Educational Psychology, 91*, 284–300.

Graesser, A. C., Cai, Z., Louwerse, M. M., & Daniel, F. (2006). Question Understanding Aid (QUAID): A web facility that tests question comprehensibility *Public Opinion Quarterly, 70*(1), 3–22.

Graue, M. E. (1993). Integrating theory and practice through instructional assessment. *Educational Assessment, 1*, 293–309.

Heritage, M. (2007). Formative assessment: What do teachers need to know and do? *Phi Delta Kappan, 89*(2), 140–145.

Mokhtari, K., & Reichard, C. A. (2002). Assessing students' metacognitive awareness of reading strategies. *Journal of Educational Psychology, 94*(2), 249–259.

Ogle, D. M. (1986). K-W-L: A teaching model that develops active reading expository text. *The Reading Teacher, 39*(6), 564–570.

Pelligrino, J. W., Chudowsky, N., & Glaser, R. (2001). *Knowing what students know: The science and design of educational assessment.* Washington, DC: National Academy Press.

Piaget, J. (1969). *Psychology of intelligence*. Totowa, NJ: Littlefield, Adams.

Piaget, J., & Inhelder, B. (1973). *Memory and intelligence.* New York: Basic Books.

Pintrich, P. R., & De Groot, E. V. (1990). Motivational and self-regulated learning components of classroom academic performance. *Journal of Educational Psychology, 82*(1), 33–40.

Pintrich, P. R., & Schrauben, B. (1992). Student's motivational beliefs and their cognitive engagement in academic tasks. In D. Schunk & J. Meece (Eds.), *Students' perceptions in the classroom: Causes and consequences* (pp. 149–183). Hillsdale, NJ: Lawrence Erlbaum Associates.

Pressley, M., & McCormick, C. B. (1995). *Advanced educational psychology: For educators, researchers, and policymakers.* New York: HarperCollins College Publishers.

Resnick, L. B. (1987). *Education and learning to think.* Washington, DC: National Academy Press.

Roth, K. J. (1990). Developing meaningful conceptual understanding in science. In B. F. Jones & L. Idol (Eds.), *Dimensions of thinking and cognitive instruction*. Hillsdale, NJ: Lawrence Erlbaum Associates.

Roth, K. J., & Anderson, C. W. (1987). *The power plant: Teacher's guide to photosynthesis. Occasional Paper no. 112. Institute for Research on Teaching.* East Lansing: Michigan State University.

Sadler, D. R. (1998). Formative assessment: Revisiting the territory. *Assessment in Education: Principles, Policy and Practice, 5,* 77–84.

Shepard, L. A. (1997). *Measuring achievement: What does it mean to test for robust understanding?* Princeton, NJ: Educational Testing Service, Policy Information Center.

Shepard, L. A. (2000). The role of assessment in a learning culture. *Educational Research, 29*(7), 4–14.

Siegler, R. S. (1998). *Children's thinking* (3rd ed.). Upper Saddle River, NJ: Prentice Hall.

Stobart, G. (2008). *Testing times: The uses and abuses of assessment.* London: Routledge.

Thorndike, E. L. (1924). Mental discipline in high school studies. *Journal of Educational Psychology,* 15, 1–22.

Verschaffel, L., Greer, B., & De Corte, E. (2000). *Making sense of word problems*. Lisse, The Netherlands: Swets and Zeitlinger.

Von Glasserfeld, E. (1989). Cognition, construction of knowledge, and teaching. *Syntheses, 80,* 121–140.

Wiggins, G. (1992). Creating tests worth taking. *Educational Leadership, 49,* 26–33.

Woloshyn, V. E., Paivio, A., & Pressley, M. (1994). Use of elaborative interrogation to help students acquire information consistent with prior knowledge and information inconsistent with prior knowledge. *Journal of Educational Psychology, 86*(1), 79–89.

CHAPTER 12

Grading

THROUGHOUT THIS BOOK we have discussed approaches to evaluating performance on an individual assignment, whether it be a performance assessment, written essay, or multiple-choice test. In this chapter, we turn our attention to summative grading practices of the type that you would give for an end-of-the-semester report. In the long run your students will talk about your teaching style, warm personality, and your ability to interact well; but in the short term, the first thing your students will bring up when discussing their experience with you is the grade they received in your class. In this chapter, we will introduce a philosophy of grading, aspects of grading to consider, communicating grades, and the notion of using self-grading as a way to reinforce what was learned. Because most school districts use some sort of web-based electronic grading system, we will illustrate how they work. We end with a discussion of how to evaluate group versus individual performance.

■ On the Nature of Learning in Public Schools

If one considers what an optimal learning environment might look like, one attribute that would be on everyone's list is that the curriculum would be tailored to students' skill levels. Children enter school with different achievement levels, abilities, and interests, so it would only make sense to start them from where they *are*, their entering behaviors, not from where they *should be*. Clearly some *activities* might group students by age level, ability, or interest areas, but these factors need not be the sole basis for arranging students. Other factors might be the need for remediation or enrichment. In any event, grouping is never fixed in the sense that students are classified according to some criterion level and then remain in that group for the remainder of the term. Rather, if grouping were used, it would be for certain activities and adapted to the pupil's needs at a given time such as interest, remedial requirements, enrichment activities, and so on.

A given child's learning is influenced by any number of variables and, as a result, is a highly individual event. To be most effective, student progress in learning should be closely monitored by teachers to enable students to progress at their own pace. It is unnecessary to be concerned where other students are in the curriculum as it has little impact on the teacher's work when working with one particular individual. Grading and grades, under these optimal conditions, would be adapted to the characteristics of individual learners.

However, in public school settings, student progress in learning is managed in groups of 22–30. The typical grade level is such that students *are* grouped primarily by age level, sometimes by ability (within age level), and occasionally by interest. In a normal classroom environment, teachers must establish a pace that will allow them to cover a relatively prescribed curriculum in 180 classroom days. If the content is taught at some average pace, approximately 20 percent of the students will find it too fast and 20 percent will find it too slow. Whether subjectively judged as desirable or not, assignments and grades serve a genuine purpose; they comprise a benchmark to signal collective "progress" through the curriculum. Because grading is done in "clumps," teachers often have to resort to arbitrary rules to manage the progress of the group (e.g., "Papers turned in late will be penalized on two points per day").

Why Grade?

Given that grading and grades are a fairly well acculturated aspect of most schools, it may seem a bit superfluous to ask the question, "Why grade"? But it is nonetheless a good question because it is the practice of *classroom* grading that is uniquely associated with most of our experiences and perspectives regarding education. For example, when grading "on the curve," why should one use students in the classroom as a comparison base? Why not a wider, more heterogeneous group (e.g., all students in the school or district)? Why would you use a bell-shaped curve as a distribution for grading? Why not some other shape?

When grading on an absolute scale, who said that 90 percent constitutes the lower threshold for an A? Why couldn't it be something different? There is nothing magical about classroom comparisons and the use of the bell-shaped curve in determining the cut-points for letter grades. Whether you choose a normative or absolute basis for determining grades, the use of grades is a universally accepted way to communicate performance levels of students.

Because assigning grades will probably take up to 10 percent of your time, it might be helpful to gain a better understanding of what functions are served by grades. Here are a few (Haladyna, 1999):

- *Credit.* This is akin to certification. The grade in a course is both a record of having taken the course and an indication of the proficiency level required to achieve some goal (such as fulfilling a prerequisite requirement for more advanced grade levels, more advanced courses, or high school graduation).
- *Feedback to teachers and students.* On a periodic basis (e.g., every nine weeks, end of the semester, and so on) grades can provide feedback on student performance. They are capable of providing feedback on how both instructional practice (time spent on topics, instructional strategies, and so on) and student capability (readiness and effort) in studying relative to instructional practice has paid off. By careful analysis grades can be useful indicators of remedial resources, if any, that must be made available if the student is to sustain performance, subgoals to be achieved if progress is to be maintained, and, of course, which students would profit by enrichment.
- *Feedback to parents.* Parents are interested in the progress of their children in school. The traditional practice has been to send the report card home for the parents' signature as assurance that the parent was informed of their child's progress. Some school districts ask teachers to post grades and send them to parents on a weekly basis as a way to keep them informed of student performance. Parents can take appropriate steps, or work with the teacher to take appropriate steps, to facilitate school performance if it does not meet their expectations.
- *Feedback to administrators and teachers.* If tied to goals and objectives, grades can help teachers and administrators determine, at the curricular level, the nature of the content of

subject-matter areas to be taught and any revisions in instructional measures necessary for achieving intended outcomes. Such practices as reorganizing the elementary school and high school into primary, elementary, middle, and high school is an example of the way administrators stratify different hierarchical levels in response to student achievement patterns.

- *Placement.* Nationally, our children are grouped by grade and often tracked by ability (more on this later). Identifiable grade patterns have been used by researchers, teachers, and administrators to make decisions about new school placements that are in the best interest of students. On various occasions different grouping patterns have been tried out to examine their feasibility for enabling student progress according to their needs. Over the years, we have seen the emergence of such plans as nongraded plans, progressive learning, or mastery learning. Individualized instruction used in special education is an example in which learning of children with special needs is guided by the Individualized Education Program (IEP) developed collaboratively for specific students by teachers, parents, school administrators, and related services personnel. The procedure has been extended in some schools with students who score below grade level on standardized tests (Schargel & Smink, 2001). As another example, the structure of the nongraded plan permits children to progress along a continuum of simple through more complex content in the first three grades at their own rates. The intent is that they are to make continuous progress rather than being promoted to the next grade at the end of a school year (note that *nongraded* does not refer to assessment but to the structure of the first three grade levels of schooling) (Cotton, 2001).

- *Admissions.* Admission to specialty high schools, vocational schools, or college is often contingent on overall GPA or a pattern of grades in a specialty area (e.g., science) from earlier grade levels. For college admission, other criteria are often employed (e.g., SAT scores, letters of recommendation), but considerable weight is given to grades earned in high school, which in many studies have been found to be as highly related to first-year college grades as other criteria, including standardized test scores.
- *Awards and honors.* Grades can form the basis of, or be used as a criterion for, scholastic awards and honors. In high school, the class valedictorian is often selected as the individual with the highest overall GPA.

- *Selection*. Selection into academic programs may be based on grades. For example, one of the considerations for entering a gifted program will be grades earned in previous years.
- *Academic and career counseling*. Colleges and universities provide pathways to different career options. So, for instance, the way to become an engineer is to go through an engineering program at a college or university that has one. These programs specify prerequisite courses that one must take and the minimum grades that must be earned for serious program admission consideration. They are the basis for educational counseling in career choices for elementary (which high school curricula to pursue) and secondary (matching career choices with educational plans) students as well.
- *Motivation*. When used appropriately, grades can be a motivator for students. The psychological literature makes the distinction between *extrinsic* and *intrinsic* motivation. Paying someone for good performance would be an example of an extrinsic motivator because the payment constitutes a secondary reinforcer that can be used for other pleasurable things (primary reinforcers). Receiving applause for a good performance is considered an intrinsic motivator because the recognition cannot be converted to other primary reinforcers. Educators typically try to use intrinsic motivators because they can be generalized to a variety of situations. So, if you are intrinsically motivated, good performance in an academic area is something that, in and of itself, you want to strive for. If grades directly reflect degrees of performance or learning, then they can be a source of intrinsic motivation. If the link to learning is a bit more tenuous (i.e., grades include attendance or reflect in-class social behavior), then they may not be reinforcers at all (Hargis, 2003). Intrinsic motivation is clearly compromised when parents pay their children for good grades.
- *Employment criterion*. Particularly in the professional fields, grades may be used as a screening mechanism for prospective employees.

Placing Students Along an Achievement Continuum

Basically there are two approaches to grading—one is to determine where one falls in a distribution of others (sorting) and the other is to certify that one can perform at a certain proficiency level (mastery). Which approach you choose is a function of what you think you have to know about the individual. So for instance, would you rather know that the pilot guiding your airplane was in the top 5 percent of his or her class or that he or she was certified to take off properly, fly according to a registered flight plan, and land the plane safely? Most people would opt for the latter (mastery).

Up until about 40 years ago, the primary function of grades was to sort students by their level of performance so that only the best students would take valuable seats at the higher grade levels. In college, the introductory class for a subject major was designed to sort "the wheat from the chaff" in order that only the highest-performing students would pursue subsequent coursework in that discipline. All of this was predicated on the notion that postsecondary opportunities were limited, and only those who merited it through their grades in prior coursework should go on for additional education. Today, the assumption is that most people will attempt college work at some point in their lives and that the opportunity to do so will be ubiquitous. While many colleges are still competitive with regard to grade-point admission requirements, others have an "open door" policy that provides even minimally prepared students the chance to participate in postsecondary education. As a societal mechanism for distributing valuable resources, the use of grades for sorting students has limited utility and appeal.

Still, you will hear references to grading on the curve, in which an instructor will model grade distributions on a normal (Gaussian or bell-shaped) curve. The normal curve is based on the observation that many things in nature distribute themselves with a frequency distribution that looks very similar to Figure 12.1. For example, score distributions on IQ tests are

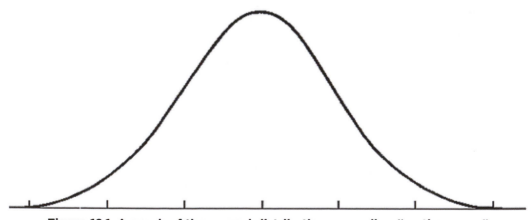

Figure 12.1. A graph of the normal distribution or grading "on the curve."

well modeled by the normal curve. The quality of written English papers or scores on a 50-point multiple-choice test composed of moderately difficult questions might be characterized in the same way. The problem is that the grade assigned to a student is not necessarily a function of what he or she can do, but rather how well other students in the class or comparison group performed. So if the mean score on a 50-point exam was 49 with a standard deviation of 0.75, then a score of 45 would be comparatively poor even though the individual answered 90 percent of the questions correctly.

Can Everyone Achieve Mastery?

Mastery is based on the philosophy that most skills or content knowledge can be broken down in such a way that virtually everyone can learn them. The common adage here is that "everyone should be able to learn to tie a shoelace." This philosophy is the basis for Individually Programmed Instruction (IPI). The approach seems intuitive for a curriculum that is explicitly hierarchical in nature, but may break down in areas that involve creativity or a synthesis of skills. Nevertheless, the majority of public school curricula would be amenable to a mastery learning approach.

With mastery learning, the key is to create assessments that determine whether you are proficient in the particular skill or not (e.g., multiplying two 2-digit numbers). Moreover, you would need to determine a proficiency level for the distribution of grades. Most school districts have chosen a general rule of thumb that goes like this: 90–100 percent = A, 80–89 percent = B, 70–79 percent = C, and so on. These percentages are based on an agreed upon convention and do not necessarily have an empirical base. There are some skills where the risks demand a higher standard of proficiency—for instance, airline pilots need to be able to perform their skills with (perhaps) 100 percent proficiency before they can be certified to fly—but most of these do not apply to public school situations. The field of educational measurement has developed techniques to derive an empirical basis for making what are essentially value judgments about where standards (cut-offs) should be set for a particular domain. This standard-setting technology provides a mechanism whereby the judgments could be replicated if openly challenged (Cizek & Bunch, 2006).

Grading What?

Your college instructors may base their final grade assignments on the basis of a relatively limited sample of your work—a midterm exam, a final exam, and a final paper, for example. Most school districts, however, will require a larger sample of performance (e.g., nine graded products per nine-week grading period). Moreover you will have to weight each product so that the sum of weighted products is equal to 100 percent.

Haladyna (1999) provides several lists of products or attributes that have been used for grading in the past. His list is divided into three parts: supportable, arguable, and unsupportable. These are displayed in Table 12.1.

Supportable criteria for grading include:

- *Homework*. These are assignments that are designed to be completed at home to reinforce the ideas and skills that were learned in class. They are typically of moderate difficulty.
- *Classroom activities or exercises*. These are the same as homework except that they are completed as part of the in-class lesson plan.
- *Individual or group projects*. These are products that often are of a long-term duration, require a synthesis of skills, and are designed to be challenging. The end product should illustrate the student's best work for the class at that point in time.

Table 12.1. Criteria for Grading

Supportable	*Arguable*	*Unsupportable*
Homework	Violation of a deadline	Conformance to teacher's rules
Classroom activities or exercises	Class participation	Effort, enthusiasm, attitude
Individual or group projects	Extra credit	Neatness
Quizzes	Improvement over the grading period	Mental ability
Tests and final exams	Attendance	Verbal ability
Papers, essays, reviews, critiques	Subjective assessment	Standardized test scores
Performance		Departmental standards
Demonstrations		Creativity
Exhibitions		Appearance
Experiments		Hygiene
		Personality
		Interpersonal skills
		Emotional need
		Reputation
		Gender, ethnicity, race, disability, religion

Source: Haladyna, 1999.

- *Quizzes*. These are short tests to determine if students have done either prerequisite work or reading in preparation for a class. Test items are usually very easy.
- *Tests and final exams*. These are tests that cover materials for a prescribed period of time (i.e., weekly, nine weeks, semester). They are designed to be comprehensive and of moderate difficulty.
- *Papers, essays, reviews, critiques*. These may have as their sole focus the evaluation of writing skill development (e.g., as in an English class) or may serve as a vehicle for assessing knowledge or skills in another area (e.g., social studies). Depending on their purpose, they can range in difficulty level from easy to hard.
- *Performance*. This is used to assess a skill or a set of skills by having students actually perform them. Performances can range from easy to difficult depending on the level of synthesis or integration required.
- *Demonstration*. This can either be an asynchronous performance (i.e., not done in real time) or a product created to illustrate a concept or set of concepts. Like a project, these are constructed to show a student's best efforts.
- *Exhibitions*. These are like demonstrations in that they illustrate a student's best work, but may not be created to illustrate a concept. Typically reserved for art or related fields.
- *Experiment*. This is a technique used by students to explore basic principles in a discipline by controlling some aspects of their study and systematically varying other aspects of it. These typically range from moderately difficult to difficult.

All items in the arguable category are listed because their relationship to actual student performance is vague. You will have to decide (and be ready to defend) your consideration of these behaviors when assigning grades.

- *Violation of a deadline*. Just because an assignment is late doesn't diminish the student's actual work or performance. In school, no one drops dead for failing to meet a *deadline*— this is a real-world contrivance based on common business practices. You may have administrative constraints to move your class at a given pace or organized in a way that prevents you from reasonably giving sympathetic consideration to those who might present late work. But be prepared to hear a lot of very sad (and often true) stories. There is no empirical basis for penalizing a student one grade for "every day that they are late with their work." You would have unjustifiably invented that rule. If you adopt it you will need to continually remind your students how your policy will impact their grade.

- *Class participation*. Teachers often use this as a leveraging mechanism when a discussion mode is their preferred style of teaching. Keep in mind that the discussion technique is your preference and does not necessarily reflect the learning style of your students, who in fact may function quite well in a more passive mode of learning. You can expect that some students will more actively participate than others, but their level of participation may be unrelated to their accomplishments on the kinds of supportable assignments listed in the first column of Table 12.1.

- *Extra credit*. This is really a proxy for hard work in which work volume is supposed to offset deficiencies in regular academic achievement. Unfortunately this approach is rarely successful either in school or later on in life. Employers would rather have you work smarter than harder. Ideally, of course, they would prefer to see you work both smarter and harder. In any event, the extra credit work detracts for the teacher's evaluation of your regular class performance and may be biased against students who have other time demands in their lives (e.g., sports).

- *Improvement over the grading period*. While improvement over the grading period may reflect a variety of positive attributes (hard work, industriousness, learning), it nevertheless detracts from the assessment of the current performance level. From a performance standpoint, why would one reward someone who went from a D to an A more than an individual who maintained a grade level of A for the entire grading period? You would be rewarding inconsistent performance over consistently high performance. Again, we introduce the caveat that, if you decide to use such rules, they should be used judiciously out of concern for the outcomes.

- *Attendance*. This is required in elementary and secondary settings, so it really does not act as a differentiating mechanism. Even at the postsecondary level, it is not particularly discriminating. Those who rarely show up, rarely do well on the assignments anyway. The basic question here is, if students were to perform well on your class assessments without attending your class, is there a justifiable reason (other than one's ego) for penalizing them?

- *Subjective assessment*. These are often based on a students' circumstances and not linked to actual performance. As such, they lack predictive power.

In the final column from Table 12.1 is a list of unsupportable criteria that have been used in the past. These have no relationship to actual student performance and may be related more to a teacher's need to exert control over the classroom environment or biases. They include conformance to teacher's rules; effort, enthusiasm, or attitude; neatness; mental ability; verbal ability; standardized test scores; departmental standards; creativity; appearance; hygiene; personality; interpersonal skills; emotional need; reputation; and gender, ethnicity, race, disability, or religion (Haladyna, 1999). It is recommended that you never use them as you will not be able to create a rationale to justify their application.

Weighting Grades

In our discussion on test planning in Chapter 2, we suggested that you would do well to match the proportion of the test (usually the number of test items) to the amount of instruction given to the unit being assessed. So if you spent 15 percent of your instructional time on the Bill of Rights for an eighth-grade social studies class, students would expect that 15 percent of the test would address issues regarding the Bill of Rights. In a similar vein, you want to have your grading weighted by the amount of time students spend working on the various products for your class. If they spend 10 percent of their time preparing for quizzes, then the weighted contribution of quizzes to the overall grade should be approximately 10 percent.

If there is an unbalance in the weighting of grades, it may be because you are unaware of how your students are actually spending their time. For example, students quite often spend 60 percent of their time completing homework assignments, yet it may only count for 20 percent of their overall grade. They quickly figure out the nature of the unbalance and reallocate their time to other products which count more in your grading scheme, but would normally require less time. As a consequence the product that is not worth it either does not get done or is performed poorly. If homework practice is a key element in learning the material but it takes more time, give it the appropriate weight even though it may not sound as worthy or impressive as a final exam or term paper.

■ Technology Applied to Grading

Many school districts ask teachers to e-mail or post grades on a secure web server so that students and parents can keep up to date with the achievement progress of students. The software teachers use typically comes in the form of an electronic gradebook or spreadsheet in which teachers list assignment categories (e.g., tests, papers, homework), the weights associated with each category, the actual assignments (e.g., Paper 1, Paper 2), due dates, and grading standards. As a convenience, most software packages allow teachers to import class rosters provided by the district. Figure 12.2 shows how one class is set up using the software package Micrograde 6.1.2. In this class the teacher has listed two exams, one paper, and several entries for class participation. Figure 12.3 is an illustration of the grades entered for one student in the course. Micrograde allows the e-mailing of grades to students, or they can log into a secure web server with a password and look at their grades at any time during the term. Figure 12.4 shows how the grades for one test were distributed. Micrograde has this as a summary feature for teachers who wish to share this information with their students, parents, or administrators.

Group versus Individual Grades

Though workers in many jobs are often evaluated independently, there are a number of positions in which teamwork may be more highly valued than individual performance. Evaluating performance in software engineering is a good example here.

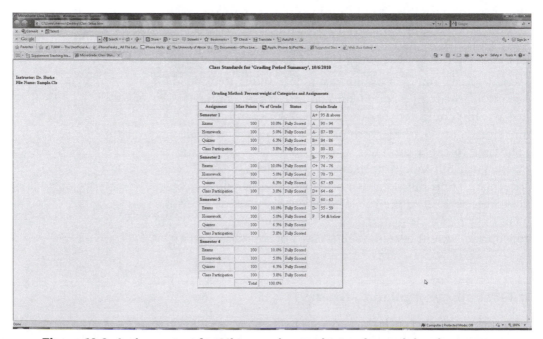

Figure 12.2. A class setup for Micrograde, an electronic gradebook program.

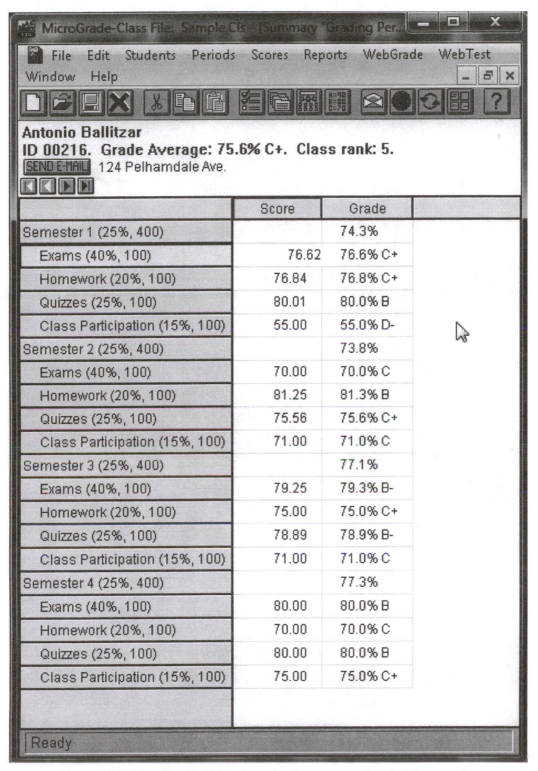

Figure 12.3. The distribution of grades for one student in Micrograde.

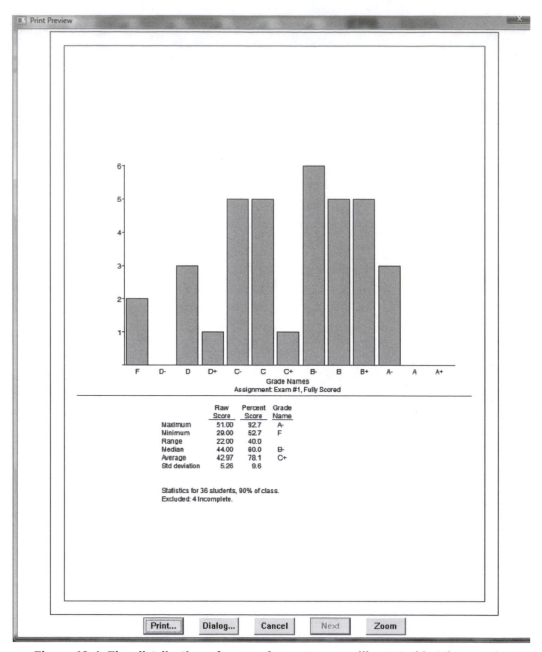

Figure 12.4. The distribution of scores for an exam as illustrated in Micrograde.

A software product is largely the result of the efforts of many programmers. It is certainly the case that creative and proficient programmers may have made larger or more important contributions to the project, but the ultimate criterion for selling the software is that it meets a market need and works flawlessly. Even if one seemingly trivial aspect of a product fails to perform well, potential customers are likely to shy away from it. A situation has been created where the efforts of the group will outweigh those of an individual no matter how important that individual contribution may have been.

Are there parallels for such considerations in a school setting? Group performance is a commonly used situation in schools and ranges from evaluating lab partners in a science class to rating a choir performance in music. The final product is a function of the successful collaboration among members of the group. In order to address the grading issues, it is important to decide on the focus of assessment: Does the final product define performance or is the major concern centered on individual contributions to it, or both?

If the performance defines the product, then it might be evaluated as if it were generated by one individual. In a statewide music competition, it is the choir that is graded, not individuals within it. Individual contributions, beyond singing in the choir, may or may not be related to vocal performance. That is, some choir members may be able to read music better than others (more related to vocal performance), but other contributors may simply be better social organizers (less related). If assessment takes into consideration these other factors, then they should be clearly specified in advance.

Occasionally individual contributions can strongly influence how an overall group effort is evaluated. In a play performance, the acting of the leads can make or break the reviews for a theatrical production. An assessment of these individuals may reflect their greater contributions to the success of the show when contrasted to cast members who may have played only a supporting part. Note that those who had supporting roles had less of an opportunity to make a more significant contribution.

Typically with group performances assessments are weighted, with a portion devoted to the individual's contribution and a portion devoted to the merits of the group performance. The weights may vary and should be agreed upon in advance.

■ Reporting Grades: The Report Card

The compilation of the multitude of grades that can be obtained is typically recorded by the teacher either in daily logs or weekly summaries. The purpose of careful assessment and of keeping these records is the need to (a) clarify the student's progress in learning, (b) maintain a record of progress that can follow the student from grade to grade, and (c) provide a basis for communication. Periodically, perhaps at the end of the month or term, the grades are summarized into a number that carries with it the progress (or lack of progress) in subject-matter areas and behavioral areas considered important for understanding progress in learning.

These facets of grading, of course, describe summative evaluation as it is represented in a report card. In an earlier era, the report card was a fairly simple matter. It probably had a listing of four or five subject-matter areas, with marks from A to F or in some cases in percentage points. The card was sent home to the parent for the parent's signature and brought back to the teacher. Today's report card is remarkably different. In response to continual revision for accurate communication, it is more detailed and is expected to be optimally informative to the parent as well as to other users who do their part in facilitating student progress. A typical report card is shown in Figure 12.5 (please keep in mind that this is but one variation, there are others that depart from this one in varying degrees; however, their overall structure is similar).

As you can see the report card provides a summary of how well the student has progressed in specific curricular areas. As an aside, the fact that a student's learning status or progress over a lengthy period of time can be even marginally summarized in a single number or two is in itself a rather outstanding achievement. Additionally, the report card in Figure 12.5 provides an analytical summary of progress in a content area as the subparts contribute to the total estimate of progress.

The goal in making report cards meaningful is to provide feedback by providing information that emphasizes remediation if needed by slower learners or staying on course for the more successful student. Thus, it is expected that students will shy away from comments such as "what mark did you get in that course?" "the marking period," "marks on my report card," and so on. Such comments tend to show that the single number, represented by a mark on the report card, despite the constant debate, is revered by all and feared by some—attitudes that are, perhaps, tempered by the more detailed reports.

Reported grades become significant in virtually all parts of the student's academic life from the preschool years through graduate school. It has been that way for decades. But the mystery of why it is successful in view of its limited representation is never approached. There is, among the general population, little debate about what the report card represents. The debate appears to center around the possibility that those responsible for measurements that go into grades may not be doing the measurement correctly, that the measurements are not representative of student

HARBOUR ELEMENTARY SCHOOL REPORT CARD

Grade 4

Student _____ Teacher _____ Principal _____

Grading Key: E = Excellent   S = Satisfactory   P = Making Progress   I = Needs Improvement

Learning/Social Behavior
Demonstrates Responsibility for own Learning
_____ Demonstrates self control
_____ Attends to the task at hand
_____ Completes class work
_____ Completes homework
_____ Completes tasks independently

Responds to Teacher-directed Activities
_____ Follows Directions
_____ Uses Active Listening
_____ Participates in activities & discussions
_____ Works to produce a quality Object
_____ Speaks and acts respectfully to others

Social Studies
_____ Takes part in social studies discussions
_____ Understand concepts or asks questions
_____ Completes social studies activities

Fine Arts
Art
_____ Skill development
_____ Appropriate conduct
_____ Effort
Music
_____ Skill development
_____ Appropriate conduct
_____ Effort

Reading
_____ Independently reads and comphrehends grade appropriate material
_____ Selects and reads books during independent reading times
_____ Understands the meaning of the text
_____ Formulates questions with guidance regarding the text
_____ Summarizes chapters and short stories
_____ Reads books assigned from a variety of genres
_____ Writes quality responeses from text
_____ Leads or takes part in text discussions

Writing
Grammar and Usage
_____ Write complete sentences with proper structure
_____ Uses grade-level grammatical concepts in writing
_____ Uses quotation marks and commas when appropriate

Writing Process & Personal Sytle
_____ Uses a variety of pre writing techniques that help structure ideas
_____ Writes focused ideas with mechanically sound paragraphs
_____ Proofreads and edits own writing
_____ Revises own draft using written and oral feedback

Spelling
_____ Correctly spells words in reading and writing using a variety of stategies

Handwriting
_____ Writes neatly and legibly in cursive and print

Mathematics
Basic facts:
_____ Addition
_____ Subtraction
_____ Multiplication
_____ Division
_____ Estimation
_____ Computation
_____ Graphing
_____ Patterns
_____ Geometry
_____ Spatial sense
_____ Measurement
_____ Time
_____ Money
_____ Fractions
_____ Problem solving
_____ Probability
_____ Desctibe and justify math concepts in writing

Science
_____ Scientific inquiry process
_____ Earth and geology studies
_____ Space studies
_____ Plant studies
_____ Atmosphere and weather studies
_____ Animal studies
_____ Human body
_____ Nutrition
_____ Technology
_____ Ability to write or draw science concepts

Health/Phsyical Education
_____ Skills development
_____ Appropriate conduct
_____ Knowledge of health concepts
_____ Works well with other students
_____ Effort

Teacher Comments:

Teacher Signature: _____   Date: _____

Figure 12.5. An example of a current day report card.

performance, or that the measures do not do justice to one district or another. As you have seen in the presentation in this chapter, one thing is certain—the popular grade, for whatever performance, is a highly complex entity not entirely appreciated by those who are directly involved. This lack of appreciation is manifest in most educational settings where, following an important test, students elbow their way to the bulletin board where the grade is posted to see what grade they got; they still compare their grades with others ("What grade did you get? I got . . ."), rationalizing or taking pride in the number ("That was an easy test," "I know just what the teacher wants on these tests," "I never do well on those tests," or "I just can't seem to get good grades in this course or any course"). The use of *good* or *bad* in speaking about scores received (parents say, "Did you get good grades?") implies a restricted notion of what the grades mean. These perceptions of grades reflect the limited meanings attached to them by stakeholders, but more important for our purposes here is that such attitudes surrounding grades reflect the need for understanding the way they are arrived at as well as understanding that they are communicative devices intended to provide information to the student and other stakeholders about progress.

What seems to be lacking is the fact that the numbers in themselves are relative, not absolute. Their meanings are many. It is critical that teachers and others who produce scores about student performance are well informed about the characteristics of scores and communicate the nature and functions of grades to others concerned with them, including parents and students. In fact, it is almost a necessity that the parent become as much of a knowledgeable expert in assessment as other stakeholders—give the technical knowledge of assessment away to the stakeholders. Simply sending a report card home with a bunch of numbers for the signature of an uninformed parent does not appear to be an efficient procedure. As public school teachers, one of us has observed in our experience with elementary and high school parents that the report card may be given little more than a glance by the parent(s). But without considerable prodding by teachers, principals, or other parents, perhaps even the student themselves, the implications of the grades are not requested. Occasional comments offered by the parent to their child, such as "When I was your age, I didn't do as well as you (or I did better than you)" are not reflective of effective feedback; we suspect such comments are made more out of not knowing the purpose of the grades than a deliberate unwillingness to put them to good use. And there are reports of parents opposing the use of report cards, which we suspect is due to either misinformation or misperceptions of the purpose of grading. (We are aware that these illustrations of subjective experiences with parents are not representative of the entire population of parents and that parental reactions to report cards vary according to district, regional, or broader contexts as well as within a given context.)

From the discussion of grades in this chapter you can see that grading is a complex enterprise. The value of grades for any and all of their functions is dependent on an understanding of what went into the grades—estimates, observational data, test scores—of what was measured—effort, motivation, conceptualization levels—and of the interpretation of the grades. In short, what the grade really represents goes far beyond being a score or mark. That single number summarizing some performance of the student over a period of time represents a multitude of factors, including some that are classified as affective and some that are cognitive. They represent not only the student's performance but also instructional effectiveness, as well as other factors such as the contexts in which the child lives.

Within any of these categories there are a multitude of other factors represented. At the affective level there might be included attitudes, mood, motivation, attention, and interest. For example, restricting our discussion to the cognitive factors, the grade might have been based on measures of factual retention, conceptual understanding, transfer to applications, or any combination of these. Because of these influences scores can never be interpreted consistently in the same way by different stakeholders, a feature that accounts for misunderstandings of grades or scores, the intent of grading, or the way the grades can be most useful.

The ways that interpretations of a single grade can be distorted as a result of these factors are innumerable. Although distortions are unlikely to be removed entirely, they can be minimized by the simple measure of making stakeholders using grades informed users; the stakeholders must know how the grades were obtained, what the grades mean, their potential uses and functions for optimal utility, their limitations, an obvious but often neglected or ignored preventative measure. Unfortunately a grade, as a number or even fleshed out with comments, cannot be all things to all people.

■ Beyond Grades

Grades perform a valuable function, and there is nothing on the immediate horizon that suggests they are going away any time soon. While the interpretive basis for grading may have shifted from the bell curve to mastery of objectives, one of the continuing functions of a teacher is to provide feedback for his or her students. But is this all that can be done?

Consider the professional workplace. We may work in environments in which there will always be someone better skilled than us who will provide supervision, guidance, and future direction. However, at some point you may be asked to be *that* person. Can you communicate the attributes of the products you produce that make them good or poor? If you can, you will have at least one critical skill mastered in your new leadership position.

In Chapter 5 we discussed the pros and cons of using a portfolio as a way of allowing students to collect their best work. One of the variations of portfolio assessment is to ask students to reflect on the artifacts that they produce and enter—what was impressive about them and what was lacking. Initially their reflections are often superficial (e.g., "This paper would have been better if I had more time to work on it"), but after some experience with this mode of assessment they can share their expertise with you (e.g., "The conflict between the protagonist and antagonist in this story was really 'much ado about nothing'"). In addition students also can suggest next steps in order to further their skill development.

Stiggins (2001) incorporates portfolio assessment in an extension of the traditional grading process that he calls *Student Centered Assessment*. He advocates for a student-led parent–teacher conference in which the student uses portfolio artifacts and reflections as a way to communicate what was accomplished during the term, why it was good or bad, and what skill development is needed in the future to improve the products. Instead of hearing exclusively from the teacher, the parent receives most of the feedback on the subject (or an array of subjects) from the student. The goal is to develop an expertise level for students in order for them to "take charge" of their own education.

Class Exercise

Listed below are seven beliefs about grading that are discussed in detail by Haladyna (1999). Break into 14 small teams, with two teams agreeing to debate each belief. One team takes the pro side of the statement and the other team agrees to argue the con. Each side has two minutes to present its side (pro or con) of the belief.

Commonly Held Beliefs about Student Grading
1. Grades can be used to motivate students.
2. Grades can be used to punish students or otherwise control them.
3. High grades reflect effective teaching, if grading criteria are fair.
4. High standards promote high achievement, hence high grades.
5. High grades reflect lenient grading standards.

6. The quest for high grades may promote superficial learning
7. Grading may affect self-esteem.

■ Summary

Grades are complex communicative devices serving many functions. They are the result of the several events included in the range, anchored by the quality of instruction at one end and student effort at the other. The functions served by grades are many, including the basis for assigning credit and certification for having completed a course; providing feedback about learning and learning-related behaviors; placing and admitting students in grades or instructional settings related to their instructional needs; awarding honors and scholarships; and making selections for specific career programs. Indirectly, they can serve the function of motivating students by providing both intrinsic and extrinsic feedback to the recipient.

Cutting across the functions served by grades is the need to clearly and accurately communicate their role in assessment, how the grades were determined, the facets of performance being measured, and how the grade was affected by instruction. The correct words and terminology regarding both the assessment methodology and the student performance need to be conveyed to the stakeholders.

Each score on a report card is more than a number to be casually received with interpretation assumed. It is, in reality, a composite of scores derived from several assessment procedures including observations of student performance, short tests used for measuring on-the-spot performance during or following lessons, alternative measures of the teacher's choosing for measuring some student performances, tests that assume prior knowledge in measuring higher-order cognitive skills (such as understanding and conceptualizations), and tests of applications of a broad knowledge base (including transferability and problem-solving)—all of which are clearly defined in terms of objectives that reflect the professional standards for that grade level. The reader of the report must understand the performances and tasks represented in the report. If the communication is to be effective we should be able to answer such questions as, "Was the student able to communicate taxonomic processes and details at the end of the lesson better than at the beginning of the lesson?" or "Has the student acquired the ability to classify new 'bugs' into appropriate taxonomic categories?" Assignment of grades to serve all of the potential functions asked of them is clearly a serious matter. It is also asking much of a single number or two about a course.

Thus, it must be recognized that the grade, as a number, is of no consequence; it is simply a datum. Secondly, as a datum it requires interpretation. If it isn't uniformly interpretable or if its interpretation is not made available by the source (teacher), it will undeniably be uninterpretable or incorrectly interpreted by the recipients (stakeholders). To clarify the interpretation of grades such factors as the following are to be considered: Is the grade a status measure of average performance or a measure of progress? Is the grade a measure of the effectiveness of instruction or a measure of the student's capacity for learning? Is the grade to be interpreted as a comparison with all students within in the class with a given teacher or as a measure of how a student compares with all the children in the district who have taken the test? What were the bases of the grades—subjective observations, classroom tests, and/or standardized tests?

As an integral part of instruction the target of successful instruction is the progress the student makes from one marking period to the next. Thus, for the student the report card grades should not only permit interpretation of progress made from the time of the last report, but of in what ways the progress has been made, what accounted for the progress (or lack of progress), and what remediation is indicated to get back on track. The student should not be left with a poorly interpreted, ubiquitous grade of 60 percent, D, or any other score. Grades on report cards go to permanent files that follow students from one grade level to the next; unfortunately, a bad year may cumulate needlessly into many bad years when the grade is not functionally useful due to poor interpretations.

For the parent, a report card that promotes an accurate picture can provide the means required to help a student struggling with math or reading. It can help them know what they need to do to help the student and what remedial help or enrichment is needed. Just as important, the report card can provide an indication of what the student is working on in the curriculum at any given time. In parent-teacher conferences, a well-considered report of student progress provides defensible justification for an assigned grade. It can be shown that the preparation of objectives and skills closely matched what the teacher has taught and how it was taught. By knowing the students' strengths and weaknesses a teacher is enabled to meaningfully answer such questions as "Abigail doesn't appear to be getting the high scores in social studies that her brother Dan got. Do you think it's because she is not as smart as Dan?"

For the teacher, the preparation of a clear report of grades can be an enabling step toward individualizing instruction. In the preparation of grades and reports, the teacher defines and becomes aware of what progress the student has made from the time of the last report, what the student has or has not learned, and which objectives have or have not been met. In the course of conscientious preparation of a report card, the knowledge, understanding, and skills the student should know and be capable of knowing become defined. Through the many assessment procedures, including observation, dialogue, or asking for a demonstration or a written response, teachers must examine student responses from the perspective of what they show about the students' conceptions, misconceptions, skills, and knowledge about their ability to retain organized information, to make classifications, to organize, to analyze—all of the processes that enter higher-order learning. It is critical, of course, that the analysis is made in relation to the criteria for success. You need to know the precise gap in knowledge if you are to set challenging tasks—tasks that are too difficult (due to too wide a gap) lead to anxiety and frustration; tasks that are too easy (due to no gap and repetition of what one already knows) lead to boredom and ennui. Either mood can be a detriment to progress.

■ References

Cizek, G. J., & Bunch, M. B. (2006). *Standard setting: A guide to establishing and evaluating performance standards on tests.* Thousand Oaks, CA: Sage.

Cotton, K. (2001). Nongraded primary education. *NWREL School Improvement Research Series (SIRS): Research You Can Use,* Close-up #14. Retrieved October 25, 2007, from www.nwrel.org/scpd/sirs/7/cu14.html.

Haladyna, T. M. (1999). *A complete guide to student grading.* Boston: Allyn and Bacon.

Hargis, C. H. (2003). *Grades and grading practices* (2nd ed.). Springfield, IL: Charles C. Thomas, Ltd.

Schargel, F. P., & Smink, J. (2001). *Strategies to help solve our school dropout problem.* Larchmont, NY: Eye on Education.

Stiggins, R. J. (2001). *Student-involved classroom assessment* (3rd ed.). Upper Saddle River, NJ: Prentice-Hall.

CHAPTER 13

Supplementary Assessments of Individual Differences

THIS CHAPTER EXTENDS the available assessment plans in preceding chapters to the kinds of measures that provide useful supplements to classroom assessment—measures that are typically not used in standardized tests or in summative assessment. They have the potential of informing the teacher of the characteristics of the classroom context that (a) contribute to successful (or unsuccessful) instruction and (b) facilitate decisions about strategies for remedying instructional methods that seem less than optimally successful.

These supplementary techniques "help individual [teachers] to obtain useful feedback on what, how much, and how well their students are learning [as well as understanding how the variables that make up the classroom structure are affecting learning and instruction]. [Instructors] can then use this information to refocus their teaching to help students make their learning more efficient and effective" (Angelo & Cross, 1993).

Beyond assessment of subject-matter achievement as it is related to content, these assessments provide sources of information about student capability, effort, attitudes, and motivation; classroom climate; and similar concerns that affect learning outcomes. Additionally, you will find ways of constructing alternative formats for rating scales, graphic displays, and case studies, thereby extending our discussion of these concerns in earlier chapters.

■ A Classroom Model Underlying Assessment

Consider the rich contexts comprised of four components of classroom learning and instruction—the status characteristics of the learner, what the learner knows and does, what the teacher

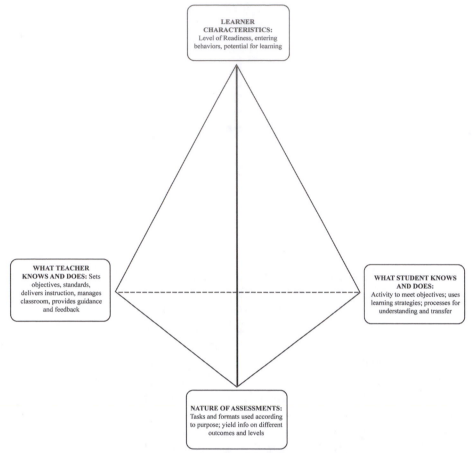

Figure 13.1. The interaction of instructional components. This figure is a modification of the tetrahedral model (Darling-Hammond & Bransford, 2005, p. 19, Figure 1.3) intended as an outline of the contents in the present chapter.

know and does, and the assessments that are made. One such model is based on four distinct features of learning; note that any one of them affects each of the other. This model, graphically displayed in Figure 13.1, is intended to be analogous to one developed by Jenkins (1978) and applied to instruction and learning by Bransford (Bransford, 1979; Darling-Hammond & Bransford, 2005).

This is an all-inclusive model that applies to most learning situations. You will recognize the relationship of each component to courses in teacher preparation you have taken or will take; for instance, you have learned about *learner characteristics* as they relate to readiness for learning in courses on human or child development (e.g., development of ability and concepts) and about *instructional activity* in courses on instructional methods (e.g., entering behaviors or readiness).

The four conceptualizations (a) can be extended to include specific activities (e.g., what the teacher does can include classroom management and making assignments) and (b) suggest characteristics (e.g., learning ability, motivation) that have the potential of being measured as individual differences. For example, *learner characteristics* that cannot be changed or are not easily changed, but that can be measured, certainly include age, physical characteristics, and the like. Those that are situationally determined or can be changed still are amenable to being measured. They include motivation, interests, self-efficacy, attitudes, and the like. Similarly, *learner activity*, what the *learner does*, includes strategies or other procedures a student uses while processing problems, making applications, or completing other assignments, which can be observed through a variety of measures.

What the teacher knows and does includes any theoretical analysis of teaching methods, of measures based on the observation of teaching in action, of the nature of instructional practices used, or of what goes on in teachers' thinking while instructing (Hativa & Goodyear, 2002; Zohar, 2004). The delivery of instructional activities, including the setting objectives or goals, affects student perceptions in a variable called classroom climate (e.g., a classification of the classroom as learner- or performance-oriented)—an important influence on student motivations.

Assessment Tasks

The objectives served by a measure, what it measures or its validity, determine the nature of the inferences and the implications that can be made from the test (measure) results. Formats vary according to the other variables in the model (e.g., what the learner knows about assessment of his or her performance, what level of characteristics is present, and what the teacher knows about assessment). Recognition and recall tasks may use different formats than tasks requiring problem solving, understanding, and so on. Also, achievement measures will require different formats than opinion surveys or interest inventories.

Assessment measure formats are important considerations in determining what one is able to read or infer from student responses. For example, a self-rating of one's degree of interest in a topic formatted as

Example No. 1:
Do you like to do math? __ Yes __ No

would present a more singular view of student interest than an item such as Example 2 that taps the *level* of interest in math,

Example No. 2:
Circle the amount of agreement for the activity indicated in the statement:

I like to do math over almost any other subject.
Strongly agree
Agree somewhat
Neutral
Disagree somewhat
Strongly disagree

or a format such as Example 3 that makes a *comparison* among activities within math,

Example No. 3:
Circle the activity in which you would be more interested:
a. Working on novel and creative math problems
b. Doing math homework assigned by my teacher
c. Trying to get a better score in math than do other students

Assessment of Classroom Components

The contemporary view of instruction and assessment is that they are integrated into a virtually seamless construction for the most part, as depicted in Figure 13.1, within the contexts of the classroom, the community, and the domain of knowledge being taught.

The assessments to be described in this chapter tap the variety of individual differences that emerge within the course of instruction and potentially affect classroom performance in the present or future. For example, the theory of multiple intelligences (a learner characteristic) suggests that there are individual proclivities (learning styles, inclinations, or predispositions) for learning modalities including visual, auditory, linguistic, naturalistic, and so on. (We discuss this framework later in the chapter.) It therefore provides an alternative view of intelligence as well as an alternative measurement format compared to the classic unitary view of general intelligence as measured by intelligence tests. By using information about individual differences in learning styles, teachers adjust instruction by providing different means of presentation; for example, if students believe they profit by visual presentations, teachers may choose to decrease the use of verbal description (if that had been the instructional delivery used) and increase the use of graphic models or examples.

In addition to considering the learning styles of the learner we can consider the measurement of *activities used by the learner*, the procedural knowledge used in learning, including:

- *Learning strategies.* Procedures applied to reading, solving math problems, general decision making, studying, and so on.
- *Metacognitions.* The all-important mental accompaniments of learning including the awareness of available strategies, what choices are useable at a given place in learning, and how they are used for learning in typical learning situations.

Other measures of individual differences are those for measuring affective variables such as those involved in classroom climate, motivation, confidence (self-efficacy) in one's ability at performing tasks, and volition (willingness) to complete assignments.

Two common conceptualizations of classroom climate are (a) climates that are *learning-oriented* and emphasize progress in learning and acquisition; and (b) climates that are *performance-oriented* and emphasize performance in response to grading practices (Adelman & Taylor, 2006). Climates are established by the teacher and are somewhat predictable from one day to the next regarding what methods a teacher emphasizes (e.g., whether the teacher focuses on student learning needs or on criteria to be reached). For measuring climate one might ask such questions as

Example No. 4:
In this class I am more interested in:
   a. How well I do in comparison to the other pupils in this class (a pupil checking this option implies a *performance* orientation)
   b. Understanding and comprehending the subject matter (a pupil checking this option implies a *learning* orientation)

These examples provide illustrations of alternative formats available for assessments, formats that contribute to understanding the classroom context. The use of measures in these categories is not mandatory. However, awareness of their availability provides a resource of alternative assessment procedures that can be useful to inform teachers of the classroom context as it affects student progress.

Although these formats are often used informally and sometimes frequently within the classroom, we propose that they should be used judiciously and thoughtfully, with consideration of the important dimensions underlying test construction. Rating scales, for example, should be constructed as validly and reliably as needed for your immediate purposes. Indeed, their reliability and validity should be considered in making interpretations of the responses. They should discriminate differences among students on dimensions intended (e.g., learning styles, ability to categorize). These qualities, as in any measure, ultimately affect interpretations that can be made of the results. To accomplish this objective we present illustrations in this chapter of measures of:

- Individual differences in motivation
- Assessments of multiple intelligences and learning styles
- Social structures in the classroom useful for classroom management and based on graphic representations
- Response to intervention (RTI) as a unique view of assessment based on responsiveness of learners to quality instruction
- Dynamic assessment in which learning potential (zone of proximal development) and interventions are coordinated to determine achievable levels of student acquisition

More complex outcomes of measurement can be inferred when:

- Assessments of student outcomes are coordinated with assumptions about instructional design through understanding if and how individual differences interact with instructional methods
- Several sources of information are coordinated and integrated in case studies or individual educational plans

■ Using Measures of Individual Differences

The procedures to be described can be identified in many behavioral conceptualizations such as test anxiety, self-esteem, self-efficacy, self-regulation of learning, and beliefs about learning (epistemological beliefs). As you have learned, the most comprehensive compilation of these exists in Buros's

Mental Measurements Yearbooks. They supplement the usual data obtained by observation, interviews, protocols, classroom tests, surveys, portfolios, and standardized tests.

A practical approach to validity for measures limited to classroom use is to focus on *content* validity, that is, the extent to which the content of the test represents an adequate sampling of the attitudes or perspectives taught in the course. A measure might be designed to encompass different classroom perspectives, contexts, or environments (e.g., attitudes toward the scientific method in a science course). Defining the subareas will assist you in making certain that the items are related to objectives and that all areas are covered. Repeated administrations of the measure will provide a basis for estimating reliability of the measures.

Each example in this chapter is intended to illustrate unique perspectives. They will provide awareness of the alternatives available for making full-scale assessments of the student. By focusing on the range of assessment alternatives you will have a perspective of assessment that goes beyond an understanding derived from limited informal observations of classroom components.

■ Categories of Individual Differences

Three classes of individual differences with which teachers are concerned are distinguished by the contributions they make to academic performance. These classes include measures of:

1. *Aptitudes, achievement, and capacities* that represent the student's abilities; that is, capabilities to perform academic tasks
2. *Motivations* that represent willingness to devote energy to a task and to focus attention to the task, attraction (interest) to a task, and willingness to pursue a task to completion (volition); involved in motivation are many facets of self-perceptions (self-concept, self-esteem, self-efficacy, and self-regulation)
3. The *knowledge base* of acquired content knowledge (declarative knowledge) and strategies (procedural knowledge), the extent to which each has been learned (factual acquisition and understanding), and their relevance to performance in other subject matter areas (transferability); we have referred to the knowledge base in other parts of this text as *prior knowledge* and *cognitive structure*

■ Culture as a Source of Individual Differences

Cultural differences underlie all assessments, affecting what is measured, how it is measured, and how the measurements are interpreted. Being rooted in culture, background, community, and family, such differences have the potential of preparing children differently for school learning whether the learning is in language, social studies, science, or math. Importantly, cultural differences affect student perceptions and interpretations.

These differences are especially considered in the teacher's accommodation to individual differences (a later section is devoted entirely to accommodation). Parental roles in education are recognized as being different among cultures: for instance, a good parent in Asian American families is one whose children are successful in school. In another culture it might be one whose children get along socially. In another it might be one whose children are loyal to authoritative sources. With these differing perceptions, each will clearly approach school learning quite differently.

Beliefs regarding *how* people learn also differ across cultures. In some cultures "being smart is cool; working hard in school is dumb; answering the teacher's questions is showing off" (Okagaki, 2001). Cultural attitudes may either increase resistance to schooling or increase persistence in learning, depending on predispositions.

The beliefs about what to learn deserve attention: In some societies children learn multiple languages; in others loyalty to a single language is the norm. These have effects on differences in attitudes toward language. Strong monolingual children in a different primary language than English may be perceived by teachers as students having limited English proficiency (LEP) when in an American school. All cultural differences prepare children differently for school. They affect performance on any instrument used for assessment and need to be considered in what is measured, how it is measured, and, particularly, in the interpretation of the measures.

■ Measuring by Use of Self-Reports: Assessment of Affect and Learner Motivations

Measures of affective (sometimes referred to as noncognitive) variables are concerns of teachers, although rarely assessed formally for classroom use. Typical of such concerns are facets of motivation that are unique to the:

- *Task*—its attractiveness and interest to the student
- *Student's behavior*—volition, or willingness with which the student engages in specific school tasks; dispositions, or student pursuit of one task over another; and personal goals or motives, that is, ends to be achieved by attending school or by setting performance standards (why does he or she want to do well in school?)
- *Classroom climate*—perceptions of the classroom environment or context due to the dynamics involved in the interaction and motivational systems of the classroom

Measures related to motivation include measures of attributions (conditions perceived to be causes for success or failure), self-efficacy (self views of how effective one is in performing tasks), self-concept (level of worth of one's self), locus of control (whether one is in control of things that happen to him or her or is being controlled by others), interests (choices based on preferences tasks and activities), and a variety of personality variables.

Why would you want to measure these variables? They may have subtle, unnoticed influences on student effort and engagement that you should know about in order to improve your instruction. For example, the narrowing of the curriculum may have an undue negative influence on student motivational inclinations (Adelman & Taylor, 2006). An emphasis only on grades creates a climate in which students emphasize scores on a test—a *performance-based* classroom climate—rather than progress in learning—a *learning-based* classroom climate. Increasing the perceptions of the merit of the curriculum can be achieved by the student and the teacher perceiving tests as feedback devices that provide copious suggestions for improvement. Measures can be used to gather specific evidence for such outcomes so that constructive steps can be taken to make whatever changes are required to improve instruction and learning.

One can develop measures that target whether the emphasis is on student progress (learner-oriented) or on a fixed performance level (performance-oriented). Increasing the transparency of the assessment objectives can be achieved by engaging students and other stakeholders in the planning and construction of tests and measures and in explaining and interpreting their results. Increasing transparency of assessment procedures helps to avoid the fear-provoking anticipation of being measured or tested. Perceptions of tests as punitive devices (punishment for poor performance) often demand undue attention to getting a passing grade. They tend to narrow the curriculum by causing teachers and students to spend large amounts of time on practice with test items in an attempt to improve studying for tests and test-taking practices in anticipation of taking high-stakes tests such as statewide tests.

Measures of Motivation

We use a readily available measure of student motivation (Pintrich & Schrauben, 1992) to illustrate the development of scales for self-reports and the several facets of motivation. As the name denotes, the rating scale is the basic format for responding; in other words, students rate activities according to their use of the activity or their reaction to the learning tasks by (a) agreeing or disagreeing with the statement, (b) indicating the frequency with which the task is performed, or (c) rating the time spent on the task. Typical response formats (which are useful to know for developing your own rating scales to meet other objectives) are:

- *Agreement.* "I think grades are the most important reason for studying hard" is used with agreement response formats. For example: *1 = strongly agree* to *5 = strongly disagree.*
- *Frequency.* "When you study for a test, how often do you write items of the sort that you think might be on the test?" is a typical format for frequency ratings. For example: *1 = always* to *5 = never.*
- *Duration.* "How much time do you spend on surveying a chapter assignment before you begin studying it?" is used for duration ratings. For example: *1 = very little of the time* to *5 = most of the time.*

Self-report measures share methodological features with survey research, including limitations in reliability and validity (Duncan & McKeachie, 2005). When the limitations are recognized, self-reports can provide useful assessments of perceptions regarding what *use is made of learning strategies* (for studying, planning, and goal setting); *how students view themselves as learners* (self-efficacy in performing classroom assignments, perceptions of their competence, and how much they desire to achieve and succeed in school); *perceptions of the learning tasks* (difficulty, effort students believe is necessary to learn the task); *how students adapt to learning situations* (metacognitions about controlling learning and controlling effort); and general *motivation* (value or interest in school matters, intrinsic and extrinsic outcomes of studying, and so on) (Pintrich & Schrauben, 1992).

The McKeachie-Pintrich Motivated Strategies for Learning Questionnaire (MSLQ)

An excerpt of the *Motivated Strategies for Learning Question-naire (MSLQ)* (Pintrich, Smith, Garcia, & McKeachie, 1991) is shown in Theory to Practice Box 13.1. (The category labels and the definitions are not used in the actual administration of the questionnaire. They are presented in the box to show the cat-egories represented.) The items were selected from the 50-item scale to illustrate four categories of motivation:

> (a) *task value* (the course or course material is interest-ing, challenging, rewarding, important), (b) *metacogni-tions* (planning, monitoring and self-regulation), (c) *beliefs* about control of learning (how effort is used and how much the effort helps), (d) *expectancies* for success, self-efficacy, at tasks involved in learning and studying (how competent one is in acquiring the course materials or in performing the tasks involved), and (e) *affect* (anxiety and worry regarding competencies in carrying out course requirements). (Schunk, 2005, p. 90)

Before learning occurs, these self-perceptions identify the student's expectations as they modify estimates of cognitive ability. That is, a student who is intellectually prepared (capacity or ability) to acquire course objectives may not be motivation-ally ready and therefore is apt to perform poorly. Conversely, a student who may not have high ability may be willing to be intensely engaged in the task and will perform well. As learn-ing is taking place, that is, *during learning*, motivational assess-ments can be useful in understanding how students approach a task, the extent of their engagement in the task, the value they attach to the coursework, and their choice of preferred strat-egies. Using measures such as these *after learning* determines how students perceive, in retrospect, their learning experiences.

The MSLQ can be used in its entirety (to calculate a total score) as a measure of general motivation when taking a course, Or you can use it to arrive at subscores representing the dif-ferent categories shown in italics. Such scales are important assessments to supplement cognitive and standardized mea-sures of ability. They provide otherwise ignored or neglected contexts when diagnostic measures are used for student advis-ing and counseling. They are useful as well for developing or placing students in remedial courses. You can use these scales for learning individual or group approaches to course work (a

Theory to Practice Box 13.1

ILLUSTRATIONS OF MSLQ ITEMS FOR CATEGORIES REPRESENTED IN THE SCALE

The general instructions are to rate each of the items on "how well it describes you" by using the following scale:

1 = not at all true of me
2 = mostly untrue of me
3 = somewhat untrue of me
4 = neither true or untrue of me
5 = somewhat true of me
6 = mostly true of me
7 = very true of me

Self-Efficacy: The items in this category refer to the student's perceptions of his or her own effectiveness, that is, confidence in one's ability.

I am able to understand the most difficult concepts presented in the assignments for this course.

I have no concerns about mastering the skills the instructor expects us to learn in this course.

Task value: The items in this category refer to the student's perceptions of the extent of the course's value to him or her, the extent to which it meets his or her expectations, its usefulness, and his or her interest in it.

I am hopeful that I will be able to use what I learn in this course in other courses.

The course material in this class is important to learn for broadening my education.

Metacognitive self-regulation: The items in this category refer to the student's views of the extent to which the course contributes to his or her ability to control and use learning strategies in learning, reaching objectives, or performing tasks.

When reading for this course, I make up questions to help focus my reading.

I know how to review and change my strategies when I do not comprehend what I am reading.

Before I study new course material thoroughly, I often skim it to see how it is organized.

Affect: This category of items refer to the affectivity that the student might experience during any phase of course work: his or her anxiety, perceptions of motivational lapses, worry, concern in taking exams, and so on.

When I take a test I think about items on other parts of the test I can't answer.

I feel my heart beating fast when I take an exam.

Source: Based on Pintrich, Smith, Garcia, and McKeachie (1991).

student in different content areas), for learning about motivations of target populations (high school, nursing students, or engineers), or for learning about subpopulations based on combinations of variables (e.g., female undergraduates in engineering). And, as importantly, the *MSLQ* is only one of the many measures that can be used for measuring motivational areas including test anxiety, self-regulation of learning, self-esteem, and classroom climates.

Assessment by Graphic Displays: Sociograms and Concept Maps

A frequently neglected instrument in assessment is the graphic display of relations among concepts, people, or characteristics. Graphics can be used for assessing how students organize the concepts they have learned, that is, the relationships among concepts through displays of hierarchical or linear relations in networks or concept maps. Additionally, they can be used for assessing social structures. Finally, they can be used for showing profiles of data acquired about learner interests or other characteristics.

Why Use Sociograms?

We use the sociogram to illustrate how graphic displays have been used to diagram social structure in the classroom and the interactive relationships among students in a classroom or other environment. Knowing the social interactions among individuals can be important information to have when making seatwork assignments or when employing cooperative or competitive learning situations. For example, you might want to identify any of the following for use in classroom management: *leaders* (students who are selected by majority); *followers* (students who select others); *cliques* (students who select one another), *isolates* (students who are not selected by any others), and so on.

The information might be used in pairing a student-as-tutor with another student who might profit from tutoring. You can use the information in composing student dyads for computer assignments. An outcome of understanding the relations among individuals in the classroom is that it will also provide a basis for identifying neglected students who are overlooked by most of the class or those students who lack the ability to relate well to other students and need to develop social skills.

Bases for Making Sociograms

The sociogram is based on student choices of other students with whom they would like to work (other choice-tasks are possible). Because interactions differ by situations—in the classroom, on projects, in the laboratory, on the playground, or out of school—the assessment instrument might also include a framework within which to make the selection. An illustration of an item is as follows:

We'll work with teams of four members on a cooperative learning project. Write in the names of three persons with whom you like most to work: 1. _____ 2. _____ 3. _____

Or, as an item for a computer-based assignment:

We'll work in teams of two on a computer-based assignment. Write in the names of two students with whom you would most like to work: 1. _____ 2. _____

Other kinds of questions might include:

• Who would you select to be a member of your favorite school club?
• With whom would you like to join at the next baseball game?

Questions can be based on social roles and structures:

• Who does everyone think is the class leader?
• Who do you think is the best all-round friend to most kids in class?
• Who do you think is the computer whiz in this class?

Table 13.1. A Matrix of Nomination Data for Five Members of a Class

| Students Selecting | Students Receiving | | | | |
	Sam	John	Carlos	Maria	Alice
Sam		1st	2nd		
John	1st		2nd		
Carlos		1st		2nd	
Maria		2nd			1st
Alice		2nd	1st		

Summarizing Results

One format for summarizing results is shown in the display in Table 13.1. This display is simply a summary of choices made by five members of a class. They have been ranked as first and second choices and are displayed accordingly. In addition, the number of nominations or times chosen by other members of the class can be shown. Other ways for depicting class structure, including computer programs for more elaborate analyses, are described by Walsh (Walsh's Classroom Sociometrics, 2004; also see Smith, 2004, p. 4, Figures 1 and 2).

In this case, the teacher had seen these five students together in several situations. She thought that she might want to use them in a cooperative group for studying international relations. However, she was not certain who the leader was. Accordingly, in a more comprehensive questionnaire she included the opportunity for identifying the structure of this group. And, indeed, her predictions were correct; these students selected one another as first and second choices. On the basis of the number of their first choices she identified two "leaders" shown in Figure 13.2 as *stars*.

A map display, shown in Figure 13.2, presents the data in graphic form. A view of these five as a group make apparent some social relations of interest. In particular, John and Carlos seem to be the dominant figures in the group and perhaps are "pals." Alice is selected by Maria, but by no other one in the group; Alice probably belongs to another group. This information could be obtained from a summarization of choices made by the entire class. The questions shown in Theory to Practice Box 13.2 will help in understanding the use of the sociogram.

The results of an analysis of the sociogram are useful for *matching* or *mismatching* in interactive settings (Smith, 2004, p. 4, Figures 1 and 2). For example, leaders could be assigned to groups with those who voted for them (matching), or

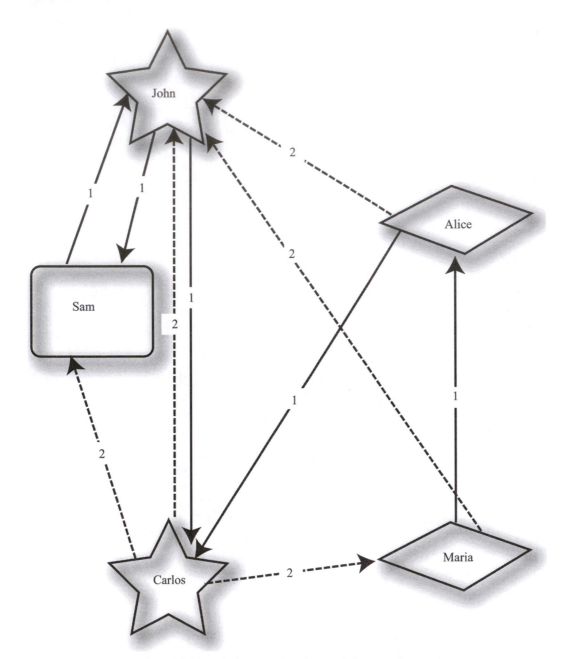

Figure 13.2. A graphic display of the nominations of five students. Star = most votes; diamond = girls; rectangle = boys; 1 = 1st choice; 2 = second choice; solid line = 1st choice; dashed line = 2nd choice; arrowhead is on the chosen person.

leaders could be paired with students who had few or no votes to compose mixed (mismatched) groups comprised of popular and unpopular students or of students who are voted as having high and low knowledge. Other bases might be used, depending on the activities you plan for reaching classroom objectives. For example, three students who pick one another to

Theory to Practice Box 13.2
QUESTIONS TO HELP INTERPRET SOCIOGRAMS

Refer to Figure 13.2 or other sociogram.

- What social structures can you identify in Figure 13.4? (Hint: pals, pairs, cliques, nonmembers of the informal group.)
- Do you agree with the stars for the most popular members of this group as determined by the number of choices from their peers? Is there more than one popular member? Explain.
- What reasons can you suggest why Alice has no nominations and Maria has one nomination? The reasons might be quite different. What other data would you need for a clearer answer?
- How would you structure a team based on these five students for working on a computer project?
- Go to the source cited in the text to view more extensive sociograms of entire classes. What other interactions of interest can you glean from them?

form a tightly knit triad might represent a clique, in which case you might wish to retain the group as one in which all three could work with one another or you might want to split them up so that they will learn to work with others. The data can also be used to identify popular or neglected children (those receiving very few nominations).

Cautions in the Use of Sociograms

It should be noted that the data obtained by sociometric devices do not explain *why* the student is perceived in a certain way (Smith, 2004); for example, it cannot tell directly why a child in a class receives no or very few nominations. The sociogram can be useful for understanding some aspects of the social structure of the classroom or the relations among the students composing the class. The reasons for the linkages among students will require interpretation.

The sociogram is most appropriately used when it serves a constructive purpose in interactive settings or in understanding the students' social skills. Difficulties can be avoided by using only positive nominations such as "With whom would you most like to work?" rather than negative nominations such as "With whom would you least like to work?" Avoid implying negative connotations as are involved in most-to-least preferences. Although the method can be useful, it must be used cautiously, with seriousness of purpose, or not at all. If scores are made public, for example, the teacher runs the risk of having them misinterpreted or becoming the basis of stereotypes such as "John is unpopular" or "John is not liked."

■ Graphic Organizers of Course Content Achievement

Opportunities for graphic displays exist in cognitive areas, whether science or literature. In literature, for example, characters can be displayed as they are engaged in power relations, leadership roles, maintaining hierarchical status, and so on. In any area, graphics can be used to determine the depth of understanding concepts, as illustrated in Figure 13.3 later in the chapter.

Graphic Displays of Assessment of Understanding Literature

A technique described by Johnson and Louis (1987) for mapping social interaction in literature parallels the one we have described for sociograms. For example, students may have been assigned a novel in which the interactions among the characters are laid out. To assess understanding of the text, the student is assigned the task of graphically displaying the relations among the characters. The instructions place the central character at the center with other characters around him or her. The students' arrangement of characters and connecting arrows are scored according to rubrics such as the following:

- Relations among characters are clear and accurately displayed. Lines are drawn to connect those that are somehow related. The line is labeled to show the relationship (leader, expert, follower, learner, etc.).
- Psychological relations between or among characters are understood. Distance between them is correctly displayed to represent psychological proximity.
- Importance of the character (central, dominant, subordinate, etc.) is shown. The size of the box or other shape in which the name is enclosed represents the importance of the character.
- Direction of influence, if any, is accurately displayed. The direction is shown by arrows connecting characters.
- The role(s) of the characters have been identified; for instance, protagonists and antagonists, if a part of the story, are identified by placing them appropriately (one side or the other) with reference to the central character.

- Time relations are shown if a part of the story; for example, parallel displays might be used to show the relation among the characters before and after an event such as an election or a conflict.

Perceiving Relations among Events

Graphic displays can be used to assess the degree to which students perceive important relations among events described in newspapers, television programs, and movies, as well as in literary works (Johnson & Louis, 1987) and classroom interventions. Used in this way, graphic organizers provide a map of the student's perceptions and thinking of knowledge and events. Furthermore, the character of the organization significantly influences remembering and transfer (application) in context. Thus, assessment that uses graphic displays can be very useful for understanding such facets of thinking as how well the students understand the structures underlying the content learned, how well the students' organization of content corresponds to the scholarly base of the content, how well they can elaborate on the information newly learned in class assignments, how well they will be able to remember the concepts, and under what circumstances they can transfer the knowledge to new situations.

Teaching Students to Use Graphic Organizers

When employing this form of assessment it is important that the student knows how to make the necessary graphic displays for organizing information and how to apply the technique to what has been learned. In being trained to use this procedure, students can be shown the many ways for presenting such information, for example, as Venn diagrams, hierarchies, concentric circles, spider webs, networks, and the like (Sinatra, 2000). They can also be shown that displays can be used to display many types of organization, for example, to show ideas related to signals (in the first place, in the second place, etc.), to show causes and effects, to show development of reasoning, to show classifications, to show sequences or steps in a process, to aid in elaboration (adding what they know to what has been taught), to make comparisons and contrasts, and to show analogies or other forms of valuing (Sinatra, 2000). Each can provide a basis for assessments that go beyond recall of facts and lead to an emphasis on a facet of understanding.

Drawing a Concept Map

An example of how students might respond to an assignment requiring a concept map is shown in Figure 13.3. The illustration depicts the responses of two students following a lesson on minerals. The class was instructed to draw a map organizing the relation among the concepts they had learned in studying minerals,

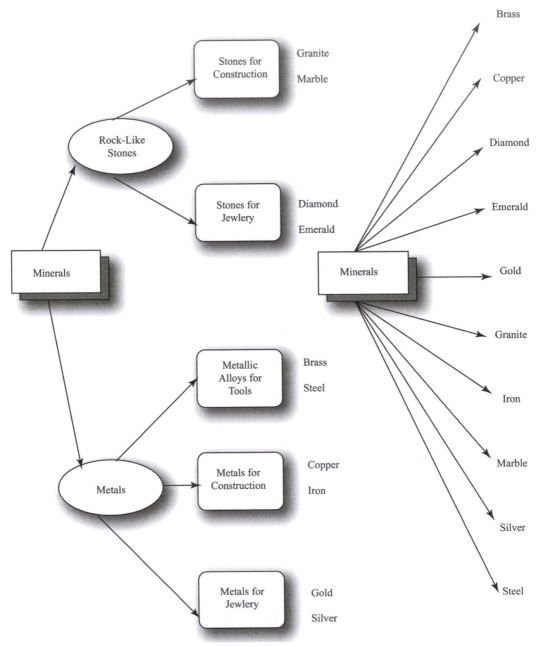

Figure 13.3. Concept maps of minerals as drawn by two students. Ben's concept map is on the left and Al's is on the right. (see also Exercise 13.1).

including such items as the subcategories of minerals, which contain instances of iron, silver, gold, lead, diamond, marble, quartz, and ruby. Rubrics for scoring might include (a) the degree of accurate differentiation within the maps, (b) the accuracy of labeling categories and subcategories, and (c) the meaningfulness of the organizational basis.

Making Inferences from Student Concept Maps

Knowing these pieces of information, the teacher would be able to infer the strategy the individual is using for recalling information, which items are related to one another, and how they are related. Scores are based on teacher-based criteria or scientifically based criteria. Inferences from results provide bases from which remedial work could be planned. If concept maps are used before and after a lesson the differences between the two, based on the same rubrics, can be used to determine the change in student understanding.

Exercise 13.1: Questions for Interpreting Figure 13.3

What is Al's basis for organizing the concepts? What is Ben's basis for organizing the information? Which student do you think has a better understanding of the concept of minerals? Why do you think so? How do you know from their responses? Who will remember better? Can you give reasons why this might be so? In what ways does the figure suggest the two students recalled information? Who will probably be better able to apply the information? Why? Under what contexts would they be able to retrieve information equally well?

■ Assessment Based on Multiple Intelligences

Most often we think of intelligence as a unitary characteristic of human thinking. The intelligence quotient, for example, is probably our first experience with the formal definition of intelligence and represents a general characteristic of behavior. It is found to be one of the best predictors of later performance. But the potential for scoring the test in various ways suggests that general intelligence may be subdivided into other components, such as verbal or quantitative, reflecting the possibility that, in addition to being a measure of general aptitude, intelligence may be composed of specific intelligences.

In thinking about the assessment of individual differences in intelligence Gardner (1993; cf. Smith, 2002) theorizes that the single score of "intelligence" is too inclusive and that intelligence may take many forms (also see Sternberg & Grigorenko, 2002). This view questions the psychometric soundness of the single score as a predictor of success in school and suggests that its authenticity for a full description of intellectual capacity may be limited. The alternative is that if teachers are to obtain a full description of intelligence they must consider the nature of intelligence required to serve the ways intelligence functions in different work situations (also see Sternberg [2007] for a description of the triarchic theory of intelligence, which advocates a three-pronged approach to studying intelligence).

In everyday observation of people at work, you too may have noticed that they can be intelligent in different ways; each excels in their own unique ways. You may have said one "is *musically* inclined," "has superb *social skills*," is "a *mathematical* thinker," "is good in languages," "learns best through *visual* presentations," or other characterization. Based on such observations, Gardner (1983) reasoned that the usefulness of single-score intelligence might be enhanced for predicting performance by considering the distinctive kinds of intelligences that exist in a variety of work situations; individuals are not equally expert in all situations.

Multiple Intelligences

Emerging from this framework, the intelligences that constitute the classification of multiple intelligences are illustrated in Table 13.2 (Gardner, 1983) and elaborate upon Gardner's (1991) descriptions of the multiple intelligences.

How Multiple Intelligences Are Used in Curriculum Development

This classification holds promise for curriculum development. The first two intelligences listed in the box will be recognized as cognitive domains. The others have received less attention despite the likelihood that many, if not all, are represented in any given classroom.

Instructional methods appeal to more than one of the intelligences. Any topic can be presented with integrity in a number of ways. Instruction can provide opportunities for matching instruction to existing capabilities of students despite differences in multiple intelligences. By varying forms of delivery according to these dispositions, you will provide opportunity for reaching each student in some way.

Table 13.2. Characteristics and Manifestations of Multiple Intelligences

Kind of Intelligence	What It Involves	How It Is Manifested in Typical Behavior	Occupations Emphasizing this Intelligence
Linguistic	Sounds, rhythms, language functions, meanings of words, use of metaphor, analogies for reaching goals, ability to learn language	Using words and linguistics in patterns, storytelling, word games, reporting (journalism), writing poetry, discussion	Poet, author, journalist, critic, speaker/lecturer, lawyer, interpreter, rapper, librarian, teacher
Logical mathematical	Interpreting logical and numerical patterns (graphs), reasoning, problem solving, cryptography, Socratic dialogue	Number games, calculating costs in relation to selling price, debit-credit sheets, balancing check books, conducting small experiments, discovery, creativity, investigation, solving mysteries	Mathematician, logician, scientist, computer programmer, banker, accountant, statistician, code decipherer
Spatial	Finding and manipulating patterns in dimensional space, visualizing, imagery, picture interpretation	Conceptual maps; graphic organizers; use of video, diagrammatic, and other pictorial displays; jigsaw puzzles	Cartographer, artist, cartoonist, photographer, chess player, architect, surgeon (see kinesthetic)
Musical	Musical expression; dynamics; emphasis on pitch, tone, timbre; skill in performing; composing musical patterns (see kinesthetic)	Singing, music perception (clapping), music appreciation (recognizing key structure), phrasing, music appreciation	Composer, musician, singer
Kinesthetic	Physical movement, large and small muscle cues, gross and fine motor skills	Conveying messages nonverbally (posture, etc.), physical awareness, tactile materials and experiences, manipulatives, games, field trips, simulators, audiovisual games	Driver; physical therapist; athlete; dancer; surgeon (see spatial); actor; occupations that use equipment, apparatus, or tools; crafts; signaling; computers; musicians

(continued)

Table 13.2. (*continued*)

Kind of Intelligence	What It Involves	How It Is Manifested in Typical Behavior	Occupations Emphasizing this Intelligence
Interpersonal	Relations with others, communication, social aptitude, responding to moods of others	Jigsaw classrooms, tutoring, cognitive apprenticeships, scaffolding, conflict resolution, community work	Labor/industry mediator, social worker, anthropologist, politician, managerial position, therapist
Intrapersonal	Understanding self, self-esteem, self-regulation, confidence, in sync with one's own feelings, emotions, empathy, accurate self-knowledge	Self-insight, independent work, planning, life course decisions, lifelong learning, coping exercises	Involved as affective component of other intelligences. Involved in aesthetics, morals, values, ethics
Naturalistic	Identify natural forms of categorization (birdlike, animal-like), developing taxonomies	Encoding in symbol systems; capturing identifying features in hieroglyphics, classifying plants, animals, and geographic features (e.g., children's preoccupation with classifying dinosaurs)	Botanist, biologist, environmentalist, physical scientist

Source: Figure from p. 6 Gardner and Hatch (1989) and adaptations of that figure based on Gardner (1999).

Using Different Modalities

Curricula can be devised or modified, regardless of the school subject, to facilitate development of each of the intelligences. The list in Table 13.2 provides clues for different approaches to instructional methods. Concepts in any course can be presented in different modalities. Instruction on the musical songs of birds, for example, can deliver the content in a visual mode (seeing the musical score for the song), auditory mode (hearing the song), or linguistic mode (translating the songs to wordlike syllabic sounds). Creative possibilities exist for presentations in kinesthetic (whistling the song), interactive (replying to a song with the appropriate sequence of notes), or affective (singing louder or softer, quickly or slowly to denote happiness, for example, or sadness) modes. Such variations provide curricular adaptations to student capabilities that have typically been ignored or neglected. Existing capabilities or predispositions can be exploited, nurtured, or developed to facilitate acquisition and the ways in which the outcomes (understandings) are demonstrated on achievement tests (Gardner, 1999).

Spatial Reasoning

As one might expect, the typical ways of measuring intelligence within this framework are limited in their usefulness, so alternative assessments such as portfolios, rubrics, and other performance measures are used (Gardner, 1993; Gardner & Hatch, 1989). Thus, to evaluate spatial intelligence the student gets the opportunity to take apart and reassemble some common object with many parts but the skill required is within the student's capability (also being culture-fair in the course of doing so). You will recognize the need for spatial intelligence in many construction toys (e.g., robotic assemblies, Legos, and so on) for building mechanical devices, houses, and moving objects. It is also engaged in such activities as assembling furniture, connecting parts of a computer system, assembling a bicycle, and so on.

In the course of assembling and disassembling objects (or any other task), a number of mental processes are brought into play that are certain to have an enduring effect on what the student learns beyond the task's specific contribution to the content knowledge base. In these manual performances, students' developmental representations (abstract mental pictures or images) of the plan, the appearance of parts, the final goal (the way the object will look when assembled), the names of the parts, the sequence in which the parts go together, and the strategies to facilitate assembly are developed. Some reliance on verbal information would be necessary, but most effort will engage spatial representations of parts, models, and working mechanisms. In an earlier era and in some cultures children learned such skills as learning to dance and sing, also taking part in building houses and in disassembling and reassembling farm machinery in many modalities (intelligences) through apprenticeship learning with the expectation that those skills would serve them well in carrying out adult responsibilities.

Linguistic Ability

In comparison with manual performances, linguistic ability, too, has many potential assessment alternatives. It would not be measured solely by the typical classroom test based on word definitions, syllabification, or sentence construction. Rather, it would be measured by providing props or contexts such as pictures or toys that require verbal participation in the form of initiating story telling (author), reporting of an incident (journalist), or review of an event (critic). Again, as you can see, the assessment would require the student to anticipate a story plan, an *image* of the events, a *linguistic* framework representing those events, a *spatial image* of the unfolding of events to correspond to the story plan, and transformations of mental images into *verbal* expressions in reaching the goal of having told a story. Ratings would be obtained by judging the performance against a set of rubrics.

School Programs Based on Assessment of Multiple Intelligences

Educational programs based on this approach employ assessments that feature sets of exercises and curriculum activities paralleling the intelligences. Among these is an arts-based program, Art PROPEL (Gardner & Hatch, 1989). The products are in the forms of drafts, sketches, writings, and other formats collected into portfolios and serving as a basis for assessment. Similar programs at the elementary level are based on themes such as "Man and His Environment" and "Changes in Time and Space." The products, in the forms of presentations, displays, science fairs, and similar activities, are videotaped for assessment by such criteria as project conceptualization, effectiveness of presentation, technical quality, and originality (Olson, 1988, as reported in Gardner & Hatch, 1989).

Assessing Multiple Intelligences

Assessment Contexts

Instead of measuring any of the intelligences solely in abstract terms, each is measured in terms of the student's *ability to use it* within a framework in which it is engaged. Teachers in science can observe the student's dependence on spatial relations (a) in the laboratory (assembling apparatus for an experiment as compared to learning from verbal descriptions alone); (b) in exploring unknown territory (finding one's way in a local cave or around a park) where one path is not a sufficient answer; or (c) in *representing* numbers or quantities (to show increases in population growth, budgetary allotments, or gas consumption of automobiles). Each of the observations can be transformed into graphic representations.

Portfolios

Evaluative data can be found in portfolios documenting these activities for external review. Exhibits provide opportunities for audio recording of presentations or for photographs or videos capturing the visual qualities of a display. Journal entries reflect the logical development and emergence of the different stages of an activity from the time it is initiated to its completion. Whether the account is visual as in an exhibit, written as in a journal, or manual as in assembling an object, it can be assessed for *interpersonal* as well as *intrapersonal* intelligence (collaborative efforts, cooperation, discussions, or perceptions of self-efficacy). Virtually any classroom activity provides opportunities for discovering relations, classifying components, and experimenting as tests of *logical* intelligence, and any movement exercises, including ballet steps, basketball activities, and typing on a computer keyboard, provide the basis for tests of *kinesthetic* intelligence. And, even in teaching about Gothic arches, kinesthetic intelligence might be engaged by having students form aisles and connect the aisles by grasping hands to form an arch. All emphasize how content is to be taught in delivering instruction.

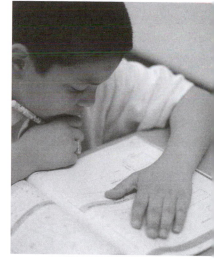

Affordances for Multiple Intelligences

Although instructional settings provide opportunities for assessing multiple intelligences, some opportunities must be planned; they don't occur naturally or spontaneously. In other words, the instruction must be geared to afford opportunity for the intelligence to be engaged. High-affordance environments consist of materials, replicas, and events displayed or presented so that they invite the engagement of a particular intelligence (Gardner & Hatch, 1989), that is, afford the opportunity for it to be used. (You may wish to refer back to our discussion of the ways instruction might engage multiple intelligences in teaching bird songs.) The instruction is arranged to allow students to engage "their several intelligences, even as teachers have the chance unobtrusively to observe and assess children's strengths, interests, and proclivities" (Gardner & Hatch, 1989, p. 7).

■ Self-Reports of Preferences: Assessment of Learning Styles

Both learning styles and multiple intelligences are similar in their assumptions that students do have measurable preferences (styles) for modes of learning. These tendencies can be used advantageously in creating classroom presentations corresponding to the student's preferred or best way of learning. Gardner (1999) indicates that some of the intelligences suggest the learner's style, or preferred way of learning.

A typical measure of learner style is illustrated in the *Learning Style Profile* (Dunn & Dunn, 1978). It is based on a definition of style in terms of self-perceptions of how or under what conditions one learns best. Note the differences from the categories of multiple intelligences in the following style categories. Preference is related to:

- Environmental variables (sound, light, temperature, classroom design)
- Affective variables (motivation, persistence, responsibility)
- Social variables (peers, groups, teams)
- Delivery modalities (perceptual—auditory, visual, tactual, kinesthetic)

The outcomes of this assessment are employed in matching instruction to learning style on the assumption that the matching of the two (in terms of time on task, how one is best motivated, whether one likes to learn solitarily or in groups) leads to the most efficient learning. The questionable assumption in using such measures is whether individuals are capable of making reliable and valid judgments or observations of themselves, a criticism equally applicable to self-ratings made of the multiple intelligences.

The distinction between multiple intelligences and learning style is in the emphases on which perceptions are based. In assessments of multiple intelligences, an item intended to measure naturalistic intelligence would be in the form: "I tend to examine new environments from a biological position" or "I try to learn from the people and their ways." Note the emphasis is on the "what": the content and the ability to use it as implied in the definition of the intelligence. In style inventories, on the other hand, the items would emphasize the preferred conditions of studying or working, conditions that may transcend two or more intelligences or content areas; for example, "I remember things best when they are presented in a pictorial form." Similarly, the use of a style is assumed to apply over a range of subject-matter areas.

■ Response to Intervention (RTI): A System for Instruction-Based Assessment

A proposal for a formal system of adapting instruction to individual differences is known as RTI ("response to instruction" or "response to intervention"). The assessment procedure is interesting because instruction is adapted to those students who depart from ability to profit from quality (i.e., evidence-based instruction) or general standards-aligned instruction. Good assessment is critical to this systematic approach to instruction. The aim is to eliminate a quality evidence-based core curriculum as the source of a student's learning difficulties by assessing all students and identifying, from the group, those who are unresponsive to the general education curriculum. The unresponsive students are assigned to strategically designed or intensive instruction.

RTI is part of the 2004 reauthorization of the Individuals with Disabilities Education Act (IDEA), originally enacted in 1975 and most recently reauthorized (2004) as the Individuals with Disabilities Education Improvement Act (IDEIA or IDEA 2004). It specifically authorizes the use of RTI standards in disability identification and makes funding available for RTI implementation. The following discussion is based on a comprehensive exposition of RTI by Burns, Christ, Kovaleski, Shapiro, and Ysseldyke (Renaissance Learning, 2009) to which you may wish to refer for complete details (also see reports on the Internet for the National Center for Learning Disabilities' RTI Action Network at rtinetwork.org).

The Components of RTI

RTI is an individualized, comprehensive assessment and intervention process. Student academic difficulties are addressed by instructing them through effective, efficient, research-based instructional practices. The procedure is initiated with evidence-based interventions (instruction); that is, identification of individual differences is made from measures administered to students following high-quality instruction. The RTI approach requires the school to know the dimensions of high-quality instruction and the ways of measuring the outcomes. The measures must be sufficiently diagnostic to warrant interpretation of the kinds of instruction that should be used for students who do not profit from the instruction. In general, the process may be linked to the Zone of Proximal Development (Vygotsky, 1978), which relates the potential for educational achievement to the student's ability and instructional procedures; most students will profit from some level of instruction, whether direct, with few hints, or with many hints. However, some students will not profit from traditional instruction outside of their zone of potential development and will require special instruction such as tutorial or individualized instruction.

Although the RTI framework is a useful way of perceiving formative assessment in a number of areas, the current formal focus on RTI has concentrated on math and reading in the early grades, as these are essential components of IDEA legislation. An understanding of this procedure is valuable for all teachers because it demonstrates the way in which objective data can contribute to effective classroom instruction as well as understanding the necessary collaboration with the special education community in monitoring student progress.

The assessment is concerned with the development and implementation of:

- Evidence-based, quality *classroom instruction and management* effective for 80–85 percent of students in achieving learning outcomes in general education
- Use of evidence-based *strategic academic or behavioral interventions* targeting identified learning difficulties for instructing about 10–15 percent of students who are not fully responsive to quality instructional practices in the general education classroom
- *Intensive interventions*—one-on-one, tutorial, or small group instruction for about 5 percent of students who are persistently or significantly nonresponsive to interventions, including students with disabilities.

These components of RTI can be represented as a multilevel system that integrates assessment and intervention to maximize student achievement. Using RTI, schools *identify* students at risk for poor learning outcomes (students with learning disabilities), *monitor* student progress, *provide* evidence-based interventions, and *adjust* those interventions to the student's responsiveness to instruction. A graphic depiction of the tiers is displayed in Figure 13.4.

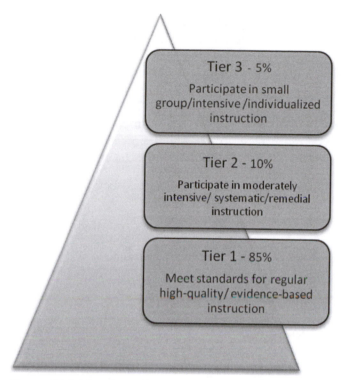

Figure 13.4. The three tiers of response to intervention.

The Three Tiers of RTI

As shown in Figure 13.4 RTI is often conceptualized as a three-tiered system of assessment, placement, and instruction of students (Gersten et al., 2008).

Tier I

The system is initiated by making certain that the classrooms where RTI is to be used are meeting standards for high-quality, evidence-based instruction. By using well-constructed instruments, diagnostic assessments are made to identify students who are not learning at the expected rate for their grade level. This may require two screenings of all students for potential learning (reading or math) problems: once at the beginning of the year and again in the middle of the year. The progress of students identified as being at elevated risk is monitored. About 15 percent of students are typically found to not meet the basic standards. These are considered for placement in Tier II instruction.

Tier II

About 10–15 percent of the general student population in an RTI school might participate in Tier II instruction. Here they participate in moderately intensive, systematic instruction for remediation in identifiable deficiencies (e.g., in basic reading skills). For example, students who did not reach benchmark scores on important foundational reading skills such as decoding and vocabulary would receive five weeks of instruction, three to five times a week for 20–40 minutes. Their progress would be monitored at least once a month, if not more often. The data on their progress (which represent response to intervention) would be used to determine the student's responsiveness to the instruction.

After a reasonable time at this tier, Tier II students who demonstrate improvement return to Tier I. They receive continued monitoring to ensure that they are adequately profiting from general classroom instruction. Other students found to be making insufficient progress in Tier II will receive additional intervention by being placed in Tier III.

Tier III

The 5 percent of students assigned to Tier III receive small-group instruction or individualized instruction. The plan for Tier III instruction provides for intensive daily instruction that promotes the development of various components of (reading) proficiency. "Although student [reading] programs should be individualized, they should be viewed as more than one-on-one instruction. In particular, [in listening and reading comprehension and vocabulary development] small group instruction makes sense" (Gersten et al., 2008).

The Challenges of RTI for Schools

RTI may be a challenge for implementation in some schools because the framework does not involve one practice or strategy but multiple processes and resources for administering the instruction and assessments involved. Some of the components that must be in place for RTI to be effective are discussed in the following paragraphs (based on Stepanek, 2008).

Research-Based Core Curriculum and Instruction

Decisions regarding the selection of the curriculum are expected to be based on addressing important components of instruction as they relate to students' needs and developmental levels. If a large number of students struggle under the general core program, the implementation might be questioned on the basis of

(a) the *conditions* (frequency, duration, intensity) of the implementation; (b) *adequacy of design* for student level; (c) *students' understanding* of the intervention (how, when, and why it was to be used); and (d) *administration* of the intervention (were students given sufficient practice and was practice given in relevant contexts?) to produce a change in achievement. These questions address the reasons for lack of response to the intervention; that is, was it due to the way the core program was implemented or to the program itself?

Assessment Tools

Central to the use of RTI are the screening and evaluation tools used to identify student achievement progress and learning needs. Monitoring the amount and the rate of growth in each student's performance in Tiers II and III needs to be done periodically. These assessments will yield large databanks on student progress, placing unusual demands for efficiently storing the data and for making meaningful analyses and summaries for teachers.

Research-Based Interventions

To support students in Tiers II and III, teachers must have a variety of interventions for facilitating learning that can be targeted to students' needs. Typical Tier II interventions include supplemental instruction and small-group tutoring. Tier III interventions might involve unique (a) modeling of skills to be learned, (b) corrective feedback, or (c) provision of incentives. Tracking assessment data from progress monitoring also aids teachers in evaluating the success of the interventions used and the periodic adjustments for efficient instruction.

Validity and Fidelity of Measures

The use of such phrases as *evidence-based*, *research supported*, *accurate prediction of success*, and *research validated measures* in describing RTI emphasizes the critical attention to assessment in this system of instruction. Assessments enter into RTI at several places to determine whether the intervention is the correct one (the intervention's validity or fidelity); whether the intervention is correctly implemented; and whether the measures of student progress provide data that can be usefully interpreted. In meeting the usual demands for reliable and valid assessments it is important to consider that any lack of student progress is the result of a *mismatch of the intervention to the student's level of development* and not the result of an ineffective intervention. The questions to be answered here are:

- Is the current intervention producing results?
- If so, is additional intervention required?

If not:

- Was the intervention implemented correctly and was it of high quality?
- Was the intervention implemented with sufficient AET (including practice time)?
- Is additional skill analysis required to determine why it is not working?
- Is additional intervention and more time required after a reasonable length of time?

The Use of Technology in RTI

The systematic requirements of the RTI model are efficiently implemented at all levels of the system—the evidence-based instruction, the selection of measures, and the use of the assessments in diagnosis and monitoring as well as in the analysis of the data (Fuchs & Fuchs, 2009). The instruments for screening, progress monitoring, and diagnoses are computerized for administration and reporting of student data. Technology is used to maintain and consolidate data for screening, monitoring, and referral. Benchmarks and cut-off scores are used to group students, for example, those who are at or above the benchmark, who are potentially at risk or are at risk and on watch, or for referral to one of the tiers for immediate intervention.

■ Dynamic Assessment: Measuring Change and Potential for Learning

Typically we think of measures of intelligence or of potential for learning in terms of such tests as the standardized tests of intelligence. Within the framework of dynamic assessment these traditional assessments are referred to as static measures, characteristic of an individual's performance at a given time and having some unchanging properties such as high reliability, stable item characteristics, and validity. The static quality is emphasized in the test's administration under controlled, standardized conditions including specific time limitations, unyielding instructions to the student, and standardized situational requirements.

An assumption of advocates of dynamic assessment is that traditional conditions are poorly adapted to assessing the student's *potential* for improvement or change; standard tests index a given level of performance at a given time, which may not be the best predictor of future performance or readiness.

These views parallel those in Vygotsky's (1978) conceptualization of the Zone of Proximal Development (ZOPD). An easy way to understand ZOPD is to consider the student taking a test, such as an intelligence test, under ordinary circumstances with no help. The score is recorded. Then, he or she takes the test again, but this time when he or she has difficulty he or she will be given a hint. If correct, that score is recorded. If incorrect, he or she is given another hint and so on. The hints can be graded in such terms as subtle or directly blunt. Then the score is calculated in terms of both the number correct with no hints and the number correct with hints and their directness required for arriving at the correct answer. The difference between the score under no help and the score with help represents the zone of proximal development. This zone can be interpreted in terms of how the student would respond to instruction (see discussion of RTI). A small or no difference between the two scores would indicate low probability of meeting learning standards with traditional teaching methods; a large difference would indicate high potential for profiting from traditional instruction when sufficient elaborations and extensions are provided.

Dynamic testing is based on similar assumptions as those made in ZOPD; measures need not be obtained or used in only one way, that is, by taking a test under highly standardized conditions. Rather they can be compared with scores obtained when taking it with the guidance (hints) of a knowledgeable peer or adult. The two scores will be different, of course; the latter will typically be higher than the former. The score from the standardized administration represents the student's ability to learn without aid. The score from the guided administration represents the basic ability of the student plus ability with guidance. The difference between the two measures represents the potential for learning. To reiterate, when few hints are required there is higher potential for independent learning (less external help needed); when more hints are required there is less potential (more external help needed). It should be noted that assessments of the current ability of the student compared with assessments of what he or she can learn with expert help is a

Table 13.3. Distinctions between Static and Dynamic Testing

Characteristics on Which the Types of Testing Are Compared	Type of Testing	
	Static testing	Dynamic testing
Products	Measure of preexisting, already developed state	Measure of developing process or other change
Feedback	Test is structured and prearranged according to test construction principles; no feedback on quality of performance	Feedback, implicit or explicit, to progressively increasing challenging tasks
Administration	Examiner is neutral, uninvolved, and adheres strictly to detailed administration procedures without departure	Highly interactive; the general climate is one of aiding and guiding the student to make the most of a challenging situation

Source: Adapted from Sternberg and Grigorenko (2002).

description of instruction. The differences between traditional assessment and dynamic assessment are shown in Table 13.3.

Dynamic assessment assumes a range of learning potential for classroom settings: Some students will need more or less assistance than others and some will gain more from given levels of assistance than others. In principle, the difference between the measure of performance status and performance with guidance is assumed to be a better indicator of readiness to learn than the performance under static learning conditions alone. For example, championship spelling competitions (spelling bees) are static measures of ability. Nevertheless, assessments with aids (feedback, interaction, definitions) are permitted to help realize the participant's potential for spelling. The participant may have a word repeated, phonetically segmented, or defined—all of which provide hints and reduction of ambiguity and eventually the realization of the full potential. A detailed example is shown in the Theory to Practice Box 13.3.

Although they achieve their purposes in different ways, dynamic and formative assessment are similar in their objectives. However, formative assessment focuses on feedback from assessment to improve instructional methods, whereas dynamic assessment focuses on feedback from assessment procedures to promote change in the student's potential for learning. It assumes that instruction proceeds best when the teacher knows the extent to which the student can change given the opportunity to do so. The focus is on how much detail, explanation, or other guidance is required for the student to realize his or her potential.

Theory to Practice Box 13.3
DYNAMIC TESTING FOR HELPING A LOW-COMPETENCE STUDENT TO ASK GOOD QUESTIONS

These examples show the acquisition of *question asking* by a remedial seventh-grade student (Charles).

Day 1

Text: *The water moccasin, somewhat longer than the copperhead, is found in the southeastern states. It lives in swampy regions. It belongs, as do also the copperhead and rattlesnake, to a group of poisonous snakes called pit vipers. They have pits between their eyes and their nostrils which, because they are sensitive to heat, help the snake tell when they are near a warm-blooded animal. Another name for the water moccasin is "cottonmouth." This name comes from the white lining of the snake's mouth.*

S: What is found in the southeastern states, also the copperhead, rattlesnakes, vipers they have—I'm not doing this right.

T: All right. Do you want to know about the pit vipers?

S: Yeah.

T: What would be a good question about the pit vipers that starts with the word "why"?

S: *(No response)*

T: How about, "Why are the snakes called pit vipers?"

S: Why do they want to know that they are called pit vipers?

T: Try it again.

S: Why do they, pit vipers in a pit?

T: How about, "Why do they call the snakes pit vipers?"

S: Why do they call the snakes pit vipers?

T: There you go! Good for you.

Day 4

Text: *Spinner's mate is much smaller than she, and his body is dull brown. He spends most of his time sitting at one side of her web.*

S: *(No question)*

T: What's this paragraph about?

S: Spinner's mate. How do spinner's mate. . . .

T: That's good. Keep going.

(continued)

Theory to Practice Box 13.3
(Continued)

S: How do spinner's mate is smaller than. . . . How am I going to say that?

T: Take your time with it. You want to ask a question about spinner's mate and what he does, beginning with the word "how."

S: How do they spend most of his time sitting?

T: You're very close. The question would be, "How does spinner's mate spend most of. . . ." Now, you ask it.

S: How does spinner's mate spend most of his time?

Day 7

Text: *Perhaps you were wondering where the lava and other volcanic prod-ucts come from. Deep within our earth there are pockets of molten rock called magma. Forced upward in part by gas pressure, this molten rock continually tries to reach the surface. Eventually—by means of cracks in the crustal rocks or some similar zone of weakness—the magma may break out of the ground. It then flows from the vent as lava, or spews skyward as dense clouds of lava particles.*

S: How does the pressure from below push the mass of hot rock against the opening? Is that it?

T: Not quite. Start your question with, "What happens when?"

S: What happens when the pressure from below pushes the mass of hot rock against the opening?

T: Good for you! Good job.

Day 11

Text: *One of the most interesting of the insect-eating plants is the Venus's flytrap. This plant lives in only one small area of the world—the coastal marshes of North and South Carolina. The Venus's flytrap doesn't look unusual. Its habits, however, make it a truly plant wonder.*

S: What is the most interesting of the insect-eating plants, and where do the plants live at?

T: Two excellent questions! They are both clear and important questions. Ask us one at a time now.

Day 15

Text: *Scientists also come to the South Pole to study the strange lights that glow overhead during the Antarctic night. (It's a cold and lonely world for the few*

hardy people who "winter over" the polar night.) These "southern lights" are caused by the Earth acting like a magnet on electrical particles in the air. They are clues that may help us understand the earth's core and the upper edges of its blanket of air.

S: Why do scientists come to the South Pole to study?

T: Excellent question! That is what this paragraph is all about.

Source: Campione and Brown (1987, Appendix C, pp. 112–113).

Teachers using dynamic assessment provide guidance (Palinscar, Brown, & Campione, 1991), as needed, on:

- *Content* (known related facts)
- *Modality* (whether the material is presented in a visual or auditory mode)
- *Phases* (input, elaboration, and output)
- *Operations* (strategies or procedures used)
- *Complexity* (quantity and quality of information processed or to be processed)

In the course of dynamic assessment the teacher continually assesses the potential of the student to learn what is taught, to provide guidance, and to reasonably use what is learned. *Guidance*, either by the use of hints or interventions, supports the student's ability and learning style as does the provision of *content* (facts, concepts, etc.) or *procedures* (strategies, retrieval routines, procedures for conceptualizing, problem solving, critiquing, and so on) needed for learning new material. For these purposes and contexts, dynamic assessment and the tests employed appear to have advantages over the use of static measures alone for helping students realize their performance potential (Day, Engelhardt, Maxwell, & Bolig, 1997; Sternberg & Grigorenko, 2002).

■ Integrating Assessments: The Case Study

Legal regulations have been in place for more than a quarter of a century to provide for the educational needs of children with physical and learning disabilities. These range from autism to hearing, orthopedic, and visual impairments to mental retardation and traumatic brain injury. IDEA establishes procedures for evaluating and identifying children who are eligible to have an Individualized Education Plan (IEP) in order to understand the requirements and services for meeting the child's unique educational needs. Decisions about individual placements in appropriate school settings (resource room, special classes, inclusion, and the like) are made on the basis of the plan, *not* on the basis of a disability category.

We discuss the IEP here as it represents the format of a well-prepared case study. It provides a general structure for integrating assessments from a variety of sources. The IEP should also be recognized as an aspect of assessment in which every teacher will be involved.

Legislation for Exceptional Students

The IEP must be understood in relation to the Rehabilitation Act (1973), which merged into the Education for All Handicapped Children Act (1975), later amended in 1986. It was followed by IDEA in 1990, with amendments in 1992 and 1997. The most recent legislation, as you know from other chapters in this book, is the No Child Left Behind Act (NCLB) of 2001.

These acts mandate states to provide for the educational needs of children with disabilities. While allowing the states flexibility in specifying standards and procedures, they are held accountable; that is, they must meet standards in order to receive funding. An emphasis in the last version of the act is on reading—every child reading by the third grade—including reading for students whose first language is not English, that is, who are learning English as they enter the educational system. At the center of this legislation is the required assessment of eligibility for a free appropriate public education coupled with the development of an individualized plan for each student who is entitled to this education.

Structure of Individual Education Programs (IEP)

The content of the IEP is structured to provide a sound basis for making educational decisions about the student, consistent with the mandate of the legislation. The preparation of the IEP begins with joint meetings of team members who discuss the assessments of the child and record all findings. On the basis of this record statements are made in sections that parallel legal requirements for summarizing the findings and decisions of the committee regarding:

- The composition of the IEP team
- Assessments of the child's level of performance in educational settings
- Assessments of the child's functioning in the general classroom as it is affected by the disability
- Short-term achievement goals
- Long-term achievement progress
- Educational inclusion and mainstream requirements as well as participation with other children with disabilities
- Criteria and objectives for necessary educational and support services

To meet the legal requirements, the IEP summarizes findings regarding an eligible child on a number of considerations, including the following: assessments of the child's level of performance in an educational setting; instructional expectations based on assessment of needs and capabilities; special educational services to be provided; ways of obtaining evidence that the instructional objectives are being achieved; and schedules for initiation of services, duration, and assessments.

A summary of these findings is then made in the recommended format as shown for the case study of Curt, described as a ninth-grade low achiever who is poorly motivated and has a disciplinary problem. Curt is characterized as a discouraged, frustrated student with learning disabilities, particularly in language arts (Bateman & Linden, 1998, p. 126). The completed summary based on the team's discussion of Curt's diagnosis is shown in Table 13.4.

A successful IEP (for our purposes here, the case study) presents all facts about the student and considers the available services for meeting the student needs. By understanding the placement of students and the provisions of special services you will come to understand the assessments involved for planning instruction for other students. Planning programs for children with disabilities directs attention to their amenability to profit from alternative forms of instruction. Conversely, alternative forms of assessment available for traditional students direct attention to their usefulness in assessments of diverse children, children with disabilities, and other children with special needs. Beginning with planning for meeting the unique needs of individual students and ending with the evaluation of the services recommended, the IEP highlights the potential of integrating assessment information for general educational planning.

Table 13.4. Example of an Individualized Education Program for Curt (student)

Unique Educational Needs, Characteristics, and Present Levels of Performance (PLOPs) (including how the disability affects the student's ability to progress in the general curriculum)	Special Education, Related Services, Supplemental Aids and Services, Assistive Technology, Program Modifications, Support for Personnel (including frequency, duration, and location)	Measurable Annual Goals and Short-Term Objectives or Benchmarks • To enable student to participate in the general curriculum • To meet other needs resulting from the disability (including how to progress toward goals will be measured)
Present Level of Social Skills: Curt lashes out violently when not able to complete work, uses profanity, and refuses to follow further directions from adults. Social Needs: • To learn anger management skills, especially regarding swearing • To learn to comply with requests	1. Teacher and/or counselor consult with behavior specialist regarding techniques and programs for teaching skills, especially anger management. 2. Provide anger management instruction to Curt. Services 3 times/week, 30 minutes. 3. Establish a peer group which involves role playing, etc., so Curt can see positive role models and practice newly learned anger management skills. Services 2 times/week, 30 minutes. 4. Develop a behavioral plan for Curt that gives him responsibility for charting his own behavior. 5. Provide a teacher or some other adult mentor to spend time with Curt (talking, game playing, physical activity, etc.). Services 2 times/week, 30 minutes. 6. Provide training for the mentor regarding Curt's needs/goals.	*Goal:* During the last quarter of the academic year, Curt will have 2 or fewer detentions for any reason. Obj. 1: At the end of the 1st quarter, Curt will have had 10 or fewer detentions. Obj. 2: At the end of the 2nd quarter, Curt will have had 7 or fewer detentions. Obj. 3: At the end of the 3rd quarter, Curt will have had 4 or fewer detentions. *Goal:* Curt will manage his behavior and language in a reasonably acceptable manner as reported by faculty and peers. Obj. 1: At 2 weeks, when asked at the end of class if Curt's behavior and language were acceptable, 3 out of 6 teachers will say "acceptable." Obj. 2: At 6 weeks, asked the same question, 4 out of 6 teachers will say "acceptable." Obj. 3: At 12 weeks, asked the same question, 6 out of 6 teachers will say "acceptable."

Unique Educational Needs, Characteristics, and Present Levels of Performance (PLOPs) (including how the disability affects the student's ability to progress in the general curriculum)	Special Education, Related Services, Supplemental Aids and Services, Assistive Technology, Program Modifications, Support for Personnel (including frequency, duration, and location)	Measurable Annual Goals and Short-Term Objectives or Benchmarks • To enable student to participate in the general curriculum • To meet other needs resulting from the disability (including how to progress toward goals will be measured)

Study Skills/Organizational Needs:
• How to read text
• Note taking
• How to study notes
• Memory work
• Be prepared for class, with materials
• Lengthen and improve attention span and on-task behavior
 	
Present Level:
Curt currently lacks skill in all these areas.
	1. Speech/language therapist, resource room teacher, and content area teachers will provide Curt with direct and specific teaching of study skills, i.e.,
	  • Note taking from lectures
	  • Note taking while reading text
	  • How to study notes for a test
	  • Memorization hints
	  • Strategies for reading text to retain information
	2. Assign a "study buddy" for Curt in each content-area class.
	3. Prepare a motivation system for Curt to be prepared for class with all necessary materials.
	4. Develop a motivational plan to encourage Curt to lengthen his attention span and time on task.
	5. Provide aid to monitor on-task behaviors in first month or so of plan and teach Curt self-monitoring techniques.
	6. Provide motivational system and self-recording for completion of academic tasks in each class.
		Goal: At the end of the academic year, Curt will have better grades and, by his own report, will have learned new study skills.
		
		Obj. 1: Given a 20–30 min. lecture/oral lesson, Curt will take appropriate notes as judged by that teacher.
		
		Obj. 2: Given 10–15 pp. of text to read, Curt will employ an appropriate strategy for retaining info—i.e., mapping, webbing, outlining, notes, etc.—as judged by the teacher.
		
		Obj. 3: Given notes to study for a test, Curt will do so successfully as evidenced by his test score.
		
		Goal: Curt will improve his on-task behavior from 37% to 80% as measured by a qualified observer at year's end.
		
		Obj. 1: By 1 month, Curt's on-task behavior will increase to 45%.
		
		Obj. 2: By 3 months, Curt's on-task behavior will increase to 60%.
		
		Obj. 3: By 6 months, Curt's on-task behavior will increase to 80% and maintain or improve until end of year.

(continued)

Table 13.4. (continued)

Unique Educational Needs, Characteristics, and Present Levels of Performance (PLOPs) (including how the disability affects the student's ability to progress in the general curriculum)	Special Education, Related Services, Supplemental Aids and Services, Assistive Technology, Program Modifications, Support for Personnel (including frequency, duration, and location)	Measurable Annual Goals and Short-Term Objectives or Benchmarks • To enable student to participate in the general curriculum • To meet other needs resulting from the disability (including how to progress toward goals will be measured)
Academic Needs/Written Language: Curt needs strong remedial help in spelling, punctuation, and usage. Present Level: Curt is approximately 2 grade levels behind his peers in these skills.	7. Provide direct instruction in written language skills (punctuation, capitalization, usage, spelling) by using a highly structured, well-sequenced program. Services provided in small groups of no more than four students in the resource room, 50 minutes/day. 8. Build in continuous and cumulative review to help with short-term rote memory difficulty. 9. Develop a list of commonly used words in student writing (or use one of many published lists) for Curt's spelling program.	*Goal:* Within one academic year, Curt will improve his written language skills by 1.5 or 2 full grade levels. Obj. 1: Given 10 sentences of diction at his current level of instruction, Curt will punctuate and capitalize with 90% accuracy (checked at the end of each unit taught). Obj. 2: Given 30 sentences with choices of usage at his current instructional level, Curt will perform with 90% accuracy. Obj. 3: Given a list of 150 commonly used words in writing, Curt will spell with 90% accuracy.

Source: From Bateman and Linden (1998, Figure 29a, b, and c, Curt. pp. 127–129).

■ Summary

Assessment in recent years has developed a collective system of unique measures that go beyond the usual single-trait measures. They encourage the intertwining of measures with curriculum, emphasizing the importance of adapting instruction and the curriculum to individual differences. Beyond measures of general achievement, there now is concern with specific assessments of understanding underlying the acquisition of content and skills.

Similarly, multiple-trait theories are being considered as supplementing traditional trait theories, as exemplified by multiple intelligences. How individuals learn and what their inclinations are toward ways of learning are coming to the forefront as considerations in designing and delivering instruction as well as adapting to individual differences.

In these endeavors the format of assessment is an important consideration. We have illustrated several different formats that teachers might consider in developing assessments. Some of these will appear in reports that might be shared in committees dealing with individual educational plans or other diagnostic summaries. Among these formats are graphic displays, rating scales, and case studies.

Some theories extend the measurement of a single-score view of intelligence to incorporate multiple intelligences and affective components known as learning styles. Other plans are based on systems of coupling assessment and instruction.

RTI is a system of assessment coupled with instruction for adapting to the needs of children with disabilities. Central to the implementation of this system is the base of quality evidence-based instruction. The assessment consists of the student's ability to succeed with that instruction. If not, then the student is assigned intensive remedial instruction.

Dynamic assessment is similar. It identifies the Zone of Proximal Development, focuses on feedback and guidance in areas where students are deficient, and is directed to promote change in the students' potential for learning.

Legislative efforts have brought into play a variety of procedures for integrating measures of individual differences in making full assessments through case studies. In these efforts both standardized and authentic measures are used. Not only are tests adapted and employed at all levels and for a variety of purposes, but the decisions based on the test are made by teachers and panels who use interview data, observation in work and play, portfolios, and summative evaluations.

Many of the recent innovations have involved case studies of students put to the service of interventions used for remedial purposes. IEPs and RTIs are based on multiple sources of assessment. They aid in the diagnosis of students at risk. The resulting diagnoses facilitate the selection of instructional interventions that directly target learning weaknesses identified in the assessment data. In all of these settings, the importance of evidence-based, quality-driven instruction integrated with similarly characterized assessments is highlighted.

■ References

Adelman, H. S., & Taylor, L. (2006). *The school leader's guide to student learning supports: New directions for addressing barriers to learning.* Thousand Oaks, CA: Corwin Press.

Angelo, T. A., & Cross, K. P. (1993). *Classroom assessment techniques: A handbook for college teachers.* San Francisco: Jossey-Bass.

Bateman, B. D., & Linden, M. A. (1998). *Better IEPs: How to develop legally correct and educationally useful programs* (3rd ed.) Longmont, CO: Sopris West.

Bransford, J. D. (1979). *Human cognition: Learning, understanding, and remembering.* Belmont, CA: Wadsworth.

Campione, J. D., & Brown, A. L. (1987). Linking dynamic assessment with school achievement. In C. S. Lidz (Ed.), *Dynamic assessment: An interactional approach to evaluating learning potential* (pp. 82–115). New York: Guilford Press.

Darling-Hammond, L., & Bransford, J. D. (Eds.). (2005). *Preparing teachers for a changing world: What teachers should learn and be able to do.* San Francisco: Jossey-Bass.

Day, J. D., Engelhardt, J. L., Maxwell, S. E., & Bolig, E. E. (1997). Comparison of static and dynamic assessment procedures and their relation to independent performance. *Journal of Educational Psychology, 89*(2), 358–368.

Duncan, T. G., & McKeachie, W. J. (2005). The making of the Motivated Strategies for Learning Questionnaire. *Educational Psychologist, 40*(2), 117–128.

Dunn, R., & Dunn, K. (1978). *Teaching students through their individual learning styles: A practical approach.* Reston, VA: Reston Publishing.

Fuchs, L., & Fuchs, D. (2009). *Manual: Using curriculum-based measurements in Response-to-Intervention frameworks. Introduction to using CBM.* Washington, DC: National Center on Student Progress.

Gardner, H. (1983). *Frames of mind: The theory of multiple intelligences.* New York: Basic Books.

Gardner, H. (1991). *The unschooled mind: How children think and schools should teach.* New York: Basic Books.

Gardner, H. (1993). *Multiple intelligences: The theory in practice.* New York: Basic Books.

Gardner, H. (1999). *Intelligence reframed: Multiple intelligences for the 21st Century.* New York: Basic Books.

Gardner, H., & Hatch, T. (1989). Multiple intelligences go to school. *Educational Researcher, 18*(8), 4–10.

Gersten, R., Compton, D., Connor, C. M., Dimino, J., Santoro, L., Linan-Thompson, S., et al. (2008). *Assisting students struggling with reading: Response to Intervention and multi-tier intervention for reading in the primary grades.* Washington, DC: National Center for Education Evaluation and Regional Assistance, Institute of Education Sciences, U.S. Department of Education.

Hativa, N., & Goodyear, P. (Eds.). (2002). *Teacher thinking, beliefs and knowledge in higher education*. New York: Springer.

Jenkins, J. J. (1978). Four points to remember: A tetrahedral model of memory experiments. In L. S. Cermak & F. I. M. Craik (Eds.), *Levels of processing and human memory*. Hillsdale, NJ: Lawrence Erlbaum Associates.

Johnson, T. D., & Louis, D. R. (1987). *Literacy through literature*. London: Methuen.

Okagaki, L. (2001). Triarchic model of minority children's school achievement. *Educational Psychologist, 36*(1), 9–20.

Olson, L. (1988). Children flourish here: 8 teachers and a theory changed a school world. *Education Week, 18*(1), 18–19.

Palinscar, A. S., Brown, A. L., & Campione, J. D. (1991). Dynamic assessment. In H. L. Swanson (Ed.), *Handbook on the assessment of learning disabilities: Theory, research and practice* (pp. 75–94). Austin, TX: Pro-Ed.

Pintrich, P. R., & Schrauben, B. (1992). Student's motivational beliefs and their cognitive engagement in academic tasks. In D. Schunk & J. Meece (Eds.), *Students' perceptions in the classroom: Causes and consequences* (pp. 149–183). Hillsdale, NJ: Lawerence Erlbaum Associates.

Pintrich, P. R., Smith, D. A. F., Garcia, T., & McKeachie, W. J. (1991). *A manual for the use of the Motivated Strategies for Learning Questionnaire (MSLQ)*. Ann Arbor, MI: National Center for Research to Improve Postsecondary Teaching and Learning.

Renaissance Learning. (2009). *Making RTI work: A practical guide to using data for a successful "response to intervention" program*. Wisconsin Rapids, WI: Author.

Schunk, D. H. (2005). Self-regulated learning: The educational legacy of Paul R. Pintrich. *Educational Psychologist, 40*(2), 85–94.

Sinatra, R. (2000). Teaching learners to think, read, and write more effectively in content subjects. *The Clearing House, 73*(5), 266–273.

Smith, D. (2004). Practical classroom strategies that work: Using sociograms as a behaviour management tool. Retrieved August 31, 2005, from http://aase.edu.au/2004_conf_papers/practica%20classroom%20strategies%20that%20work%20-%20D.pdf.

Smith, M. K. (2002, January 28). Howard Gardner and multiple intelligences. *The Encyclopedia of Informal Education*. Retrieved August 30, 2005, from www.infed.org/thinkers/gardner.htm.

Stepanek, J. (2008). RTI: Tiered instruction goes mainstream. *Response to Intervention: An Overview*. Retrieved June 2, 2009, from www.nwrel.org/nwedu/14-01/features/rti.php.

Sternberg, R. J. (2007). *Wisdom, intelligence, and creativity synthesized*. New York: Cambridge University Press.

Sternberg, R. J., & Grigorenko, E. L. (2002). *Dynamic testing: The nature and measurement of learning potential*. Cambridge, MA: Cambridge University Press.

Vygotsky, L. S. (1978). *Mind in society: The development of the higher psychological processes.* Cambridge, MA: Harvard University Press.

Walsh's Classroom Sociometrics. (2004). Classroom sociometrics. Retrieved August 30, 2005, from www.classroomsociometrics .com.

Zohar, A. (2004). *Higher order students' thinking in science classrooms: Students' learning and teacher's professional development.* New York: Springer/Kluwer Academic Publishers.

CHAPTER 14

High-Stakes Testing: Policy and Accountability

A SSESSMENT AFFECTS EDUCATION beyond its use in the classroom. So, today, it is critical for teachers to know about the assessments that are currently known collectively as *high-stakes testing*. They comprise a tool for federal and state governments to judge educational accountability. Through educational policy, legislation, and standards, they have a widespread influence on local school curricula[1] in which you play important roles.

High-stakes testing is part of a more comprehensive process sometimes referred to as *standards-based school reform*. This process is aimed at making sure that students are prepared as well as we expect them to be—preparation being defined in terms of fundamental knowledge, understanding, and performance proficiency in the content areas. The general idea, simply, is to use the results of assessment for improving education. As many critics indicate (e.g., see Popham, 2002), although accountability programs may fail in their mission, they are intended to achieve excellent instruction (through feedback they provide) that facilitates learning.

In the following sections, it will be seen that these assessments can provide useful bases for formative assessment of instruction; they provide data for examining the effects of

---

1. The NAEP and NCLB described in this chapter are illustrations of assessments and policies. The information was selected around assessment frameworks of importance to teachers. Details of importance to other areas such as curriculum development and teacher training will need reference to other sources. The presentation here was based on information in place at the time of publication. Because the specifics are bound to change rapidly, individuals needing specific information for planning, funding, and the like should seek information online or from legal federal and state documents.

potentially influential variables (such as instruction or student characteristics) through student achievement and performance.

Large-scale, standardized tests have distinctly different purposes than do classroom tests. Widely used, standardized tests, including national and state assessments, are intended to answer broad policy questions. Within that framework, the products are constrained in their potential use and interpretation of results (Pelligrino, Chudowsky, & Glaser, 2001) to serving the broader standards.

However, because of their importance they have an effect on what goes on in the school, exerting an effect on what teachers do. They are externally designed to answer questions from a distance, with minimal interference in the daily activity of the school. The measures meet stringent technical requirements of good measures and are useable with students having widely differing characteristics and with students who attend schools under widely different circumstances (such as regions of the United States).

The very characteristics that make externally administered tests uniquely useable for policy purposes can also serve teachers in making instructional decisions. Underlying this application is the need for understanding: the purpose and context in which the test is to be used; how the test is designed and tailored to meet those purposes; the bases for standardizing the test, including administration of the tests; and the standards used for technical accuracy in both the content and the psychometric characteristics of the test. Although the content of standardized tests is relatively focused on the policy objectives for which the tests are to serve, it is still adaptable to various regions where they may be administered. To meet the special populations that exist across states, some tests are constructed under state auspices. Consequently, because policy and classroom tests serve different purposes, statewide tests must, obviously, still differ in their characteristics from classroom tests.

■ An Overview

The high-stakes tests are represented in standardized statewide reading, math, and science comprehensive tests (this may be referred to, in your state, as the XCAT—where X is a symbol for the state in which the measure is used). Teachers, parents, and other stakeholders are familiar with these tests not only through communication with the school but through the media, which report on them frequently. Schools, teachers, students, and parents know the test through direct involvement in preparing students for the examination, explaining its purpose, making interpretations of the tests, and reporting outcomes to stakeholders.

High-stakes assessments are most often known through testing associated with the No Child Left Behind (NCLB) Act, a federally mandated program administered through the statewide comprehensive tests. The tests are required of all students in the third to 10th grades. They are called "high-stakes" because of their implications for accountability of educational programs and personnel involved. The result for students, for example, is that they must pass the test at one grade level (e.g., the third-grade level) if they are to be admitted to the next grade (e.g., the fourth grade). Similarly, students are required to perform successfully on tests in order to graduate from high school. The performance of a school on statewide tests may determine whether the school is to receive or will be denied funding for its programs.

Students whose primary language is a language other than English (students with limited English proficiency and students with learning disabilities) are included when schools are graded on the examination. These students, too, must pass the test if they are to advance to the next grade or are to graduate if they are high school seniors. In recognition of the fact that language can be an important barrier to successful performance, the law provides that accommodations must be made in administration of the tests to these students. Any accommodation (Chapter 16 is devoted to the topic of accommodations) must simply remove a barrier that does not provide an advantage over other students in task-related material. But, out of fairness to schools, where funding is based on ratings of school performance, the scores need not be included in the school ratings until certain criteria (e.g., students having taken the test twice or have been at the school fewer than two years) have been reached.

Professionals concerned with the national and statewide tests, at any level, must recognize the difficulties encountered by English for students who are speakers of other languages (ESOL) and make compensations for them. For example, long comprehensive examinations take more time for translation by students with another language than English. In accommodating for this outcome, schools not only use accommodations during testing, but may attempt to build test-taking skills through after-school tutorial sessions with students, workshops to provide parents with ways of helping their children, and informing parents of the nature of the test and test-related information in both English and the primary language used in the home (e.g., Spanish, Chinese, Creole, and so on).

In line with requirements for accommodations, teachers must learn how to deal with students with other languages, to understand their thinking. They must learn to work with students by complementing their instruction with visual aids, by teaching students to employ writing skills in response to prompts for essays, or by encouraging students to work individually and in cooperation with others who speak their native language. They may also find they are inadvertently introducing content-related terms that may not be familiar to their students.

You will note that the characteristics of the test itself—what it measures, its format, and how it is scored—do not make it a "high-stakes" test. The label *high-stakes* is derived from the way the test is used, its interpretation, and any policies associated with it: The rewards and sanctions are based on ratings of the school's performance. Test scores are graded from A to F according to the performance of students on the exam. National or state funds are awarded to schools based on the grade the school receives. Because scoring and grading are done at remote sites, the interpretation of the scores depends on the school's (stakeholders', from state officials' to students') understanding of the standards used, what the test is measuring, and how the results are to be used, as well as the political (policy and legislation) and social contexts (diversity, geography, districts, and so on). When the limitations of the tests are misunderstood or improperly conveyed the tests may be open to controversy or misused.

■ Policy and Accountability

Policy, in general terms, is composed of a set of guidelines and principles that govern decision making. As can be seen in Figure 14.1, policy may include definitions of the issue, outcomes to be achieved, ways of dealing with the issue to achieve the outcomes, ways of identifying whether the outcomes have been achieved, and rewards or sanctions for achievement or lack of achievement.

Accountability

Specific assessment criteria are established for accountability to determine whether the policy is working as intended. Usually these criteria are embodied in policies for statewide standardized tests. There are rewards for meeting the criteria and sanctions for not meeting them, as shown in Figure 14.1. All personnel have much at stake when tests are used to hold them

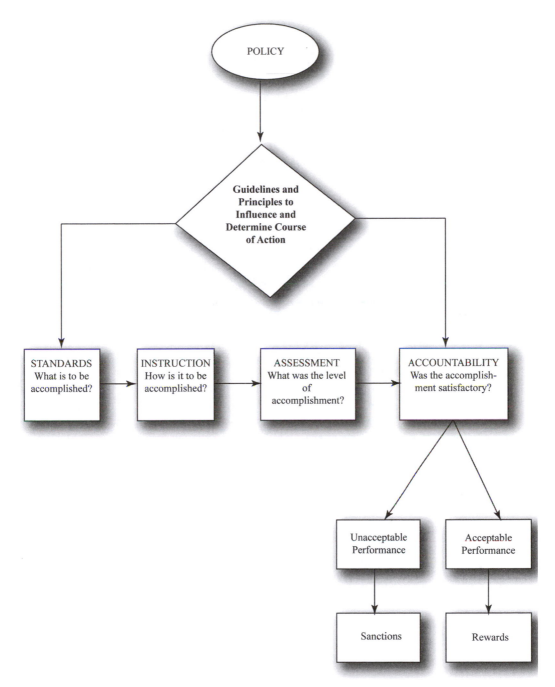

Figure 14.1. Educational policy in accountability.

accountable for their apparent successes and failures in closing the achievement gap. In addressing accountability, by definition, we find such examples as "the purpose of NCLB is to close the achievement gap and raise standards of student academic proficiency," "the policy mandates that schools . . . [must] ensure all students to perform at grade level," "the methods [for measuring grade level proficiency are determined] by states" and, "consequences of the policy [should] align theoretically with established educational best practice" (Davies, 2007, p. 2).

High Stakes

You already know, through your own experience as a student or teacher, a good deal about the importance of what it means to be involved in high-stakes testing. If you received public education in a state where comprehensive examinations are given regularly, you know that a school may have received a letter grade from A to F (you might have checked the daily newspaper, watched for radio or TV newscasts, or seen the bulletin board on the school lawn for reports of a grade received by a school). Students in those schools are quite aware of the importance of the statewide comprehensive examinations and the fact that the school made demands on time and normal general instruction to prepare for the examination. Perhaps parents were also engaged in the process; they may have taken pride if the school earned an A or become alarmed if the school received an F. The grades earned by schools are the subject of media coverage and may be followed by attempts (often misdirected or incompletely understood) to highlight what are thought to be the reasons; to restructure the personnel or curriculum; and to demand resources to improve student achievement on subsequent test administrations. These attempts are made because the stakes were high; schools or districts not only earned praise for success or blame for failure, but might also have received (if they met standards) or been denied (if they didn't meet standards) extra funding.

Stakeholders

Every student, teacher, principal, and school district is involved in educational policy, and all are affected by accountability requirements, whether as the instigator (legislators) or the recipient (schools and students) of the policy. Students are expected to achieve levels of attainment imposed by policy and measured by the tests. Teachers are expected to use high-quality instruction to achieve the desired results. Administrators are expected to hire personnel who can guide the development of curricula that will meet more than minimal standards. School districts are expected to create the proper conditions for achievement and monitor school performance. And the states themselves, through their specific policies and tests, are held accountable for establishing school systems that prepare students to become intelligent users of knowledge and responsible citizens. Everyone has something to gain—or lose.

Intent

The intent is to create change through the promotion of good teaching practices that lead to high student achievement. Accountability standards make it clear that schools cannot be satisfied with simple factual acquisition by students, although such acquisition is recognized as basic to many content areas. Rather, the ultimate aim is to achieve instructional levels that promote understanding, comprehension, application, and creation of new knowledge (invention, creativity, artistry, writing, research).

Education, as an institution, plays a critical part in individual success and makes a major contribution to the success of the democratic process in general. It should come as no surprise, then, that the school is constantly scrutinized and governed to become as effective as possible. Although it is expected that schools will promote high levels of achievement, the decision regarding appropriate instructional methods and curricula is that of the individual school or district (National Assessment Governing Board, 2002b). It is desirable that both the professional psychometrician building national or statewide comprehension tests and teachers building classroom examination are sensitive to the requirements of their constituencies for making meaningful assessments. It might be something as simple as knowing the effects of changing the format of questions or what objectives are measured, for example, revising the format of a question following a laboratory experiment from:

Item 1. "Did you see the green precipitate after you combined the two compounds?"

which requires only a "yes" or "no" answer, to:

Item 2. "Describe your observations of what happened when you combined the two compounds."

Item 3. "What conclusions can you make from your observations?"

Item 4. "In technical terms, describe the experiment and its outcome."

These transformed questions make different cognitive demands in answering the test item and thus measure quite different outcomes. The first example (Item 1) requires only a confirmation of what might have occurred; it can even prompt an answer based on understanding that would otherwise have been neglected in knowledge about chemical reactions. The remaining questions (Items 2–4) require more technically sophisticated observation as well as application and understanding of chemical reactions.

In this regard, professional standards are under continual scrutiny and revision by relevant professional groups including the National Academy of Sciences, the National Assessment of Educational Progress, and the National Council of Teachers of Mathematics. In playing increasingly influential roles in achieving valid outcomes of high-stakes tests, these organizations are as essential to promoting appropriate test use as are the legal guides of policymakers.

Policy in High-Stakes Testing

The policies associated with educational accountability funnel down from the federal or state government as legislative mandates for action. The key elements (Abrams & Madaus, 2003; Hamilton, Stecher, & Klein, 2002) of the educational policies behind high-stakes testing are:

- *Standards* for the knowledge, ideas, understandings, and application skills in the curriculum at all levels
- *Measures* (tests, rubrics, performance) of student achievement, status, from which progress in reaching objectives for the knowledge base and skills may be inferred
- *Targeted objectives* performance targets or proficiency categories that specify grade level expectations regarding achievement levels: quality (basic, proficient, advanced); conceptual understanding (factual reasoning, problem solving, reasoning and proof, making connections, and representation); and performance (applications, transfer, skill development) (Goldsmith & Mark, 1999)
- *Intrinsic and extrinsic incentives* in all motivational categories, including *sanctions for failing* to achieve high scores on state or national tests and *rewards for succeeding* in achieving high scores

For a better idea of how these elements all come into play, we examine an important development in educational policy: the National Assessment of Educational Progress (NAEP).

■ Assessment for Educational Policy and Accountability: The National Assessment of Educational Progress

Accountability in education has been around for a number of years in one form or another. We won't attempt a complete history, but it is important to recognize the recent thrusts that emphasize assessment. Important in initiating this thrust was the establishment of a national assessment program based on a uniform standardized measure that was administered nationally. The results were summarized a few years later in a report describing the gradual erosion of the educational institutions, along with implications and recommendations for remedial actions. Following this report were legislative actions affecting education in all of the states.

A National Testing Program: The NAEP

Legislative action establishing the National Assessment of Educational Progress (NAEP) (Raju, Pellegrino, Bertenthal, Mitchell, & Jones, 2000) was a milestone in nationwide assessment of educational programs. It is sometimes referred to as the "nation's report card" of student achievement and school accomplishment. *Although we begin our discussion of high-stakes tests with the NAEP, it is* not *itself an assessment aimed at accountability or high stakes.* We describe it here, with the help of the *NAEP Guide* (Ballator, 1996), because it shares with high-stakes tests the development and use of a *standardized* formal test program for providing data about the national educational system. Although schools and districts decide on their own to participate in the NAEP program, all schools that receive Title 1 funding must participate in the program. But keep in mind our earlier comment to the effect that the term *high stakes* is not a characteristic of a specific test, but, rather, is a label attached to the way the test is used; in principle, *any* test can be a high-stakes test if it is used as a basis for sanctions. Thus, although the NAEP is a source of data used to corroborate the results of statewide testing program, the results are not the basis for decisions about school accountability.

The NAEP is important for teachers to know about because it contributes to an understanding of the achievement of a national representation of students in public and private schools. Continuing assessment show trends in what American students know and can do in various subject areas over time. NAEP assessments are conducted at scheduled, periodic intervals in grades 4, 8, and 12 in mathematics, reading, science, writing, the arts, civics, economics, geography, and U.S. history. A sample item from an early form of the test is displayed in Theory to Practice Box 14.1.

Establishing the Assessment Program

Legislative action responsible for the NAEP school assessment program occurred in the 1960s. The mandate was for continual internal and external appraisal of the nation's educational programs to provide policymakers and educators with information related to the status of education throughout the United States.

Theory to Practice Box 14.1
WHAT IS THE TEST LIKE? AN ITEM FROM THE NAEP EXAM FOR GRADE 4

Subject: History
Grade: 4
Difficulty level: Medium
Item base: A house divided against itself cannot stand. I believe this government cannot endure permanently half slave and half free. I do not expect the Union to be dissolved—I do not expect the house to fall—but I do expect it will cease to be divided.

—Abraham Lincoln, 1858

Question: What did Abraham Lincoln mean in this speech?
 a. The South should be allowed to separate from the United States. (17%)
 b. The government should support slavery in the South. (15%)
 c. Sometime in the future slavery would disappear from the United States. (46%)*
 d. Americans would not be willing to fight a war over slavery. (19%)
 Omitted (3%)

*Correct alternative. The percentages following each alternative are percentage of all students taking the test who chose that alternative. The average scale score on the entire exam of students who chose (c) was 224—the upper boundary of *basic* achievement. Those who chose other alternatives or who omitted the item had scale scores on the entire exam below 224 but higher than 195 (except for the 3 percent who omitted the item; their average scale score was 194).

Source: NAEP (2006).

The NAEP tests are administered nationally to thousands of students each year. Because the data in specific subject-matter areas are collected in cycles of every four or five years, they reflect large-scale trends in student performance. Norms are based on the entire sample but are also developed by disaggregation (separation of data according to levels of a variable such as gender or ethnicity) of results in order to provide useful bases (norms) for comparison of students with different demographic and geographic characteristics. The norms are based on statistically selected national samples designed to provide a national overview of U.S. student achievement over time (Heubert & Hauser, 1999).

A concerted effort is made to maintain the integrity and utility of the program for evaluating student progress in reading, science, mathematics, computer skills, and other school areas. The administrative procedures are continually reviewed and criticized by external agencies to assure policy makers they receive the best available evidence regarding the methods employed and the ways the tests are implemented. Standards are under constant review by the profession, test content is examined to see that it corresponds to the standards, and items are constructed according to sound scientific principles of assessment.

Monitoring the Policy

The National Assessment Governing Board (NAGB) sets the policy for the NAEP (NAGB, 2002a, 2002b). We cite the responsibilities of the NAGB because they represent requirements in the development of any viable test, whether developed by corporations or by the state for their comprehensive examinations serving the NCLB requirements, adding to your knowledge of test construction. Thus, you will note that the bases of these responsibilities are embedded in the many principles of good assessment development described in previous chapters. The NAGB (2002b) responsibilities include:

- Select subject areas to be assessed
- Set student achievement levels appropriate to the age group to be tested
- Develop a plan stating assessment objectives and test specifications
- Developing a process for the review of the assessment
- Design the assessment methodology to be used
- Develop guidelines for reporting (NAEP) results

- Develop standards and procedures for making comparisons (interstate, regional, and national)
- Determine the appropriateness of all assessment items and ensure that the assessment items are free from bias
- Plan for taking action for continual improvement of the form, content, use, and reporting of results

(Responsibilities cited were taken, with slight modification, from statements by the National Assessment Governing Board retrieved March 19, 2008, from www.nagb.org/.)

Determining Achievement Levels: Policy Support

The NAEP results are divided into three categories: *basic*, *proficient*, and *advanced*. These items and scale (standardized) scores are intended to describe how well students' actual achievement matches each of the achievement levels. The general definitions of the three levels are displayed in Table 14.1, and examples of the ways these are implemented for achievement in history are shown in Text Box 14.1. The three achievement levels apply to each grade (grades 4, 8, and 12) assessed by NAEP.

In practice, scale scores are used to indicate the lowest score for a subject-matter area. An example of the application of these levels for the history portion of the test appears in the Text Box 14.1 for fourth-grade students. This example enables you to see how the three achievement levels are described *within* a grade, in this case grade 4. A subsection of Text Box 14.1 provides an illustration that will allow you to compare the criteria for the basic level *across* grades 4, 8, and 12.

The objective of the NAEP goes beyond the accumulation or averaging of test scores. The data are made available to researchers who examine the relation of both school and student variables to performance. For example, the results of the

Table 14.1. Achievement-Level Policy Definitions

Basic	*Partial mastery* of prerequisite knowledge and skills that is fundamental for proficient work at each grade.
Proficient	*Solid academic performance* for each grade assessed. Students reaching this level have demonstrated competency over challenging subject matter, including subject-matter knowledge, application of such knowledge to real-world situations, and analytical skills appropriate to the subject matter.
Advanced	Superior performance.

Source: IES National Center for Educational Statistics. Mathematics: The NAEP Mathematics Achievement Levels by Grade (Grades 4, 8, 12). Retrieved May 1, 2008, from http://nces.ed.gov/nationsreportcard/mathematics/achieveall.asp.

Text Box 14.1 Descriptions of NAEP U.S. History Achievement Levels for Grade 4

Basic (Scale Score 195)*

Fourth-grade students performing at the **Basic level** should be able to identify and describe a few of the most familiar people, places, events, ideas, and documents in American history. They should be able to explain the reasons for celebrating most national holidays, have some familiarity with the geography of their own state and the United States, and be able to express in writing a few ideas about a familiar theme in American history.

Proficient (Scale Score 243)

Fourth-grade students performing at the **Proficient level** should be able to identify, describe, and comment on the significance of many historical people, places, ideas, events, and documents. They should interpret information from a variety of sources, including texts, maps, pictures, and timelines. They should be able to construct a simple timeline from data. These students should recognize the role of invention and technological change in history. They should also recognize the ways in which geographic and environmental factors have influenced life and work.

Advanced (Scale Score 276)

Fourth-grade students performing at the **Advanced level** should have a beginning understanding of the relationship between people, places, ideas, events, and documents. They should know where to look for information, including reference books, maps, local museums, interviews with family and neighbors, and other sources. They should be able to use historical themes to organize and interpret historical topics, and to incorporate insights from beyond the classroom into their understanding of history. These students should understand and explain the role of invention and technological change in history. They should also understand and explain the ways in which geographic and environmental factors have influenced life and work.

Basic Score Criteria for Advanced Grades

For comparison with the fourth grade the scores and standards for *Grades 8 and 12* are presented. Notice the changes in the statements of expectations for performance.

Descriptions of NAEP U.S. History Basic Achievement Levels for Grade 8 (252)

Eighth grade students performing at the Basic level should be able to identify and place in context a range of historical people, places, events, ideas, and documents.

(continued)

Text Box 14.1 (*Continued*)

They should be able to distinguish between primary and secondary sources. They should have a beginning understanding of the diversity of the American people and the ways in which people from a wide variety of national and cultural heritages have become part of a single nation. Keep in mind that the scale scores above are for fourth grade students. *Eighth grade* students, at the Basic level, should also have a beginning understanding of the fundamental political ideas and institutions of American life and their historical origins. They should be able to explain the significance of some major historical events which brings the lowest scale score in this category to 252 for *eighth grade* students. Students with scale scores below 252 are simply described as "below basic performance."

Descriptions of NAEP U.S. History Basic Achievement Level for *Grade 12* (294)

Twelfth-grade students performing at the Basic level should be able to identify the significance of many people, places, events, dates, ideas, and documents in U.S. history. They should also recognize the importance of unity and diversity in the social and cultural history of the United States, and an awareness of American's changing relationships with the rest of the world. They should have a sense of continuity and change in history and be able to relate relevant experience from the past to their understanding of contemporary issues. They should recognize that history is subject to interpretation and should understand the role of evidence in making an historical argument. The lowest score for this category at *Grade 12* is 294.

*The numbers shown in each heading indicate scale (standardized) scores for that grade level.

Source: National Assessment Governing Board (2002b).

tests led to policy and practice in the use of accommodations in testing special groups. Additionally, the investigations have shown, for example, that student performance in a number of areas may be lower than in some other countries or that reading performance has shown a national improvement for grade 4 over the previous testing.

In addition to detailed analyses of performance in subject-matter areas at the district, state, regional, or national level, the data are used by researchers to relate performance differences to available resources (such as reading matter, TVs, or computers) and to such other variables as the manner in which students spend their free time. At the school level, performance outcomes can be related to the curriculum, including its content, the amount of time devoted to various topics, the kind and amount of homework assignments, and the type of instruction or classroom climate.

Influence of the NAEP

The program's influence goes beyond the accumulation of data regarding student performance; it promotes interaction among practitioners (teachers and schools), the community (localities and districts), and the scientific communities (professional researchers) who evaluate the data. The current impact of NAEP on educational practice remains high. By making objective information on student performance available to policy makers at the national, state, and local levels, NAEP is an important part of our nation's evaluation of the condition and progress of education).

Exercise 14.1

We have provided only selected examples of the NAEP test's characteristics. We urge you to visit the website for a broader, more exacting view of the very important NAEP test. Because you will certainly be engaged with it or other standardized tests such as the XCAT (statewide test in your state), examine the test characteristics for the nature of the item formats (we have shown only the multiple-choice format), of the levels of understanding measured (we have shown these for history; look for the representation of the levels in other subjects), of the ways the data are analyzed both for achievement levels and for disaggregation of the data (analysis of subgroups, such as districts and gender), and of the uses of the data made by government officials, and so on.

You may compare the NAEP data with similar data that may appear on state websites for the XCAT used in your state (these may not be readily available for all states, in which case you may wish to access data, if available, for a neighboring or other nearby state).

To begin your search for descriptions of the NAEP test and analysis of data, the URL is http://nces.ed.gov/nationsreport card/itmrls/startsearch.asp. Your instructor may make other assignments in conjunction with this suggestion.

■ Assessment in Policy for Accountability: The No Child Left Behind (NCLB) Legislation

Policy makers use assessment for accountability—the process of holding educators and students responsible for student achievement. In this context, assessment measures, together with statewide standardized tests, help policy makers:

- Set standards and goals
- Monitor educational quality and assign quality grades to schools or districts
- Reward successful practices and allocate financial resources
- Formulate general policy

The Legislation

The No Child Left Behind Act is an illustration of how policy-makers use assessment. The NCLB mandates that all children have a fundamental right to a high-quality education and that they should be proficient in basic learning areas by the academic year 2013–2014. The central focus of NCLB requires states to (a) ensure that highly qualified teachers are in every classroom, (b) use research-based practices as the foundation of instruction, (c) develop tests to assess students so that data-driven decisions become a key component of the educational system, and (d) hold schools accountable for the performance of all students (Yell & Drasgow, 2005).

Such legislation strongly determines the way states get graded for the performance of their schools. The legislation affects assessments of the schools at the local level as well as at the state level, which in turn raises questions about the consequences of such legislation as to its effectiveness. To illustrate the effect of such policies, some views regarding the No Child Left Behind Act are summarized here. They show the potential effect such legislation has on you, as a teacher, regarding how you will assess your students, how you will budget time for assessment, and how your school and you will be affected by the state assessment.

The No Child Left Behind Act

In 1983 the National Commission on Excellence in Education produced the document *A Nation at Risk: The Imperative for Educational Reform*. The report, based on results of the NAEP, advocated (but did not engage in) accountability of schools reflected in stringent educational standards and extensive testing aimed at educational improvement. Standards were to be set for every subject, with careful specification of what students should know at every grade level. *A Nation at Risk* was only one of the first documents of many to be developed for inspiring standards-based reforms during the latter part of the 20th century (Ravitch, 2002).

Relation of the NAEP to NCLB

The No Child Left Behind Act of 2001 required mandatory state participation in biennial reading and mathematics assessments in grade 4 and grade 8. However, the assessment so authorized prohibited its

> use by an agent or agents of the Federal Government to establish, require, or influence the standards, assessments, curriculum, including lesson plans, textbooks, or classroom materials, or instructional practices of States or local educational agencies. (No Child Left Behind Act of 2001, 2002, p. 1)

The following examples of the inclusion of the use of the NAEP in this policy illustrates recognition of the NAEP's impact on educational practice:

- The policy must provide an influence on testing, as it has for decades, by exemplifying high-quality, standards-based reporting, and cutting-edge use of test technology.
- States may look to NAEP when contemplating changes in their own assessment programs without urging from federal agencies, and may even seek technical help from the federal government.
- Teachers may decide to download test questions and data from the NAEP website for use with their students. Curriculum planners may choose to examine NAEP frameworks when updating internal documents about subject-area content coverage. Others who are involved in or concerned about education may look to NAEP for useful information. As a public resource, the NAEP program should be responsive in helping those who, by their own choice, want to make use of NAEP.
- Agents of the federal government may provide data on the association or correlation between achievement on NAEP and instructional variables. They may not disseminate reports about how to teach a particular subject, basing the report on the association between achievement on NAEP and instructional variables.

Since the development of the NAEP and the publication of *The Nation's Report Card*, every state has been concerned with rigorous academic requirements, evidence based on testing, and the consequent implications for accountability within school districts and for teacher certification requirements (Bierlin, 1993). The primary source of federal aid to K–12 education is to be found in the Elementary and Secondary Education Act (ESEA), particularly its Title I, Part A Program of Education for the Disadvantaged, initially enacted in 1965.

Assessments for Accountability

The 1965 ESEA was amended and reauthorized in 2001 by the No Child Left Behind Act. The aim in that amendment was to increase the accountability of public school systems and individual public schools for improving the achievement outcomes of all pupils (K–12) as measured by adequate yearly progress (AYP). The far-reaching programs included instruction for improvement of achievements by disadvantaged, migrant, and LEP students; teacher recruitment and professional development; school practices such as after-school instruction; services for Native Americans; and school organization, including forms of public school choice (charter schools, etc.).

The Role of the States under NCLB

Under the NCLB, states are required to (a) set standards for subject-matter objectives and (b) develop tests to measure the achievement of the standards. States are to select and design assessments of their own choosing. A sample of students in each state is to be assessed annually with the National Assessment of Educational Progress (NAEP) fourth- and eighth-grade assessment in reading and math. While allowing flexibility in implementing means of improving student performance, the act also mandates *evidence-based* accountability. When large discrepancies are found between the results of statewide tests and the NAEP, the state is required to reexamine its standards and tests.

Accountability and Funding

The act aimed at improving achievements of America's most disadvantaged students, improving the teaching and learning of children in high-poverty schools, and enabling those children to meet challenging state academic content and performance standards. The allocation of funds by the federal government is in accordance with accountability, measured against such standards as the following:

Students in all groups (ethnic, poverty, language differences) must:

- Meet high standards consistent with clear, measurable goals focused on basic skills and essential knowledge.
- Meet the stated goals as reflected in the annual state assessments in math and reading in grades 3–8.
- Demonstrate continuous improvement on the annual assessments.

The law states that schools failing to make sufficient progress should receive special assistance. Further, students should not be forced to attend persistently failing schools, and they must at some point be freed to attend adequate schools. The implementation of sanctions and rewards is the mechanism for holding districts and schools accountable for improving academic achievement, as shown in these statements, based on the text of the act:

- States that establish a comprehensive reading program anchored in scientific research from kindergarten to second grade will be eligible for grants under a new Reading First initiative.
- States participating in the Reading First program will have the option to receive funding from a new Early Reading First program to implement research-based prereading methods in preschool programs, including Head Start centers.
- Each state must establish instructional plans that result in all students achieving proficiency in reading and math by the year 2014. In the course of educational improvement, each state established its own standards and means of assessment.

Uses of Statewide Tests by Stakeholders

Ideally, the construction of tests by professionals is guided by standards for subject-matter content associated with levels of accomplishment. The standards are uniformly applied across the state, providing a uniform, stable basis for comparison of schools and their achievements. Also, the tests are constructed with technical accuracy to yield tests with evidence-based reliability and validity.

How Teachers Can Use the Test Results

The test results can assist teachers by providing information about the effectiveness of their methods and curricula. The results are particularly useful for providing information about alignment with state standards. Poor performance may imply the need for changes in teaching objectives, content, or instructional methods. The results for individual students provide the opportunity for diagnostic analysis and potential or alternative interventions.

How Principals Can Use the Test Results

The results of accountability assessments can help principals by providing information about the performance of teachers through the progress made by their students. The test information can also be useful in the development of school programs and curricula and in the planning of in-service workshops and seminars for professional development of teachers. Test outcomes can alert principals to seek additional resources required for good instruction.

Overall, test results for schools have the potential of showing principals how their school is performing relative to all others, not only as a whole, but in terms of differentiated groups represented in the student body and in relation to specific subject-matter areas. Data on these matters can help principals enhance what the school is doing well and address weakness in student performance levels, curricular opportunities, or available resources.

How Parents Can Use the Test Results

Parents can use the information from accountability assessments to bolster the community's contributions to school improvement. In particular, statewide assessments help parents know how to ask the right questions. Parents can ask such questions as:

• How do the results of statewide assessment affect our students, our teachers, and the school?
• What do the results mean for the school and school district?
• How does the faculty review the results of the assessment?
• Are the state standards well known by teachers and students?
• What have the assessments revealed about the school's weaknesses and strengths?

- What is being done in curriculum development and in instruction to assure that students are learning?
- How do the results of the statewide testing programs affect actions taken for professional development, curriculum development, selection of instructional resources and materials, and opportunities for learning in the content areas?

Accountability: Rewards and Sanctions—Pros and Cons

Accountability is accomplished by the use of tangible and intangible rewards and sanctions. An illustration from an explicit governing statement in Title 1 is presented in Text Box 14.2. (It should be noted that some of the points in this summary have been made in other contexts within this chapter.)

Avoiding the Use of Single Test Scores for Educational Decisions

To repeat a caveat in the use of any test, including standardized tests, the interpretation of scores from a single test is not unequivocal. For example, in a comparison of state performances on the nationally administered NAEP, the correspondence between measures of proficiency on the national and the statewide tests for grades 4 and 8 was found to be relatively low. *The results of the state comprehensive tests for only a very few states (a half dozen) matched the NAEP proficiency ratings.* These considerations raise the issue of how accountability is to be administered. Sirotnik and Kimball (1999, p. 211), for example, say:

> Common sense suggests that scores on one test (which itself is only a sample of many possible performances) cannot possibly represent all that is going on in a school. . . . Making inferential leaps from test results to the causes of those test results is foolish in the extreme. . . . There are a number of factors that can affect the scores of a single test. They include:
>
> *Student factors*: race/ethnicity, economic status, attendance rates, mobility, suspension and expulsion rates, placements in tracks, course enrollment patterns, special education placements, scores on other tests, and the usual array of opportunity-to-learn indicators.
>
> *Faculty factors*: we might find race/ethnicity, years of teaching experience, number of teachers teaching out of

---

Text Box 14.2 Rewards and Sanctions in Accountability

- **Increase Accountability for Student Performance:** *States, districts, and schools that improve achievement will be rewarded. Failure will be sanctioned.* Parents will know how well their child is learning, and that schools are held accountable for their effectiveness with annual state reading and math assessments in grades 3–8.
- **Focus on What Works:** *Federal dollars will be spent on effective, research based programs and practices. Funds will be targeted to improve schools and enhance teacher quality.*
- **Reduce Bureaucracy and Increase Flexibility:** Additional flexibility will be provided to states and school districts, and *flexible funding will be increased at the local level.*
- **Empower Parents:** Parents will have more information about the quality of their child's school. *Students in persistently low-performing schools will be given choice.*
- **Rewards for Closing the Achievement Gap:** *High performing states that* narrow the achievement gap and *improve overall student achievement will be rewarded.*
- **Accountability Bonus for States:** *Each state will be offered a one-time bonus if it meets accountability requirements,* including establishing annual assessments in grades 3–8, within two years of enacting this plan.
- **"No Child Left Behind" School Rewards:** Successful schools that have made the greatest progress in improving the achievement of disadvantaged students will be recognized and *rewarded with "No Child Left Behind" bonuses.*
- **Consequences for Failure:** The Secretary of Education will be authorized to *reduce federal funds* available to a state for administrative expenses if a state fails to meet their performance objectives and demonstrate results in academic achievement.

Note: Also see *Fact Sheet: Six Years of Student Achievement under No Child Left Behind* (January 2008) for White House news release, at www.whitehouse.gov/news/releases/2008/01/20080107-1.html.

Source: White House. (2008, January 8). Foreword by George W. Bush. Transforming the Federal Role in Education. Retrieved March 20, 2008, from www.whitehouse.gov/infocus/education/ and www.whitehouse.gov/news/reports/no-child-left-behind.html#3.

---

field, and hours of paid in-school time set aside for planning to be useful indicators.

Principal factors: leadership skills, experience and frequency of principal turnover

Other factors: parental involvement at the school, the instructional resources available per student, and the quality of those instructional resources.

When these factors are neglected, schools or teachers may dwell primarily on increasing test scores and may fail to use instructional procedures that adapt effectively to students' differences. Perhaps the most malicious of misperceptions regarding high-stakes or other standardized tests is the focus on state standards as represented by the test or test items and too little focus on the more meaningful underlying standards that the test items represent, keeping in mind that any test, however flexible it may be, can only be a sample of a standard's domain.

Sensitivity to How Test Scores Are Interpreted

In the long run, beyond the immediate concern of accountability, there is also the issue of how an assessment, single test score, or other related event is interpreted by the user, that is, the teacher, parent, or administrator. To say that improvement will occur automatically is a distortion of the reality. The interpretation of success or failure consequences is determined by the perceptions of the test events and sanctions.

Thus, whether or not the desired outcome for improvement occurs depends, in large part, on the mediators ("intervening thoughts or events"), and the nature and effectiveness of the mediators depend on how well-informed those who are making the decisions are about the nature of education and educational goals. To ensure that low-achieving schools improve performance, teachers and other educators should insist that all facets of assessment be explained as specifically and thoroughly as possible.

The kinds of information that play important parts in perceptions and interpretations can be seen in differences in the knowledge base. Try your hand in explaining how the differences in the following list might differentially affect understanding and perspectives to the extent of creating some dissension among participants.

- Policy makers are informed by legal statutes and political considerations.
- Professional educators are informed by research.
- Test constructors are informed by methodology and applied research.
- Teachers are informed by teacher preparation programs and in-service programs.
- Parents are informed by informal observations of school practices and their own interpretations of the consequences of these practices for their children.

Each level of personnel has its own source of information affecting the interpretation of what tests are about and what the scores mean. That information differs in quality and level. The differences are certain to affect the perceptions of the assessment and the usefulness of decisions made and will often result in a lack of consensus about their value.

Negative Impact on Instruction of Limited Interpretations of Test Scores

So pervasive are the outcomes of high-stake testing that schools attempt strategies for boosting scores in ways that have negative impacts. The hidden effects of teachers' behavior, beliefs, and self-efficacy may result in a disguised form of poor practice by teachers who try to improve their students' test scores by using actual items taken from a current or recent form of a high-stakes test or items available in test preparation manuals. Popham (2002, pp. 310–314) provides an insightful analysis of rules as a guide for test preparation. In summary, they are:

- *Test preparation must produce educationally useful outcomes.* A practice that doesn't contribute to acquisition of the subject-matter objectives is a waste of time. Practice on previous forms of a test is an example. On the other hand, when similar or varied formats used in statewide tests are integrated into instruction, they have instructional value.
- *Test preparation must be consistent with ethical considerations.* The use of a current form of a high-stakes test is not only totally wrong, but should be viewed with suspicion (Popham, 2002). Current forms are not available for practice. If one is used, it is certain that it would have been acquired by illegal, dishonest means (theft, cheating, etc.). Its use would be violating test security measures while simultaneously compromising the value of the test.

Other examples of practices that can be viewed within the context of these two rules follow.

Coaching for the Test

Coaching students on ways to answer test items, specific or very similar to those on the test, amounts to little more than making students familiar with the mechanics of responding to given item formats. Scores from tests in which students have been coached on how to answer specific items may not be useful data for any purpose.

Preparation for taking a test, when based on single items, does little more than increase the probability of a correct answer if that same item (or something similar to it) appears on the test. If the item had been deliberately borrowed from the upcoming test, drill, or practice on that item would be additionally unethical. Nevertheless, if it is understood that the test item represents a test format for measuring deeper understanding, with transfer capabilities, of the concept or standard represented by the item, the procedure can make a useful contribution to improving learning.

Teaching the test format can also be useful to the extent that it removes a source of error variance from the test scores, but this effect can be obtained in a short preparation on test-taking strategies in order to help the students become comfortable in dealing with different test formats. (Note that practice items provided on many standardized tests are intended to serve a similar function.) Extended time (some schools spend a semester) adds little to the gains achieved in the first hour or two of test preparation (Pedulla et al., 2003).

Coaching while Taking the Test

Other forms of unacceptable teacher practices that occur when administering standardized tests occasionally emerge from good intentions—for example, giving students a little more time to take the test; signalling the student surreptitiously by a smile or other nonverbal behavior to indicate whether the student is on the right track; allowing students to review finished tests after time has run out; and inadvertently urging students to rethink their answers to certain questions, or revise their responses in certain ways. Although these practices are often dismissed as well-intentioned, they are inappropriate forms of coaching. The practices distort the test results and destroy the purposes of standardization.

Boosting Scores When Grading

When high test scores, rather than learning outcomes, become the overriding goal of classroom instruction, distortions of curriculum and instruction are likely results, and such practices risk eventual student failure (Koretz, Linn, Dunbar, & Shepard, 1991). (In an earlier discussion, we referred to this event as "narrowing the curriculum.") When the intent of high-stakes tests is poorly understood or perceived, they tend to encourage curricula and instruction that are aimed at producing high scores on the tests. In doing so, they squeeze out other, more important (effective) methods of instruction related to learning, thereby constraining (narrowing) the curriculum (Shepard et al., 2005). Teachers may modify instruction to coincide with their perceptions of the content emphasized in the test, often seeing simply the facts rather than the concepts or understandings underlying the items. This practice may also misdirect instruction by encouraging the teaching of the content superficially, for example, surfing over many topics superficially rather than fewer topics with conceptual, in-depth understanding (Hillocks, 2002).

Sound Use of the Results of High-Stakes Testing Programs

Text Box 14.3 offers a number of recommendations from the American Educational Research Association (2000) for the proper use of high-stake tests.

Text Box 14.3 A Dozen Conditions for the Sound Use of High-Stakes Programs

The following conditions, stated in a document by the American Educational Research Association, are essential to sound implementation of high-stakes educational testing programs. Although adopted for the specific purposes of high-stakes programs, these conditions provide useful and logical guides for (a) the use of any assessment, whether teacher-made or standardized; (b) the use of any test, whether for formative assessment or for accountability; and (c) the selection of a test. You will recognize statements about the importance of validity, reliability, and psychometric characteristics to well-constructed and properly used tests.

1. Protection against high-stakes decisions based on a single test
2. Adequate resources and opportunity to learn
3. Validation for each separate intended use
4. Full disclosure of likely negative consequences of high-stakes testing programs
5. Alignment between the test and the curriculum
6. Validity of passing scores and achievement levels
7. Meaningful remediation opportunities for examinees who fail high-stakes tests
8. Appropriate attention to language differences among examinees
9. Appropriate attention to students with disabilities
10. Careful adherence to explicit rules for determining which students are to be tested
11. Sufficient reliability for each intended use
12. Ongoing evaluation of intended and unintended effects of high-stakes testing

Source: Condensed from American Educational Research Association (2000).

Implementing Change Based on High-Stakes Testing

The recommendations in Text Box 14.3 are based on thoughtful and evidence-based considerations. They should be carefully heeded, not only for the administration of high-stakes tests but for the use of tests in general. The very characteristics that make standardized tests uniquely different from classroom tests are the ones that can be used advantageously for improving instruction and learning. Some of these characteristics are that purposes are clearly stated for their orientation (as such the orientation must be accurately informed, communicated, and interpreted); the test is constructed by professionals to achieve high technical characteristics supported by evidence for such qualities as reliability, equivalence of forms, and validity; content-area scores are broken down into subcategories (e.g., arithmetic facts, operators, understandings); results are displayed as raw scores, grade equivalents, and percentiles; and norms are disaggregated.

These characteristics suggest the kinds of comparisons among variables that can be made from standardized tests, including high-stakes tests, for example:

- They are given periodically over time so they can be used to chart trends.
- Disaggregated norms for grade levels, ethnicity, socioeconomic status, language differences, or districts (national, state or local districts) enable comparison among schools in different localities or to show differential trends in the progress of these groups.
- The scores for subject-matter areas are often broken down into subscores, allowing comparisons of student abilities in content objectives both across areas (e.g., science and math) and within areas (e.g., factual acquisition and conceptual understanding).

Merely examining the data for changes in performance patterns is insufficient without corresponding attempts at interpreting these changes and finding informed ways to incorporate the implied changes in the curriculum or in instruction. When students are performing poorly against a national average, the ways in which high or low scores in a content area are achieved by the students can be examined through the subscores: look for peaks or unusual conditions that accompany peaks or depressions in trends or that correlate (being certain not to attribute causation) with high or low scores. For example, by analysis of subscores, it might be found that higher scores were obtained in factual information but lower scores in conceptual understanding. Or the analysis may reveal weaknesses (or strengths) in making inferences, estimation, generalizations (transfer) to other contexts, or finding main ideas. Such findings might then be translated into more intensive instruction aimed at student understanding.

Pros and Cons of the Legislation

From both idealistic and political viewpoints, it is difficult, indeed, to argue against the basic premises of NCLB. All want children to learn in schools with high-quality teachers and excellent resources. It would be reassuring to know that the curriculum, instructional methods, and assessments employed in the school were formulated from information discovered using scientific methodology. The goals of NCLB are worthy ones to pursue even though the assessment may require continued surveillance for revision, formulation, construction, function, and employment for improving education.

What NCLB Means to You

The prevailing political view is that students (in the elementary and secondary level, as a group) who fail do so because of poor instruction and that teachers who bear primary responsibility for learning are to be blamed for the students' failures. Basically, in today's climate, the legislation directly links the performance of students to the teacher's (and school's) performance. The demand to adapt to cognitive and noncognitive needs is highly complex, but the NCLB clearly implies that teachers must work around any other limitations that might challenge the performance of students (Yell & Drasgow, 2005). One author (Abernathy, 2007) has argued that this expectation is somewhat unique to teaching.

Recent data show that some of the desired changes are correlated with the administration of the test. These are displayed in Figure 14.2, which shows that in 2008, 66 percent of all students in grades 3–10 were performing at or above Achievement Level 3 (on grade level and above) on the Florida Comprehensive Achievement Test (FCAT)'s test in mathematics. This is an increase from 50 percent in 2001, 51 percent in 2002, 54 percent in 2003, 56 percent in 2004, 59 percent in 2005, 61 percent in 2006, and 63 percent in 2007. In 2008, 15 percent of all students in grades 3–10 were performing at Achievement Level 1 on the FCAT mathematics test. This is a decrease from 29 percent in 2001, 27 percent in 2002, 24 percent in 2003, 22

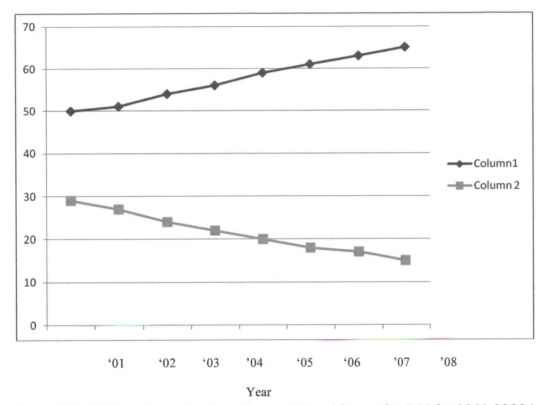

Figure 14.2. FCAT mathematics by achievement level for grades 3–10 for 2001–2008.*
Source: K20 Education Data Warehouse Florida Department of Education, June 2008.

*Column 1 = Increases in percentage at Achievement Level 3; Column 2 = decreases in percentage at Achievement Level 1.

percent in 2004, 20 percent in 2005, 18 percent in 2006, and 17 percent in 2007.

It is unlikely that these results were obtained through brute-force training in how to take tests (using the same items in practicing for the test). Although it is not possible to tell the exact cause, it is more likely that the improvements were achieved by the use of instructional procedures aimed at conceptual understanding underlying the content-based standards and objectives.

Summary of the Current NCLB Act

The current (2010) NCLB act can, in retrospect, be seen to have several characteristic features. In general it is quite inflexible in its requirements. The implementation of the act relies heavily on assessment tools, as can be seen in the following summary of some features related to assessment.

States are required to test students through their own state tests, known as the (State) Comprehensive Achievement Tests.

The focus of these tests is grade-level proficiency. Students are to be tested annually in grades 3–8 and at least once in high school. The focus is on reaching 100 percent proficiency in reading and math by the year 2014. The number of students in each grade level who are declared proficient in reading and math is used as the basic formula. States define their target levels. When schools do not reach levels of proficiency they are labeled simply as failing.

Outcomes on this test are reported for subgroups such as special education and ELL students as well as for all students in the school. Thus, the overall data for the reports were disaggregated for the special groups.

The act emphasizes punitive measures for low-performing schools over rewards for well-performing schools. Schools that miss achievement targets need improvement; that is, if they are not making adequate yearly progress, they are subject to serious negative sanctions. One such provision requires that schools failing to achieve proficiency targets are required to provide students with tutoring or with the parental option to transfer to better-performing schools.

The lowest tier, comprised of the 5 percent of lowest-performing schools, must use the Department of Education's turnaround models (see the section titled "Tier Models") employed in the Title 1 improvement program. The next-to-the-lowest tier receives a warning and must take steps to improve using evidence-based interventions. The turnaround models can be used, but it is not mandatory for schools in this tier to do so.

Federal funding is formula based; for example, funding is available for schools in districts with high concentrations of poverty. This is an important measure, as poverty is related to achievement, but it leaves open the nature of the measure to be used in the formula—such as whether to use percentages or numbers of disadvantaged children and whether they are in low-population rural or high-population urban and suburban districts.

The Future of NCLB

The extent to which the NCLB legislation has positive effects remains an important research issue.

The Debate

The debate regarding the existing legislation is ongoing. The legislation has become unpopular for some lawmakers because, they say, it is too punitive on students who fail to meet program goals. Accordingly, it is likely to undergo revision by the incumbent administration. Such revisions will require studies of how failures and successes directly or indirectly affected by the legislation improve instruction and how to assure that school grades are fairly assigned based on the assessments used.

An earlier position regarding the future of the NCLB is presented in Text Box 14.4.

Race to the Top

More recently, a change in the legislation is beginning to be expressed. The revised program is earning the label of *Race to the Top*. The emergence of a framework, though not firm, appears to be providing the groundwork for the new legislation, so we tentatively list for your consideration and guidance some of the proposals now being considered.

The summary that follows is based on several sources available at this writing, including a presidential speech (*New York Times,* 2010) and articles published on websites by the media (Douglass, 2010; *New York Times,* 2010; Terry, 2010). The proposed changes and actions are certain to be revised.

Potential Targets and Changes in Race to the Top (RttP)

It is our intention in this presentation that the list of revised targets increases your understanding of the far-reaching effects of legislative actions where knowledge of assessment practices is essential to that understanding. Additionally, this discussion provides a background to guide your further study of the emerging legislation, which is certain to have a major impact on school, curriculum, instruction, and individual professional development.

Assessment Schedules

Assessments will provide the database on which decisions are made and implemented. The yearly schedule for assessing students carries over from the Title 1 mandate. The assessment will include a broader knowledge base than reading, science, and math.

Preparation Targets

The standard of proficiency will focus on preparation for college and careers by the time students graduate from high school. A

Text Box 14.4 The Future of NCLB

No Child Left Behind is a monument to what we can accomplish when we bring accountability, high standards, and unprecedented funding to our schools. And as all your analysts ultimately agreed, it is a monument we must stand behind ("Do We Repair the Monument?" *Forum*, Spring 2005).

NCLB starts with the premise that all students, regardless of race, income, or special need, can and should achieve high standards. If you believe every child can learn in school, then it makes perfect sense to expect every child to be proficient in reading and math by 2014. To call this goal unrealistic is to abandon millions of children to what President Bush has so aptly termed the soft bigotry of low expectations.

While we want to be as flexible as possible, we will not backtrack and lower standards. If we do, children will fall behind, and our monument will stand for nothing but an empty promise. That would be a terrible shame because we can already see that this law is making a difference. Across the country, scores are rising, and the achievement gap is closing.

It is like the saying, what gets measured gets done. We must continue to assess every student every year. But let me be clear: We do not believe in a federal test. No Child Left Behind calls for each state to set its own academic standards in the best interests of its own students. We simply provide the funds for these assessments and ask for accountability for results in return.

Already we are seeing the states make real progress. Pennsylvania has gone from 61 percent of schools meeting their academic goals to 81 percent; California, from 54 percent to 64 percent; and Georgia, from 64 percent to 78 percent.

Now we want to bring the benefits of this law to our high schools by expanding on its principles of accountability, flexibility, choice, and research-based practices. Using those pillars, we can help ensure that a high-school diploma once again represents a ticket to success.

We face serious challenges. Just 68 out of every 100 9th graders will graduate from high school on time. And the vast majority of these students are unprepared for higher education. As a result, out of those 100 original 9th-grade students, only 27 are still enrolled in college in their sophomore year. With 80 percent of the fastest-growing jobs requiring some postsecondary education, we face a crisis.

That is why the president has proposed a $1.5 billion High School Initiative to ensure every student graduates ready for college or to be able to function in the workforce of the 21st century. We need to annually assess our high-school students, so we can intervene before a problem sets a student behind for life.

Now is not the time to chisel away at No Child Left Behind. We need to build on its foundations and extend the promise of high standards and accountability to all of our students. Together, we can give every child a quality education.

Chris Doherty
Chief of Staff
Office of Elementary and Secondary Education
U.S. Department of Education

Source: Reprinted with permission from *Education Next* (Summer 2005, Volume 5, Number 3).

common core of courses and standards is suggested. The focus is on the skills and understandings students will need in continued schooling and/or their career development. Schools that miss targets would not be required to provide parental options (e.g., transfer of students to other schools).

Test Aims

The tests will be used to measure student progress, that is, each student's academic growth, regardless of the performance level at which he or she starts. This is an important replacement for the current measure of achievement proficiency levels.

School Subjects Tested

In addition to the present reading and math tests required under NCLB, schools would have the alternative of reporting student performance in other subjects as part of overall measurements of progress. The new proposal emphasizes the importance of the broader goals related to being well educated.

Sanctions

Evaluations of schools would provide increased attention to rewards. A tier system would identify the lowest tier, the 5 percent of schools struggling the most in each state. Credit would be given when outcomes show that student performance has improved, even if the target is missed. Financial rewards and greater flexibility would be awarded to personnel, schools, or school districts that show large improvements in student learning.

Tier Models

A system of models for improving the performance of the lowest-performing schools would be retained from the Title 1 mandate. Brief descriptions follow:

- *Turn around the framework of the school organization.* Some recommendations would be to replace inefficient key staff (e.g., principals, department heads, and so on), and provide for improved administrative flexibility (e.g., staffing, calendar and time schedules, and budgets).
- *Restart the school in a different organizational framework.* The process might be initiated by closing the school, perhaps

to be reopened in another form of educational organization such as a charter school.

- *Close the school.* A decision to close the school would simultaneously provide enrollment of students in a high-achieving school.
- *Transform some aspect of the school.* Implement the three strategies above in ways that are most effective, including replacing key staff, initiating comprehensive reforms, increasing learning time, providing administrative flexibility, and providing sustained reform.

Other tiers include schools facing less-severe challenges than the lowest tier. The next-to-the-lowest tier receives a warning to improve performance with the use of evidence-based practices. Other tiers would have local and state flexibility in the interventions used.

Assessment Technology in Understanding Teacher and Principal Effectiveness

States would be encouraged to engage in the assessments, development, and improvement of teacher and principal effectiveness, and of programs in teacher preparation as they are related to student progress. Technology could be used to develop data-driven systems that support the recognition of the contributions of effective educators and the assessment of teacher-preparation programs.

■ Summary

The emphasis on federal concern with school achievement is an ongoing process and involves both policy established at the national level for descriptive purposes (NAEP) and at the state level for accountability (NCLB). The NAEP shows where students from several norm groups are in their educational development. Its development is guided by the National Assessment Governing Board, which formulates policy guidelines for selecting subject matter to be assessed, setting performance levels, developing assessment objects and test specifications, designing methodology, developing standards and procedures, and making certain the test and test items are free of bias.

Research is continually conducted on the NAEP, including comparisons among subgroups such as districts or states, poverty levels, ethnicities, or language priorities. The many studies that have been conducted have resulted in a report of progress made nationally for improving instruction in reading, math, science, and literacy. We have noted that the legislation deliberately specifies that the NAEP is to be used only for describing the achievement of subgroups and setting performance standards.

Although the interpretation and appropriate use of NAEP results is clearly presented in *The Nation's Report Card*, more consideration is warranted to fulfill the functions of formative assessment. That is, the data and reports tell us how well students are doing in school, but more discussion is required to understand how schools need to be organized and how instruction needs to be designed and delivered for effective instruction.

Importantly, the assessments we have discussed are professionally monitored according to the latest methodology in good assessment, measurement, and evaluation. They are constructed to permit valid comparisons from year to year. Overall, the NAEP program has informed educational practice but has not produced programs that have widespread applicability for education and that effectively produce achievement gains that we expect in meeting performance standards. Knowledge is needed about which instructional procedures, from the current armamentarium of instructional and learning strategies, are capable of producing which results for which groups.

The NCLB Act has separately built into the national assessment a legislative requirement in which the states develop their own unique programs for educational improvement in their schools. They set their standards for subject-matter areas and develop strong assessments according to the same principles as those that are conducted by the National Assessment Governing Board. Simply put, they use the latest scientific and professional knowledge about assessment methodology in the construction of assessment procedures.

State tests developed within the NCLB are known mainly as the (State) Comprehensive Achievement Test (state CAT = XCAT). Unlike the NAEP, the state tests incorporate specific requirements for assessing disadvantaged children, rural children, and children with a first language other than English. Accommodations are permissible, provided, of course, that they do not bias performance on the test (discussed in Chapter 16). To implement change, states must demonstrate on their assessment measures that student achievement levels are being maintained or improved. Schools that are initially nonproductive are provided aid to improve staff and instruction for a period of three years. If they are unsuccessful in those years, then funding may be withdrawn or parents may choose to move their children to more successful programs. If the schools show maintenance and/or improvement in student achievement they may be rewarded by additional recognition or funding.

Regardless of the nature of the test, whether for descriptive or accountability purposes, the ultimate use of any test or pattern of test scores should be judged against the criterion of alignment with the curriculum (Weiss, Knapp, Hollweg, & Burrill, 2002). Interpretation of test results is often done without regard to the influence of variables other than instruction. Scores can fluctuate in accordance with factors such as ethnicity, attendance, mobility, retention (in grade), administrative or organizational implementation (track, nongraded plans, etc.), curriculum offerings, class size, amounts of standardized test experience, Parent Teacher Association participation, attendance, and psychological services. The influence of any of these factors may go unrecognized; all have the potential of producing variability in averages. And, as a final note, decisions about accountability must be based on multiple measures, not single test scores; on strong support and monitoring of the provision of learning opportunities for a diverse student body; on understanding the reciprocity of the relation between teaching and learning; on measures taken in many contexts and useful for monitoring; and on the fair use of rewards for accomplishment and support for schools having difficulty (Sirotnic & Kimball, 1999).

Exercise 14.2: Reviewing the Results of Statewide Tests
Obtain the three most recent publicly available summaries of the statewide tests for a school and grade level of your choosing (alternatively your instructor may provide you with these data). Select a school that did not earn a high grade overall. Also select the summaries for a subject-matter area and grade level near the one in which you intend to teach. Write a review of the results to reflect your understanding of statewide and standardized tests. Your review should be based on a comparison of the results of the three periods for the variables suggested in this chapter.

Your report should summarize one or more of the following: Identify peaks and valleys or trends on subscores across the three periods. Identify the norms available and indicate the ones appropriate for your selected school or grade level. Compare the school you selected with the various norms and any other data available, such as media reports for the public.

Was the school or grade low (or high) on all subscores? What strengths or weaknesses did you find? What instructional change (alternative methods) would you make on the basis of your analysis? What instruction would you retain? How do your interpretations stack up to those you found in any media (news or TV) report that you can find? What is missing in the media reports that might misdirect or misuse the test results? Outline the presentation that you might make to parents at a meeting with them. Use any other evidence for points made in this chapter for your review.

■ References

Abernathy, S. F. (2007). *No Child Left Behind and the public schools.* Ann Arbor: University of Michigan Press.

Abrams, L. M., & Madaus, G. F. (2003). The lessons of high-stakes testing. *Educational Leadership, 61*(13), 31–35.

American Educational Research Association. (2000). *High-stakes testing in PreK–12 education.* AERA position statement. Retrieved March 20, 2008, from www.aera.net/policyandprograms/?id=378.

Ballator, N. (1996). *The NAEP Guide* (rev. ed.). Washington, DC: National Center for Education Statistics.

Bierlin, A. B. (1993). *Controversial issues in educational policy.* Thousand Oaks, CA: Sage.

Davies, R. (2007, April). *Education accountability policy: Leaving children behind by definition.* Paper presented at the Midwest Political Science Association, Chicago, IL.

Douglass, J. N. (March 14, 2010). No Child Left Behind overhaul: Five key things would change. *The Christian Science Monitor.* Retrieved July 25, 2010, from www.csmonitor.com.

Goldsmith, L. T., & Mark, J. (1999). What is a standards-based mathematics curriculum? *Educational Leadership, 57*(3), 40–44.

Hamilton, L., Stecher, B., & Klein, S. (Eds.). (2002). *Making sense of test-based accountability in education.* Santa Monica, CA: Rand.

Hillocks, G. (2002). *The testing trap: How state writing assessments control learning.* New York: Teachers College Press.

Heubert, J. P., & Hauser, R. M. (Eds.). (1999). *High stakes testing for tracking, promotion, and graduation.* Washington, DC: National Academy Press.

Koretz, D. M., Linn, R. L., Dunbar, S. B., & Shepard, L. A. (1991, April 3-7). *The effects of high-stakes testing on achievement: Preliminary findings about generalization across tests.* Paper presented at the American Educational Research Association and the National Council on Measurement in Education, Chicago, IL.

National Assessment Governing Board. (2002a). Prohibition on using NAEP to influence state and local standards, tests, and curricula [white paper]. Retrieved April 1, 2008, from www.nagb.org/release/white_paper.doc.

National Assessment Governing Board. (2002b). *U.S. history framework for the 1994 and 2001 NAEP.* Retrieved April 1, 2008, from http://nces.ed.gov/nationsreportcard/ushistory/results/interpret-results.asp.

National Assessment of Educational Progress. (2006). *The Nation's Report Card: U.S. history report card (sample questions in*

U.S. history, grade 4). Retrieved May 1, 2008, from http://nationsreportcard.gov/ushistory_2006/h0111.asp.

New York Times. (March 16, 2010) The No Child Left Behind act. Retrieved July 26, 2010, from http://topics.nytimes.com/top/reference/timestopics/.

No Child Left Behind Act of 2001. Public Law No. 107-110. 115 Stat 1444-1446 C.F.R. (2002).

Office of the Press Secretary, The White House. (March 1, 2010). Remarks by the President at the America's Promise Alliance Education event. Retrieved July 25, 2010 from www.whitehouse.gov.

Pedulla, J. J., Abrams, L. M., Madaus, G. F., Russell, M. K., Ramos, M. A., & Miao, J. (2003). *Perceived effects of state-mandated testing programs on teaching and learning: Findings from a national survey of teachers.* Boston: National Board on Educational Classroom Uses of Accountability, Assessments, Testing, and Public Policy, Boston College.

Pelligrino, J. W., Chudowsky, N., & Glaser, R. (2001). *Knowing what students know: The science and design of educational assessment.* Washington, DC: National Academy Press.

Popham, W. J. (2002). *Classroom assessment: What teachers need to know.* (3rd ed.). Boston: Allyn and Bacon.

Raju, N. S., Pellegrino, J. W., Bertenthal, M. W., Mitchell, K. J., & Jones, L. R. (Eds.). (2000). *Grading the nation's report card: Research from the evaluation of NAEP.* Washington, DC: National Academy Press.

Ravitch, D. (2002). *Brookings papers on educational policy.* Washington, DC: Brookings Institution Press.

Shepard, L., Hammerness, K., Darling-Hammond, L., Snowden, J. B., Gordon, E., Gutierrez, C., et al. (2005). Chapter eight: Assessment. In L. Darling-Hammond, J. D. Bransford, P. LePage, K. Hammerness, & H. Duffy (Eds.), *Preparing teachers for a changing world: What teachers should learn and be able to do.* San Francisco: Jossey-Bass, a Wiley Imprint.

Sirotnik, K. A., & Kimball, K. (1999). Standards for standards-based accountability systems. *Phi Delta Kappa International, 81*(3), 209–214. Retrieved September 15, 2007 from www.pdkintl.org/kappan.

Terry, D. (2010) *What's possible: Turning around America's lowest achieving schools.* U. S. Department of Education, Office of Communications and Outreach. Retrieved July 25, 2010, from www.ed.gov/blog/2010/03/.

Weiss, I. R., Knapp, M. S., Hollweg, K. S., & Burrill, G. (Eds.). (2002). *Investigating the influence of standards: A framework for research in mathematics, science, and technology education.* Washington, DC: National Academy Press.

Yell, M. L., & Drasgow, E. (2005). *No Child Left Behind: A guide for professionals.* Upper Saddle River, NJ: Pearson Merrill Prentice Hall.

CHAPTER 15

Assessment and Best Practices

WITH THE PERSPECTIVES provided by increasingly sophisticated theoretical perspectives amid the findings reported in the research literature, assessment of school programs has been increasingly informed by empirically based decision making regarding the integration of assessment with instruction, curriculum, and policy. This orientation, through either expert judgment or research investigation, relates evaluation and measurement to the process and practices involved in producing educational excellence rather than the sheer isolated emphasis on outcome or result (e.g., the student grade report card). This orientation has become known as best practices studies.

Most readers will be familiar with such frequent and redundant journalistic reports as "the goal of the state comprehensive assessment test provides an oversight presence that can have a beneficial effect," "some schools have improved from an F to a D," "math and science offer the greatest opportunities for improvement," and "one half to one quarter of the classes remain behind." In these reports and editorials, despite their frequency, no mention is made of the work to be done or of the practices to be initiated for the improvement of learning by students who struggle the most. The study of best practices offers, at the least, a constructive beginning to workable solutions, solutions that go beyond the recommendation that schools need to maintain their hard work to get the job done. Understand that, despite the promise of the orientation, the methods of best practices are still not totally defined and should be considered a work in progress.

■ Purposes Served by Best Practices Studies

Ross and Morrison (2009) propose that different objectives can be achieved at various stages of the educational process for the purpose of understanding what factors are at work to produce changes and at which points changes can be made for most effective improvement:

- *Formative stage.* This is the developmental, ongoing, or during-instruction stage. Assessment at this stage informs the teacher or school about the practices being used at a given time for achieving instructional goals. The concern is on practices that are in effect as the student is engaged in the educational process and is responsive to instruction for new learning—for instance, one might ask, "How is the instruction working? Is the student making the progress expected? What practices accounted for the effects? What changes need to be made?" At this stage, the instructional practices can be flexibly modified as they are found to be effective or ineffective in achieving objectives. This phase is captured, in part, by response to intervention, described in Chapter 13.
- *Summative stage.* This is the immediate postinstruction stage, one with which most people are most familiar. It is a period of instruction defined by the completion of a unit of work, such as promotion to a new grade or graduation. It informs the educator, parent, or other stakeholder of the progress made in achievement of standards or other general objectives. The emphasis here is on the practices that were accountable for student achievement (cognitions, affective tendencies, and skills). Here, one might ask such questions as, "Were the standards or benchmarks met by the student (or school)? What were the processes, practices, or curricula that contributed to the success (or failure) in meeting expectations?" Because this is summative, the practices related to effective or ineffective programs can only be modified to take effect in ongoing or future educational settings.
- *Confirmative stage.* This period is often neglected in thinking about the effectiveness of schooling. It is an important addition to perspectives on assessment and the study of best practices as it follows the point at which formal instruction is defined as completed. It informs the stakeholder of the extent to which education has had enduring effects, beyond the point where education is generally considered

as having been completed (e.g., graduation). Best practices research would enable answers to such questions as, "Were the effects temporary or long-lasting (successful placement in jobs or success in college or contributions to lifelong learning)? Were the effects due to practices in the educational setting or to other factors external to education (for example, changes due to changes in the knowledge base of cohorts—people of the same generation—technology, or cultural concerns might affect practices or their outcomes)? What practices can be exploited to continue the success of students beyond formal education? Which effects were associated with cultural changes and what do they mean for curriculum and instruction?"

The *confirmative assessment* stage is obviously more complicated than the other two stages. Practices that are due to education and that contribute to outcomes beyond schooling need to be identified. As in the previous phase, when they are identified they are restricted to use in future educational settings.

■ Teacher Preparation for Assessment Practices

Within a similar framework, Shepard and colleagues (2005) have thoughtfully considered the components of assessment as they are related to practices that might be infused in curricula for the preparation of teachers (Shepard, 2005, pp. 275–276). In particular, a base knowledge of the relation of assessment to instructional practice can be useful in (a) selecting and choosing ways of evaluating student proficiency from the many alternative ways of using criterion-based performance measures; and (b) becoming informed about high-stakes tests, their positive and negative effects, and how well they align with content standards and curriculum goals.

To accomplish these ends Shepard and colleagues indicate several general practices, some of which are based on statements prepared by the PACT (Performance Assessment for California Teachers) consortium, a project piloted by several California universities for helping teachers develop the skills necessary for integrating assessment with instruction. A summary of recommendations is displayed in Theory to Practice Box 15.1. Keep in mind that these practices are assumed to be *integrated* within instruction, as a part of every instructional practice, rather than attached to instruction as isolated or independent events.

Theory to Practice Box 15.1
TEACHER PRACTICES FOR LEARNING TO INTEGRATE ASSESSMENT AND INSTRUCTION

Observing and Analyzing Student Performance over Longer Intervals of Time. Using the processes of practical and useful observation (see earlier chapters), analyze student work for *trends* in progress including writing, lab work, and math. Recognize the ways in which the outcomes of observations affect what is done in instruction. Evaluate how these outcomes inform what is known about the relation of student strengths and weaknesses to learning progress and interventions that affect learning progress. Understand how instruction affected these outcomes.

Planning the Assessment. Infusing assessment throughout the instructional plan or design is a critical part of using assessments to improve instruction. "Mapping backward" (Wiggins and McTighe, 1998) is a process that initiates the instructional plan with statements about outcomes and making certain that all educational experiences of the student leading up to the goal are targeted to, or connected with, the goal. Assessment decisions will include a variety of assessments to inform instructional practice. Consideration of the psychometric characteristics (reliability, validity, and practicality) underlying selected assessments would be important in making effective decisions.

Relating Assessment to Learning and instructional Goals. Formative assessments require understanding the ways in which assessment characteristics (the use of rubrics, feedback, alternative assessments, and so on) differentially affect motivation, metacognitions, and assignment criteria.

Using Standards, Assessment and Accountability—the High-Stakes Road. The rather complicated idea of *domain mapping* suggests that teachers map the subject-matter domain represented by the state standards. These are reflected in the statewide tests, curriculum frameworks, or national content standards and, subsequently, are incorporated into instruction. Obviously, the teachers' own curriculum and standards, in relation to the state standards, would be a part of the mapping process. On the basis of such analyses, teachers determine the strands covered in their own curriculum and plan their own classroom instruction. To become familiar with the externally administered tests, teachers might take, themselves, available subparts of the high-stakes tests (real items) to enable an understanding of the test and what it measures. On the basis of that experience, tests would be analyzed for their limitations (e.g., do test items target only the more easily measured content?).

Source: Adapted from Shepard et al. (2005, pp. 315–322).

■ Benchmarking as a Component of Best Practice Studies

By accurately characterizing processes in learning and instruction, teachers are in the favorable position of knowing what to observe and how to assess behaviors and processes related to improvement in learning. When some status variable (e.g., cognitive ability, personality trait) is identified as potentially detrimental to effective learning or teaching, informed teachers know how to diagnose its presence in a student and what remedial measures are necessary either for the teacher in instruction or for the student in learning.

The Nature of Benchmarks

These premises are incorporated in the outline of a plan for comprehensive school reform presented here because it introduces the process known as *benchmarking* (see Table 15.1). Benchmarking provides a base set of criteria, for example, of instructional practices used by schools with exemplary performance, against which other schools (your school, perhaps) can be compared and for suggesting practices that are not currently being used in the "other" schools.

As noted in Table 15.1, comparisons between schools are initiated from a base for comparison, the *benchmark*, characterized in a unit (e.g., a school or district) by some measurable quality of high achievement—one which might be informally judged as a top quality, a best-in-class, or a cost-effective unit (e.g., school or district). This form of assessment works backward from the benchmark; that is, to understand how each preceding instructional component has contributed to reaching the high performance.

Practices that Contribute to the Benchmark's Performance

The practices that characteristically contribute to the benchmark performance may emphasize the role instruction plays in achieving educational goals. By further extrapolation the administrator or other stakeholder can hypothesize how high quality was achieved so that the hypothesized practices can be recommended for improving the performance of other schools (e.g., poorly performing schools—those that might be reported in the media as "schools with F standings," "schools lagging behind the NCLB criteria for adequate yearly progress," and so on).

Table 15.1. Identifying and Using Benchmarks: Illustrations of Phases and Their Implementation in Comprehensive School Reform

Phase	*Implementation*
Establish benchmarks for implementation	Based on provider's experience in many schools. Develop or select existing evaluation tools. Outline all components of a design or model to be implemented.
Identify benchmarks	Equalize school with benchmark schools on the basis of such demographics as SES data, student stability (stable students divided by total number of students enrolled), percent of minority students (e.g., all nonwhite)
Identify program to be implemented and the degree of fit between program and school needs	Identify program to be incorporated into school curricula as potentially beneficial to improvement; programs may include established programs such as Reading Recovery or Success for All to meet school needs. Science programs may include Geometer's Tutor programs in incorporating technology.
Schools establish need and expectations about student outcomes	Establish base levels in relevant area(s)' achievement levels and student progress over a period of time (pre/post). Estimate how long it will take to reach levels of implementation for each component. Use rubrics to describe different levels of implementation.
Assess progress toward benchmarks	Evaluate student outcomes annually or semi-annually: achievement, teacher or student retention, student attendance, parental involvement, levels of new program implementation, use of good teaching practices, and so on.
Use a variety of assessment tools	Assessment tools include questionnaires, observation, focus groups, individual interviews, and school and classroom observation protocols. Measure skills and knowledge in multiple ways against content standards.
Communicate findings regarding expectations and intentions of program implementation	Improvement on factors considered responsive to change: instructional practices, levels of new program implementation; ability of students to articulate expectations and reasons why activities are engaged in; interactive teaching to facilitate constructive processes and to help students explore topics; and so on.

Phase	Implementation
Feed evaluation findings back to school as a means of encouraging continuous improvement.	Provide results of assessment; evaluative information on processes and outcomes directly addressed in the concerns of users. Information is provided about the practicality and consequences of their change efforts.
Enhance commitment of school staff to the change process.	Teachers see themselves as mastering the process and perceive that their students are improving. Teachers develop problem coping strategies and a sustained mindfulness, leading to further diagnosis and action taking.

Source: Adapted from Ross (2000); Rowan, Camburn, & Barnes (2004).

■ Best Practices Research

Best practices research is not the exclusive domain of educators. It is used by large corporations—for instance, those which investigate how high-quality administration is achieved by leadership practices that increase productivity. Educators, similarly, can attempt to identify practices contributing to productivity (school organization, administration, instruction, or other aspects of education). The study of best practices contributes to the improvement of schools through recommendations offered by practices believed to be on-target, yet within the limits of practicality, capable of being successfully reached by teachers or schools.

The Study of Best Practices

Two frequently employed research techniques are used for identifying such practices. One is the *method of comparison*. It begins with the identification of benchmarks and compares the practices of teachers, administrators, schools, districts, or other units in one school (e.g., one considered poor performing) with those in another school deemed to be experts or exemplars of expertise according to assessments of their performance. The other method is the *method of meta-analysis*. It begins with the practices and appraises their excellence (or lack thereof) through available empirical evidence regarding the effectiveness of a practice or practices in a variety of settings. The use of these practices is then suggested for use by schools wanting to improve their performance. Some examples of each method are presented in this chapter.

There is no single guide for best practices studies and, in fact, some may be conducted informally. Nevertheless, any method of studying best practices is oriented to the improvement of some aspect of education. Within the classroom, each begins with a common concern, that is, the need to clearly state the relation of instructional practices to intended outcomes of instruction. From that point on, assessment needs to be planned and consistently managed to result in identification of practices that are validly related to productivity (learning improvement).

Meta-analysis for Identifying Best Practices

Meta-analysis begins with identification of available studies conducted on a targeted practice or subject-matter area—for instance, one problem might be to develop a summary of available research specifically related to the effects of repeated testing (the practice) on student achievement of factual knowledge. The summary of results of these studies is then examined (perhaps statistically) for consistency and strength of effects across all studies: What does the research suggest regarding specific teaching techniques that will help students reach stated standards? In well-conducted meta-analyses the studies are initially accumulated for their relevance to the objectives of concern and screened for their compliance with rigorous research demands. Because the studies selected are typically conducted in very different contexts, the results that emerge are probably unrelated to situational demands; the researcher may conclude that strong effects imply or suggest that the effects are not due to differences in contexts but to the processes under investigation and, thus, may have wider applicability than a single study limited in sample size, location, and the like.

One such analysis has led to the finding of the class-size effect. Across a range of school contexts, a consistent finding is that performance (test scores) is inversely related to class size (i.e., small class sizes earn higher scores than larger classes). (It should be noted that this effect is described here as an illustration of best practice research. Although the finding does not answer the question of what it is about class size that contributes to this effect, the finding has influenced legislation limiting class size in some states.)

Somewhat similar to the meta-analytic studies are the reviews of the literature conducted by experts who compare and contrast the findings from a selection of studies. The expert then draws conclusions about the importance of the practices within the framework of validity of the findings.

A comparison of two sets of practices is illustrated in Table 15.2.

Table 15.2. A Comparison of Two Methods for Identifying Good Practices

1. Example of Benchmarks Used for Identifying Best Practices in Teacher Preparation

The process begins with benchmarks either from informed expertise or by informing experts who base their identification of best practices on top-performing units. It assumes the knowledge that any assessment samples the actual knowledge, skills, and dispositions expected in given situations. Benchmarks are based on the ways knowledge of learners, community values and contexts, and standards affect outcomes. The process articulates beliefs regarding good practices of instruction and issues regarding standards and how they are assessed. One set of partial implications of training in assessment for teacher preparation is summarized here.*

- Plan standards; integrate lesson plans; attend to issues of content pedagogy, general pedagogy, and content knowledge.
- Use multiple formats for assessment tools—observation, traditional tools, portfolios, research and inquiry, case studies. Use assessments frequently; respect diversity.
- Involve participants as appropriate in the development and conduct of assessment.
- Implications and inferences regarding good practice are the outcomes affecting the purposes at different stages of assessment and instruction.
- Assessment is as much assessment of curricula and instruction as it is of student performance.
- Provide for feedback adjusted to stakeholders' interests; developmental level, level of learner's performance; and diagnosis of area requiring attention and instruction; this promotes and provides for self-assessment.

*The full report should be read for complete details of the study of successful, powerful teacher-education programs.

Source: Adapted from Darling-Hammond (2006, Chapter 5, pp. 113–151).

2. Example of Meta-analysis Used for Identifying Practices: What Works Best in Writing?

The emphasis in meta-analysis is the identification of what research suggests regarding teaching or other techniques associated with schooling—what will help student reach stated standards in a subject-matter area or what works best at a given developmental level. Meta-analysis requires good planning, searching the literature, conducting statistical analyses, and summarizing. The partial results of one literature search are summarized below.

- Multiple types of lessons, teaching component skills through methods such as *sentence combining*, while taking advantage of *word processing* and other supporting technologies. Using technology such as word processing provides opportunity for added skills related to editing, rewriting, and writing to learn.
- Integrated assessment, providing clear *rubrics* for quality writing and *models* of good writing.
- Integrated instruction connecting writing to meaningful goals in classroom and beyond, through the use of *prewriting, inquiry activities*, and *writing across the curriculum*.
- Explicit *strategy instruction* not only in general writing processes but in specific, critical writing tasks such as *writing for real audiences* and *cycles of planning, reviewing, and summarization*.
- Fostering *collaborative writing* by adopting a *process writing approach* and structuring classroom activities to make writing a natural, shared task for achieving a variety of instructional goals.

Meta-analysis may sometimes identify negative practices; for example in this study, it was found in 10 studies that traditional grammar instruction, such as parts of speech and sentence structure, had negative or neutral effects on writing improvement.

Source: Adapted from Graham & Perin (2007).

Method of Comparison

The method of comparison is probably the one most associated with best practices. It begins with (a) *identification* from informed observation of events, behaviors, practices, and processes that are related to educational goals of interest; (b) *descriptions of the effects* of these events such as the results or reactions of teacher or students to instructional events; and (c) *explanations*, insofar as possible, stating the underlying reasons confirming the event's relation to the targeted links.

A generalized series of steps is presented below. Compare these with the steps shown in Table 15.1; these steps are in most respects similar to or an extension of those on benchmarking.

1. *Statement of purpose*. The purposes correspond to targeted objectives for initiating the study; for instance, "Identify schools or teachers whose students perform with excellence." The objectives or criteria being targeted are implied in such questions as, "Which teachers have students whose performance is in the top quartile of NAEP scores?" "Which schools have a large proportion of graduates who go on to college?" "Which teachers of math have larger proportions of students who are most successful in advanced courses?" "Which schools have received A grades on successive administrations of statewide comprehensive test?" or, "How is writing being taught in the best-performing schools?" "What are the content standards and how are they taught in schools where students excel in meeting basic content area standards?"

2. *Obtain data on all schools characterized by quality of outcome*. Once the objectives are clearly stated, the data on a set of schools, characterized by a set of criteria that define them, are obtained. For example, data could be obtained on the number of graduates from schools with limited resources who are admitted to college; or on advanced math course grades of college students who have taken introductory courses with a given teacher.

3. *Data sources*. To the extent of their availability, data are obtained from multiple sources of evidence such as observations, interviews, objective tests, statewide tests, performance measures, and authentic measures. Sampling of knowledge, skills, and dispositions in authentic contexts is a useful, generally accepted procedure. The sampling of data from several sources would constitute a planned and integrated set of assessments. The researcher would avoid poor research

practices resulting in undefined, fragmented, or isolated data such as the exclusive use of objective test data because it was all that was available, or of data restricted to the acquisition of factual knowledge alone.

4. *Rank units being studied on the basis of data obtained.* Once the data has been obtained for schools or teachers or other units, the units are ranked from high to low on the criteria selected for targeting. These become the basis for benchmarking; for instance, the top 10 schools or the top 10 percent of schools across the state provide the basis for identifying the practices they use, with the expectation that these practices are the ones contributing to the unit's success.

5. *Select benchmark schools.* The selection of the top schools can be a complicated process. A school selected as a benchmark for studying classroom practices is selected based on the assumption that it is best because of its instructional practices and not due to such demographics as high socioeconomic status, ethnicity, or similar variables. If the achievements are found to be the result of variables other than instruction, these must be clearly identified. The idea of benchmarking is to identify experts (e.g., master teachers) or expertise (schools or districts) that contribute to outstanding performance and, in addition, are exemplars of excellence on some attribute (e.g., "A-grade" schools for three successive years). If the performance record is due to other variables such as section of the country (e.g., northwest or southeast), the results are disaggregated on that variable.

6. *Identify positive and negative practices contributing to objectives.* Evidence and data regarding the practice of these experts in the area of concern (instruction, resources, administration) are collected. The practices are also collected for the schools or teachers ranked as the bottom quartile, poorest, or most in need of improvement (i.e., in the poor-performing schools). The best practices are determined by a comparison of those practices used by the schools at the top and bottom ranks with similar demographics. The practices unique to the top group are considered successful or best and those unique to the bottom group are considered as potential hindrances to good performance. Such comparisons permit examination of events having the potential of being negative practices that contribute to poor performance. Each set of unique practices is examined more thoroughly for theoretical and empirical support that might be reported in the literature.

7. *Implement practices for improvement of instruction.* Those practices identified as best, supported by theoretical considerations, and based on evidence are recommended for implementation across schools as having potential for improving current practices. The practices must be linked to standards and implemented by tasks designed to achieve desired performance levels.

■ Best Practices for Educational Improvement

In a changing view of assessment, the study of best practices is legitimately considered as a part of educational reform, a reform manifested in both the intent underlying the use of assessment and the purposes to be achieved by assessment. This orientation is unlike that of an earlier era in which summative evaluation dominated the scene. The teacher's and the system's responsibility were, at best, displaced; the responsibility was passed on to the student, whose low grades were due to his or her lack of responsiveness to instruction, but he or she could improve those scores by "working hard enough." The prevailing reasoning went something like the following: The simple act of giving tests and grades would in itself reliably induce student anxiety. Students would be motivated to perform well in order to avoid the dire consequences of low grades. Or, simultaneously, anxiety might be induced by comparing a student's grades with others in his class. The low-performing students would be motivated to do better in order to avoid the stigma of being at the bottom of their class. Whatever the reasoning, test anxiety induced by grading was a means of inducing the student to study harder and to memorize better and probably, at that time, was considered a "best practice." Although the current evidence and view is that these effects are minimal, the same view seems to prevail today among administrators, teachers, pupils, and parents; they often believe that remediating the behavioral outcome is less a result of instructional intervention and more a consequence endured by the student. (However, one can find increasing evidence in the media as well as in group discussion that instructional responsibilities also apply.)

More modern approaches (Chappuis & Stiggins, 2004) take the view that a critical element of assessment is the provision of data for facilitating learning. Not only does it involve both teachers and students in setting objectives for promoting meaningful learning, but it is also used as a basis for revealing the practices of each instructional component associated with good (or poor) progress in learning and achievement. Good teaching practices that may be considered as best practices include those involved in typical day-to-day decisions about instruction; for example:

- Identifying the best stage to evaluate the achievement of objectives
- Diagnosing student requirements for learning such as when and how to practice a skill or strategy
- Knowing or being aware of the availability of learning strategies
- Teaching self-regulation in the use of learning strategies
- Diagnosing teaching effectiveness
- Relating specific teaching practices to specific objectives (imparting facts, developing skills, forming attitudes, and understanding)
- Timing the introduction of specific teaching practices (peer tutoring, jigsaw classroom, or instructional technology)
- Knowing the bases for implementing practices (e.g., oppositional matching, that is, the matching of students who learn by understanding with students who appear to be learning by rote means)

The question in the use of best practices is not simply "What level of achievement has a school or school district or other unit attained?" but, rather, "How did they get there?" "What practices permitted them to get there?" and "Are these the best way, or are there better ways?" In addition, best practices research adds the question of whether these practices would be of general use to other schools where student performance is not average or lower than average.

The Best Practices Knowledge Base

The idea behind best practices is that there are *reasons* why schools are or are not performing well. These reasons provide a basis for changing the ways teachers teach and students learn. In view of the many activities in which teachers engage and the many decisions they make hour to hour, it is notable that over time the best practices can easily be overlooked while issues of the moment take priority. These are brought to the fore in studies focusing on finding best practices. For either students or teachers such reasons involve knowing (a) *where students are in their learning* (Are they learning facts? Making associations? Improving in their understanding?), (b) *what the learning targets are* (Are they simply trying to pass a test?

Making applications? Thinking creatively?), and (c) *what steps are needed for achieving those targets* (e.g., do you want to add understanding or organization to the students' knowledge base? Do you want to add problem solving strategies? Do you want to improve study skills?).

Some of these practices are evident, on a more informal basis, in teachers' daily activity. Students, too, are often engaged in finding their best practices for getting along in school. Without guidance, the involvement of either student or teacher results in much incidental learning, much of which may be a misrepresentation of what it is that affects achievement. From assessment feedback teachers can infer student views (and their correspondence to teacher views) regarding:

- *Goal setting* (simply to find out where they stand versus what they hope to achieve)
- *Attributes of good learning* (inert rote memory versus understanding or application)
- *Evaluation of their own performance* (against a criterion of good performance versus comparison with others in the class)
- *Steps in learning* (study details versus generalizations versus understanding)
- *Use of examples*
- *Criteria involved in achieving high scores*
- *Expectations* about what is to be learned from given teachers
- *Expectations* of what is to be learned from test content and format
- *Ways of revising* their own work
- *Reasoning* for making revisions

But it is desirable that teachers back up their inferences using evidence-based (empirical) studies of best practices to understand the reasons behind current trends in education, what practices uniquely characterize good and poorer performing schools, what their schools are doing right already, which of the practices they are using could stand improvement, how improvements might be made, or what corrective practices should be made. Best practices are intended to be a research-based method of obtaining evidence about tools, methods, and materials that have proven to support effective teaching and achievement. They are a way of improving teaching and learning through research-based strategies. The starting point for the process of evidence-based identification of best practices is identifying a basis for comparison (the benchmark).

A Case Study

A best practices study framework (based on NCEA, 2008) is represented by the Just for the Kids (J4TK) study of nearly 500 school systems across the nation, on which the following description is based. It is a framework to identify a summary of activities found to distinguish consistently high-performing schools from average- or low-performing schools. Although some elements of good practices exist in average-performing schools, there may be difficulty in identifying them because their use in average-performing schools may be insufficiently institutionalized to be reflected in student achievement.

The J4TK framework is *not* the only framework possible, but it provides a unique set of components for identifying best practices. As the authors state, the practices studied do not refer to specific instructional issues such as which reading program to buy, whether to allow calculators in mathematics classes, or how best to teach English language learners to divide fractions. Rather, they refer to the broad principles of a school system's work that are most directly related to teaching and learning. The framework does not attempt to include everything that school systems do.

Certain levels of a school system have more activities located outside their framework than other levels. For example, district activities that are fundamentally instructional tasks are described in the framework, while other required activities (such as maintaining relationships with the community or school board) are not discussed. Teachers at the classroom level, on the other hand, are deeply involved in the instructional program of the school but still may take on some activities, such as sponsoring extracurricular activities that fall outside the research framework. Although activities that relate only indirectly to instruction can be important to schools and may, in fact, serve critical support roles for instruction, they do so in different ways than are represented in the objectives of the study. For example, there may well be a best way to run food services or transportation systems, but, as you would expect, those administrative and support functions are not the focus of the best practice framework.

The best practice framework has been used in a number of states, using it to focus on practices and strategies found in benchmark schools. It is critical here to note that the benchmark schools are those schools in a district judged to be high performing. They can be used as bases for comparison with average or below-average performing schools. The practices that are identified as unique to them are identified or demonstrated to be the best practices. The best practices then are assumed to be the practices that have contributed to their above-average performance. (See www.just4kids.org/bestpractice/research _methodolgoy.cfm?sub=methodology for details in which you might be interested but that do not appear in our description or for details that may be unique to particular states in which the studies have been conducted.)

Both quantitative data and qualitative data are obtained (a) for information defined by the professional or content standards, (b) for the alignments of programs and practices, and (c) for monitoring purposes aimed at intervention and adjustments. *Quantitative* data are obtained through assessments based on tests, particularly standardized measures that are aligned with the curriculum. *Qualitative* data are based on observation of classrooms; document analysis; and phone and individual interviews with teachers, principals, and parents. These considerations are of concern whenever the results of a study are compiled into a case study report.

A typical summary of findings based on observations from schools in one state is summarized in Theory to Practice Box 15.2. The topics comprising the framework are reflected in the display.

Different Purposes Served by Best Practice Research

A slightly different approach from the J4TK's student is represented in a current study being conducted by the American Psychological Association (Belar, 2009). It focuses on "a sample of 5000 graduates of specialized high schools in science, math and technology" and compares them with "1000 students with similar characteristic who are graduates of traditional high schools" (both sets are comprised of graduates in the last four to six years). The intent is to identify the career and educational consequences of their participation in the two educational tracks. In addition, the objectives of the study are to "provide insight into the educational practices that appear to be most strongly associated with these outcomes" (Belar, 2009, p. 301).

Although the reasoning in both the APA and the J4TK studies is similar to that underlying formative assessment, best practice studies begin with identification of high-performing schools (or other criteria). The high-performing schools are used as a comparative base with low-performing schools (or other criteria) to determine unique factors that contribute to the performance of each.

Theory to Practice Box 15.2
AN ILLUSTRATION OF ONE BEST PRACTICES SUMMARY REPORT*

Researchers conducted site visits to 15 elementary schools in New York identified through the NCEA analysis. Summaries of the findings of those practices that appeared to distinguish consistently higher-performing elementary schools from average-performing ones are presented below by theme.

Curriculum and Academic Goals

In the higher performing schools, the [State] Learning Standards were positively presented as a powerful tool to serve all students and guide improvement. The delivery of the curriculum in every classroom . . . was both expected and monitored while teachers retained the ability to be creative in instructional approaches to that delivery.

Staff Selection, Leadership, and Capacity Building

Stable and strong instructional leadership existed . . . in higher performing school systems; principals and district office personnel were "focused on student learning." Collaboration focused on curricular and instructional issues.

Instructional Programs, Practices, and Arrangements

Instructional programs were primarily mandated at the district level. Teachers supplemented adopted programs with appropriate classroom materials. The primary instructional strategy noted at the consistently higher performing schools was "differentiated instruction."

Monitoring: Compilation, Analysis, and Use of Data

Collective accountability across school levels as well as within schools marked the culture of consistently higher performing schools. Monitoring of student achievement was varied and ongoing, being initiated well before any state testing occurred. Data were organized and available, and staff were both highly dependent on and skilled at using data to make informed decisions about teaching and learning.

Recognition, Intervention, and Adjustment

Recognition of students and teachers was centered on improvement in academic achievement in consistently higher performing schools. Interventions for students needing assistance were immediate and well established. Interventions were planned both within and outside the individual classrooms.

*This summary is an adapted version of the original for illustrative purposes. Some details or practices have been omitted. The reader may wish to refer to the full report, which provides details of the research methods used and the description of each of the 10 schools on which the summary is based, as well as more complete details of the summary.

Source: The above material was retrieved on August 15, 2009, from the more complete report for New York schools at www.just4kids.org/en/research_policy/best_practices/executive_summaries.cfm. The reader may wish to read reports for schools in their state by accessing the same website.

In formative assessment one identifies, in the course of teaching, the performance of a class and then examines why the class is performing well or poorly in terms of a particular known standard. Knowing that, the decision is based on the question: "What can be done to improve or retain the instructional level?" The answers are to be found, generally, through reasoned decisions based upon the teacher's understanding of how people learn leadership, policy, and other related information. Best practices, on the other hand, assume that we can identify a well-performing unit or benchmark based upon some measure or reference against which comparisons are made. Knowing that, the question is, "What practices are uniquely associated with that unit's performance?" The answer, obviously, is found in identifying the practices unique to that unit, not shared by a less effective unit.

A form of best practices study conducted differently from the one described in Theory to Practice Box 15.2, rather than being based on a benchmark begins with a series of evidence-based beliefs about best practices for educational purposes (Ross, 2000; Ross & Morrison, 2009). An example of such beliefs might be the existence of a given classroom climate (e.g., learning-oriented or performance-oriented). Then parents, teachers, and administrators rate their degree of agreement (on a Likert rating scale of *1 = strongly agree* to *5 = strongly disagree*) that the school is characterized by that climate. The productivity (student achievement) is then examined for its correlation with the presence of a given classroom climate. Ratings would only be one of a number of possible assessments for identifying classroom climate. The difficulty with the use of a rating scale is that statements about classroom climate, as related to learning, may be supported by the research literature but do not have the opportunity to surface within the experience of a respondent and so can't be observed.

In line with good research methodology, the results of best practices studies are critically analyzed for the reliability and validity of findings to minimize differences in their interpretation: Assessments may be inappropriate for determining whether a practice is a good one, and, even if it has been identified as one associated with the best-performing schools, it may be difficult to determine whether it has a direct relation to instructional outcomes. Nevertheless, when carefully conducted, the best practices format can be a useful form of research for helping schools improve performance:

> When properly implemented best practices research . . . is initiated with assessment. As they regularly assess

themselves schools can use the information constructively taking the opportunity to learn how to improve their practices, how to monitor their progress, and communicate the results to others. Gear assessment to promote success rather than simply measure it as is sometimes attributed to state assessment practices. (Shepard, 2001)

And, we have noted elsewhere, conclusions from best practices research can provide useful feedback regarding instructional and curricular goals. Chappuis and Stiggins (2004), in applying the work of Black and Wiliam (1998), say,

> When teachers use the principles of assessment implied in formative and best-practices approaches students demonstrate unprecedented score gains on standardized assessments . . . they make feedback about the goals of assessment, descriptive and informative . . . becoming a school improvement tool aiding the school . . . to become a body composed of responsible, engaged, and self-directed learners.

Most measures in education, such as statewide tests and the NAEP, have generated considerable information about schools and students over a number of years and can be considered as bases for identifying benchmark schools and the practices they use. Many schools have improved considerably during that period, whereas others have stood still. It is the interest of best practice researchers to determine the associated practices related to such differences in progress of schools.

■ Using Best Practices in Teacher Education

Informed feedback from best practices studies, then, can be helpful to teachers and schools for enhancing their instructional capabilities in teaching subject-matter content. Often it is simply a matter of increasing awareness of alternative empirically based practices. These practices and the abilities associated with them may have been overlooked in education, or perhaps some teachers did not have the opportunity to develop appreciation of these practices in their experience.

Best practices formats suggest a focus on the use of authentic tasks in tests for teacher selection or teacher accomplishment rather than simply on the multiple-choice formats sometimes used for these purposes. A focus on authentic instructional tasks permits examination of the extent to which high-quality instructional practices have been acquired, whether they can be used within the perspective of subject-matter standards, and whether they can be applied in the context of real students in real schools. Such studies enable the examination of the interface of teachers interacting with real students, parents, and administrators. When they are focused on norms for good teaching shared by the profession they can become the basis for teachers' individual development of career portfolios as well as in the development of in-service programs for teachers.

Informing Instruction

The intended outcomes of best practices do not occur automatically. The program must be initiated and implemented with the complete cooperation (and understanding) of schools in the ongoing operation of investigation and research; the expectation should be that returns from investigations occur slowly over time.

In the course of employing investigations and applications of best practices, teachers must expect to hone existing skills or learn new ones. They become aware of new developments through the professional literature. They develop new perspectives of their classroom and interaction with their students through collaboration with their peers. When the best practices model is fully and optimally implemented by teachers and schools they can demonstrate the extent to which a school program has made progress in improvement of learning and has met policy requirements.

Good Research Practice in Best Practices Studies

Obviously, best practices research can contribute to the in-service training of teachers beyond the settings in which it has been conducted. It can be used to facilitate development of new skills and knowledge needed to help students learn in other settings—whether in the immediate district or nationally. It can instill the expectation that instructors and administrators everywhere can make improvements to instruction and curricular programs.

Nevertheless, it is critical that administrators and stakeholders recognize the potential for downfalls either in the research or implementation of the programs. For example, in designing studies for benchmarks, the locations of schools should be proportionately sampled in terms of ethnicity or diversity. The resources available to districts must be known. Some schools may have resources contributing to their success that others do not have, such as proximity to libraries or higher education opportunities. The method of assessment of schools must be carefully considered as well as the validity and reliability of the measures used. Respondents (teachers or administrators) reporting on their practices must be trained so that practices employed are understood and, when data is collected on them, the data can be translated into practices that teachers can employ in definable ways.

Overall, the implementation of the best practices model must follow the regulations of good research. Requirements or variables similar to those represented in the research phase must also be present when the schools that are to benefit from the research begin incorporating new practices into their programs.

It is not beyond the scope of reality that when offered a new practice to follow, a teacher or administrator will modify it to make it "better." They must be guided in employing the practice conscientiously in the manner intended without such extensions in modification that the practice becomes a different one than that identified as best. Sometimes personnel (teachers and administrators) are unwilling to accept a new practice, favoring a traditional one that may no longer be useful. In such cases, actual deployment of a program must be delayed until such time as the dispositions of the personnel involved have been changed to adopt the practice effectively. (You may want to refer to Table 15.2 for an example of how best practice studies in writing identified a traditional practice that does not provide the same outcome as the newer practices.)

Another interesting, though negative, outcome of assessment policy has surfaced. It is a practice somewhat like teaching the test and is reported upon in a news article (Breitenstein, 2009). The article focuses on the similarity of about 50 schools from several school districts within a state in the writing of essays for the XCAT writing tests. The similarity was not due to the sharing of answers during the test or preparation on identical XCAT test material prior to the test; they couldn't be easily shared since several school districts were involved. Rather, the similarity was due to the way the students were taught. The teachers used a template for teaching writing in ways that were believed to be consistent with performing the test task. Template writing was the instructional practice of choice. Evidently, it was used by teachers across districts in attempts to facilitate improvement in their student's writing skills. The test task, in the statewide comprehensive examination, is ordinarily introduced by providing a prompt (i.e., the way the writing was to proceed).

The difficulty was noticed by the readers of the essays; they noticed that the students (fourth-grade students) in the schools, across districts, followed the same pattern without differentiating their writing according to the prompt (e.g., expository or narrative). According to the report the schools were using the template framework for

the five paragraph essay,
- *an introduction* [e.g., give the writing a focal point],
- *three supporting paragraphs* [e.g., arguments to support the event, help the reader understand, or give explanations], and
- *conclusion* [e.g., a decision]. (Breitenstein, 2009)

The practice itself, or even the possibility that students were sharing answers, was *not* the cause for concern. Rather, it was the fact that the essays followed precisely the same patterns without concern for the prompt that was to guide the answer; the same "words, phrases, and imagery" appeared across essays from students in the same schools and districts. Students were not accused of cheating, but the instruction had simply bypassed the intent of the statewide tests for measuring students' writing skills. Stereotyped products did not meet state standards for good writing. As a result of their instruction, student essays were unimaginative and lacking in originality, obviously tailored to fit the template they had been taught so well in preparation for the test. In their use of catch phrases, similar transition sentences, analogies, and uses of imagery, the students were not meeting the standard of writing skillfully; in their adherence to the format hammered in during instruction, they were not showing the extent of their ability for making a writing style work well or convincingly.

Lessons in Using Assessments

The foregoing anecdote illustrates some important points regarding best practices. First, when a best practice is employed rigidly, without understanding, it has the potential of producing negative rather than positive results, results that have been described earlier as narrowing the curriculum through teaching to the test. Secondly, when test results are skillfully analyzed, the analysis can reveal difficulties in the instructional process that need remediation.

The weaknesses of the assessment process are also revealed in the context of the anecdote: The instructional remediation required for beginning writers is to build flexibility into the student's use of writing skills, *not to prepare for the purposes of assessment incorrectly perceived* (i.e., we should attend to the administration of a test as an instrument for assessing student achievement rather than simply as an instrument to find out who is capable of earning a high score). To be reasonable in our evaluation of the practice, accessories such as templates can provide beginners in writing with a potentially useable plan. Perhaps some tangential benefits of self-acquired metacognitions about writing and beginning to write are also acquired along the way. However, when learning is used in the manner described in the anecdote, the strategy becomes something of a crutch. In future learning, there must be a transition from the use of templates as rigid guides to their meaningful use in adapting writing to certain circumstances or relinquishing the guides in favor of some other strategy to achieve creativity. Accordingly, students learn that writing style is used differently and flexibly according to genre (description for expository, compare and contrast for evaluation, and so on). Thirdly, the relation of the test questions, the standards underlying them, and best methods for achieving the standards must be correctly perceived. In this example, it became obvious that the teachers, across 50 schools, were influenced by uninformed perceptions of test purposes (or, perhaps, the pressure of dealing with individual differences) and as a consequence were inappropriately modifying their instruction.

In reacting to these possibilities, test constructors responsibly examine test results for suggestions or recommendations for instruction. They bring any anticipated difficulties before the teachers and demonstrate ways of instructing students such that they will meet the state standards in producing original writing products. Further, the analysis of test products is instrumental in bringing to the attention of assessment experts the extent to which the test results were an accurate representation of the students' writing skills, rather than, as in this case, an ability to follow a template or the same writing technique for *all* prompts. It should be noted that, in this case, the revision of the assessment led to an instructional focus on tasks that discouraged the use of overrehearsed, robotic patterns of writing.

■ Summary

Best practices studies are, in some ways, comparable to program evaluation. Both attempt to provide evidence regarding the practices being used in schooling that make a difference. These studies may not, for everyday purposes, adhere strictly to specific, well-known experimental or similar research designs. Nevertheless, when these studies are conducted for applications across districts they are expected to be conducted rigorously and credibly. Evidence is gathered to compare the practices of high-performing with average- or low-performing schools. The data are carefully collected and interpreted to enable the objective and unbiased identification of strong instructional practices.

As shown in this chapter, such evaluation can take place at various phases of instruction—before, during, or after instruction or delayed until some time following the completion of instruction. In the initial phases, practices are evaluated formatively to provide feedback to instructors regarding their success in the development of learning products. As instruction proceeds, remedial measures can be introduced or interventions can be changed if necessary. Recall that one of the practices of high-performing schools in the Just for the Kids study was the availability of a "pyramid of intervention practices"—a feature of the high-performing schools. The practices could be implemented if formative assessment suggested that need. At the conclusion of instruction, summative evaluation provides a basis for determining the extent to which the completed instruction produced the intended outcomes—for example, was the instruction standards based? Did it produce learning and achievement outcomes consistent with the standards?

In all applications there is the need to examine how the principles from the laboratory fare when field applications are made. The practice must be justified by the learning environments for which it was intended. Best practices studies go beyond the degree to which students acquire factual knowledge (although such outcomes are not discounted, of course, when they play a justifiable role in preparation for later phases of cognitive development).

One framework for evaluation (Ross & Morrison, 2009) described instructional effectiveness on the basis of such characteristics as interaction with students (sharing responsibilities, setting goals, establishing remedial interventions, evaluation of outcomes); qualities of instruction (assessment used; standards or bases of assessments; use of assessments once made; communications or reporting to community, parents, and students), and, importantly, the degree to which students are engaged in schooling (motivation, interest, perseverance, receptivity to feedback).

In best practices field studies, students are one of the central data sources. They complete surveys; they comment on schools, teachers, and instruction; and they respond to testing at every phase (diagnostic tests, teacher-made tests, standardized tests, alternative tests, statewide comprehensive tests, all pre/post tests, etc.) Teachers, too, are a major source of data. They evaluate instructional practices, the quality of the practice for intended goals (from processes for acquisition of content to processes facilitating higher order thinking processes), the degree to which practices are effective and effectively implemented, the quality of learning outcomes associated with the practice, and the motivational attributes of students as they are affected by the instructional practice.

Products from best practice research (see National Center for Educational Accountability, 2005a, 2005b, 2008 as examples) emphasize strategies for school improvement: (a) reports describing the characteristics of high performing schools compared with similar but average-performing or poorer-performing schools; and (b) descriptions of what research says to the teacher (including what research says for the principal, the superintendent, the community, or the policy). Models based on practices and policies in high-performing and average-performing schools guide the preparation of manuals. They provide the practices in high-performing schools that might be influential in improving the performance of average- or under-performing schools.

■ References

Belar, C. (2009). Bringing psychology to teaching and learning. *American Psychologist, 64,* 301.

Black, P., & Wiliam, D. (1998). Inside the black box: Raising standards through classroom assessment. *Phi Delta Kappan, 80*(2), 139–148.

Breitenstein, D. (2009, July 22). Schools warned on FCAT: Lee students' essays appear to be unoriginal. *The News-Press, Nation & World,* pp. A1, A3.

Chappuis, S., & Stiggins, R. J. (2004). Classroom assessment for learning. Retrieved February, 2004, from http://curriculum.risd41.org/committee/best_practices/files/mod2_day1/Nov1%20MagArticle.doc.

Darling-Hammond, L. (2006). *Powerful teacher education: Lessons from exemplary programs.* San Francisco: Jossey-Bass.

Graham, S., & Perin, D. (2007). *Writing next: Effective strategies to improve writing of adolescents in middle and high schools—a report to Carnegie Corporation of New York.* Washington, DC: Alliance for Excellent Education.

National Center for Educational Accountability. (2005a). Best practices framework for Arkansas. Retrieved February 16, 2005, from www.just4kids.org/bestpractice/study_framework,cfn?byb+state&stydt=Arkansas.

National Center for Educational Accountability. (2005b). Best practices of high performing school systems by the National Center for Educational Achievement: Methodology. Retrieved February 16, 2005, from www.just4kids.org/bestpractice/research_methodolgoy.cfm?sub=methodology.

National Center for Educational Achievement. (2008). Research & policy: Best practices framework. About the framework. About the themes. Retrieved May 1, 2008, from http://just4kids.org/en/research_policy/best_practices/about_practice.cfm.

Ross, S. M. (2000). *How to evaluate comprehensive school reform models*. Arlington, VA: New American Schools.

Ross, S. M., & Morrison, G. R. (2009). The role of evaluation in instructional design. In K. H. Silber & W. R. Foshay (Eds.), *Handbook of improving performance in the workplace. Instructional design and training delivery* (Vol. 1, pp. 554–576). San Francisco: Pfeiffer.

Rowan, B., Camburn, E., & Barnes, C. (2004). *Benefiting from comprehensive school reform: A review of research on CSR implementation*. Washington, DC: National Clearinghouse for Comprehensive School Reform.

Shepard, L. A. (2001, July). *Using assessment to help students think about learning*. Paper presented at the Assessment Training Institute Summer Conference, Portland, OR.

Shepard, L. A., Hammerness, K., Darling-Hammond, L., Snowden, J. B., Godon, E., Gutierrez, C., et al. (2005). Assessment. In L. Darling-Hammond, J. D. Bransford, P. LePage, K. Hammerness & H. Duffy (Eds.), *Preparing teachers for a changing world: What teachers should learn and be able to do* (Chapter 8). San Francisco: Jossey-Bass.

Wiggins, G., & McTighe, J. (1998). *Understanding by design*. Alexandria, VA: Association for Supervision and Curriculum Development.

CHAPTER 16

Test Bias, Fairness, and Testing Accommodations

V ALIDITY AND RELIABILITY are important qualities of assessment measures and can be easily compromised. This is not unique to educational or psychological measurement. Even those measures with which we are most familiar in daily life and those used in the sciences, such as measures of length, height, and weight, have the potential for measurement errors. That is, the measurements can be biased in unsuspected ways when used by the less-informed person or when used casually without the necessity for precision (e.g., we might say, "he weighs about 150 lbs."). But in most cases dependably precise measures are needed, and even tiny distortions may be unacceptable. This need for dependable instruments is evident almost daily in reports of local school grades on results from statewide high-stakes accountability tests. In the physics laboratory, measures from a precisely calibrated balance (scale) for weighing milligrams can give biased measures because of dust settling on it. To *accommodate* for such distortion, balances in physics laboratories are kept in enclosures. Similarly, if a precisely calibrated meter stick were to be made of a metal with an unduly large expansion rate, there is the possibility of distorted measurements due to fluctuations in temperature affecting the length of the instrument. To *accommodate* for this source of bias, precise measuring instruments (meter sticks) are made of materials that are stable under temperature changes. Other similar examples are found in all sciences, including physical anthropology, chemistry, astronomy, seismology, or meteorology.

Regardless of how well-developed an educational assessment might be, the outcomes of its use are subject to the influence of a number of variables resulting in biased scores. However, as in the sciences, with knowledge of the reasons for the existence of such errors, steps can be taken to minimize them. The aim in assessment of students as indicated in legal statements is to remove those sources of variability that result in scores that are too low because of systematic errors (due to bias and obstacles such as visual problems). Scores that are too low because of random errors due to carelessness, lack of motivation, and so on can also be reduced by the way the test is constructed, by the scheduling of the test, or by the way it is administered.

■ Obtained Scores, True Scores, and Error

Hypothetically, if the student were to take the same test repeatedly, with no learning taking place between administrations of the test, one might guess that the obtained score would be identical from one occasion to the next; it would be a "true" measure. The reality is that the score rarely, if ever, remains precisely the same when administered on separate occasions.

If an infinite number of samples (groups) of measurements were taken from the same group on several sessions, a range of scores with different means would be obtained. Scores for one session might be higher or lower than the overall mean because of changes in the examinees' motivation, attention, or physical condition. Some variation even occurs because of the influence of chance factors such as guessing the correct answer or some more identifiable experience related to the test question that sensitized the student to the correct answer. Different factors become engaged at different times, resulting in further changes in scores. These variations among observation samples are balanced in the mean across sessions; the overall mean of several testing situations is said to approximate the true score on that measure.

Components of the Obtained Score

The *obtained score* is the first outcome considered in judging the pupil's performance based on an assessment. Other scores (rankings, percentiles, standardized scores, and so on) are derived from it.

The obtained score is the base score that the student earns on a test, a rating, or other basic measure. It is the one you record, the one that represents the number right, the one that needs interpretation, or the one in a test manual with which to begin comparison with the norms for a standardized test such as a statewide examination. It is often called a *raw score*. It is perhaps true that most teachers accept it as a correct representation of the student's performance level and so assign and accept marks (A to F) accordingly.

True Score

But the raw score represents more than the "real" performance level; it is theoretically comprised of both (a) a measure of the student's true ability on the construct the test is supposed to measure, *and* (b) a number of variables existing at the time the student takes the test. The latter might involve affective states (such as feelings or motivations), challenges (such as perceptions of difficulty or need to excel), or physical states (such as health or disabilities) of the student taking the test, as well as the situational characteristics (such as demographics, characteristics, and setting) of the context in which the test is taken. Other factors include the processes or strategies employed and perceptions of test taking, either or both of which can potentially influence performance.

The factors of personal characteristics; situational, contextual, or environmental features; and some strategies used in test taking are extraneous, *construct–irrelevant* factors that become a part of the obtained score. These extraneous influences on the test score contribute to variations in scores and are assigned the term *measurement errors*.

Random Error

Some of the error is random, differing in unpredictable ways from one occasion to another. Although present for all the test takers, these sources of error may affect test takers differently. For example, the presence of other students may be distracting to one test taker, while another may be completely oblivious to their presence and remain unaffected.

Differences in ethnicity may have effects in many ways. One illustration is that different groups view testing differently. Such differences in perception of the assessment may have effects on (a) feelings of self-confidence or self-efficacy, (b) estimations of time for taking the test or time spent on an item (some students, given no time limit, may remain at a test for double the length of time taken by other students), and (c) particular information retrieved for any item. (It should be noted that these differences, though used as an example for ethnic groups, are not exclusive to any group; differences in perceptions have the potential of influencing the performance of any group or individual.)

In summary, the test score embraces the ability being measured (i.e., the validity of the test or its true score) and any

number of other known, unknown, inadvertent, or unaccountable factors that contribute to the score; these sources of error are known as *error variance*. Such factors include reactions to unpredictable variations in the conditions surrounding the test (noise, heat, light, time of day); responses to inadvertent procedures in administering the test; the unknown variations in the strategies used (guessing, eliminations of alternatives, etc.); the varying perceptions of the test; the strategies used in taking the test; effects of test formatting (types of test items, ordering from easy to difficult or vice versa, etc.), and the altered administration procedures from one assessment session to another.

Systematic Error

Some sources of influence on scores are systematic; they affect most if not all respondents of selected groups predictably and equally. For example, girls might be found to achieve higher grades in a subject-matter area than boys, or students from a cultural group taking a test that is dependent on their second language may earn consistently lower scores than a group whose first language is the same as the one on which the test is based.

An assessment biased in predictable ways may still be used fairly if we know *how* the bias affects the test score. Suppose, for example, that a test is consistently biased such that people from District A consistently score five points higher on the average than do those from District B. In such cases, five points would be added, as a constant, to the observed scores of the people from District B. That score might then be used fairly in making decisions about students in either group.

Summary

The obtained test score, consisting of two parts, the *true score* (the actual measured score) and *error* (due to factors contributing to the variation in the scores), is commonly represented in the expression:

$$\text{Obtained score} = \text{True score (T)} + \\ [\text{Random Error (RE)} + \text{Systematic error (SE)}]$$

■ Student Characteristics and Normative Comparisons

In some test development, norms for interpreting scores of individuals are based on scores of all people who had taken the test, for example, of students across the nation or state. Such wide-spread norms are often found to be biased against subgroups of students because of age, grade, or ethnic differences. As a result, test results vary in their ability to predict some targeted objective for some groups. The variation often depends on the characteristics of a group; for instance, a language test aimed at English-speaking students will be a better predictor of reading achievement when English is a first language than when Spanish is a first language. Such observations led to the need for establishing disaggregated norms.

Disaggregated Norms

Disaggregated norms are, simply, subnorms summarizing the performance of groups making up the total group. For example, the global norms for all students in the United States may consist of many subgroups such as (a) sections of the country—far west, northeast, southeast, central states, and so on; (b) ethnicity—including Hispanics, Native Americans, Asians, and so on; (c) rural versus urban; or (d) socioeconomic status represented in occupational groups. The disaggregated norms provide a more authentic base for making educational decisions than do the global norms because they consider the influences that contribute to measurement error.

Demographic Influences

A more subtle source of bias is rooted in the assumed role of such variables as family or cultural attitudes toward schooling and ways of learning. Primary-language culture, learning context, ethnicity, and socioeconomic status are all related to perceptions of the objectives of schooling, strategies for learning, or the value of assessment. All are direct or indirect influences on learning and performance and, as a result, on test scores.

Differences in Culture and Ethnicity

Unique experiences within a cultural or ethnic group affect what is learned, which in turn directly influences assessment outcomes. These experiences can contribute to a measure's reliability, validity, predictability, or utility for one population but not another. They can extend from specific educational circumstances, such as the students' or the teachers' ways of questioning, to the differences associated with the learning experiences in the home or cultural group. And, when considered by the test constructors, they can affect construction of tests and the interpretation of scores, whether positively or negatively.

Teacher Beliefs

Cultural differences are represented in teacher beliefs, too. They in turn may affect ways of testing as well as teaching. They certainly affect expectations regarding classwork assignments and other aspects of schooling. Such expectations may be disadvantageous to some groups (Hofer & Pintrich, 1977). For example, teachers may believe some students to be smarter or better learners, and as a result they are more generally favored over the students who are believed to be less successful learners. Beliefs regarding individual students may challenge teachers to adjust the level of difficulty for the entire class ("I need to make this test easier, because it wouldn't be fair to kids like Johnny," or "this test can be a little more difficult to make it challenging for Ernest.")

As has been shown with the "Pygmalion Effect," also known as the Rosenthal Effect (Jussim & Harber, 2005; Rosenthal & Jacobson, 1968/1992), perceptions can produce other outcomes. (The Pygmalion Effect refers to the phenomenon that teacher expectations affect student performance.) Thus, when students are believed to be smart, teachers tend to give them more attention than others in a class, thereby facilitating their potential for development. The consequence is that the student believed to be smart gets more help, guidance, or feedback than those believed to be not as smart (or, conversely, teachers might say, "I give up on them; they will never learn!"). The help given to the former group may take any number of forms extending from items included on a test to such activity as selection of tests for placement or other academic purposes, administration of the test (providing nonverbal cues), laxity in scoring (making suppositions that the student actually knew the answer though the answer was partially wrong), or interpretation of scores ("the student is a good student; he or she deserves encouragement by a higher score").

An illustration of cultural influences that affect student interpretations of test items is shown in Theory to Practice Box 16.1.

■ Bias in the Construction of Assessments

Assessments, in instruction and schooling, are, of course, cultural products, developed within a culture by teachers and test

Theory to Practice Box 16.1
ILLUSTRATION OF THE INFLUENCE OF CULTURAL BIAS ON INTERPRETATION OF TEST ITEMS

Solano-Flores and Trumbull (2003) examined potential differences in interpretations of test items by using the following "Lunch Money" item from the National Assessment of Educational Progress (1966).

Test Item: *Sam can purchase his lunch at school. Each day he wants to have juice that costs 50 cents, a sandwich that costs 90 cents, and fruit that costs 35 cents. His mother has only $1.00 bills. What is the least number of $1.00 bills that his mother should give him so he will have enough money to buy lunch for 5 days?*

Interpretations by Children: Students from low-income families interpreted the item as if they were being asked "What can Sam buy with $1.00?" The concern was with the lack of money ($1.75) for buying lunch (i.e., "what can I purchase now?") rather than with figuring out how many bills of the same denomination are needed for a week (i.e., "how can I plan my spending for the future?").

Follow-up interviews (abstracted from Solano-Flores & Trumbull, 2003) yielded different interpretations. Some student replies to the researchers' questions were:

- "The question is about Sam. He wants to buy juice, sandwich, and fruits."
- "He was hungry, but I think his mom didn't have enough money."
- "The question says she only had one dollar bill."
- "To answer the question I had to do the math problems, like, how much money he needed for five days and how much juice and sandwich and fruit costs and his mother only had one dollar bill."

constructors representing the culture. Students taking the tests are also from a culture—perhaps the same as the teacher's but as often, one different from that of the teacher or test constructor. They bring to both the learning and the test-taking situation their own knowledge base, the knowledge they access to develop their own constructions of what is being taught, and ultimately, the organization of those constructions in the form of knowledge structures. When the two—the student's and the teacher's cultural attitudes—are incongruent, assessment can be biased. Equitable assessment requires respect for the cultures represented in the classroom, such as those of English language learners (ELLs) and students from culturally nonmainstream backgrounds (Solano-Flores & Trumbull, 2003).

Cultural Influences on Assessment Construction

Some ways of reducing or avoiding cultural bias in test construction include awareness of the complexity of perceptions of a test (Weisen, 2002).

Reading Level

The reading level of assignments and assessments should correspond to the students' reading level. An interesting observation made by Weisen (2002) is that assignments or assessment requirements that are difficult to understand may lead to student misunderstanding and consequent distortion of the requirements and interpretations of a test item—answering a different question than the one intended; on the other hand, if an item or test is too easy students will make snap judgments rather than studying the details or requirements to answer an item correctly.

Instructional Preparation

It is essential that language employed in the test and the performance requirements correspond to instructional objectives. Adequate preparations for tests should provide sufficient familiarity to assure realistic test expectations. This outcome can be achieved through assignments, reading lists, and other activities related to assessments.

■ Bias through Question Formats

The lesson here is to use neutral content and wording. Avoiding bias, in this instance, can often be achieved by simply avoiding emotionally laden words. Be sensitive to the meanings assigned to words by different people or groups. For example, *bass*—as in fishing—and *bass*—as in band instruments—would be differentially accessed by the fishing-minded versus the music-minded student. Other words that might be thought to reflect the "with-itness" of the teacher, such as "fair-haired child," "teacher's pet," "geek," or "nerd," can have differential effects on children of varying personalities, especially when used to denote appeal or when suggesting a favored characteristic of the teacher or parent. "The gentleman's grade of C" suggests that reaching for higher grades is not favored. Emotionally laden words should be avoided, even if they have only a hint of potential for unintentional bias.

Problem Statements Can Bias Responses to Assessment Tasks

When constructing tests, it is common for test constructors to shorten the time spent in developing items by asking, "Which of the following is incorrect?" or "With which of the following do you disagree?" When this procedure is used, you introduce the possibility of double negatives, leading to an answer based on other reasons than knowing the information. Take the following example (Tercent, 2005):

Poor: Which of the following is not true of birds?
    a. Live in caves
    b. Do not have feathers
    c. Lay eggs
    d. Have wings

The difficulty here is that interpretation of the question leads to the need for complex processing: "it is not true that birds do not have feathers" requires the learner to unravel a sentence into a different question than the one intended. The correct alternative in the item also hints that the correct answer is the longest of the four alternatives. If the question was intended to simply ask, "What are the characteristics of birds?" an improved item might look something like the following:

Better: Which of the following is a distinguishing characteristic of birds?
    a. Skin
    b. Hooves
    c. Feathers
    d. Scales

Other bias that affects responses can be introduced by consistent typography that provides cues to the correct (or incorrect) answers. For example, consistently positioning the correct answer (always first or last in the set of alternatives) or always stating items with correct alternatives as positive and those with incorrect alternatives as negative, are quickly learned as position effects by the students taking the test.

Tricky Questions

Although there are few studies regarding tricky questions, there is sufficient evidence to suggest that the overzealous test constructor may, sometimes deliberately or sometimes inadvertently, increase item difficulty or defensive incidents to outwit the test taker or to make the test more difficult. Occasionally students attempt to outwit the test constructor by identifying the way a test constructor makes item alternatives.

Students may sometimes rationalize their poor performance by blaming the test constructor, attributing to him or her the characteristic of producing tricky questions. For example, they may justify poor performance by evaluating alternatives as unfair in their requirements (such as "we didn't cover that" or "we didn't learn it that way"), as requiring the respondent to make finer discriminations than they had learned, or as putting a twist on the items to permit more than a single interpretation. On such bases, students make the judgment that the questions were "tricky."

Sometimes teachers may feel that the students ought to be able to use the material taught in quite a different way than it was taught or that the students ought to be able to think about the material from many vantage points. They accordingly construct items that, without deliberate intention, appear to the student unaware of the objectives as though they were intended to be tricky. Even with the best of teacher intentions, an item perceived as outside of instructional objectives has the potential of being a tricky item. It is easy to see that such claims, especially if they occur while the test is being taken, introduce an inadvertent source of bias (error).

Two illustrations of tricky questions come from the "Ask Marilyn" column in *Parade Magazine*:

> *If Mary's mother has four daughters, and the names of the first three daughters are Penny, Nickel and Dime, what is the name of the fourth daughter?* James Dunbar, Floral Park, N.Y. Ans. *Mary*. (Vos Savant, May 25, 2003, p. 15)

> *Which word doesn't belong in this list: irredeemable, irreducible, irreligious, irrevocable, irremovable, irrepressible, irreversible?* (From: Harold Beg, Lemon Grove, Calif. to M. Vos Savant) Ans. *Irrevocable* (the only word pronounced with the accent on the second syllable not the third). (Vos Savant, November 13, 2005, p. 26)

As you can see, each question establishes a response set through wording that implies a given category of responses different from those that produce the correct answer: The first example subtly incorporates coin names for children's names and the second incorporates a distinction based on meaning. Either question might be viewed as tricky because the respondent is deliberately misguided by the framework. In these puzzle situations the intent is to "force" the wrong answer and so the questions are properly labeled tricky. Thus, the reader was made to respond in terms of the imposed context—coins in the first example; the next daughter ought to be named "Quarter." This network of ideas results in forgetting that Mary is one of the daughters as explicitly established in the first sentence of the question.

A similar principle is present in this analogy:

If 1 : 5 : : Washington : X. What is X?

What answer would you give? You probably have noted that by inserting Washington the context becomes ambiguous; "1" and "5" could be either values of money or part of a chronological series of historical figures. If the context was perceived as a monetary one, the answer would be "Lincoln"; if as a presidential order, the answer would be "Monroe." These are clear sources of bias, in these cases introduced playfully to produce tricky items and make good party activities. When such processes are introduced into tests, however, arriving at the correct answer to such questions is related more, or as much, to test-taking skills or outwitting the test constructor as it is to what the student knows.

The above discussion illustrates the nature of tricky questions and the biases they produce. Roberts (1993) derived, more formally, some characteristics of tricky questions. He said that tricky questions were produced by the introduction of:

- *Intention.* The items intentionally mislead or confuse the respondent.
- *Trivial content.* The answer focuses on trivialities to which the respondent might have been exposed but is unlikely to have learned.
- *Discrimination.* The instruction focused on approximations or generalized information but the test requires precise distinctions.
- *Noise.* The test constructor uses stems that are "noisy," containing irrelevant information deliberately used to make the item appear difficult.
- *Multiple correct answers.* There is more than one correct answer to an item, and the item is stated so as to elicit the more salient choice, whereas the correct answer is the less

salient one. (See the examples above of the four daughters, the accented pronunciation, and the analogy problem.)

• *Ambiguity and opposites*: The item is constructed to capitalize on what might confuse even the best students, such as capitalizing on student expectations and then introducing the opposite as the correct answer, as in the examples above.

In the final analysis whether an item is a tricky one or not depends on how the respondent perceives an item. Any suggestion that items are tricky is counterproductive to good assessment.

Context

The research on tricky questions suggests the importance of contextual cues. Cues that are extraneous to the instructional and assessment objectives can change the perceptions of tests. Sometimes teachers attempt to measure transfer by introducing contexts that may not be relevant to the question or for which students are not prepared. If students have not been prepared to use context, don't expect them to have learned its use when instruction was oriented only toward drill and practice exercises. Drill (overpreparation) on specific test items or formats used in standardized tests results in a narrowing of ability to just those items or formats, indicating a major difficulty in the use of that practice. It is well established that when students learn with visual supplements (e.g., pictures of the heart) they perform better on visual tests than on verbal tests and vice versa (see, e.g., Lin, Dwyer, & Swain, 2006).

From another standpoint, such contexts as those used in teaching or testing a principle in the physics of mechanics can introduce biases. The salience of different components of the principle will differ as a result of student interest, learning style, or gender. Similarly, the salience of the components of a principle of math taught within the framework of import and export balance sheets will be viewed differently than those in a teaching context emphasizing budgetary expenditures in travel. Test performance will vary accordingly. Although, in the interest of efficiency in education, we would like "far-transfer" (Barnard, 2005) of learning, the fact is that we cannot assume students can perform within a new context on a test if it has not been part of the instructional context.

■ Bias in the Administration of Assessments

Any assessment must target realistic expectations about the students' abilities following instruction. That is, given the instruction the student receives, he or she should be capable of meeting the requirements in taking the test. The implication is that the language and format of any assessment should match the student's level of capability.

Administration-Imposed Bias

Bias can be introduced in the administration of the test, whether in written or oral instructions or conditions during the test. The following are variables that have been discussed in the foregoing presentation that have the potential of influencing test-taking behaviors, scores, and grades, resulting in scores that are too low. You will note that these indicate either biases such as favoritism or suggestions of negative motivation. The categories are:

- *Cues, words, or phrases.* Don't use suggestions that will be perceived negatively by students as suggesting their *lack of* preparation, their inability to *make correct interpretations* or their *unfavorable attitudes* (e.g., comments indicating a lack of knowledge of the criteria—"You don't know what this test is about," "You don't know what we are trying to do with tests," or "You probably won't do well since you weren't very attentive in classwork").
- *Motivating some students over others.* Don't introduce bias or favoritism by posturing to encourage motivation in some students. Such activities as the use of coaching signals when correct answers are approximated, providing signs of progress such as assuring efficacy, or providing feedback implied by smiling or nodding approval when a student's response is seen to be correct or scowling or shaking head in disapproval when incorrect are sources of bias to be avoided.
- *Expressions of beliefs.* Particularly avoid those that belittle or denigrate the value of testing, the value of preparation for the test, or time taken in completing the test. Such expressions include "You either know it or you don't," "You get the answers immediately or not at all," "Good learners are born, not taught," or "We know you don't believe in the value of tests but we give them anyway" (Hofer & Pintrich, 1977).

Respondent-Imposed Bias

Some bias may be imposed by respondents themselves. Students may tend to select options according to the position of the alternative ("with this teacher, the correct alternative is always in the middle") or they may make consistent judgments such as selecting negatively worded items or the longest of the items as the "correct" alternative. The common description of multiple-choice items as "multiple guess" is an example of student perceptions that deteriorate the testing setting. Similarly, a common student response set in answering essay tests is to write longer essays in the belief that the teacher assigns higher grades to the papers that weigh the most.

Despite the ill effects on test taking of student-imposed biases, there are positive effects when students know legitimate strategies of taking tests efficiently. By using such knowledge the student can direct his or her attention to course content and demonstrating what he or she knows about that course content rather than being trapped by considerations that have little to do with evidence of learning course content.

Testwiseness

The strategies incidentally learned for routine ways of adapting to test-taking situations are sometimes referred to as response sets. These response sets fall under the category of "testwiseness." Their influence is induced in several ways: Textbooks often induce response sets by providing rules on how to use item characteristics that provide clues to the correct answers; manuals provide students with strategies for taking tests that get results; students are coached on using understandings of the mechanics of test construction; and students communicate their own ways of getting higher test scores with a given teacher. We have described the negative consequences (such as narrowing the curriculum) of similar routines in our discussion in Chapter 15 about teachers' use of templates for helping students prepare for a writing test.

There are numerous principles on which testwiseness is based. A study by Millman and colleagues (1965) provides excellent illustrations of the technical reasoning underlying an understanding of this source of bias. Some of these reasonings are illustrated in Theory to Practice Box 16.2.

Leading Questions

How assessments are constructed or administered can affect the way students respond to the test (Tercent, 2005). The student may be led to a response by what researchers consider "leading" or "loaded" questions. For example (Loftus & Palmer, 1974), after showing a movie of an automobile accident, the question might be asked: "Did you see the glass on the ground in front of

Theory to Practice Box 16.2
EXAMPLES OF TESTWISENESS

The student eliminates options that are not consistent with the stem.
Example:

The state with the highest total population in the United States in 1950 was:
  (a) New York,* (b) Chicago, (c) Michigan, (d) California.

Since b is not a state, the question is now a three-choice rather than a four-choice item. Michigan can be eliminated on knowledge that the Eastern states were growing more rapidly during that period.

The student uses relevant content information in many test items and options.
Examples:

Which one of the following four animals is warm blooded? (a) snake, (b) frog,
  (c) bird,* (d) lizard.
Which one of the following four animals is cold blooded? (a) snake,* (b) dog,
  (c) kangaroo, (d) whale.

A bird is warm blooded. All animals are one or the other but not both. A snake is present in both items, so snake should be picked in the second.

The student sees that an inexperienced test maker includes foils of familiar (or unfamiliar) terms or phrases.
Example:

Behavior for which the specific eliciting stimulus is not determined is called:
  (a) operant,* (b) operational, (c) apopathetic, (d) prehensory.

A student who sat through the lectures and skimmed the text recalls seeing the word *operant* and not the others.

The student uses any resemblances between the stem and the alternatives to identify the correct answer.
Example:

The aeronautics board which has jurisdiction over civil aircraft is called: (a) Civil Aeronautics Board, (b) Committee to Investigate Airlines, (c) Division of Passenger Airways, (d) International Military Aviation Committee.

The correct alternative is a direct repetition of words and phrases in the stem.

(continued)

Theory to Practice Box 16.2
(Continued)

The student finds one of the options bears a conceptual relationship to the stem whereas the other options do not.
Example:

What is the chief obstacle to effective homogeneous grouping of pupils on the basis of their educational ability? (a) resistance of children and parents to discriminations on the basis of ability, (b) difficulty of developing suitably different teaching techniques for the various levels, (c) increased costs of instruction as the number of groups increases and their average size decreases, (d) wide differences in the level of development of various abilities within individual pupils.*

The correct alternative is the only one related to educational ability within the framework of a course in educational measurement. Children's resistance, instructional methods, and cost efficiency do not have the same relation to the stem.

Source: Based on Millman, Bishop, & Ebel (1965, pp. 717–724).

the car with the damaged front fender?" Even though no broken glass appeared near the front fender, some respondents, taking the cue from the question (which indicated the front fender was damaged) were inclined to assume there was broken glass because the front fender was damaged near the front headlight. The students tended to answer "yes"—a response biased by the way the question was asked. (Please note that this is not a veridical description of the study cited. The situation and interpretation have been changed from the one reported in the study for purposes of our illustration here.)

Grading Criteria

Both students and teachers will find it advantageous for reporting, defending, or explaining grades to students and parents when criteria for grading or scoring are clearly defined and free of unrelated behaviors (e.g., posture of student in making an oral presentation might not be an appropriate measure, whereas enunciation and inflection might be critical to the quality of the oral presentation). The characteristics to be measured should be easily observed or identified in whatever assessment format is used. Statements of criteria, such as rubrics used in scoring, should be understood, available, and easily inferred from scores or ratings.

A source of bias associated with scoring or assigning grades is the irrelevancy of criteria to learning outcomes to be measured. The malicious characteristic of this bias is that it occurs unknowingly by the one doing the grading. For example, if not taught deliberately or stated as an objective of the assessment, scores on written compositions would be unfair if the composition was judged on neatness, length, or creative formats. Frequently, teachers may deliberately or inadvertently use items that are related to the construct being measured, but that were not part of the instruction.

■ Fairness

Fairness in testing is closely related to bias. Indeed, some of the same principles apply and some of the examples used in discussing bias apply equally to fairness. When content and performance standards that went into the test are unclear or when they favor one group over another, the test should be examined for its fairness. The bases for test scores must be transparent.

Fairness in Tests

A useful start to determining the test's fairness is to employ the simple ethic of considering the ways the learner's characteristics not associated with the knowledge, attitudes, or skills being tested affect responding to the test.

Language and Genre

The test constructor should be certain to use the language and genre with which the student is familiar. For language, ask the question, "How does the respondent use the language used in the test?" A native speaker can be simply defined by the language typically used in speaking about one's self. For evaluating possible effects of genre, ask the question, "What is the style of expression typically used by respondent?" If the respondent typically uses a narrative style in expressing him- or herself, he or she may have difficulty in adapting to a test written in an expository style; individuals most familiar with personalized, conversational styles may have difficulty in adapting to an objective formal or technical presentation (Mayer et al., 2004). If the writing and student preferences or experience with the genre differ from the objective being measured, and those differences are reflected in lower test performance, then an inference that the student's performance on the test was poor would be unfair.

Ability Levels

Any assessment should be based on knowledge of content or performance skills in which the student has had experience (instruction). If knowledge or skills are beyond the student's level, or if the student is physically or mentally ill-equipped for the test tasks, then an inference of poor achievement based on a low score would be unfair to that student (i.e., the resulting score would be too low).

Cultural Context

Test scores for a student in one cultural context should be interpreted against norms based on performance of people in that or similar cultures with similar characteristics. If the norms are based on an entirely different subculture known to have higher scores in general, then an interpretation of poor performance would be unfair to that student.

Directed Instruction for Performance Improvement

Schools under pressure to comply with accountability measures and earn high scores may succumb to teaching to the test to get quick results. Often they will set aside considerable amounts of time to do so. It is a sufficiently pervasive practice that test constructors should be sensitive to the problem and take whatever steps are necessary to limit or eliminate the practice. They should also be aware that the practices sometimes used in preparation for test taking can contribute to furthering of the negative consequences.

Popham (2001b), in an insightful analysis of how preparation for high-stakes tests can go wrong, suggests several remedial measures to help avoid improperly directed instruction, that is, avoid teaching to the test or teaching to test items, discussed in the following sections.

Adverse Effects of Teaching to the Test

Adverse effects include boosting scores and narrowing the curriculum. Preparation for taking high-stakes tests may involve practice on items identical to those to be used in testing. Such preparation *may* lead to higher scores if there is high similarity between the content of practice and actual test items, not because of increased understanding of the construct being measured, but because of practice. Avoid this practice to the extent possible. It takes valuable time from effective instruction. Additionally, the predictability of the test score (i.e., its validity) for any criterion of educational value is compromised.

Assessments and Instruction Should Be Aligned with Standards and Objectives

Ensure that tests and test items are aligned with content standards especially if they are supposed to emphasize understanding, conceptualization, and problem solving. Items measuring rote learning are sometimes overemphasized because such items are easier to construct. Items that measure rote learning or inert knowledge exclusively tend to have minimal transfer value and should be used only to the extent they contribute to the broader educational objectives related to understanding.

Conversely, overly generalized objectives such as "students should think scientifically, inferentially, with good judgment, and critically" are too ambiguous. How would you construct a test, performance or otherwise, for measuring achievement of this objective? Objectives stated in overly general terms are lacking in clear instructional guidance. They don't help in determining content to be taught or in selecting instructional methods. As Popham (2002b) notes, overly general objectives are discouraged because they could apply equally well to any form of scientific endeavor, to reading any kind of literature, or to solving any kind of social or political problem. They tend to circumvent the alignment of test tasks to those specific to an area of study—for instance, the ways of doing experiments in different sciences (doing a laboratory experiment in chemistry versus one in physics) or in reading works with different genres (reading a newspaper versus reading a novel).

When Preparation for Assessment Can Be Useful

Any fair test of the standards will reflect improvement in performance if good teaching practices have been used. Preparing students for taking a high-stakes test, for example, can be justified if the preparation is aimed at analyzing the content of the item and making selections on the basis of understanding the content. Again base your test preparation practices on your objectives. Prepare clear descriptions of curriculum standards, make certain that your instructional methods implement those objectives, and ensure that assessment is based on both the standards and instruction. Aiming solely at higher test scores through answering specific test items or test-taking skills has little effect on overall performance. Similarly, the main effects of these limited practices are acquired with a few hours of training, rather than the weeks of preparation sometimes devoted to them. Unless the descriptions of curriculum and instruction are clear, inferences made of performance measures resulting from practice on tests will be invalid (Popham, 2001a).

Summary

It is not uncommon to find reports in the media that student scores on a high-stakes test jump dramatically from one year to the next. The reason for the spurt in performance is often challenged. Did it result from a corresponding change in instruction and learning, the result of coaching or some other means of improving test scores? The potential for unfair or biasing influences exists in any form of assessment, whether it is the use of objective tests, completion tests, essay tests, or performance measures. Sometimes such influences are not recognized and, as often, they may be inadvertent. Fortunately, we are becoming sufficiently informed about these biasing influences that their effects can be minimized by a little forethought in planning. All stakeholders must be sufficiently well informed to be sensitive to variables that may work against the fairness of assessments, whether in their construction, their administration, or the inferences made in grading them. Many sources of bias have subtle influences, the effects of which are not immediately apparent unless one is well informed about the assessment process both from the standpoints of the examinee and the test constructor. Among the ways of avoiding unfair tests, whatever the sources that make them unfair, is *accommodation*, a legal requirement in the instruction of students with special needs.

■ Testing Accommodations

The work on test bias and fairness is clearly represented in current concerns about the assessments of students with disabilities and English language learners. Especially critical is the issue of whether the special groups are treated equitably and justly when standardized tests are used for placement, for individual plans, or for accountability purposes and where high stakes are involved. There is a concern for the potential difficulties placed on students taking statewide tests that are ordinarily constructed to serve the needs of students without disabilities and whose primary language is English.

Accommodations are viewed as necessary to make certain the tests are fair for students with special needs. The use of accommodation is intended to permit the assessment to reflect full potential in reaching learning objectives. Similarly, reducing the performance gap (e.g., between English language learners and English-proficient students) is desirable, but, concurrently, the accommodations should not give an unfair advantage to those students receiving the accommodations (Shepard, Taylor, & Betebenner, 1998)

Policy Requirements for Accommodation

The importance of considering accommodations for students with physical, mental, or developmental impairment is recognized in several formal documents, but most notably in the Standards for Psychological and Educational Testing (AERA, APA, & NCME, 1999) and the official statement of the Elementary and Secondary Education Act (ESEA), the nation's major federal law related to education in grades prekindergarten through high school. (The ESEA received its most recent congressional approval in 2001 and became known as the No Child Left Behind Act—see discussion in Chapter 14.)

In order to understand the role of accommodation in education, the reader is reminded that, under NCLB, all public school students, including students with disabilities (SWDs) and English language learners (learners whose first language in not English), are tested annually in specific academic areas and grade levels. Accommodations are expected to be made when dictated by awareness of learners' disabilities. District coordinators of special education report compliance with the policy of accommodations for special education students on statewide and high-stakes tests (Zehler, Fleischman, Hopstock, & Stephenson, 2003).

The purpose of making certain students with disabilities have been given the necessary accommodations is apparent. The policy includes students with special needs in the accountability process to ensure that these students are given the educational opportunities received by all other students. If left out of the school grading programs, there is the potential that these students might be more amenable to being ignored or neglected in instruction for improvement in learning.

But inclusion in the testing program was also recognized as potentially disadvantageous for these students when taking the standardized tests required under NCLB, as follows:

> students with disabilities (those covered under the Individuals with Disabilities Education Act or Section 504 of the Rehabilitation Act) must be provided the appropriate accommodation necessary to participate effectively in these tests. . . . [As a critical component in developing a student's IEP (Section 504 Plan IEP/504)] team members must carefully decide which accommodations would be helpful in facilitating the student's ability to profit from grade level instruction and to fully participate in state/ district assessments.

Premises in Using Accommodations

A basic premise underlying the use of accommodations is the assumption that they are to compensate for the detrimental effect of a given disability or lack of language proficiency (ELLs) but at the same time will not affect the scores of students without disabilities (SWOD) or language differences.

Validity

As you would expect, any modification of the testing situation should not affect measurement of whatever construct is being measured by the test. If it did so, the validity of the test would be jeopardized. For example, if the wording of test items made the test easier for ELL students by removing a problem-solving feature, the objective measured by the test would be altered. In math tests, the math problem is often embedded within a situational context that provides a problem-like feature, whether in the first grade or later grades. Typical of such tests, abstract math operations are embedded within problem contexts. For example, the first-grade test for subtraction skills might be:

John had 8 marbles and gave 4 of them to Bill. How many
    would John now have?

To simplify the problem one might think that an abstract version of the item would be more appropriate, such as, "If you subtract 4 from 8, what is the remainder?" However, there is documentation that word problems are more difficult than abstract problems for children in American schools (Carraher, 1989). They also measure different processes than do abstract problems, which lack the surrounding contexts—a change in context, as in this case, often changes the construct measured by the test. By removing the wordings from the problems and using only the abstract problem, the problem is easier to solve for both the ELL and the non-ELL students. One alternative that might be more universally effective as an accommodation is to accompany the problem by using pictures showing John holding the eight marbles and using that format for all examinees.

Constructors of standardized tests consider how the construct (concept) is to be used and how the test items might be best constructed to represent that use. For example, a test of math achievement might be used to predict how well the student will profit from advanced courses, whether the student knows math sufficiently well to work as a store clerk, or whether the requirements to enter vocational training in accounting are met. In brief, assessments are framed with the contexts of such questions as "What is to be measured? How will it be best measured? How will the results be used? What interpretations will be made of the performance scores? What applications are implied? Who will use the test?" A definition and examples of common constructs in education are given in Text Box 16.1. Some premises on which the use of accommodations is based include those discussed in the following sections.

Text Box 16.1 Definition of *Construct*

You will find the word *construct* used frequently in discussions and presentations related to the technical characteristic of validity in testing and in its practical applications, such as in making accommodations. This term refers to the idea, concept, skill, attribute, or ability measured by the test. The definition of *construct* is close to that of *concept*. Assessments are constructed to target or represent the construct. The *Standards for Educational and Psychological Testing* (1999) begins with a discussion of constructs. That document provides examples of constructs that include math achievement, computer performance, and self-esteem, for which there are measures and which are related to some practical outcome. You might easily add to these by including reading comprehension, composition writing, creativity, English language proficiency, or historical analysis, as well as factual knowledge, skill acquisition, or problem-solving ability. Thus, as in our examples, by viewing changes in test items as a result of accommodation you might find the item changes from one that requires understanding or conceptual knowledge to one that requires only rote memorization or recognition of facts.

An Accommodation Should Not Result in Changes in Relevancy or Representation of Constructs

The accommodation must not affect the measurement of the construct itself. First, the accommodation must not neglect the construct; *that is, the construct must not be underrepresented.* If it does so, what is measured will have changed. Secondly, the changes in the performance of students should result without changing the measurement of the construct. The changes in student performance should be the result of making changes in the way the disability or lack of language proficiency had made the score lower (by removing the irrelevant factors that were causing the lower performance), *not by measuring something different than the construct intended.* Sireci (2005) notes:

> "Tests are imperfect measures of constructs because they either leave out something that should be included . . . or else include something that should be left out, or both." (Messick, 1989, p. 34 as cited in Sireci 2005, p.4)

> A test that leaves something out might *underrepresent* a portion of the intended construct (or content domain) by leaving important knowledge, skills, and abilities untested. On the other hand, a test that includes something that should be left out could conceivably measure-proficiencies *irrelevant* to the intended construct. (Sireci, Scarpati, & Li, 2005)

Based on Sireci's (2005, p. 4) insightful analysis, we can turn to some examples: Mobility or vision impairments may make a difference in standardized test scores (i.e., the impairments may be contributors to variance). Students with mobility impairment, for example, may earn lower scores because they are unable to turn pages quickly enough or don't have the agility to mark spaces as required; or students with visual impairments may earn lower scores because the print can't be seen clearly or the letters and words can't be identified correctly. In these illustrations, the difference is due to a condition extraneous (irrelevant) to what the test measures. It is not due to differences in what the test measures (the construct). In other words, the difference is due to *construct-irrelevant* variance.

To use another example, an accommodation might be made to make test materials easier to handle by examinees with motor disabilities (e.g., using a computer for administering the test). Or we might use Braille (tactile stimuli) to help a student with visual impairment read the text. If either of these accommodations were to be used with students taking a standard math exam the accommodations would be based on the assumption that changes in scores would occur without changing what the test measures or what the scores represent. Removing the barriers of mobility and vision are accommodations made by modifying the administration of the examination, thereby reducing construct-irrelevant variance and increasing test validity.

Accommodations Must Not Result in Construct Underrepresentation

If care is not taken, accommodation has the potential of changing the extent to which the test measures what it is intended to measure, that is, its validity. If the construct is changed or modified, the result is *construct underrepresentation*. For example, in accommodating a student with attention deficit disorder (ADD), we might attempt to decrease attention span requirements by reducing the number of alternatives or substituting multiple-choice questions for written answers that would require extended attention. In either of these two cases, we would endanger the cognitive requirements for successful completion of the examination. As you can see, the accommodation not only limits the attention required of the examinee, but also limits the information needed to answer the question, that is, how the construct is represented (e.g., the multiple-choice questions require only selection from a given set of alternatives; written answers require the respondent to both access potential alternatives *and* make a selection from the alternatives accessed). If whatever is intended to be measured by a test changes as a result of the modification, it is, obviously a different measure than the one originally intended.

Acceptable Accommodations

The use of an accommodation should be the result of a careful appraisal of the nature of the disability and the way it would affect the test performance; this is not an easy task. Such appraisals are not taken lightly by those involved in constructing the IEP, that is, the teacher, the school psychologist, the parent, and the student, as well as any others that might be involved, such as a director in assessment. Each state is required to identify which specific accommodations are acceptable. Most states have done so. Although there is some variation from one state to another, there is considerable agreement among them.

Some specific accommodations, taken from several sources, within each of the broader categories of strategies described in the *Standards for Educational and Psychological Testing* (AERA, APA, & NCME, 1999) are shown in Text Box 16.2. These are illustrations of specific strategies that might be used but that still do not exhaust all the possibilities. (For more informed guidance in the preparation of IEPs and for state requirements please see the suggested readings at the end of this chapter.)

The Effectiveness of Accommodations

As you can see in Text Box 16.2, the use of accommodations is important in the evaluation of students with disabilities or cultural differences. School personnel such as special education teachers or school psychologists may be interested in extended lists of available accommodations for either classification. However, we continue our discussion mainly on the characteristics of accommodations for ELL students. The discussion illustrates the effective application of accommodations in assessment for all special-needs education.

Accommodating different levels of language proficiency may involve more than one strategy. For example, it is sometimes helpful to provide ELL students with dictionaries or glossaries to compensate for lower proficiency in English. But how does this provision affect what is measured? Does the evidence negate the use of the accommodation? Which accommodations are acceptable in terms of good psychometric practice is continually being examined. The accommodations are becoming increasingly based in the findings of research evidence.

Use of Glossaries

For example, Abedi and Gandara (2006) and Abedi, Hofstetter, and Lord (2004) showed that both ELLs and English-proficient students benefited substantially from having an available glossary *plus* extra time. But students who were already proficient in English showed a greater improvement (16 percent) with this combination than did the ELL students (13 percent). Because the effect is greater for the non-ELL students than for ELL students the combination is not considered a useful accommodation and is not recommended.

Translations

Simple translations from English to the learner's language are sometimes believed to be sufficiently helpful to use the

Text Box 16.2 Accommodations

The *Standards for Educational and Psychological Testing* (1999, pp. 103–104) provides a classification for accommodation strategies that is in general use by most states' decisions for classifying specific strategies available for students with disabilities.

The strategy classification is in the left column and illustrations of some available specific modifications are in the right column. These are not for indiscriminate use and may not be appropriate for all circumstances. States and officials in charge of administering tests are informed that although a child's IEP must include the appropriate accommodations necessary to fully measure the child's academic achievement and functional performance *only accommodations that do not invalidate the score may be used for any student.*

Strategy	*Modifications*
Presentation: Modifications or changes in the way the test is presented	*Accommodations for either SWD or ELL students:* • Larger-type fonts for students with visual impairments • Braille for blind students • Oral reading of test directions for visually impaired individuals • Sign-language interpreter • Repeating test directions • Simplified directions • Test parts that are particularly challenging because of the disability are eliminated for an individual (e.g., syllabic pronunciation in a reading test taken by a student with a severe speech impediment) • Computer use to display large print • Technology to permit selection of items in print, spoken, or pictorial form *Accommodations more specific to ELL students:* • Questions presented in home language • Clarification of English words • Questions administered in first language if feasible • Manually coded items in English or American Sign Language • Use of dictionaries

(continued)

Text Box 16.2 (*Continued*)

Strategy	*Modifications*
Response: Modifications that change the way the student responds to the test.	*For selected-response formatted items (multiple-choice, true-false):* • Student provides selection orally • Student points to the correct answer • Student marks answers on test booklet • Responses made in other formats than the standardized one are transferred to machine scoreable answer sheets by qualified personnel • Manipulatives are used to demonstrate conceptual or procedural knowledge (e.g., in math or science) *For essay tests:* • Computer software of various kinds, with or without special adaptive features as judged necessary by team • Use of computer for typing answers to essays (spell checker or grammatical aids turned off if related to test answers) • Answers written in Braille • Answers dictated orally
Timing, pacing, scheduling: Modifications of time requirements or scheduling formats; extensions or changes in schedules or time limits	*For students whose primary language is other than English, for SWD such as ADD, or for students given other accommodations that may affect the time taken (such as dictating answers to a scribe):* • Allow students additional time for taking the test • Remove time limits altogether if one exists • If parts are distinguishable administer parts of the tests on separate days • Administer separate sections of the tests at different points during the day • Schedule two or more shorter sittings rather than one long one • Provide frequent or longer breaks • Choose time of day suitable to the student
Setting, situation, context: Modifications of the testing environment, setting, location, or context in which test is administered	*Students whose attention is disrupted by others around them or unduly distracted in large groups might be offered the opportunity to have the test administered:*

Strategy	Modifications
	• Individually
	• In small groups of individuals with similar disabilities
	• In separate room to eliminate distractions
	• In a private space such as a carrel
	ELL students might also profit from:
	• Seating in the front of the room (to provide best opportunity to hear or see the test administrator)

translation as an accommodation. However, a translation may result in changes in meaning, that is, in what the test measures. If the test is believed to change the meaning or to avoid the hazards of one-way translation, the translated passages or test items are translated back into the original language (back translations). Any differences between the two provide a basis for determining whether the meaning has been changed. Similar difficulties are imposed when an interpreter is used to administer the test in the student's language.

Cultural Differences

Accommodations for ELL students are associated with cultural differences. Accordingly, the attitudes of the culture in relation to the demands of testing need to be considered in making interpretations of the test-taking behavior or accommodation employed for these groups. For example, in some cultures children are reluctant to speak to adults in elaborated language (sentences, explanations, and so on). This becomes reflected in clipped, short answers or in postural changes that may be mistakenly interpreted as lack of knowledge or unwillingness to respond to tests, respectively. Cultural differences include reluctance to volunteer answers out of politeness to others or to respond as a group rather than individually. These would need to be taken into account to resist making the interpretation that the student's performance does not meet desired levels of proficiency. Reticence to respond is sometimes interpreted in the American culture as an indication that the student may be antagonistic, withdrawn, or of low mental ability rather than one respectful of cultural values.

In general, LEP students often do not receive the same attention as students with disabilities (Zehler et al., 2003). For example, just a little more than half of students with disabilities and limited English proficiency were reported to receive one or more accommodations. The accommodations are similar to those described above, consisting mainly of (a) individual or small-group administration, (b) extra time as needed to complete the test, (c) giving directions in the student's native language, and (d) making glossaries or dictionaries available.

Inclusion of ELL Students into Regular Classes

Provision of accommodations has helped to increase the rate of inclusion of ELL students (Mazzeo, Carlson, Voelkl, & Lutkus, 2000) into regular classes. However, there remain some major concerns regarding the use of accommodations for ELL students simply because of the complexity of variables characterizing ELLs. Among the most important issues are those raised in the questions, "How effective are accommodations in reducing the performance gap between ELL and non-ELL students?" and "How valid are the assessments when accommodations are used?" Unfortunately accommodations do not have an all-or-none quality. The evidence shows that their effectiveness depends on the kind of accommodation and the characteristics of the students. Due to the number of variables involved, such research is complex, often with conflicting results.

When the performance of ELL students and non-ELL students are compared under different forms of accommodation, the results suggest that some accommodations helped non-ELL students significantly but did not have much impact on the performance of ELL students. This is a cause for concern because it may invalidate the accommodated results for use in evaluating the overall performance of a school. The results of accommodations that improve the performance of *all* students may not be combined with the results of nonaccommodated assessments. Unfortunately, accommodations are often used without evidence of their utility in evaluation.

Congruency of Language Used in Instruction and in Assessment

A commonly used accommodation strategy is the translation of assessment tools (measures, performance, tests) into the student's native language. Native-language assessments are useful only when students can demonstrate their content knowledge more effectively in their native language. Otherwise translated items may confuse students who have learned content and concepts in English in their class work. For example, eighth-grade

Hispanic ELL math students taught in English or sheltered English scored higher on NAEP math items in English than their peers who received the same math items administered in Spanish (Abedi et al., 2004). In comparison, students who received their math instruction in Spanish performed higher on the Spanish-language math items than those in either modified or standard English.

Did you notice in these examples that the effectiveness of the accommodation is dependent on the congruency of the language used in both the test and in instruction? Students typically perform better on a test when the language of the test corresponds to the language used in instruction. In such circumstances, the *congruence* of the language of instruction and the language of the test contributes to understanding of the content as it is represented on the test. When this point is not considered, the result of the accommodation is a threat to the validity of assessment. If there is a lack of understanding content-related terms, a source of construct-irrelevant variance is introduced into the assessment (Messick, 1988).

Does the Accommodation Provide an Unfair Advantage for the Recipient?

An important question is whether an effective accommodation provides unfair advantage to the recipients, that is, does it alter the construct under measurement? To illustrate, some findings are:

- *Modifying the language of a test can result in better performance by the ELL students receiving a modified version of a math test than those receiving the original items* (Abedi, Lord, & Plummer, 1997). Among four accommodation strategies of extra time, glossary, linguistically modified items, and glossary plus extra time, the linguistic modification was the only accommodation that reduced the performance gap between ELL and non-ELL students (Abedi & Gandara, 2006).
- *Extra time is a common and easily implemented accommodation strategy* but may lead to higher scores for English learners (Hafner, 2000; Kopriva, 2000; Winter, Kopriva, Chen, & Emick, 2006). The results of several studies indicate that extra time helped eighth-grade English learners on NAEP math tests, but it also aided students already proficient in English, thus limiting its potential as an assessment accommodation (Abedi, 2008; Abedi et al., 1997; Hafner, 2000).

- *Dictionaries and glossaries are helpful accommodations* when they do not contain information related to the construct being measured. In eighth-grade science classes (Abedi, Lord, Kim, & Myoshi, 2000) three test formats were randomly distributed: (a) original format (no accommodation), (b) provision of an English glossary and Spanish translations in the margins, and (c) a customized English dictionary at the end of the test booklet. The customized dictionary included only words that appeared in the test items. English language learners scored highest on the customized dictionary accommodation (the mean scores for the three formats were 8.36, 8.51, and 10.18, respectively, on a 20-item test). Interestingly, although the accommodations helped the English learners score higher, there was no significant difference between the scores in the three test formats for the English proficient students, suggesting that accommodation strategies did not affect the measure of the construct.
- *Simplifying language helps ELL students* who would typically score low on standardized science and math tests (Abedi & Leon, 1999). The performance gap decreases or even disappears on math items that have relatively low language demands, such as math computation (Abedi, Leon, & Mirocha, 2003). Of several accommodations, the one that narrowed the gap between ELL and non-ELL students most was reducing the unnecessary language complexity of those test questions with excessive language demands (Abedi et al., 2000).

Whether used with ELLs or SWDs, *effective accommodations should reduce the performance gap but should not affect the performance of the non-ELL students or SWODs*. This is appropriately said to "level the playing field" (Abedi et al., 2004).

Sireci's Theory of Accommodation Effectiveness

Figure 16.1 shows the assumed results of an accommodation compared to the actual results found in studies (the figure is based on Sireci, 2005, Figure 1, p. 459, and Figure 2, p. 483). There it may be seen that the test performance of SWDs without accommodations are lower than that of the SWODs. However, the theoretical assumptions would indicate that with accommodations, the SWDs improve almost to the level of the SWODs; but, theoretically (SWOD-T), the performance of the SWODs does not change with the accommodation.

In most studies, however, it appears that most SWODs do improve, however slightly, with an otherwise acceptable

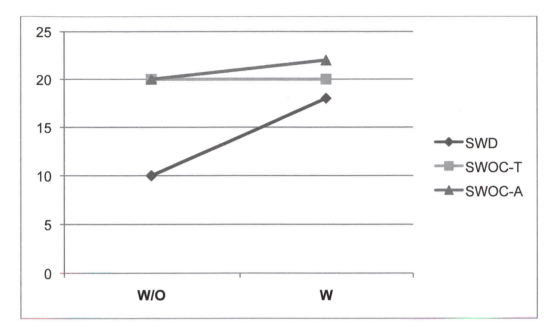

Accommodation

Figure 16.1. Hypothetical effects of test administration without (W/O) and with (W) according to characteristics of the student (students with disabilities [SWD] and without [SWOD] under theoretical [T] and actual [A] conditions). Based on Sireci, 2005, Figure 1, p. 459 and Figure 2, p.483.

accommodation (see SWOD-A), an effect that Sireci (2005) notes as an *accommodation boost* for SWODs (Fuchs et al., 2000). Because the improvement for SWDs is so much greater than the lesser boost for the SWODs, the use of the accommodation for the SWDs would still be acceptable.

Assistive Technology in Accommodation

Because of their functional flexibility and capacity for storing information, computers can provide an important way of assisting accommodations in assessment. You probably have thought of many such possibilities in reading this section. For example, in the construction of tests, the administration of trial tests can be made on computers, response data can be stored, and items can be revised accordingly. In managing accommodations, computers can deliver items in auditory or visual modalities and can also provide for "zooming" both visual and auditory presentations. They can be used for varying the order or sequence in which items are presented (easy to difficult, for example). They can provide for differentiated time limits on individual questions or on the entire test. Tactile accommodations can be made by requiring the student to use the keyboard rather than writing, or the student can use the keyboard as an alternative to Braille. Similarly, answers to questions can be given orally and stored in printed form. Alternate test forms can be provided from which a student makes a selection. Teachers can identify the order in which the questions were answered as well as the time taken on individual items or the entire test. These examples are merely illustrations of the possibilities of technology in the use of accommodations. The research on the use of technology remains limited, but the illustrations provided may suggest further creative alternatives for research or applied use of the computer, whether for constructing tests, managing the administration of tests, or making accommodations for children with special needs.

■ Summary

A number of variables affect the obtained or raw score. A part of that score is the "true" score, that is, the measure of what the test or other device is intended to measure. The remainder is the "error" score, that is, the impact of all other variables on the score, whether random or systematic. Errors might enter the error score by several routes, such as through overlooking some item characteristics by the test constructor (e.g., tricky questions), through the strategies examinees use in taking the test (e.g., testwiseness), through the situation or context in which the test is given (e.g., paced tests versus self-pacing), or through student disabilities. In most cases they are factors beyond individual control.

By considering accommodations for both classroom assignments and assessment there is the promise that assessment of what has been learned can be greatly improved. The introduction of accommodations assists IEP teams to understand and provide supports for students with special needs. The use of accommodations helps those students to demonstrate their actual ability. Coupled with monitoring of progress, valid measures allow for continual checking on individual progress as well as matching instruction to student needs.

Understanding the functional use of accommodations helps teachers and IEP teams to address the students' strengths and make adjustments for challenges students face as learners. Accommodations allow students with disabilities to participate in standard classroom instruction otherwise unavailable to them; assessments demonstrate more accurately what they have learned not only in more accurate test scores but in meeting requirements in the NCLB legislation.

Accommodations can be made in the (a) *presentation* of the test material, including using an alternative modality such as auditory presentation for accessing the test material; (b) *responses required*, that is, completing activities, assignments, and assessments in different ways or solving or organizing problems using some type of assistive device or organizer; (c) *setting, location, or conditions* in which a test is administered; or (d) *pacing, timing, or scheduling*, for instance, allowing self-pacing or increasing allowable length of time to complete a test or other assessment (Thompson, Morse, Sharpe, & Hall, 2005). For students to become familiar with the accommodations it is helpful if they are the same or similar to the ones used in the classroom, but keep in mind that often the requirements for administering statewide tests are different from those used in the classroom. It is important to know these procedures for the state in which the school resides.

The research with many types of students and many types of accommodations yields promising though not unequivocal findings regarding the use of specific accommodations (Johnstone, Altman, Thurlow, & Thompson, 2006). Empirically based recommendations for accommodations cannot be made in all cases but, borrowing from Sireci, Scarpati, and Li (2005), it is important to remember that "the provision of test accommodations is the best recommendation we have for promoting equity and validity in educational assessment" (p. 486).

Overall, the literature has shown that accommodations do have positive, construct-valid effects for certain groups of students, although questions remain regarding how the accommodations that are reasoned to work well can be implemented appropriately for all groups. There remains the need to identify which accommodations are best for specific types of students. Research has identified some accommodations that help ELL students with their English language needs and some accommodations that help students with special disabilities without compromising the validity of the assessment (Abedi & Gandara, 2006). These can be employed advantageously, with thoughtful consideration, for all special-needs students.

As explorations into the effectiveness of test accommodations continue we can expect that other increasingly valid accommodation practices will emerge. In the meantime, it seems reasonable that accommodations should be made on the basis of a thoughtful appraisal of their potential. They must compensate for the detrimental effect of a given disability or lack of language proficiency and, simultaneously, must not affect the validity of the test; that is, they must not affect the measurement of the construct (Sireci, 2005, p. 486) or substantially affect the performance of students without disabilities.

■ Suggested Readings

If you desire more details, especially for preparing IEPs, you may wish to refer to the URL www.nichcy.org/Educate Children/IEP/Pages/AccommodationsinAssessment.aspx.

An important, well-documented, and detailed list of accommodations with brief explanations of each are offered in the following sources:

- Thompson, S. J., Morse, A. B., Sharpe, M., & Hall, S. (2005, August). *Accommodations manual: How to select, administer, and evaluate use of accommodations for instruction and assessment of students with disabilities* (2nd ed.). Washington, DC: Council of Chief State School Officers. Available online at www.ccsso.org/content/pdfs/AccommodationsManual.doc.
- U.S. Department of Education. (2007, April). *Modified academic achievement standards* [non-regulatory guidance draft]. Washington, DC: Author. Available online at www.ed.gov/policy/speced/guid/nclb/twopercent.doc.

■ References

Abedi, J. (2008). Utilizing accommodations in assessment. In E. Shohamy & N. H. Hornberger (Eds.), *Encyclopedia of language and education. vol. 7: Language testing and Assessment* (2nd ed., pp. 1–17). Totowa, NJ: Springer Science+Business Media LLC.

Abedi, J., & Gandara, P. (2006). Performance of English language learners as a subgroup in large scale assessment: Interaction of research and policy. *Educational Measurement: Issues and Practice, 25*(4), 47–57.

Abedi, J., Hofstetter, C. H., & Lord, C. (2004). Assessment accommodations for English language learners: Implications for policies based empirical research. *Review of Educational Research, 74*(1), 1–28.

Abedi, J., & Leon, S. (1999). *Impact of students' language background on content-based performance: Analyses of extant data.* Los Angeles: UCLA Center for the Study of Evaluation/National Center for Research on Evaluation, Standards, and Student Testing (CRESST).

Abedi, J., Leon, S., & Mirocha, J. (2003). *Impact of student language background variables on student's NAEP performance (CSE Technical Report, Number 478).* Los Angeles: University of California, National Center for Research on Evaluation, Standards, and Student Testing (CRESST).

Abedi, J., Lord, C., Kim, C., & Myoshi, J. (2000). *The effects of accommodation on the assessment of LEP students in NAEP (CSE Technical Report Number 537).* Los Angeles: University of California, National Center for Research on Evaluation, Standards, and Student Testing (CRESST).

Abedi, J., Lord, C., & Plummer, J. (1997). *Language background as a variable in NAEP mathematics performance (CSE Tech. Rep. No. 429).* Los Angeles: University of California, National Center for Research on Evaluation, Standards, and Student Testing (CRESST).

American Educational Research Association, American Psychological Association, & National Council Measurement in Education. (1999). *Standards for educational and psychological testing.* Washington, DC: American Educational Research Association.

Barnard, J. K. (2005) The effects of a near versus far transfer of training approach on trainees' confidence to coach related and unrelated tasks. Doctoral Dissertation, College of Education, Ohio State University. Retrieved July 24, 2010, from http://etd.ohiolink.edu/send-pdf.cgi?acc_num=osu1133208874.

Carraher, T. N. (1989) The cross-fertilization of research paradigms. *Cognition and Instruction, 6(4),* 319–323.

Fuchs, L. S., Fuchs, D., Eaton, S. B., Hamlett, C., Binkley, E., & Crouch, R. (2000). Using objective data sources to enhance teacher judgments about test accommodations. *Exceptional Children, 67*(1), 67–81.

Hafner, A. L. (2000). *Evaluating the impact of test accommodations on test scores of LEP students & non-LEP students.* Paper presented at the American Educational Research Association, Seattle, WA.

Hofer, B. K., & Pintrich, P. R. (1977). The development of epistemological theories: Beliefs about knowledge and knowing and their relation to learning. *Review of Educational Research, 67*(1), 88–140.

Johnstone, C. J., Altman, L., Thurlow, M., & Thompson, S. J. (2006). *A summary of research on the effects of test accommodations: 2002 through 2004 (No. 45).* Minneapolis: University of Minnesota, National Center on Educational Outcomes.

Jussim, L., & Harber, K. D. (2005). Teacher expectations and self-fulfilling prophecies: Knowns and unknowns, resolved and unresolved controversies. *Personality and Social Psychology Review, 9*(2), 131–155.

Kopriva, R. (2000). *Ensuring accuracy in testing for English-language learners.* Washington, DC: Council of Chief State School Officers, SCASS LEP Consortium.

Lin, H., Dwyer, F., & Swain, J. (2006). The effect of varied cognitive strategies used to complement animated instruction in facilitating achievement of higher order learning objectives. *International Journal of Teaching and Learning in Higher Education*, 18(3), 155–167.

Loftus, E., & Palmer, J. C. (1974). Reconstruction of automobile destructions: An example of the interaction between language and memory. *Journal of Verbal Learning and Verbal Behavior*, 13(4), 585–589.

Mayer, R. E., Fennel, S., Farmer, L., & Campbell, J. (2004). A personalization effect in multimedia learning: Students learn better when words are in conversational style rather than formal style. *Journal of Educational Psychology*, 96(2), 389–395.

Mazzeo, J., Carlson, J. E., Voelkl, K. E., & Lutkus, A. D. (2000). *Increasing the participation of special needs students in NAEP: A report on 1996 NAEP research activities (NCES Publication No. 2000-473)*. Washington, DC: National Center for Education Statistics.

Messick, S. (1988). The once and future issue of validity: Assessing the meaning and consequences of measurement. In H. Wainer & H. I. Braum (Eds.), *Test validity* (pp. 33–45). Hillside, NJ: Lawrence Erlbaum.

Messick, S. (1989). Validity. In R. L. Linn (Ed.), *Educational measurement* (pp. 13–103). New York: Macmillan.

Millman, J., Bishop, C. H., & Ebel, R. (1965). An analysis of test-wiseness. *Educational and Psychological Measurement*, 25(3), 707–726.

Popham, W. J. (2001a). Teaching to the test? *Educational Leadership*, 58(6).

Popham, W. J. (2001b). *The truth about testing: An educator's call to action*. Alexandria, VA: Association for Supervision and Curriculum Development.

Roberts, D. M. (1993). An empirical study of the nature of trick test questions. *Journal of Educational Measurement*, 30, 331–334.

Rosenthal, R., & Jacobson, L. (1968/1992). *Pygmalion in the classroom: Teacher expectation and pupils' intellectual development*. New York: Irvington Publishers.

Shepard, L. A., Taylor, G. A., & Betebenner, D. (1998). *Inclusion of limited English proficient students in Rhode Island's grade 4 mathematics performance assessment (Center for the Study of Evaluation Technical Report No. 486)*. Los Angeles: University of California at Los Angeles, National Center for Research on Evaluation, Standards, and Student Testing (CRESST).

Sireci, S. G. (2005). Unlabeling the disabled: A perspective on flagging scores from accommodated test administrations. *Educational Researcher*, 34(1), 3–12.

Sireci, S. G., Scarpati, S. E., & Li, S. (2005). Test accommodations for students with disabilities: An analysis of the interaction hypothesis. *Review of Educational Research*, 75(4), 457–490.

Solano-Flores, G., & Trumbull, E. (2003). Examining language in context: The need for new research and practice paradigms in the testing of English language learners. *Educational Researcher*, *32*(2), 3–13.

Tercent. (2005). Response bias. *Super survey knowledge base.* Retrieved February 10, 2010, from: http://knowledge-base.supersurvey .com/response-bias.htm.

Thompson, S. J., Morse, A. B., Sharpe, M., & Hall, S. (2005). *Accommodations manual: How to select, administer, and evaluate use of accommodations for instruction and assessment of students with disabilities*. Washington, DC: Council of Chief State School Officers.

Vos Savant, M. (May 25, 2003). Ask Marilyn. *Parade Magazine*, p. 15.

Vos Savant, M. (November 13, 2005). Ask Marilyn. *Parade Magazine*, p. 26.

Weisen, J. P. (2002). *Review of written, multiple-choice test items, with some emphasis on cultural bias*. Paper presented at the 17th Annual Conference of the Society for Industrial and Organizational Psychology.

Winter, P. C., Kopriva, R. J., Chen, C. S., & Emick, J. E. (2006). Exploring individual and item factors that affect assessment validity for diverse learners: Results from a large-scale cognitive lab. *Learning and Individual Differences*, *16*(4), 267–276.

Zehler, A. M., Fleischman, H. F., Hopstock, P. J. P., & Stephenson, T. G. (2003). *Descriptive study of services to LEP students and LEP students with disabilities. Special Topic Report #4: Findings on Special Education LEP Students* [Report submitted to U.S. Department of Education, Office of English Language Acquisition]. Arlington, VA: Development Associates, Inc.

Index

Abedi, J., 508

academic counseling, 351

accommodation: construct and, 506–7; construct-irrelevant variance and, 506–7; without construct underrepresentation, 507; effectiveness of, 508, 514–15, *515*; in presentation, 509; in setting, situation, context, 510–11; summary on, 516–18; for SWD, 503–4, 506–12, 514–18, *515*; for SWD compared to SWOD, 514–15, *515*; technology in, 515–16; in timing, pacing, scheduling, 510; unfair advantages from, 513–14. *See also* testing accommodations

accountability, 439, 440; assessment for, 436; funding and, 436–37; item improvement for, 425–26; of NCLB, 421, 433–34, 436–37; policies and, 422–27, *423*; summative assessment and, 87

adequate yearly progress (AYP), 436

administration, 4, *5*, 7, 14, *406*; administration assessment bias, 494–99; administration-imposed bias, 485; cheating by, 21; feedback for, 349–50; NCLB for, 438; of standardized tests, 219, 235; summative assessment to, 86–87

admissions, grades for, 350

AES. *See* Automated Essay Scoring

affective variables measurement, 378; graphic displays for, 383–88, *385–86*; on motivation, 379–83; *MSLQ* for, 381–83; rating scales in, 380, 382–83; self-reports in, 380, 382–83. *See also* sociogram(s)

alternative assessment, 23, 122, 338; IEPs and, 411, *412–24*; validity of, 120–21. *See also* performance assessment; supplementary assessments

alternative evaluation, 169–70

alternative representations (developing representations), 328–29, *329*

American Educational Research Association, 444

American Psychological Association (APA), 472

analysis, 44, *48*, *50–51*, 71; of organizational principles, *49*; of sociograms, *385–86*, 385–87. *See also* meta-analysis

answers: rapidity of, 65, 68. *See also* short-answer questions; tests

anxiety: grades related to, 468; about learning, 312–13, 381; math anxiety, 226, *227*; test anxiety, 18, 383

APA. *See* American Psychological Association

applications, *51*; inert knowledge compared to, 330; in multiple intelligences assessment, 396–97; in objectives, 44, *48–50*; of previous information, 71; questionnaires on, 340–41; for subject-specific assessment, 305–6

archived information, 58, 78

art, 126

Arter, J., 142

artifacts: behavioral artifacts, 59–60; in observations, 55, 58–60; in portfolios, 59, 144

Art PROPEL, 396

assessment, *3*, 3–4, 12–13, 27, 276; for accountability, 436; toward benchmarks, 462–63; changing role of, 22–23; of classroom

About the Authors

Mark D. Shermis, Ph.D., is presently professor and dean in the College of Education at the University of Akron (UA). He received his B.A. at the University of Kansas and was on active duty in the U.S. Navy for three years before entering graduate school. After finishing his master's and Ph.D. from the University of Michigan, Dr. Shermis worked for a computer firm and eventually entered academe. Dr. Shermis has played a leading role in bringing computerized adaptive testing to the World Wide Web, and for the last 10 years has been involved in research on automated essay scoring. His most recent work has resulted in the seminal book on the topic, *Automated Essay Scoring: A Cross-Disciplinary Approach* (Jill Burstein, Ph.D., coeditor).

Dr. Shermis's first book, coauthored with Drs. Paul Stemmer, Carl Berger, and Ernie Anderson, entitled *Using Microcomputers in Social Science Research*, was one of the first successful texts on the topic. He has numerous publications in such journals as *Educational and Psychological Measurement, Psychological Test Bulletin, Educational Measurement: Issues and Practice*, and the *Journal of Psychoeducational Assessment*, to name a few. He was recently chair of the American Psychological Association's Continuing Education Committee and takes an active role in professional governance. He is a licensed psychologist in the states of Florida, California, Indiana, and Ohio, and is a fellow of the American Psychological Association (Division 5) and the American Educational Research Association. He is a consulting editor for the APA journal *Psychological Assessment*. Prior to coming to UA, Dr. Shermis served as professor and chair of the Department of Educational Psychology at the University of Florida and was professor and associate dean for research and grants in the Department of Educational and Psychological Studies at Florida International University.

Francis J. Di Vesta, Ph.D., has authored or coauthored books as well as a number of book chapters on development, language, and learning. In addition he has a number of research publications in technical journals including the *Journal of Educational Psychology*, *Journal of Applied Psychology*, *Contemporary Educational Psychology*, *Child Development*, *Teachers College Record*, and *Educational and Psychological Measurement*. He is fellow in the APA Divisions 7 and 15 and has been on the Boards of Consulting Editors of the *Journal of Educational Psychology* and *Educational Technology: Research and Development*. Dr. Di Vesta has held appointments at Syracuse University and The Pennsylvania State University with his latest appointments at the Florida International University.